AF248659

Adult Learning in Modern Societies

eduLIFE LIFELONG LEARNING

Series Editors: Hans-Peter Blossfeld, *European University Institute, Italy* and Sandra Buchholz, *Bamberg University, Germany*

By taking an explicit life course perspective, the *eduLIFE Lifelong Learning* series examines the ways in which individuals' educational careers unfold in relation to their family background, educational institutions, workplaces and private life events. The series focuses on four distinct and central phases of the educational career: preschool education, general schooling, vocational training and labor market entry, and adult learning and careers. For each of these four central phases of the educational career, the series will present detailed empirical facts and country-specific institutional background information for a broad number of European countries and the United States of America. This will highlight these countries' very different and distinct systems, policies, and cultures of education. Based on cross-national comparisons of educational processes, this exciting series will give readers a profound and elaborated understanding of educational processes, developments and social inequalities in modern societies as well as their country-specific differences.

Adult Learning in Modern Societies

An International Comparison from a Life-course Perspective

Edited by

Hans-Peter Blossfeld
European University Institute, Italy

Elina Kilpi-Jakonen
University of Turku, Finland

Daniela Vono de Vilhena
European University Institute, Italy

Sandra Buchholz
Bamberg University, Germany

*edu*LIFE LIFELONG LEARNING

Edward Elgar
Cheltenham, UK • Northampton, MA, USA

Published by
Edward Elgar Publishing Limited
The Lypiatts
15 Lansdown Road
Cheltenham
Glos GL50 2JA
UK

Edward Elgar Publishing, Inc.
William Pratt House
9 Dewey Court
Northampton
Massachusetts 01060
USA

A catalogue record for this book
is available from the British Library

Library of Congress Control Number: 2014932631

This book is available electronically in the ElgarOnline.com Social and Political Science Subject Collection, E-ISBN 978 1 78347 518 6

ISBN 978 1 78347 517 9

Printed and bound in Great Britain by T.J. International Ltd, Padstow

Contents

PART IV   CONCLUSION

Contributors

Paolo Barbieri is Professor in Economic Sociology at the University of Trento, Italy, where he currently also coordinates the PhD program in Sociology. His main research interests are concerned with welfare and labor market dynamics in a comparative perspective. Address: University of Trento, Department of Sociology and Social Research, Via Verdi 26, 38122, Trento, Italy. [e-mail: paolo.barbieri@unitn.it].

Carlo Barone is a Lecturer at the University of Trento. He is interested in social stratification and social mobility, education and educational policies. He has published two books and several peer-reviewed articles on these topics. Address: University of Trento, Department of Sociology and Social Research, Via Verdi 26, 38122, Trento, Italy. [e-mail: carlo.barone@unitn.it].

Hans-Peter Blossfeld was born in Munich (Germany) in 1954 and received his training in sociology, economics, social statistics and computer science at the University of Regensburg (Dipl.-Soz., 1980), the University of Mannheim (PhD, 1984), and the Free University of Berlin (Habilitation, 1987). He worked as Research Scientist at the University of Mannheim from 1980 to 1984 and as Senior Research Scientist at the Max Planck Institute for Human Development and Education. Since 2002 he is Professor and Chair of Sociology I at the University of Bamberg (where he is on leave) and since 2012 he is Professor and Chair of Sociology at the European University Institute (EUI) in Florence (Italy). His research interests include life course research, educational sociology, labor market sociology, family sociology, demography and statistical methods. Address: European University Institute, Via dei Roccettini 9, 50014 San Domenico di Fiesole, Italy. [e-mail: HP.Blossfeld@EUI.eu].

Sandra Buchholz is a Professor of Sociology at Bamberg University in Germany. Before, she served as a research scientist in various international comparative research projects. Her research especially addresses the influence of national institutions and cultures on the structure and development of social inequalities and individual life courses and she published several articles and books on this topic. Address: Otto-Friedrich-University Bamberg, P.O. Box 1549, 96045 Bamberg, Germany. [e-mail: sandra.buchholz@uni-bamberg.de].

Sandra Buchler is a Research Fellow and Lecturer at the Chair of Sociology Specializing in Quantitative Analyses of Social Change at the Goethe-University Frankfurt am Main. Her research interests include families and households, cohabitation, gender attitudes, longitudinal research and inequalities in education. While completing the research for this book Sandra was employed as a Research Fellow and Lecturer at the Chair of Sociology I at the University of Bamberg. Address: Goethe-University Frankfurt am Main, Faculty of Social Science, Chair of Sociology Specializing in Quantitative Analyses of Social Change, Grüneburgplatz 1, 60323, Frankfurt am Main, Germany. [e-mail: buchler@soz.uni-frankfurt.de].

Jenny Chesters is currently a Post-Doctoral Research Fellow at the University of Canberra. She graduated with a PhD in Sociology from the University of Queensland in 2009. Her research interests include transitions between education and employment throughout the life course and the persistence of inequality in educational attainment. Address: ESTeM Faculty, Building 6, University of Canberra, Canberra, ACT 2601, Australia. [e-mail: jenny.chesters@canberra.edu.au].

Gábor Csanádi is Professor of Sociology and Director of the Research Centre for Urban and Regional Studies at Eötvös Loránd University, Budapest. His research topics are the relations between knowledge and urban development, social segregation, socio-spatial urban policies and governance. The focus is on comparative studies in a European context with a special attention on Hungary, Eastern and Central Europe. He has participated in a number of EU-funded research projects and in numerous advisory boards. Address: Eötvös Loránd University (ELTE) Faculty of Social Sciences, Pázmány Péter sétány 1/A, H-1117 Budapest, Hungary. [e-mail: gcsanadi@tatk.elte.hu].

Adrienne Csizmady is an Associate Professor of Sociology at Eötvös Loránd University, Budapest. She holds a senior researcher position at the Research Centre for Social Sciences, Institute for Sociology of the Hungarian Academy of Sciences. The main fields of her interests are: urban social problems (including integration of poverty groups), housing and large housing estates, organizations of civil society (including young people) and lifelong learning. She has participated in several international comparative projects. Address: Institute for Sociology, Centre for Social Sciences, HAS Országház u. 30, H-1014 Budapest, Hungary. [e-mail: csizmady.adrienne@tk.mta.hu].

Giorgio Cutuli, PhD, is a Research Fellow at the Department of Sociology and Social Research of the University of Trento. His main research interests include social stratification, labor markets, income and inequality dynamics, and longitudinal and counterfactual analysis. Address: University of Trento, Department of Sociology and Social Research, Via Verdi 26, 38122 Trento, Italy. [e-mail: g.cutuli@unitn.it].

Johanna Dämmrich is a PhD researcher at the Department of Social and Political Science in the European University Institute, a member of the Comparative Life Course and Inequality Research Center at the EUI, and part of the research team on the ERC-funded international comparative research project 'Education as a Lifelong Process – Comparing Educational Trajectories in Modern Societies'. Her primary research interests involve educational systems, labor markets and welfare states in a comparative perspective as well as gender differences in educational and labor market outcomes. Address: European University Institute, Via dei Roccettini 9, 50014 San Domenico di Fiesole, Italy. [e-mail: Johanna.Dammrich@eui.eu].

Cheryl Elman is an Emeritus Professor of Sociology at The University of Akron and Scholar in Residence (History) at Duke University. She studies the effects of twentieth century social change on and over the adult life course, as produced through social institutional and organizational forms such as labor markets, school systems and households. Her publications include articles in American Journal of Sociology, American Journal of Public Health, Demography and Social Science History. Address: Department of Sociology, University of Akron, Akron, OH 44325-1905, United States of America [e-mail: cse10@duke.edu].

Dana Hamplová is a Senior Researcher in the Institute of Sociology, ASCR and an Associate Professor at the Charles University. Her main research interest lies in a topic of social inequality and she particularly focuses on the interdependence between education and family behavior. She has authored and co-authored several books and published in peer-reviewed journals such as Demography, Journal of Family Issues, Journal of Comparative Family Studies, Ethnic and Racial Studies, and others. Address: Institute of Sociology, Jilska 1, 110 00 Prague 1, Czech Republic. [e-mail: dana.hamplova@soc.cas.cz].

Michele Haynes is an Associate Professor and Leader of the Research Methods and Social Statistics Program at the Institute for Social Science Research, The University of Queensland. Haynes is also the current Chair of the Social Statistics Section of the Statistical Society of Australia and is an internationally respected authority in longitudinal analysis. Her research interests include developing methodology for modeling longitudinal social survey data, and optimal weighting strategies for longitudinal and dual-frame surveys. She has more than 20 years' experience in providing statistical advice and teaching statistical methods to researchers, public sector officers and practitioners in the social sciences and other disciplines. Address: The University of Queensland, Institute for Social Science Research, St Lucia

Campus, GPN3 (Building 39A), Level 4, Campbell Road, QLD 4072, Australia. [e-mail: m.haynes@uq.edu.au].

Angela Higginson is a Research Fellow at the Institute for Social Science Research at the University of Queensland, Australia. Her research interests are predominantly in quantitative methods for social sciences, including evaluation, systematic reviews, and longitudinal methods. She leads the Systematic Review team in the Policing and Security program, where her work focuses on the synthesis of empirical evidence for intervention effectiveness, particularly around issues of crime and justice. Address: The University of Queensland, ARC Centre of Excellence in Policing and Security (CEPS) and Institute for Social Science Research, St Lucia Campus, Building 31B, Room 111, Brisbane QLD 4072, Australia. [e-mail: a.higginson@uq.edu.au].

Elina Kilpi-Jakonen is an Academy of Finland Postdoctoral Researcher at the University of Turku. During the time of writing this book, she was a Research Fellow on the eduLIFE project, first at the University of Bamberg and then at the European University Institute. Her research interests focus on social inequalities related to social origin, migration background and gender within education and the labor market. Address: Sociology unit, Department of Social Research, Assistentinkatu 7, 20014 University of Turku, Finland. [e-mail: elina.kilpi-jakonen@utu.fi].

Yuliya Kosyakova is a PhD researcher at the Department of Social and Political Science in the European University Institute, a member of the Comparative Life Course and Inequality Research Centre at the EUI, and part of the research team on the ERC-funded international comparative research project 'Education as a Lifelong Process – Comparing Educational Trajectories in Modern Societies'. Her main research interests focus on educational inequalities over the life course, social inequality, post-socialist societies, and international comparison. Address: European University Institute, Via dei Roccettini 9, 50014 San Domenico di Fiesole, Italy. [e-mail: yuliya.kosyakova@eui.eu.].

Michele Lugo is a PhD student in Sociology and Social Research at the University of Trento, Italy. His main research areas concern social stratification and inequalities, welfare and labor market studies, occupational career analysis and family and labor market dynamics in a comparative perspective. Address: University of Trento, Department of Sociology and Social Research, Via Verdi 26, 38122 Trento, Italy. [e-mail: michele.lugo@unitn.it].

Pekka Martikainen is Professor of Demography at the Department of Social Research, University of Helsinki. He has written on socio-demographic differences in mortality in Finland, and on the health effects of unemployment and death of spouse. His current research interests include changes and causes of socioeconomic differences in cause-specific mortality, and social determinants of use of long-term care in aging populations. He is also working on the health effects of marital status and living arrangements and has been involved in cross-national comparisons of health inequalities. Address: Population Research Unit, Department of Social Research, P.O. Box 24, FIN-00014 University of Helsinki, Finland. [e-mail: pekka.martikainen@helsinki.fi].

Patricia McMullin is a PhD researcher at the Department of Social and Political Science in the European University Institute, a member of the Comparative Life Course and Inequality Research Centre at the EUI, and part of the research team on the ERC-funded international comparative research project 'Education as a Lifelong Process – Comparing Educational Trajectories in Modern Societies'. She has worked as a research assistant in the University of Bamberg, Germany and the Geary Institute, University College Dublin. Her main research interests focus on educational inequality in third-level education, employer-sponsored adult education and early childhood education. Additionally she is interested in labor market research, longitudinal data analyses, program evaluation and comparative research. Address: European University Institute, Via dei Roccettini 9, 50014 San Domenico di Fiesole, Italy. [e-mail: Patricia.McMullin@eui.eu].

Pau Miret Gamundi is a Senior Researcher at the Centre for Demographic Studies (CED) at the Autonomous University of Barcelona (UAB). His main research interests are the effect of education on family formation, labor force dynamics, and migration. Address: Centre for Demographic Studies, Campus de la Universitat Autònoma de Barcelona, Edifici E2, 08193, Bellaterra (Barcelona), Spain. [e-mail: pmiret@ced.uab.es].

Vibeke Myrup Jensen is a Senior Researcher and Director of the Education Research Group at the Danish National Centre for Social Research (SFI). Her research interests include economics of education, health economics and family economics. Address: The Danish National Centre for Social Research, Herluf Trollesgade 11, DK-1052, Copenhagen, Denmark. [e-mail: vmj@sfi.dk].

Elisabeth Reichart is a Researcher at the German Institute for Adult Education. She studied educational science at the Universities of Bamberg and Aarhus and got her Ph.D. in social and economic sciences from the University of Bremen. Her research interests include participation in adult education, adult education systems in comparative perspective, and statistics on adult education providers. Address: German Institute for Adult Education, Heinemannstr. 12-14, 53175, Bonn, Germany. [e-mail: reichart@die-bonn.de].

Peter Róbert is Professor of Sociology at Széchenyi University. He holds a senior researcher position at the Institute for Political Science, HAS. His research interests involve social stratification, educational inequalities, public opinion research and analysis on political attitudes. He has published in edited volumes by Oxford University Press, Princeton University Press, Edward Elgar, Routledge, Springer and Stanford University Press as well as in refereed journals like RSSM, ESR, European Societies, ERE. Address: Institute for Political Science, Centre for Social Sciences, HAS Országház u. 30. H-1014, Budapest Hungary. [e-mail: robert. peter@tk.mta.hu].

Eve-Liis Roosmaa is a Researcher Lecturer and a graduate student in sociology at the Institute of International and Social Studies, Tallinn University, Estonia. She is interested in the research fields of education, lifelong learning and labor market, mostly in a comparative perspective to investigate structural effects on individual outcomes. Address: Institute of International and Social Studies, Tallinn University, Uus-Sadama 5-662, Tallinn 10120, Estonia. [e-mail: eve-liis.roosmaa@iiss.ee].

Ellu Saar is a Professor at the Institute of International and Social Studies, Tallinn University, Estonia. Her research areas are social stratification and mobility, educational inequalities and life course studies. She is an editor-in-chief of the journal Studies of Transition States and Societies, a member of the editorial board of European Sociological Review and a member of the Steering Committee of the European Consortium of Sociological Research. Address: Institute of International and Social Studies, Tallinn University, Uus-Sadama 5-662, Tallinn 10120, Estonia. [e-mail: ellu.saar@iiss.ee].

Stefani Scherer is an Associate Professor in Sociology at the University of Trento, Italy. She is working on social inequalities in international comparison, the analysis of life courses, family and labor market dynamics. She is the principal investigator of the ERC-financed project "Families of Inequalities". Address: University of Trento, Department of Sociology and Social Research, Via Verdi 26, 38122 Trento, Italy. [e-mail: stefani.scherer@unitn.it].

Susanne Schührer is a PhD researcher at the Department of Social and Political Science in the European University Institute, a member of the Comparative Life Course and Inequality Research Centre at the EUI, and part of the research team on the ERC funded international comparative research project 'Education as a Lifelong Process – Comparing Educational Trajectories in Modern Societies'. Her research interests are educational sociology, sociology of the labor market, non-cognitive skills as well as methods of empirical social research. Address: European University Institute, Via dei Roccettini 9, 50014 San Domenico di Fiesole, Italy. [e-mail: susanne.schuhrer@eui.eu].

Natalie Simonová is a Senior Researcher at the Institute of Sociology, ASCR and has been associated with the ISEA think tank since 2011. Her research interests include educational inequalities, their sources and developments, and particularly educational mobility in the Czech Republic. She has written the book "Educational Inequalities in Czech Society: Development from the Early 20th Century to the Present", and edited the book "The Czech University System at the Crossroad". Her work has also been published in peer-reviewed journals such as British Journal of Sociology of Education, The Sociological Review, Sociologický časopis/Czech Sociological Review, Sociológia, Sociological Theory and Methods, and Higher Education. Address: Institute of Sociology, Jilska 1, 110 00 Prague 1, Czech Republic. [e-mail: Natalie.simonova@soc.cas.cz].

Outi Sirniö is a doctoral candidate in the Population Research Unit, University of Helsinki. Her scholarly interests include social stratification, inequality and intergenerational social mobility. Address: Population Research Unit, Department of Social Research, P.O. Box 18, FIN-00014 University of Helsinki, Finland. [e-mail: outi.sirnio@helsinki.fi].

Anders Stenberg is an Associate Professor of Economics at the Institute for Social Research, Stockholm University. Adult education has been his major research area for more than a decade, and he has published articles in world leading economics field journals. Address: Swedish Institute for Social Research, Stockholm University, 10691 Stockholm, Sweden. [e-mail: anders.stenberg@sofi.su.se].

Moris Triventi, PhD, has been post-doc researcher at the University of Milano-Bicocca from 2010 to 2013; in September 2013 he joined the eduLIFE research project as a Research Fellow at the European University Institute. He is interested in social stratification, education, and transition to the labor market in a comparative perspective. He published a book (in Italian) and several peer-reviewed articles on these topics. Address: European University Institute, Via dei Roccettini 9, 50014 San Domenico di Fiesole, Italy. [e-mail: moris.triventi@eui.eu].

Julia Unfried was a project assistant at the Department of Social and Political Science in the European University Institute working from Bamberg, a PhD researcher at the University of Bamberg and part of the research team on the ERC-funded international comparative research project 'Education as a Lifelong Process – Comparing Educational Trajectories in Modern Societies'. Her main research interests focus on Labour Market and Employment Research, Life Course Research as well as the Comparison of Different Educational Systems and Quantitative Methods. Address: Äußere Großweidenmühlstraße 25, 90419 Nürnberg, Germany. [e-mail: julia.unfried@googlemail.com].

Marge Unt is a senior researcher at the Institute of International and Social Studies, Tallinn University, Estonia. Her research interests lie in social stratification, transition from school to work, late career and retirement pathways in comparative perspective as well as methods of data analysis. Address: Institute of International and Social Studies, Tallinn University, Uus-Sadama 5-662, Tallinn 10120, Estonia. [e-mail: marge.unt@iiss.ee].

Daniela Vono de Vilhena, Ph.D., Scientific Coordinator at the Population Europe Secretariat / Max Planck Institute for Demographic Research. During the time of writing this book, she was a Research Fellow on the eduLIFE project, first at the University of Bamberg and then at the European University Institute. Her research interests focus on family and labor market dynamics over the life course. Address: Population Europe Secretariat, Markgrafenstrasse 37, 10117, Berlin, Germany. [e-mail: vono@demogr.mpg.de].

Susanne Wahler is a PhD researcher at the Department of Social and Political Science in the European University Institute, a member of the Comparative Life Course and Inequality Research Centre at the EUI, and part of the research team on the ERC-funded international comparative research project 'Education as a Lifelong Process – Comparing Educational Trajectories in Modern Societies'. Her main research interests lie in educational sociology, life course research, longitudinal research and quantitative methods. Address: European University Institute, Via dei Roccettini 9, 50014 San Domenico di Fiesole, Italy. [e-mail: susanne.wahler@eui.eu].

Felix Weiss is head of the team "German Microdata Lab" at the GESIS Leibniz Institute for Social Sciences. Before joining GESIS he was researcher at the Universities of Mannheim and Cologne. Felix studied sociology, political science and business administration at the University of Mannheim and the Chinese University of Hong Kong and obtained a Diploma in Social Sciences and a doctoral degree in Sociology from the University of Mannheim. His main research interests are sociology of the life course, social stratification in comparative perspective, educational inequality and sociology of the labor market. Address: GESIS Leibniz Institute for Social Sciences, B2,1, D-68159, Mannheim, Germany. [e-mail: felix.weiss@gesis.org].

Foreword

The present volume studies an important topic in contemporary highly-skilled societies: the issue of adult learning. Various societal trends in Western societies call for new forms of learning that fit less well in the 'standard' life cycle in which an initial educational phase in early life was followed by an employment career until (early) retirement. Rather than seeing the educational phase as a clearly demarcated life stage between early childhood and the transition to adulthood, we tend to see present-day life courses as more blurry, with periods of mixed statuses of schooling and work, and, relevant for the present volume, re-entry into learning as adults. Important societal trends include globalization, technological change, and aging workforces. Through globalization and technological change, low- and medium-skilled workers need to obtain skills that can keep them in work. Globalization has particularly affected labor market opportunities of the low skilled, as low-skilled work is often outsourced to developing countries. Both the low and medium skilled are further threatened by technological developments that may automate their job tasks, making their skills redundant. Moreover, through the exponential character of technological developments, skills acquired in initial education become obsolete more rapidly than was the case decades ago. So even among those who have obtained valuable skills in education, continued forms of formal and non-formal learning need to be organized in order to keep up with these changes. The aging workforce has made the need for prolonged working lives more urgent, and training is a way to increase participation rates of older workers in the labor force.

Thus, the volume takes up an important research question, with clear relevance for the scientific community, policy makers and politicians. The project is timely, with a preponderance of calls for 'lifelong learning' in Europe and beyond. Moreover, what is especially important is that the book takes an approach towards adult learning in the context of life courses and inequality. Echoing other studies by Hans-Peter Blossfeld and associates, a life-course approach is embraced, which helps to see the enrollment patterns in formal and non-formal adult learning as structurally determined and associated to differences in advantage in further careers. In other words, whereas the lifelong learning field tends to see adult learning mostly as an avenue towards economic growth, the current volume complements this view with a perspective in which social inequalities are, at least in part, shaped by opportunities and constraints of different groups of workers in different phases of the life course.

One particular strength of the book is that patterns of entry into adult learning, and the returns to adult learning in further careers, are studied in a comparative perspective. Societies differ substantially in many respects, concerning the economy and various institutions. The book examines the relevance of national institutions with regard to the educational system, the welfare state, and employment systems. The book is highly informative on how different institutions are able to deal with the increased need for skill acquisition over the life course, and how institutions affect inequalities in access to adult learning and in the returns to them. However, the book also clearly demonstrates that existing typologies of institutional arrangements are ill-suited to explain cross-national variation in enrollment patterns and returns to training. It is highly relevant to see that training can help to create human capital among groups that most need them, but it is also striking to realize that especially the well-educated benefit from training in many countries. The so-called Matthew effect implies that, across the life course, adult learning magnifies inequalities in labor market opportunities between skill groups; implying that it offers an educational explanation to cumulative advantages in addition to social-class-based and organizational explanations of growing differences from early adulthood to retirement.

This book is a must-read for anyone interested in education and inequalities, in life courses, in adult learning, and in the economics of work careers. Scientists and policy makers alike will learn a great deal from the abundance of empirical evidence, using many different sorts of data of many different countries.

Herman G. van de Werfhorst
University of Amsterdam, Netherlands

Preface

This volume is part of the *edu*LIFE project (Education as a Lifelong Process), funded by the European Research Council, and the first volume of the *eduLIFE Lifelong Learning Series*. This five-year project analyzes educational careers over the whole life course – from early childhood to late adulthood – in relation to family background, educational institutions, workplaces, and life events. This is achieved by focusing on four specific phases of the educational career: early childhood education, secondary and tertiary education, the transition from school to work, and adult learning. Based on detailed cross-national comparisons, *edu*LIFE aims to establish the generality of findings as well as the impact of specific institutional contexts.

The study of educational opportunities has a long tradition in sociological inequality research, and many sociologists have argued that education is the key variable for researching stratification in modern societies. Over the last decades, industrial societies have evolved into knowledge-based economies in which the role of education and the organization of educational institutions have become important in all phases of the life course. More than in the past, education is today a lifelong process in which individuals acquire skills and competences in formal and non-formal learning settings throughout the entire lifespan. However, most empirical research on education is based on cross-sectional studies (for example, the OECD's PISA and PIAAC studies) and does not analyze education as a time-dependent process.

Adult Learning in Modern Societies provides a state-of-the-art analysis of adult learning in different institutional settings. Although the importance of adult learning has been widely acknowledged over the last decades, empirical evidence on the topic is still scarce and stems mostly from studies of individual countries. Much can still be learned from the use of longitudinal data and the rigorous analysis of causal mechanisms over the life course. This volume brings together a number of cross-national and country studies (Australia, Czech Republic, Denmark, Estonia, Finland, Germany, Great Britain, Hungary, Italy, Russia, Spain, Sweden, and the United States), which were conducted in collaboration with country experts and using high-quality longitudinal data. Our main contribution to the literature consists of exploring the potential of adult learning for reducing social inequality. In order to achieve this aim, our chapters analyze how successful different countries have been in encouraging equitable participation in formal and non-formal labor-market-related adult learning and whether different types of adult learning are converted into positive labor market outcomes.

We have been very fortunate in being able to draw on the expertise of prominent researchers, who contributed country-specific and cross-national chapters to the book. We thank all our collaborators for their efforts in preparing and revising their manuscripts, and all their commitment to our shared purposes. During the preparation of the book, we have benefited from intensive debates with our collaborators at two workshops. Thanks to the creativity of the scholars involved in this project, we have achieved excellent solutions to our theoretical and methodological issues.

With regard to the preparation of the final manuscript, we are thankful for the support received from Janto McMullin in formatting the typescript and the rigorous proofreading executed by Ryan DeLaney. Their contribution has been of great value, but we as editors are solely responsible for any remaining errors. We also thank all the administrative and student assistants who have contributed to the project. We are extremely grateful for all the support received from Tim Williams and Emily Mew at Edward Elgar Publishing and the anonymous reviewers for supporting the publication of this volume. Finally, we would like to thank the financial support of the European Research Council (ERC) through the Advanced Grant awarded to Hans-Peter Blossfeld.

Hans-Peter Blossfeld

Elina Kilpi-Jakonen

Daniela Vono de Vilhena

Sandra Buchholz

PART I

Introduction

1. Adult Learning, Labor Market Outcomes, and Social Inequalities in Modern Societies

Elina Kilpi-Jakonen, Sandra Buchholz, Johanna Dämmrich, Patricia McMullin, and Hans-Peter Blossfeld

INTRODUCTION

Education continues to be a focus of discussion in the media, politics, and the research communities of modern societies and has been increasing in importance in many countries, especially since the first PISA evaluation in 2000.[1] However, adult learning has generally not received much attention from policymakers, and public investments in education have been targeted at other areas (European Commission 2011). This trend stands in spite of the fact that individuals who leave initial education and enter the labor market represent the largest share of the population. What is more, there are two important macro-developments – namely demographic aging and accelerated economic change as part of the process of globalization – that make it increasingly important for modern societies to ensure that their populations have up-to-date skills throughout the whole life course.

Adult learning has important implications for social inequality. On the one hand, giving adults the chance to increase their educational level or change their field of education has the potential to reduce inequalities that may have emerged earlier in life. Moreover, the macro-processes of globalization and demographic change are likely to have a particularly strong impact on the need for older persons and the lower qualified to take part in lifelong learning in order to update their skills to match new labor market demands (cf. OECD 2013). On the other hand, adult learning may actually increase existing inequalities if the well educated are the primary group taking advantage of these opportunities. Overall, the development of adult learning should be of interest to everyone concerned with the development of social inequality over the life course.

It can be expected, however, that the success of attempts to increase educational equality through adult learning varies strongly among modern societies. The recent results from the Survey of Adult Skills (PIAAC) point to divergences between countries not only in the skill levels of their adult populations but also in the ways in which skills are increased and maintained over the life course; whereas some countries are able to reduce social inequalities related to skills over the life course, in others these differences are reinforced (OECD 2013). The organization of adult learning also varies strongly among countries; in particular, a major source of difference comes from the way that responsibility for organizing adult learning is divided between the three main actors – the state, the market (including employers), and civil society (Rubenson 2006).

The aim of this book is to investigate how adult learning is organized in different countries, how successful these countries are in encouraging participation and skill formation, and whether adult learning is converted into positive labor market outcomes. Moreover, in answering these questions, we also aim to assess adult learning's potential for reducing social inequality. The use of longitudinal data is central to our analysis of adult learning from a life-course perspective in order to situate adult learning within individuals' current contexts as well as prior experiences.

Our focus is on learning that is related to the labor market. Adult learning encompasses many types of activities, much of which are not related to current or future jobs (Field 2000; see also Jarvis 1995). However, for the type of comparative research that we undertake, it is imperative to limit the scope of activities that we examine (cf. Jarvis 1994). Due to the centrality of employment in the societies that we live in, we have chosen to focus on learning that is related to the labor market. In this book, we use the term "adult learning" to refer to both formal and non-formal learning activities that take place after labor market entry. We use "learning" rather than "education" because the latter is often used with reference to learning activities that occur in formal settings only (for examples of the wide range of terminology used in the field of adult learning, see Jarvis 1995).

Furthermore, formal adult learning leads to recognized certificates and mirrors the normal (hierarchical) educational career that leads all the way to university degrees. It may take place entirely within the initial educational system and lead to the same qualifications or take place in separate institutions, where it may not necessarily lead to qualifications of the same value. Non-formal adult learning, by contrast, is often undertaken as part of employment and consists of shorter training courses. This type of learning is also organized, involves a teacher of some kind, and it may also be institutionalized and lead to certification – though not to full qualifications.

Adult learning can also take place informally, meaning that it is self-directed and not organized by a learning provider. We have chosen to exclude informal learning due to a current lack of longitudinal data (though see Allmendinger et al. 2011 for an effort to begin collecting this type of data in Germany).

The aim of this chapter is to develop a theoretical framework for answering our research questions. This chapter presents our expectations at the cross-national level, and the concluding chapter brings together the results from the individual countries. In addition to outlining some general expectations with regard to adult learning, we also take into consideration the effect of different institutional settings. Countries differ considerably with respect to the characteristics of their educational, training, and occupation systems; their labor market regulations; the nature of their employment-sustaining policies; and the level of decommodification[2] offered by their national welfare systems. Therefore, we examine how these institutions work together to influence individuals' trajectories of continued learning and employment.

In the next section, we discuss the influence of changes at the macro-level, namely globalization and demographic aging, which have contributed to an increasing need for lifelong learning in modern societies. We then further examine the importance of adult learning for social inequality and develop some general hypotheses about the factors influencing participation in adult learning and its effects on the labor market. Following these sections, we outline the role of various institutional settings for adult learning. The institutions that we discuss are (1) educational and occupational systems, (2) welfare regimes, and (3) production and employment regimes. Finally, we conclude by presenting the analytical strategy to be applied by the country studies of the adult learning phase of the *edu*LIFE project.[3]

MACRO-LEVEL CHANGES THAT INCREASE THE NEED FOR ADULT LEARNING IN MODERN SOCIETIES

Economic Change under Globalization

Globalization is often used as an umbrella term for a number of changes that have taken place all over the world and in various spheres of life in the past decades. More specifically, four macro-structural trends characterize the globalization process: (1) the internationalization of markets facilitated by formal global agreements and by the liberalization of financial markets; (2) the intensification of economic competition based on deregulation, privatization, and liberalization; (3) the accelerated diffusion of knowledge and the spread of global networks that connect diverse global markets via information and communication technologies (ICTs); and (4) the rising importance of markets as a coordinating mechanism for decisions as well as the vulnerability of markets to random shocks that occur all over the globe (Mills and Blossfeld 2005).

An important consequence of the globalization process is the stimulation of an increasing international division of labor that has led to the rapid reduction and transformation of older industries and to the creation of new production and service sectors in modern countries (Castells 2000). In these countries, knowledge-intensive jobs have been created and the number of jobs requiring low skills has strongly declined, which has lead to reduced employment opportunities for individuals with low skills (Maurin and Thesmar 2003; Dieckhoff, Jungblut and O'Connell 2007; OECD 2013).

Consequently, modern societies face the challenge of adapting their economies and labor forces to the new demands of a globalized world. Further education and retraining is one method of adjusting the skills and qualifications of the adult population to the needs of the changing occupational structure and of service economies (Janossy 1966); there is much discussion of "learning societies" in which continuous learning is imperative (Jarvis 1995; Field 2000). The other method is for new labor market entrants to take up the new, innovative jobs that have been created while older workers retire and leave the obsolete jobs behind – a process known as generational change (Blossfeld and Stockmann 1998/99). Modern societies tend to carry out the adjustment to new occupational demands in both ways. Nevertheless, there are considerable differences between societies and in the extent to which they invest in adult learning or, conversely, emphasize support for early retirement programs over time.

Demographic Aging and Increasing Labor Shortages

Demographic processes related to increasing life expectancy and lower fertility rates are the second crucial driving force behind the need for modern societies to move toward investing in adult learning and in extensions of working lives. These twin processes yield aging populations that are likely to strain welfare state budgets, which have already been burdened in many European countries by early retirement programs (Blossfeld, Buchholz and Hofäcker 2006).

In addition to causing financial problems for welfare state budgets, the shrinking proportion of young workers also results in increasing labor shortages (Fuchs and Dörfler 2005). This makes it necessary for governments as well as firms to encourage a larger proportion of the working-age population to be in employment (Buchholz et al. 2011) – for example, by integrating and/ or training those parts of the population that have so far been more likely to be excluded (e.g., older employees, mothers, low-qualified individuals, and migrants). Increasing the employment rate to meet national economic demand is already an important area of political concern (see, for example, the EU Lisbon Agenda, European Commission 2010) and has been foreseen as becoming all the more important in the future.

Furthermore, the political attitudes of welfare states have greatly changed in the recent past in regard to retirement. The focus of the latest political efforts is on maintaining employment and postponing the transition to retirement – for example, by raising the statutory retirement age as well as strengthening the private tier of pensions (see, for example, the EU Lisbon Agenda, European Commission 2010). Both changes in the pension system and the requirement to extend working lives lead to an increased need to keep the knowledge and skills of the entire population of working age up to date. Therefore, these developments have important implications for adult learning and, in particular, for the (re)training of the older population.

ADULT LEARNING AND SOCIAL INEQUALITY

Adult learning is important for social inequality in a number of different ways. In this volume, we examine adult learning from the point of view of its participants on the one hand and whether it leads to improved labor market outcomes on the other hand. Adult learning can reduce inequalities if it allows disadvantaged individuals (such as those who have left school with low or currently outdated qualifications) to acquire new skills. However, it is not enough to only enable the participation of disadvantaged groups; adult learning should also have a positive impact on the labor market in order to reduce social inequality. This means that it is imperative that we examine both the factors that influence participation as well as the consequences of participation on the labor market in order to fully assess the role of adult learning on social inequality patterns.

Returning to formal education (and to a lesser extent participating in non-formal training) can be considered to be a major life-course transition (Hostetler, Sweet and Moen 2006; Elman and O'Rand 2007). These decisions are embedded in individuals' current contexts as well as their prior pathways. In this regard, we focus on four key factors that shape participation: age, gender, prior education, and labor force status. All of these factors tap into different aspects of the (gendered) life course. The general expectation regarding age is that the likelihood of participation diminishes as individuals age, which is primarily due to lower perceived benefits of participation and possible incompatibility of learning with adult life-course roles (ibid.). Our expectations for the other key factors are discussed below. In addition, a number of other factors have been highlighted as being relevant for participation patterns, such as social origin and family formation (e.g., Gorard et al. 1998, 2001; Elman and O'Rand 2007). These factors are not studied comparatively but some of them are included in a number of the individual country chapters.

The distinction between formal and non-formal learning, which was made above, is important for patterns of participating in and labor market returns to adult learning. Due to the different nature of these two types of adult learning, there are likely to be substantial differences in the way that they affect social inequality patterns.

After an individual's labor market entry, employers play a major role in human capital development by sponsoring (mainly) non-formal training in order to maintain productivity (Becker 1993). There are a number of reasons that lead us to assume that more-highly educated individuals are more likely to take part in non-formal learning, particularly when it is sponsored by the employer. For example, the higher educated tend to work in more-demanding and knowledge-intensive occupations, which require more training (OECD 2013). They may also be more trainable and thus require a smaller investment than the lower educated in order to achieve productivity gains (Dieckhoff 2007; Boeren, Nicaise and Baert 2010). The positive relationship between educational attainment and participation in non-formal adult learning is confirmed by numerous studies (e.g., Pallas 2002; Dieckhoff, Jungblut and O'Connell 2007). This is also known in the literature as a "Matthew effect" (Merton 1968), or as a cumulative advantage (see DiPrete and Eirich 2006), and leads to our first hypothesis:

We expect more-highly educated individuals and those in better occupational positions to be more likely to participate in non-formal adult learning ("Matthew effect hypothesis").

With regard to formal adult education, the patterns of participation are likely to be somewhat different. Formal adult education takes place at both the secondary and tertiary level. The general expansion of the tertiary sector has also tended to draw in more mature students, though the extent to which this has happened differs across countries, and many barriers to entry remain (Schuetze and Slowey 2002). For example, one important barrier is prior educational attainment despite the fact that many educational systems offer possibilities to enter for those who do not fulfill the traditional entry requirements (ibid.). This is confirmed by research showing that individuals with earlier experience in tertiary-level studies but who have not necessarily completed their degrees are more likely to return to tertiary education as adults (Elman and O'Rand 1998, 2004; Hällsten 2011). More generally, we may expect that those who are already highly educated have few incentives to return to formal education (though in some countries the increasing proportion of tertiary educated may increase these incentives, see Brooks and Everett 2008), whereas those who have relatively low levels of education may be put off by either their prior schooling experiences (Field 2000; Illeris 2003; Rubenson and Desjardins 2009) or their lack of necessary entry qualifications. Therefore, those with medium-level qualifications should be most likely to participate in formal adult education. It should also be noted that there may be ceiling effects for some types of formal adult education, whereby it is impossible to observe those with the highest level of education gaining new qualifications above the level that they already hold.

In addition to formal entry barriers, a major impediment to participation in formal adult education is the time commitment required and therefore the opportunity costs of education. Acquiring a formal qualification normally requires at least one year of full-time study (or more years of part-time study) and can even be significantly longer, depending on the qualification. Therefore, individuals in good labor market positions are likely to be deterred by the high opportunity costs. Evidence from Sweden suggests that entry into formal adult education is associated with both unemployment experiences and relatively low earnings, especially for males (Hällsten 2011; Stenberg 2011). Therefore, our second hypothesis is as follows:

We expect medium-educated individuals and those in lower or less-stable employment positions to be most likely to participate in formal adult education ("Partial equalization hypothesis").

It is also important to consider inequalities in adult learning from the point of view of gender. It has been recognized that some of the barriers preventing participation are gendered (Boateng 2009). On the one hand, family responsibilities and discontinuous employment careers may mean that employers are less likely to invest in the non-formal training of their female employees. This effect should be even more pronounced when women have children and could lead to a "fatherhood premium in training opportunities" (Dieckhoff and Steiber 2011, p. 139): According to the traditional male breadwinner model, men specialize in labor market work and thus have more motivation for adult learning, particularly when they are or expect to become fathers, whereas mothers are likely to have less time for adult learning, particularly if they already face a dual burden of housework and paid employment. However, we also expect that women (particularly mothers) should be more likely to invest in adult learning than men precisely due to their employment interruptions and as a method of compensating for them (Jenkins 2006; Dieckhoff and Steiber 2011). Prolonged interruptions due to raising children may make women more likely to seek reentry into the labor market, particularly through formal adult education (Stenberg, de Luna and Westerlund 2011). Moreover, the male breadwinner hypothesis is also likely to mean that the opportunity costs of formal education are higher for men than for women. Our third hypothesis is:

We expect women to be more likely than men to participate in formal adult education. However, we expect men to be more likely to participate in non-formal adult learning when it is employer sponsored, but we expect women to be more likely to do so when it is non-employer sponsored ("Gendered participation hypothesis").

Turning to the labor market outcomes of adult education, it should generally be the case that both formal and non-formal adult learning have positive effects on earnings, prestige mobility, and job stability. With regard to formal education, the literature is divided into two types, depending on the group that adult learners are compared with: individuals graduating at the normative age and adults who do not participate in adult learning at all (Kilpi-Jakonen et al. 2012). From the individual point of view, the choice is unlikely to be between graduation at the normative age or later, but rather that due to unexpected changes, individuals are faced with the choice of reentering education and thus of graduating later or not at all. As a result, it can be argued that the more-meaningful comparison group is individuals who have not taken part in adult education. In these studies, formal adult education has often been found to result in improved employment outcomes, including higher earnings (Felmlee 1988; Jacobson, Lalonde and Sullivan 2005; Vanttaja and Järvinen 2006; Zhang and Palameta 2006; Hällsten 2011; Stenberg 2011; Kilpi-Jakonen et al. 2012; see Jenkins et al. 2003 and Silles 2007 for contradictory evidence). Formal adult education is expected to lead to positive employment outcomes because it is generally valued by employers due to its link to higher productivity and possibly higher motivation. Moreover, tertiary education in particular is becoming a prerequisite to entry into many higher labor market positions, thereby opening access to these positions for those who gain higher qualifications. Our fourth hypothesis therefore reads as follows:

We expect formal adult education to have a positive influence on employment outcomes when compared with non-participation ("Improved employment outcomes hypothesis").

With regard to non-formal learning, we also expect a positive relationship with employment outcomes. However, there is an issue with selectivity that may be particularly problematic for non-formal learning, namely that employers are likely to invest more in the training of employees that they perceive to be more productive, as discussed above. This practice would imply that the positive relationship between adult learning and labor market outcomes is not due solely to the effects of the learning itself but rather to the characteristics of the participants (Bassanini et al. 2005; Albert, García-Serrano and Hernanz 2010). On the other hand, it has been estimated that only between one-fifth and half of returns to training are captured by individuals as earnings increases, and the rest of the productivity increase benefits the employer (Hansson 2008), which means that even when training increases productivity, this increase does not immediately translate into better employment outcomes for the individual. However, it should also be recognized that a substantial amount of non-formal learning is statutory and does not primarily aim to increase productivity but rather, for example, to prevent accidents (Field 2000). Moreover, when participation is a result of compulsion, as it may be for some active labor market programs, the low motivation of learners may also lead to poor learning outcomes (Illeris 2003). Overall, our fifth hypothesis is:

We expect non-formal adult learning and employment outcomes to be positively related; however, we are cautious about asserting a causal impact ("Indeterminate employment outcomes hypothesis").

The benefits of adult learning may be gendered. There is mixed evidence about whether returns are higher for women than for men, with some studies finding one gender to be advantaged and other studies proposing the opposite case (e.g. Havet and Sofer 2008 for male advantage; Stenberg 2011 for female advantage). It is possible that the types of training that men and women undertake, as well as the segment of the labor market in which they are employed, have an effect on the employment outcomes related to their learning. Therefore, it is difficult to formulate general expectations about gendered outcomes. However, there may be country-specific expectations *("Gendered outcomes hypothesis").*

Overall, theories of cumulative advantage and status maintenance offer a relatively pessimistic prediction with regard to the relationship between adult learning and social inequality. These models predict that the educational and labor market trajectories that individuals set out on are relatively stable and that differences between trajectories widen over the life course (Elman and O'Rand 2004; DiPrete and Eirich 2006). The literature also suggests that returns to individuals who participate in formal adult education take time to appear. The overall picture presented is that adult learning at most helps to narrow the gap between the middle and upper strata (Elman and O'Rand 1998).

Our review of previous research and the hypotheses that we have formulated also suggest that if any equalization is to take place, it is more likely to come through formal rather than non-formal adult learning.

While these hypotheses reflect the basic logic of adult learning, it is nevertheless reasonable to assume that country differences exist. We elaborate on these differences in the subsequent section.

THE ROLE OF NATIONAL INSTITUTIONAL SETTINGS

In addition to the general processes of stratification outlined in the previous section, we recognize that national institutions play a role in influencing specific patterns in different countries (see Figure 1.1). On the one hand, the macro-processes that induce the need for increased adult learning are filtered through national institutions, thus generating country differences in participation rates, the types of learning that are most prevalent, and the social inequality patterns related to participation. On the other hand, institutional arrangements may also affect whether and to what extent adult learning affects labor market outcomes. Overall, this means that the hypotheses set out above may need to be slightly modified in different countries due to each country's specific institutional settings. In this section, we discuss the influence of the following institutions on adult learning, with some reference to education in general: (1) educational systems and the national infrastructure of adult learning, (2) welfare regimes, and (3) production regimes and employment systems. For the purpose of making hypotheses based on institutions, we discuss these institutional settings separately. However, we also recognize that there is a strong interdependence between them.

Educational Systems, Adult Learning, and Occupational Boundaries

There are a number of characteristics of educational systems that may have an effect on adult learning. Those discussed here are the level of education of the population, the organization of vocational training (particularly at the secondary level), and the openness of formal educational institutions to mature students.

The countries that we study vary widely in the general educational level of the working-age population (Figure 1.2). Liberal (including the Russian Federation and Estonia) and Nordic countries have the highest proportions of tertiary educated, whereas the Central and Southern European countries have

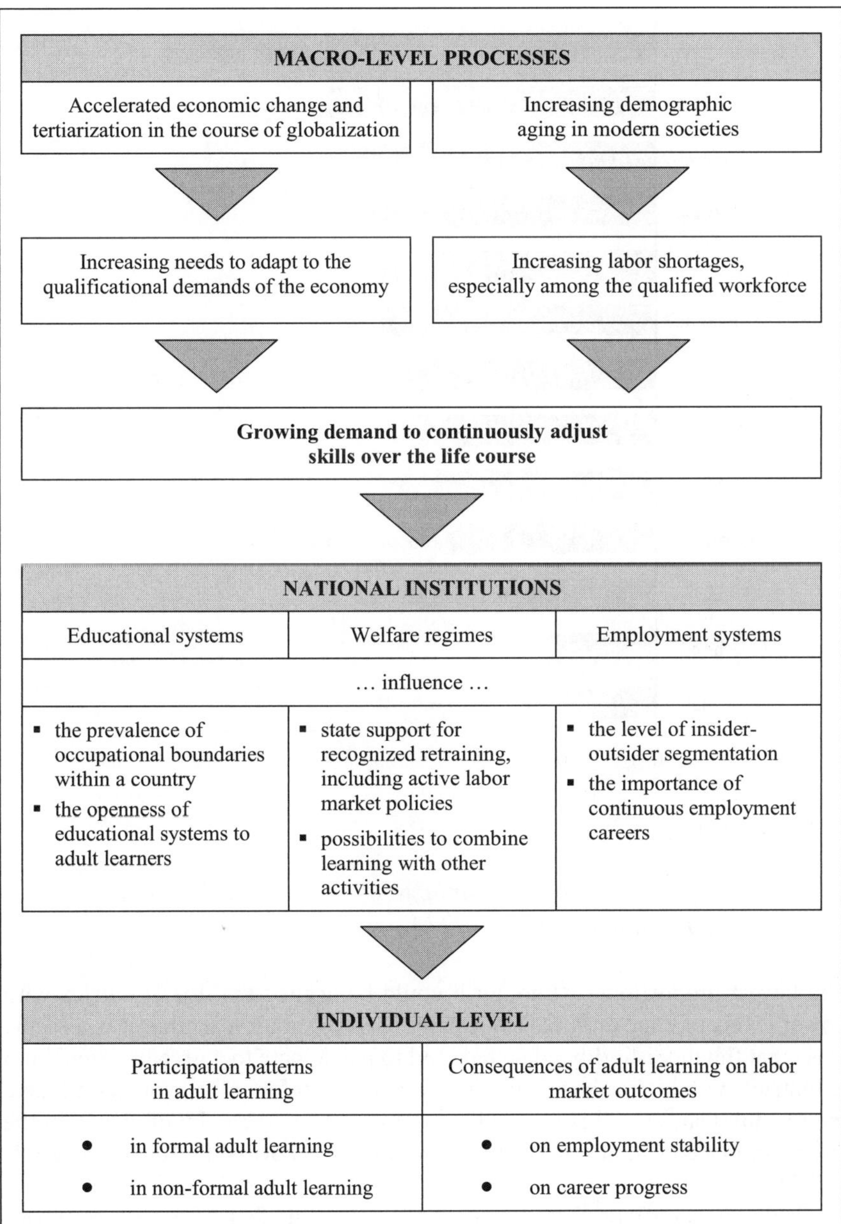

Source: Own illustration.

Figure 1.1   Adult learning and the role of various national institutions

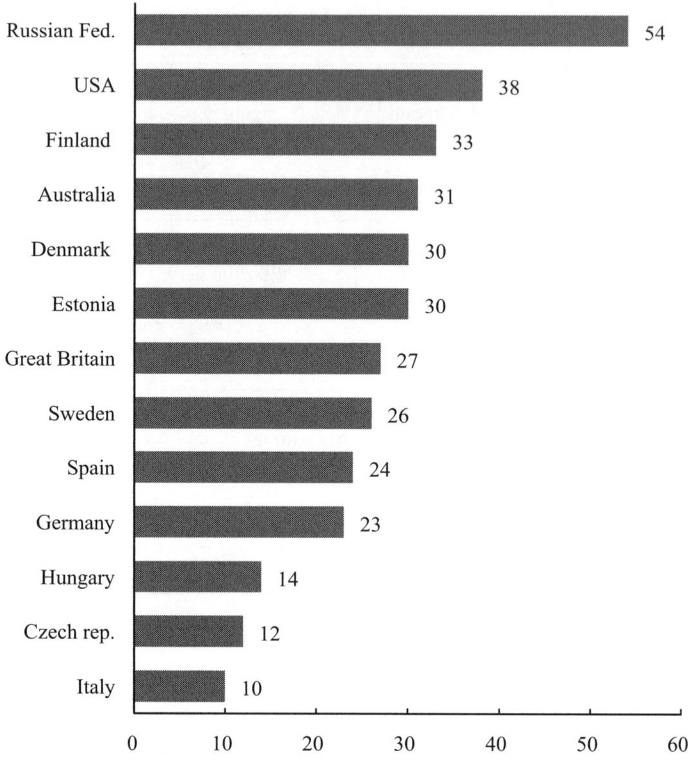

Source: OECD (2012).

*Figure 1.2   Proportion of the population (aged 25–64) with tertiary
education (ISCED 5 and 6) in 2002*

the lowest proportions. Although it could be argued that the countries with
lower levels of education have a greater need for adult learning, it is also the
case that the more-highly educated tend to participate to a greater extent, and
countries with higher levels of education are therefore also expected to have
more adult learners. This could also be argued from the point of view that the
more-highly educated tend to be more trainable (Brunello 2001; Dieckhoff
2007).

At the secondary level, the greatest differentiating factor between countries
is the way that vocational training is organized and how much focus there is
on occupational specificity versus more-general education. At one extreme,
we have comprehensive school systems in which education at the upper

secondary level can even have a strong common basis (e.g., the USA, Sweden, and Finland) and, at the other extreme, we have strongly stratified systems in which vocational education has a strong component of on-the-job training (e.g., Germany). The organization of vocational training impacts both patterns of labor market entry and occupational mobility. For example, the strong signals produced by the German system can produce smoother transitions to the labor market but may act as a barrier to mobility between jobs and occupations (e.g., Bukodi et al. 2008; Buchholz et al. 2011). This system can also produce strong differentiation over the life course between unskilled and semi-skilled workers and the vocationally trained in terms of labor market outcomes.

Some evidence exists that the arrangement of vocational training influences the prevalence of adult learning. On the one hand, in comprehensive school systems, where a common basis of knowledge is transmitted to every pupil and the amount of general education is relatively high, (upper) secondary school graduates have been found to require less training in order to meet the requirements of technical progress (Bassanini et al. 2005). On the other hand, there may also be more of a need for adult learning in comprehensive school systems, where there is less specialization during initial education (Brunello 2001; Antikainen, Harinen and Torres 2006; though see Wolbers 2005 for evidence to the contrary). Moreover, when there is a strong common core to the curriculum, gaining new qualifications should be less time consuming for individuals who return to formal education, particularly when these qualifications are at the same level (but in a different field) as ones that they have obtained previously. These considerations lead us to believe that the degree of stratification of secondary education affects participation in adult learning both between countries and between social groups within countries (Brunello 2001; Bassanini et al. 2005; Groenez, Desmedt and Nicaise 2007).

State support for adult learning is likely to affect participation levels of the population as a whole as well as those of specific (generally more-vulnerable) subgroups, as is discussed in the following section. In addition to affecting participation rates, state support and the characteristics of the educational system may also have an effect on the benefits that adult learning confers on the labor market. In particular, we may expect that more-open educational systems – i.e., those that allow for greater participation of mature students in educational types normally reserved for young persons – also reward older graduates to a greater extent than more-closed systems. One of the reasons behind this could be that participation in open systems is less "scarring" for adults than is the case when adult participation is very rare, as it is in closed systems (Kilpi-Jakonen et al. 2012).

With regard to social inequality, we expect that countries with strongly youth-oriented systems in which the opportunity to take part in recognized vocational and further education is only available directly after compulsory schooling are more likely to reproduce the social inequalities of the educational system in the labor market.[4] Thus, there is greater potential for social inequalities to be reduced by adult learning in countries in which adults have the opportunity to return to formal education at a later stage. Moreover, countries differ in the extent to which occupational status is dependent on certificates. In countries where certificates strongly regulate the entry to specific positions, it is possible that only formal adult education is useful. In countries where certificates are not as important, the opportunity to obtain higher-status positions with the help of non-formal adult learning may exist.

Welfare Regimes, Adult Learning, and Supporting Vulnerable Subgroups

Welfare state policies can be seen as having an impact on the amount of adult learning that takes place overall, on how unequally it is distributed, and on the adult learning of specific groups: women, those approaching pension age, the unemployed, and those disadvantaged in the labor market more generally. An important criterion for distinguishing welfare regimes is the way in which responsibilities are shared between the state, the market, and the family (Esping-Andersen 1999). In a similar vein, it has also been argued that the international policy discourse on lifelong learning has developed historically with regard to the roles given to the three major institutions that implement lifelong learning: the state, the market, and civil society (Rubenson 2006). Countries differ in the role that each of these three institutions assumes in terms of providing and supporting adult learning. These differences have important consequences for the participation levels of the population as a whole as well as for the participation of specific subgroups, for example the participation of vulnerable subgroups may be more reliant on state support. Earlier research has also found welfare regimes to be correlated with educational policy at the level of public expenditure (Hega and Hokenmaier 2002) as well as with adults' motivations to take part in formal adult education (Boeren et al. 2012).

Public support for adult learning is important since there tends to be a market failure in adult learning whereby individuals and firms do not invest in it to a socially optimal extent (Hansson 2008). Training as a part of active labor market programs is the type of adult learning that is most clearly linked to the welfare state. These programs are emphasized in the Nordic countries, where employment-sustaining policies have traditionally been very important (DiPrete et al. 1997).

While active labor market programs focus on the unemployed, training for the employed mainly depends on the opportunities employers offer their workforce. However, the state may also intervene in the market provision of adult learning through policies on employees' statutory and contractual rights to take paid time off for training and through monetary support for those participating in adult learning (Schömann 2002). These rights ensure that even employees not offered training directly by their employers have the opportunity to participate in training outside the workplace. The ethos of the Nordic welfare regimes to ensure employability can also be argued to influence adult learning levels in general and to result in a more-equitable distribution of employer-sponsored training (Dieckhoff, Jungblut and O'Connell 2007).

Another policy area that has been found to influence participation in adult learning relates to retirement and pensions. More specifically, the expected age of retirement has been found to negatively affect the participation rates of older persons, and countries with more-generous (early) pension systems see a steeper decline in the training of workers as they age (Bassanini et al. 2005). These results are likely due to reduced incentives for investing in the training of workers nearing the retirement age – either for the workers themselves or for their employers.

Women represent an additional subgroup whose participation in adult learning is highly influenced through public policies. Rubenson and Desjardins (2009) argue that extensive support in terms of early childhood education and care systems is particularly beneficial for the participation of women with young children. Moreover, policies that help parents combine work and family life are also likely to reduce the barriers to participation in adult learning for parents with children of all ages. The various welfare regimes tend to differ in their regulations on parental leave as well as on publicly supported childcare offerings. We expect that these differences have a direct impact on women's decisions to take part in adult learning. We expect to find a weak or non-existent difference between men's and women's participation in adult learning, especially in the Nordic countries. Instead, women's risks of potential educational losses are likely to be very high, especially in the traditional male breadwinner societies of the conservative and Southern European welfare regimes since these regimes engender discontinuous female careers.

Overall, we expect that public provision of adult learning plays an important role in reducing inequalities in participation rates between different groups and in particular that it increases the participation of otherwise vulnerable groups (Rubenson 2006; Rubenson and Desjardins 2009).

Production Regimes, Employment Systems, and the Unequal Distribution of Learning Opportunities

The final differentiating institutional factors that we consider are production regimes and the level of employment regulation, both of which influence individual employment conditions as well as possible labor market outcomes of learning. We can distinguish between "coordinated" market economies, which are characterized by reciprocal cooperation among economic actors, and "uncoordinated" ("liberal") market economies, which are primarily based on the market mechanism (Soskice 1991, 1999). Most of the research on production regimes and skills has focused on initial skill formation, but some of the arguments can also be extended to the provision of adult learning (Dieckhoff, Jungblut and O'Connell 2007).

In coordinated market economies, employment relationships tend to be longer lasting, and firing existing workers and hiring new ones is relatively difficult. This means that it is in employers' interest to continuously invest in their employees' skill development and to distribute training relatively equitably (ibid.). Moreover, coordinated market economies tend to have relatively strong unions, which are likely to negotiate more training opportunities (Booth and Francesconi 2003; Bassanini et al. 2005; Dieckhoff, Jungblut and O'Connell 2007).

However, when a coordinated economy is accompanied by a welfare regime that does not actively support full employment, a division in the labor market between "insiders" and "outsiders" may ensue. This division has also been found in countries that do not fit well with the division into coordinated and uncoordinated production regimes, e.g., the Southern European countries (Ferrera 1996). In these cases, careers of insiders are characterized by a high level of security and stability, whereas outsiders, which consist mainly of young persons, women after periods of maternity leave, and the lesser educated, have difficulties obtaining stable and secure employment and run the risk of being confined to precarious jobs or remaining unemployed (Buchholz et al. 2011).

The division in the labor markets also has consequences for adult learning opportunities. We expect that labor market insiders are the chief recipients of learning opportunities in the workplace, whereas outsiders are more likely to be dependent on publicly supported adult learning, which may be less likely to be recognized by employers. Moreover, work experience is likely to be important for the insiders, and there is likely to be a high risk that educational degrees acquired earlier in life lose importance once a person becomes non-employed. It could also be argued that in these situations the use of informal networks (social capital) is quite high, which is likely to increase informal learning but to discourage participation in formal adult education (Schuller and Field 1998).

The situation in uncoordinated market economies tends to be quite different since employment relations tend to be rather open. In these countries, the state hardly interferes with the labor market; rather, the emphasis lies on the self-regulation of the markets and short-term competitive (industrial) relations (Soskice 1999). Therefore, labor market turnover and employment mobility (between jobs, firms, and even occupations) are high (Sørensen and Tuma 1981). In contrast to insider-outsider labor markets, employment risks (and chances) in uncoordinated market economies are distributed more broadly across the entire workforce, but individual resources (including human capital) are crucial factors in determining individuals' labor market success (DiPrete et al. 1997). Low employment protection legislation means that individuals are compelled to invest in their human capital either by updating their existing knowledge or by gaining new qualifications in order to remain competitive in the labor market. However, employer-sponsored learning is likely to be firm specific partly in order to prevent the poaching of trained employees by other firms (Soskice 1999; Dieckhoff 2007).

ANALYTICAL STRATEGY AND STRUCTURE OF THE BOOK

The overall aim of this book is to investigate the relationship between adult learning and social inequality. In order to do so, the country chapters examine how adult learning is organized in different modern societies, what individual-level factors affect participation in different types of adult learning, and whether adult learning has an impact on labor market outcomes. Moreover, two comparative chapters analyze these questions from a cross-national perspective, allowing for a quantitative analysis of some of the institutional factors affecting participation and labor market outcomes. Chapter 2 presents findings that analyze participation in adult learning, whereas Chapter 3 concentrates on the short-term impacts of adult learning on income. We also return to the cross-national findings of our book in Chapter 17, where we bring together the results from all chapters and assess the evidence for the hypotheses presented in this chapter.

Many of the country studies use longitudinal data (see Table 17.1 of the concluding chapter) and apply event history models as well as other longitudinal methods to analyze learning trajectories and employment careers. These methods allow us to study these processes while taking into account the timing and ordering of events as well as considering individual characteristics and other life-cycle influences.

The labor market outcomes studied in the country chapters can be grouped under two broad headings: employment stability and career progress. The first of these includes analyses of unemployment risks and reemployment chances of the unemployed. The second includes career mobility in the form of upward and downward prestige, income, and occupational mobility, as well as occupational status, income, and prestige levels.

We organize the countries analyzed in this contribution according to their institutional settings, which we expect to have an impact on adult learning patterns (see Table 1.1). The groupings that we use are the Liberal countries (the USA – Chapter 4, Great Britain – Chapter 5, Australia – Chapter 6, Russian Federation – Chapter 7, and Estonia – Chapter 8), the Nordic countries (Sweden – Chapter 9, Finland – Chapter 10, and Denmark – Chapter 11), the Central European countries (Germany – Chapter 12, Hungary – Chapter 13, and the Czech Republic – Chapter 14), and the Southern European countries (Spain – Chapter 15 and Italy – Chapter 16). We recognize that Eastern European countries have by now become a very heterogeneous group and thus, rather than treating them as their own grouping, we have divided them into the existing typology (cf. Boeren et al. 2012).

The Liberal countries have in common their uncoordinated market economies and also share similarities in their educational systems in terms of low levels of stratification, a rather general system of secondary education, and high levels of tertiary education. The Nordic countries are connected by their strong welfare states as well as relatively similar (coordinated) production regimes and educational systems (with comprehensive schools and high levels of tertiary education), although the similarities are stronger between Finland and Sweden in comparison with Denmark. The Central European countries share stratified educational systems, more-reduced welfare states (compared with the Nordic countries), and a division of the labor market into insiders and outsiders. This last feature is particularly strong in Southern European countries, which also display educational systems that are less standardized and stratified than those of the Central European countries. These national institutions are likely to shape the extent and distribution of inequality in the countries concerned. One of our aims is to examine the extent to which these institutions also shape the relationship between adult learning and social inequality.

NOTES

1. The Programme for International Student Assessment (PISA) is run by the OECD and tests 15-year-olds in literacy, numeracy, and science literacy every three years.
2. "De-commodification occurs when a service is rendered as a matter of right, and when a person can maintain a livelihood without reliance on the market" (Esping-Andersen 1990, p. 22).
3. The *edu*LIFE project is financed by an ERC Advanced Grant for the years 2011–16. The full title of the project is "Education as a Lifelong Process – Comparing Educational Trajectories in Modern Societies". More information is available at http://edulife.eui.eu.
4. We use the term "social inequalities of the educational system" to not only refer to those inequalities produced by the educational system itself but also to those that have other causes and that are merely reflected in the inequality of educational attainment.

Table 1.1   Country groupings and expected patterns of social inequalities in modern societies

	USA, Australia, Great Britain, Russia, Estonia	Sweden, Finland, Denmark	Germany, Hungary, Czech Republic	Spain, Italy
Country studies				
Educational system	On-the-job training, low importance of certificates, few occupational boundaries, little age discrimination	Vocational schools, moderate importance of certificates, public support for retraining, little age discrimination	Dual system, high importance of certificates, strong occupational boundaries, strong youth-orientation	Vocational schools, moderate importance of certificates, strong youth-orientation
Welfare regime	Residual workfare state with strong privatization of risks	Universalistic workfare state with pronounced equality ideology	Transfer-orientated welfare state aimed at status maintenance	Fragmented welfare state with strong transfer orientation for insiders
Labor market	Highly flexible with open employment relations and privatization of risks	Coordinated with high level of state intervention	Closed employment systems with strong insider/ outsider segmentation	Closed employment systems with very strong insider/ outsider segmentation
Patterns of social inequalities	High level of inequalities, less contingent on educational and occupational degrees but rather on individuals' efforts	Efforts to actively reduce previous educational as well as labor market inequalities by state interventions	Continuation or even amplification of inequalities arising from initial education, strong differences between men and women	Strong inequalities, strong differences in returns to education between labor market insiders and labor market outsiders

Source: Own illustration.

21

REFERENCES

Albert, C., C. García-Serrano and V. Hernanz (2010), 'On-the-job training in Europe: Determinants and wage returns', *International Labour Review,* **149** (3), 315–41.

Allmendinger, Jutta, Corinna Kleinert, Manfred Antoni, Bernhard Christoph, Katrin Drasch, Florian Janik, Kathrin Leuze, Britta Matthes, Reinhard Pollak and Michael Ruland (2011), 'Adult education and lifelong learning', in Hans-Peter Blossfeld, Hans-Günther Roßbach and Jutta von Maurice (eds), *Education as a Lifelong Process: The German National Educational Panel Study. Special Issue 14/2011 of Zeitschrift für Erziehungswissenschaft,* Wiesbaden: VS Verlag, pp. 283–300.

Antikainen Ari, Paivi Harinen and Carlos Alberto Torres (eds) (2006), *In from the Margins: Adult Education, Work and Civil Society,* Rotterdam: Sense Publishers.

Bassanini, Andrea, Alison Booth, Giorgio Brunello, Maria De Paola and Edwin Leuven (2005), 'Workplace training in Europe', *IZA Discussion Paper,* No. 1640, Institute for the Study of Labor, Bonn, Germany.

Becker, Rolf (ed.) (1993), *Staatsexpansion und Karrierechancen. Berufsverläufe im öffentlichen Dienst und in der Privatwirtschaft (State Expansion and Career Chances. Occupational Careers in the Public and in the Private Sector),* Frankfurt am Main: Campus.

Blossfeld, H.-P. and R. Stockmann (1998/99), 'The German dual system in comparative perspective', *International Journal of Sociology,* **28** (4), 3–28.

Blossfeld, Hans-Peter, Sandra Buchholz and Dirk Hofäcker (eds) (2006), *Globalization, Uncertainty and Late Careers in Society,* London, UK and New York, USA: Routledge.

Boateng, S. K. (2009), 'Significant country differences in adult learning', *Eurostat statistics in focus* 44/2009, available at: http://epp.eurostat.ec.europa.eu/cache/ITY_OFFPUB/KS-SF-09-044/EN/KS-SF-09-044-EN.PDF (accessed 6.2.2012).

Boeren, E., I. Nicaise and H. Baert (2010), 'Theoretical models of participation in adult education: the need for an integrated model', *International Journal of Lifelong Education,* **29** (1), 45–61.

Boeren, E., J. Holford, I. Nicaise and H. Baert (2012), 'Why do adults learn? Developing a motivational typology across 12 European countries', *Globalisation, Societies and Education,* **10** (2), 247–69.

Booth, A. L. and M. Francesconi (2003), 'Unions, work-related training, and wages: evidence for British men', *Industrial and Labor Relations Review,* **57** (1), 68–91.

Brooks, R. and G. Everett (2008), 'The impact of higher education on lifelong learning', *International Journal of Lifelong Education,* **27** (3), 239–54.

Brunello, Giorgio (2001), 'On the complementarity between education and training in Europe', *IZA Discussion Paper,* No. 309, Institute for the Study of Labor, Bonn, Germany.

Buchholz, Sandra, Annika Rinklake, Julia Schilling, Karin Kurz, Paul Schmelzer and Hans-Peter Blossfeld (2011), 'Aging populations, globalization and the labor market: Comparing late working life and retirement in modern societies', in Hans-Peter Blossfeld, Sandra Buchholz and Karin Kurz (eds), *Aging*

Populations, Globalization and the Labor Market: Comparing Late Working Life and Retirement in Modern Societies, Cheltenham, UK and Northampton, MA, USA: Edward Elgar, pp. 3–34.

Bukodi, Erzsébet, Ellen Ebralidze, Paul Schmelzer and Hans-Peter Blossfeld (2008), 'Struggling to become an insider: Does increasing flexibility at labor market entry affect early careers?', in Hans-Peter Blossfeld, Sandra Buchholz, Erzsébet Bukodi and Karin Kurz (eds), *Young Workers, Globalization and the Labor Market: Comparing Early Working Life in Eleven Countries*, Cheltenham, UK and Northampton, MA, USA: Edward Elgar, pp. 3–27.

Castells, Manuel (ed.) (2000), *The Rise of the Network Society. The Information Age: Economy, Society And Culture,* 2nd edition, Oxford and Malden: Blackwell Publishers.

Dieckhoff, M. and N. Steiber (2011), 'A re-assessment of common theoretical approaches to explain gender differences in continuing training participation', *British Journal of Industrial Relations*, **49** (s1), 135–57.

Dieckhoff, Martina, Jean-Marie Jungblut and Philip J. O'Connell (2007), 'Job-related training in Europe: Do institutions matter?', in Duncan Gallie (ed.), *Employment Regimes and the Quality of Work*, Oxford: Oxford University Press, pp. 77–103.

DiPrete, T. A. and G. M. Eirich (2006), 'Cumulative advantage as a mechanism for inequality: A review of theoretical and empirical developments', *Annual Review of Sociology*, **32**, 271–97.

DiPrete, T. A., P. M. DeGraaf, R. Luijkx, M. Tahlin and H.-P. Blossfeld (1997), 'Collectivist versus individualist mobility regimes? Structural change and job mobility in four countries', *American Journal of Sociology*, **103**, 318–58.

Elman, C. and A. M. O'Rand (1998), 'Midlife entry into vocational training: a mobility model', *Social Science Research*, **27** (2), 128–58.

Elman, C. and A. M. O'Rand (2004), 'The race is to the swift: Socioeconomic origins, adult education, and wage attainment', *American Journal of Sociology*, **110** (1), 123–60.

Elman, C. and A. M. O'Rand (2007), 'The effects of social origins, life events, and institutional sorting on adults' school transitions', *Social Science Research*, **36** (3), 1276–99.

Esping-Andersen, Gøsta (ed.) (1990), *The Three Worlds of Welfare Capitalism*, Princeton, NJ: Princeton University Press.

Esping-Andersen, Gøsta (ed.) (1999), *Social Foundations of Postindustrial Economies*, Oxford: Oxford University Press.

European Commission (2010), *Interim EPC-SPC Joint Report on Pensions*, Brussels: European Commission, available at: http://europa.eu/epc/pdf/interim_epc-spc_joint_report_on_pensions_final_en.pdf (accessed 22.10.2013).

European Commission (2011), *Progress towards the common European Objectives in education and training. Indicators and benchmarks 2010/2011*, Brussels: European Commission, available at: http://ec.europa.eu/education/lifelong-learning-policy/doc/report10/report_en.pdf (accessed 16.11.2012).

Felmlee, D. H. (1988), 'Returning to school and women's occupational attainment', *Sociology of Education*, **61** (1), 29–41.

Ferrera, M. (1996), 'The "Southern model" of welfare in social Europe', *Journal of European Social Policy*, **6** (1), 17–37.

Field, John (2000), *Lifelong Learning and the New Educational Order*, Oakhill, Stoke on Trent, Staffordshire: Trentham Books.

Fuchs, Johann and Katrin Dörfler (2005), 'Projektion des Erwerbspersonenpotentials bis 2050. Annahmen und Datengrundlage' (Projections of the labor force potential until 2050. Assumptions and data foundation), *IAB Forschungsbericht* 25/2005, Nürnberg, Germany.

Gorard, S., G. Rees, R. Fevre and J. Furlong (1998), 'Learning trajectories: travelling towards a learning society?', *International Journal of Lifelong Education*, **17** (6), 400–10.

Gorard, S., G. Rees, R. Fevre and T. Welland (2001), 'Lifelong learning trajectories: some voices of those "in transit"', *International Journal of Lifelong Education*, **20** (3), 169–87.

Groenez, Steven, Ella Desmedt and Ides Nicaise (2007), 'Participation in lifelong learning in the EU-15: The role of macro-level determinants', *Paper for the ECER Conference*, Ghent, Belgium.

Hällsten, M. (2011), 'Late entry in Swedish tertiary education: Can the opportunity of lifelong learning promote equality over the life course?', *British Journal of Industrial Relations*, **49** (3), 537–59.

Hansson, Bo (2008), 'Job-related training and benefits for individuals: A review of evidence and explanations', *OECD Education Working Papers*, No. 19, Paris.

Havet, N. and C. Sofer (2008), 'Why do women's wages increase so slowly throughout their career? A dynamic model of statistical discrimination', *Labour*, **22** (2), 291–314.

Hega, G. M. and K. G. Hokenmaier (2002), 'The welfare state and education: a comparison of social and educational policy in advanced industrial societies', *Politikfeldanalyse*, **2** (1), 1–29.

Hostetler, A., S. Sweet and P. Moen (2006), 'Gendered career paths: a life course perspective on returning to school', *Sex Roles*, **56** (1–2), 85–103.

Illeris, K. (2003), 'Towards a contemporary and comprehensive theory of learning', *International Journal of Lifelong Education*, **22** (4), 396–406.

Jacobson, L., R. J. Lalonde and D. Sullivan (2005), 'The impact of community college restraining on older displaced workers: Should we teach old dogs new tricks?', *Industrial and Labor Relations Review*, **58** (3), 398–415.

Janossy, Ferenc (ed.) (1966), *Das Ende der Wirtschaftswunder* (The End of the Economic Miracle), Frankfurt am Main: Campus.

Jarvis, Peter (1994), 'Problems in developing the study of international comparative adult education', in Peter Jarvis and Franz Pöggeler (eds), *Developments in the Education of Adults in Europe*, Frankfurt am Main: Peter Lang, pp. 145–55.

Jarvis, Peter (1995), *Adult & Continuing Education: Theory and Practice*, 2nd edition, London, UK and New York, USA: Routledge.

Jenkins, A. (2006), 'Women, lifelong learning and transitions into employment', *Work, Employment and Society*, **20** (2), 309–28.

Jenkins, A., A. Vignoles, A. Wolf and F. Galindo-Rueda (2003), 'The determinants and labour market effects of lifelong learning', *Applied Economics*, **35** (16), 1711–21.

Kilpi-Jakonen, E., D. Vono De Vilhena, Y. Kosyakova, A. Stenberg and H.-P. Blossfeld (2012), 'The impact of formal adult education on the likelihood of being employed: a comparative overview', *Studies of Transition States and Societies*, **4** (1), 48–68.

Maurin, Eric and David Thesmar (2003), 'Changes in the functional structure of firms and the demands for skill', *CEPR Discussion Papers*, No. 3831, London.

Merton, R. K. (1968), 'The Matthew effect in science', *Science*, **159** (3810), 56–63.

Mills, Melinda and Hans-Peter Blossfeld (2005), 'Globalization, uncertainty and the early life-course. A theoretical framework', in Hans-Peter Blossfeld, Eric Klijzing, Melinda Mills and Karin Kurz (eds), *Globalization, Uncertainty and Youth in Society*, London, UK and New York, USA: Routledge, pp. 1–48.

OECD (2012), *Education at a Glance 2012: OECD Indicators*, Paris: OECD Publishing.

OECD (2013), *OECD Skills Outlook 2013: First Results from the Survey of Adult Skills*, Paris: OECD Publishing.

Pallas, A. M. (2002), 'Educational participation across the life course Do the rich get richer?', *Advances in Life Course Research,* **7**, 327–54.

Rubenson, K. (2006), 'The Nordic model of lifelong learning', *Compare: A Journal of Comparative and International Education*, **36** (3), 327–41.

Rubenson, K. and R. Desjardins (2009), 'The impact of welfare state regimes on barriers to participation in adult education: A bounded agency model', *Adult Education Quarterly*, **59** (3), 187–207.

Schömann, Klaus (2002), 'Training transitions in the EU: Different policies but similar effects?', in Schömann, Klaus and Philip J. O'Connell (eds), *Education, Training and Employment Dynamics. Transitional Labour Markets in the European Union*, Cheltenham, UK and Northampton, MA, USA: Edward Elgar, pp. 186–222.

Schuetze, H.-G. and M. Slowey (2002), 'Participation and exclusion: A comparative analysis of non-traditional students and lifelong learners in higher education', *Higher Education*, **44** (3–4), 309–27.

Schuller, T. and J. Field (1998), 'Social capital, human capital and the learning society', *International Journal of Lifelong Education*, **17** (4), 226–35.

Silles, M. (2007), 'Adult education and earnings: evidence from Britain', *Bulletin of Economic Research*, **59** (4), 313–26.

Sørensen, A. B. and N. B. Tuma (1981), 'Labor market structures and job mobility', *Research in Social Stratification and Mobility*, **1**, 67–94.

Soskice, David (1991), 'The institutional infrastructure for international competitiveness: A comparative analysis of the UK and Germany', in Anthony B. Atkinson (ed.), *Economics for the New Europe,* London: Macmillan Academic and Professional Ltd, pp. 25–66.

Soskice, David (1999), 'Divergent production regimes: coordinated and uncoordinated market economies in the 1980s and 1990s', in Herbert Kitschelt, Peter Lange, Gary Marks and John D. Stephens (eds), *Continuity and Change in Contemporary Capitalism*, New York: Cambridge University Press, pp. 101–34.

Stenberg, A. (2011), 'Using longitudinal data to evaluate publicly provided formal education for low skilled', *Economics of Education Review*, **30** (6), 1262–80.

Stenberg, Anders, Xavier de Luna and Olle Westerlund (2011), 'Does formal education for older workers increase earnings? Analyzing annual data stretching over 25 years', *SOFI working paper* 8/2011, Stockholm University.
Vanttaja, M. and T. Järvinen (2006), 'The young outsiders: the later life courses of "drop-out youths"', *International Journal of Lifelong Education*, **25** (2), 173–84.
Wolbers, M. H. J. (2005), 'Initial and further education: substitutes or complements? differences in continuing education and training over the life-course of European workers', *International Review of Education*, **51** (5–6), 459–78.
Zhang, Xuelin and Boris Palameta (2006), 'Participation in adult schooling and its earnings impact in Canada', *Analytical Studies Branch Research Paper Series 2006*, No. 276, Statistics Canada, Ottawa.

PART II

Comparative Contributions

2. Participation in Adult Learning in Europe: The Impact of Country-Level and Individual Characteristics

Johanna Dämmrich, Daniela Vono de Vilhena, and Elisabeth Reichart

INTRODUCTION

The promotion of lifelong learning has become a key issue in policy discourses in regard to both strengthening international economic competitiveness and reducing social inequalities within countries. Beyond demographic developments, accelerated technological changes and growing international interconnectedness have led to an increasing demand to update skills and knowledge over the lifespan (Heckman 2000; Cunha et al. 2006; OECD 2012; Chapter 1 of this volume). Due to these developments, a benchmark has been set within the European Union to raise the participation rate of the 25-to-64-year-old population in lifelong learning to 15 per cent by the year 2020. However, only eight member states (Austria, Denmark, Finland, Luxemburg, the Netherlands, Slovenia, Sweden, and the United Kingdom) have currently met and/or exceeded the 2010 benchmark of 12.5 per cent (European Commission 2010).

Comparative analyses of participation in adult learning have shown that there are significant country differences in overall participation rates and in the characteristics of participants. This suggests that the degree to which adult learning contributes to social equalization differs among countries. However, differences in data sources, definitions of adult learning, and varying reference periods make cross-national comparisons of adult learning difficult (Bassanini et al. 2005; Macleod and Lambe 2007; von Rosenbladt 2010). In line with that, data on adult learning that include more than one country are rare. After the International Adult Literacy Survey (IALS), which focuses on the 1990s and is used in the following chapter for analyzing returns to adult learning, the Adult Education Survey (AES) of 2007 is one of the most recent comparative datasets on adult learning. Thus, the AES facilitates the direct comparison of different types of adult learning among countries.

Using this data for 26 European countries, our chapter aims to answer the following research questions: (1) How do participation rates in job-related adult learning differ among countries and among different types of adult learning? (2) Which individual characteristics influence participation in different types of job-related adult learning? (3) Are there differences regarding the influence of gender and initial educational level among countries? (4) Which characteristics at the country level influence participation in different job-related adult learning activities?

This chapter is structured as follows: In the next section, we define different job-related adult learning activities, before taking a look at participation rates in these types of adult learning. In the following section, we provide a short overview of the literature and derive hypotheses on the characteristics that influence participation in job-related adult learning. After this, we describe the data, variables and methods. We then present our results, first regarding the influence of individual characteristics and second regarding the impact of country-level characteristics on participation in job-related adult learning. The last section summarizes the results found and concludes.

DEFINITION OF ADULT LEARNING ACTIVITIES

Definitions of adult learning vary greatly among studies, making comparisons between the findings of empirical studies difficult (Hällsten 2011). The definitions of job-related formal and non-formal adult learning applied in this chapter are based on our dataset. Accordingly, formal adult learning takes place in regular school and university systems, where the academic content is mostly based on nationally regulated curricula and the education leads to recognized certificates. Non-formal adult learning can take place both within or outside of educational institutions, the content on different topics can be more specific, and the learning activities have varying durations (European Commission 2006).

Beyond this distinction, empirical evidence further demonstrates the importance of taking the employer's involvement into account (e.g., Bassanini et al. 2005; O'Connell and Byrne 2010). Therefore, we extend the definition of adult learning and distinguish between four different types of adult learning activities in the following sections: employer-sponsored formal and non-formal adult learning, as well as formal and non-formal adult learning without employer support (see Figure 2.1). Moreover, we only focus on job-related adult learning activities.

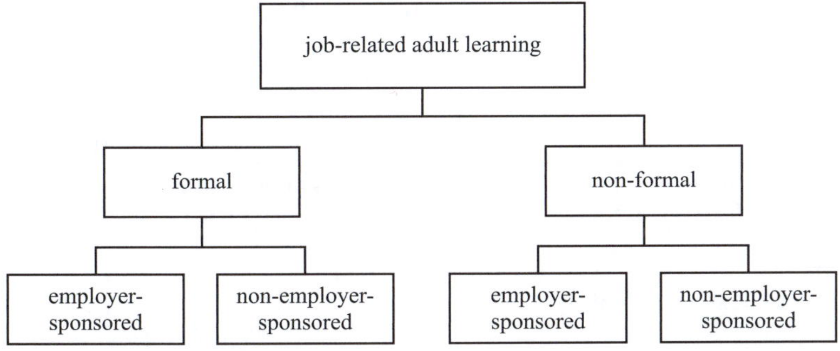

Source: Own illustration, following von Rosenbladt (2010).

Figure 2.1   Four types of job-related adult learning

PARTICIPATION RATES

The first objective of our chapter is to examine whether and to what extent countries show different participation rates in job-related adult learning and if there is significant variation regarding participation in the four distinct types. Table 2.1, which shows the participation rates for job-related formal and non-formal adult learning activities for 26 European countries, provides a response to these queries.

With the exception of the UK and Belgium, countries with high participation rates in formal adult learning also show high participation rates in non-formal adult learning activities, and vice versa. However, non-formal learning activities are attended much more often than formal ones. A further distinction between employer-sponsored and non-employer-sponsored learning activities reveals that participation in non-formal employer-sponsored adult learning is by far the highest (also found by Bassanini et al. 2005), whereas participation in formal employer-sponsored adult learning is the lowest. Using the participation rates found, countries can be grouped as follows:

1. Countries with high participation rates in all four types of job-related adult learning. These are Denmark, Finland, Norway, Sweden, and Slovenia, which have participation rates ranging between 8 and 13 per cent for formal learning activities and between 24 and 54 per cent for non-formal learning activities.

                    Adult learning in modern societies

Table 2.1   Participation rates in job-related adult learning (%)

	All formal	All non-formal	Formal employer-sponsored	Formal non-employer-sponsored	Non-formal employer-sponsored	Non-formal non-employer-sponsored
High participation rates in formal and non-formal adult learning						
DK	10.2	25.6	5.1	4.9	25.0	2.3
FI	10.1	36.3	3.8	6.4	34.0	8.4
NO	9.9	40.2	4.8	5.1	39.1	4.5
SE	13.0	53.2	3.0	10.0	51.2	5.8
SI	8.7	24.0	2.9	5.8	23.5	2.6
Moderate participation rates in formal and non-formal adult learning						
AT	4.1	22.7	1.0	3.1	21.4	7.3
DE	5.3	28.9	1.5	3.7	26.6	10.0
EE	4.9	25.2	2.6	2.4	24.8	2.4
LT	6.3	20.1	2.3	4.1	19.4	4.2
NL	6.8	25.4	1.6	1.2	24.5	4.5
Low participation rates in formal and non-formal adult learning						
BG	2.7	8.9	1.2	1.6	8.8	1.5
CY	2.9	12.0	0.6	2.3	11.4	6.1
CZ	3.9	5.1	1.6	2.3	5.0	1.9
ES	5.9	10.8	1.5	4.5	10.3	5.4
FR	1.7	17.8	n.a.	n.a.	16.3	8.5
GR	2.3	5.0	0.8	1.6	4.9	2.6
HR	4.5	5.6	1.8	2.6	8.5	1.1
HU	2.5	2.1	1.0	1.5	2.1	1.1
IT	4.4	5.8	0.7	3.5	5.6	4.8
LV	5.4	14.4	2.8	2.5	14.0	2.7
PL	5.5	n.a.	1.5	4.1	n.a.	n.a.
PT	6.5	3.6	1.7	4.9	3.6	1.9
RO	3.2	1.2	0.9	2.3	1.2	0.6
SK	6.1	3.3	2.5	3.5	3.2	2.4
High participation rate in formal, but low rate in non-formal adult learning						
BE	12.7	15.3	5.5	7.2	14.7	4.2
UK	15.2	9.1	7.9	5.5	8.7	4.3
Total ^	6.3	16.9	2.4	3.9	16.3	4.0

Notes: ^ We consider all countries as a single entity to which each individual country contributes proportionally to the participation rate in adult learning; weighted values used; Legend: AT = Austria; BE = Belgium; BG = Bulgaria; CY = Cyprus; CZ = Czech Republic; DE = Germany; DK = Denmark; EE = Estonia; ES = Spain; FI = Finland; FR = France; GR = Greece; HR = Croatia; HU = Hungary; IT = Italy; LT = Lithuania; LV = Latvia; NL = Netherlands; NO = Norway; PL = Poland; PT = Portugal; RO = Romania; SE = Sweden; SI = Slovenia; SK = Slovak Republic; UK = United Kingdom.

Source: Own calculations based on the Adult Education Survey 2007 (Eurostat).

2. Countries with moderate participation rates between 4 and 7 per cent in job-related formal adult learning and moderate participation rates between 20 and 29 per cent in job-related non-formal adult learning. These are Austria, Germany, Estonia, Lithuania, and the Netherlands.
3. Countries with low participation rates in all four types of job-related adult learning, which are Bulgaria, Cyprus, the Czech Republic, Spain, France, Greece, Croatia, Hungary, Italy, Latvia, Poland, Portugal, Romania, and the Slovak Republic. In these countries, attending formal adult learning ranges between 1 and 7 per cent, while participation in non-formal learning activities lies between 1 and 18 per cent.
4. Two countries, Belgium and the UK, show high participation in formal adult learning between 12 and 16 per cent, but low participation in non-formal adult learning between 9 and 16 per cent.

Interestingly, the resulting country grouping of participation patterns is similar to the well-known welfare state typology (see Esping-Andersen 1990; Arts and Gelissen 2002; Fenger 2007) and confirms our conclusion about similarities and differences among countries in Chapter 1. The Nordic (social-democratic) welfare states show the highest participation rates. The group with moderate participation rates consists mainly of Central (conservative) European countries. Countries normally grouped into the Southern welfare regime type show lower participation rates. Moreover, the majority of post-socialist countries have quite low participation rates. Due to this similarity with the welfare state typology, it seems plausible to assume that characteristics at the country level that lead to different welfare regimes also produce differences in participation rates among countries.

PARTICIPATION IN ADULT LEARNING: LITERATURE REVIEW AND HYPOTHESES

In the following section, we take a look at the literature concerning the influencing factors of adult learning and derive some hypotheses about the influence of individual and country-specific characteristics on participation. When analyzing adult learning, it is important to bear in mind that various factors at different levels might influence participation rates. Figure 2.2 offers a systematic overview of characteristics that previous studies have found to be relevant.

While the influence of macro-level characteristics (such as characteristics of the educational system or the labor market) has been less thoroughly explored, the influence of micro-level characteristics on adult learning has

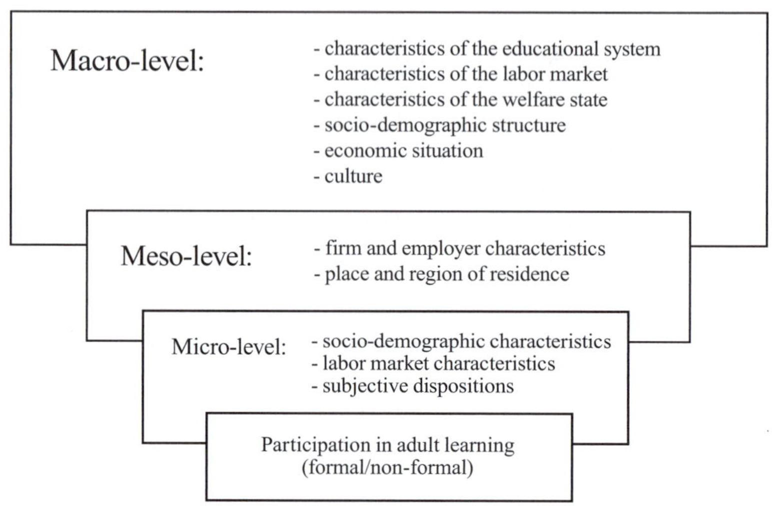

Source: Own illustration.

*Figure 2.2 Characteristics of participation in adult learning at the micro-,
              meso-, and macro-level*

more often been examined. In the following, we refer first briefly to micro-level characteristics before discussing the influence of macro-level factors on adult learning.

Socio-demographic characteristics of individuals (such as age, gender, educational background, marital status, and children) on the one hand and labor market-related individual characteristics (such as seniority or type of occupation) on the other hand have been found to significantly influence participation in formal (e.g., Egerton 2001; Elman and O'Rand 2002; Fouarge and Schils 2009; Hällsten 2011; Kilpi-Jakonen et al. 2012) and non-formal (e.g., Pallas 2002; Dieckhoff and Steiber 2011; Görlitz and Tamm 2012) adult learning activities. Moreover, individual dispositional barriers have been discussed to hinder participation (Cross 1981). Regarding meso-level factors (such as firm and employer characteristics), empirical studies for formal (e.g., Hällsten 2011; Kilpi-Jakonen et al. 2012 for Russia) and non-formal (e.g., Dieckhoff, Jungblut and O'Connell 2007; Dieckhoff and Steiber 2011) adult learning activities have in fact shown that characteristics of the employer, the firm, and the place of residence contribute further to the explanation of participation in adult learning.

Among the individual characteristics, we are particularly interested in the influence of initial education and gender. Considering the discussion in

Chapter 1, these two characteristics are central to the question of whether countries reduce or increase educational equality through adult learning.

In accordance with the *"partial equalizing hypothesis"* (see Chapter 1), some studies have found lower-educated individuals to be more likely to participate in formal adult learning than higher-educated individuals (Egerton 2001 for the UK; Elman and O'Rand 2002 for the US; Kilpi-Jakonen et al. 2012 for Russia and the UK). Yet, in contrast to this evidence, there are also findings that report a higher probability for better-educated individuals to participate in formal adult learning in different countries (Jenkins et al. 2003 for the UK; Zhang and Palameta 2006 for Canada; Cai 2011 for Canada; Kilpi-Jakonen et al. 2012 for Spain and Sweden). These contradictory findings suggest that country-specific mechanisms and the general patterns of social inequality are likely to influence differences among countries regarding the participation rate of individuals with different educational levels.

More specifically, Nordic and liberal countries show low levels of stratification of their educational systems (Gries et al. 2005; OECD 2007). Thus, barriers to participation in adult learning in the form of educational certificates received in school should play a minor role. In addition, these countries generally show very minor age discrimination in the educational system. Together, these characteristics are likely to facilitate particularly lower-educated individuals to go back into formal education. Moreover, Central European countries show a high stratification, which is likely to make it more difficult to participate in formal adult learning compared to countries with low stratification and a strong common core to the curriculum. This should apply especially for the lower-educated who do not fulfill the formal entry requirements derived from the educational system (OECD 2007; Chapter 1). Thus, *we expect that differences between lower- and higher-educated individuals in their probability of participation in job-related formal adult learning should be smaller in Nordic and liberal countries than in Central and Southern countries ("Country-specific partial equalization hypothesis").*

Many studies have shown that better-educated individuals have a higher probability of participating in non-formal adult learning than lower-educated individuals, regardless of the country analyzed (e.g., Albert, García-Serrano and Hernanz 2010 for the UK, Spain, Italy, and France; Bellmann, Hohendanner and Hujer 2010 for Germany; Dieckhoff and Steiber 2011 in a cross-national study including 23 countries; Cai 2011 for Canada). This is in line with the *"Matthew effect hypothesis"* of Chapter 1 and leads us to our second hypothesis: *We expect individuals with higher initial education to be more likely to participate in job-related non-formal adult learning than lower-educated individuals ("Matthew effect hypothesis").*

The second variable we want to explore in depth is gender. In this context, the literature suggests that employers' investment is of crucial importance in explaining gendered patterns of participation. Overall, studies report a higher probability for women to participate in formal adult learning (Elman and O'Rand 2002 for the US; Fouarge and Schils 2009 for 13 European countries; Cai 2011 for Canada; Kilpi-Jakonen et al. 2012 for Russia and Sweden). In contrast, men have been found to be more likely to attend non-formal adult learning with employer support (Evertsson 2004 for Sweden; Albert, García-Serrano and Hernanz 2010 for Italy and France). There is some evidence in the literature that men also have a higher probability of attending non-formal adult learning when measured without the distinction of employer support (Arulampalam and Booth 1998 for the UK; Dieckhoff and Steiber 2011 in a cross-national study including 23 countries). However, it should be noted that the majority of non-formal adult learning is indeed likely to be sponsored or at least organized by the employer (Booth and Bryan 2007; Dieckhoff and Steiber 2011). Returning to the discussion of Chapter 1, we assume that women are more likely to participate in non-employer-sponsored adult learning. This expectation is particularly based upon the fact that women have a greater need to update knowledge and skills after family-related employment interruptions in order to become more competitive and to demonstrate their job motivation (Dieckhoff and Steiber 2011; Stenberg, de Luna and Westerlund 2011). In turn, employers are more likely to invest in men because men are less likely to interrupt their career to take care of their family and children (Dieckhoff and Steiber 2011). In sum, we expect *that women should be more likely than men to participate in job-related formal and non-formal adult learning without employer support, whereas men should be more likely to attend job-related employer-sponsored formal and non-formal adult learning ("Gendered participation hypothesis").*

However, gender differences are also likely to be influenced by different institutional settings. In countries that facilitate combining work and family and that emphasize gender equality (i.e., the Nordic countries), the gendered pattern in participation should be less pronounced. Liberal countries are likely to show similar, less-pronounced gendered patterns due to high labor market competition with low state support for individuals out of the labor market, resulting in traditionally high employment rates for women. In these countries, it is difficult for women to interrupt employment for a longer period. As women consequently have less long employment interruptions, employers reluctance to invest in women should be reduced, resulting in lower gender differences. In contrast, in countries that show more orientation toward the male breadwinner model (i.e., Southern and Central European countries), it is more likely for employers to invest in men. This may be because women interrupt their careers due to childcare more often and for a longer time span. On the contrary, women's need to update their skills and knowledge and to show high motivation should be more pronounced in these countries, resulting in higher participation in non-employer-sponsored adult learning (see discussion above). Taken together, we expect *that differences in the probability of participation in job-related adult learning between men and women should be smaller in Nordic and liberal countries than in Southern and Central European countries ("Country-specific gendered participation hypothesis").*

In addition to individual and meso-level characteristics, this chapter focuses on the influence of country-specific characteristics. Following Rubenson and Desjardins (2009), structural conditions and targeted policy measures produce an opportunity structure that is individually perceived and interpreted, resulting in individual decisions to participate in adult learning. In other words, country-level characteristics not only influence the structures within a country but also directly affect individuals in their decision whether to attend adult learning or not.

At a theoretical level, previous research has combined welfare states' characteristics with participation rates in order to build typologies (Green 2002; Markowitsch and Hefler 2007; Holford and Mleczko 2010). Empirical studies in turn have used several characteristics at the country level: characteristics of the (adult) educational system (Wolbers 2005; Groenez, Desmedt and Nicaise 2007; Almeida and Aterido 2008), union density (Brunello 2001; Coulombe and Tremblay 2007; Dieckhoff, Jungblut and O'Connell 2007), expenditures on research and development (R&D) (Bassanini et al. 2005; Coulombe and Tremblay 2007), unemployment rates (Wolbers 2005; Coulombe and Tremblay 2007), labor market flexibility (Brunello 2001; Bassanini et al. 2005; Almeida and Aterido 2008), wage compression (Coulombe and Tremblay 2007), and Gross Domestic Product (GDP) (Groenez, Desmedt and Nicaise 2007). In most of these papers, a clear distinction between formal and non-formal adult learning activities was unfortunately not made.

While country-specific variables regarding the adult learning system should represent the most important institutional factors explaining participation patterns, to our knowledge, only Groenez, Desmedt and Nicaise (2007) have included these specific measurements. By testing one indicator for coherence and one for the comprehensiveness of lifelong learning policies, the authors found positive effects on participation levels for both variables. Other studies have included the share of upper-secondary students in vocational education (Wolbers 2005) and the years of schooling of the population (Almeida and Aterido 2008) as education-related country characteristics. Beyond education, expenditures on R&D at the country level are often hypothesized to increase participation in adult learning because the more that innovations are adopted, the higher the need for new qualifications and knowledge among the workforce is. However, empirical evidence is scarce. While multivariate analyses have not yet shown a clear influence (Coloumbe and Tremblay 2007), at least a positive correlation between R&D expenditures and adult learning participation has been found (Bassanini et al. 2005). Summing up, regarding education and innovation-related indicators, *we expect that a greater emphasis on these two aspects in a country is likely to increase participation in job-related adult learning. Thus, we hypothesize that the more open a country is toward adult learning, and the higher the public expenditures for education and for research and development are, the more likely participation in job-related adult learning in a country should be ("Education and innovation hypotheses").*

Beyond characteristics related to education and innovations, labor market and welfare state aspects are also likely to influence participation rates in adult learning. First, the existence of strong unions should lead to higher participation in adult learning because unions bargain directly over training opportunities (Booth, Francesconi and Zoega 2003). Indeed, some publications have reported positive significant effects of union density on participation in adult learning (Brunello 2001; Dieckhoff, Jungblut and O'Connell 2007), while, however, other publications report no significant effects (Coloumbe and Tremblay 2007). Second, to capture the overall economic context, the influence of unemployment rates on participation levels has been examined. It has been found that participation in adult learning decreases in times of high unemployment (Wolbers 2005), which could be due to a lack of financial resources of employers and employees (Bassanini et al. 2005). Third, the expenditures on social protection are likely to influence participation rates in adult learning without employer support. Individuals who enjoy some degree of welfare state protection are more likely to engage in risky but profitable activities, such as education (Rillaers 2001). Thus, we expect that individuals who can rely on the guaranteed social security of the welfare state are more likely to invest resources (including time and money) in adult learning due to their more secure life situation. Taken together, *we expect union density to be likely to heighten participation rates in job-related employer-sponsored adult learning, whereas high unemployment rates are likely to reduce participation in job-related adult learning. The more that states spend on social protection, the more likely the participation in job-related non-employer-sponsored adult learning should be ("Labor market and welfare state hypotheses").*

DATA AND METHODS

We use the Adult Education Survey 2007 (AES 2007),[1] which was coordinated by Eurostat and is part of the EU Statistics on lifelong learning. In total, the survey was carried out by 29 European countries. For our analysis, we received data from 26 countries. The sample includes individuals between 25 and 64 years in private households.[2]

In order to analyze the impact of individual characteristics on the probability of participation in each of the four types of adult learning, we first carry out separate logistic regression analyses for each country and each adult learning activity. Second, given the hierarchical data structure (with individuals nested in countries), we apply multilevel analysis (Hox 1995, 1998; Snijders and Bosker 1999; Rabe-Hesketh and Skrondal 2008). To study the impact of country-specific variables, we include theoretically relevant macro-variables separately in the multilevel model while controlling for the individual characteristics that have been found to be relevant.[3] We use random-intercept models in which only the intercept is allowed to vary randomly (see, e.g., Snijders and Bosker 1999).

As has been previously mentioned, we distinguish between four different job-related adult learning activities that are used as binary dependent variables for the multivariate analysis (the reference category is no participation in this type of adult learning). When the learning activity took place during working hours or when the (prospective) employer paid (fully or partly) for expenses related to this activity (tuition, fees, books, etc.), we define the adult learning activity as being employer-sponsored. Non-employer-sponsored learning activities are characterized by no employer investment (neither working time nor expenses). The reference period for participation in all four adult learning activities is the 12 months prior to the survey. Formal adult learning always leads (per se) to a qualification and is therefore labor market related. Non-formal learning activities, however, might not always be job related. Therefore, we only investigate non-formal adult learning activities for which the respondent has indicated job relevance.

Models for adult learning activities without employer investments are measured for all individuals aged 25–64. For the analysis of employer-sponsored learning activities, we restrict our sample to employed persons with a job duration of at least one year (to control that this person was already employed when starting the adult learning activity). In these models, we also include job-specific variables.[4]

We use the following individual characteristics as independent variables: gender, age (for the multilevel regressions: age centered), age squared (for the multilevel regressions: age squared centered), highest initial educational level, having children up to age five in the household, the country of birth, and the degree of urbanization of the area a person lives in. As job-related indicators (only used in models for employer-sponsored adult learning) we take firm size, permanency of the job (fixed-term or permanent), and working time (full-time or part-time work) into account.[5] In order to test if education and gender has different influence on the participation in different country groups, we further include interaction terms between education and country groups and between gender and country groups.

The classification of countries into groups mirrors institutional aspects of the welfare state as a whole and is based on the dimensions of Chapter 1 and on recent welfare state literature. For most of the post-socialist countries we build a separate category, although we are aware of the fact that these countries are very diverse. Thus, we distinguish between five different country groups:

1. Nordic countries (DK, FI, NO, SE)
2. Central European countries (AT, BE, DE, FR, NL)
3. Liberal countries (EE, UK)
4. Southern European countries (CY, CZ, ES, GR, HU, IT, PT)
5. Residual post-socialist countries (BG, HR, LV, LT, PO, RO, SI, SK)

To investigate the influence of country-specific characteristics, we focus on six macro-indicators: an indicator for the "adult learning framework", expenditures in education, expenditures on R&D, the unemployment rate, expenditures on social protection, and union density. All variables except the adult learning framework and union density were retrieved from Eurostat (reference year: one year before the survey was conducted). Union density was retrieved from the OECD database (reference year: one year before the survey was conducted) and the European Trade Union Institute (ETUI) (reference year: 2009).

The first three indicators are used as proxies for the emphasis a country places on education and efforts toward an innovative society: (1) adult learning framework measures a country's openness to adult learning; (2) public expenditures in education reveals a country's general orientation toward education; and (3) expenditures on R&D captures the efforts and policies of governments and firms toward innovations and a knowledge-based society.

The adult learning framework is based on a study of the impact of ongoing reforms in education and training on the adult learning sector. By analyzing both quantitative and qualitative data, the authors provide estimations of each country's score for the following five criteria (European Commission 2010): barriers to participation, existence of a historically well-developed adult learning system, favorable demographic structures and economic situation, existence of a coherent structural framework, and availability of financial resources for adult learning. We translated these country assessments into a numeric measure and built a summary index ranging from 0 to 10 for each country (European Commission 2010).

The remaining three indicators represent our "labor market and welfare state" variables: (1) the unemployment rate serves as a proxy for the macro-economic national situation; (2) expenditures on social protection measures how well individuals are protected against a defined set of risks and needs by the welfare state; and (3) union density reflects the role of unions as bargaining institution of employees.

The indicator expenditures on social protection is defined as "all interventions from public or private bodies intended to relieve households and individuals of the burden of a defined set of risks or needs, provided that there is neither a simultaneous reciprocal nor an individual arrangement involved" (Eurostat 2008, p. 9). These interventions include sickness/health care, disability, old age, survivors, family/children, unemployment, housing, and social exclusion. The focus of this indicator lies on income maintenance and support in cash or kind (Eurostat 2008).

RESULTS

The Influence of Individual Characteristics on Participation in Adult Learning

In the following, the results of the multilevel models regarding the influence of individual characteristics on participation in job-related formal (Table 2.2) and non-formal (Table 2.3) adult learning are presented. Before discussing the effect of education and gender on participation in adult learning as well as their varying influence in different country groups (Models 2 and 3), we will shortly refer to the impact of the other included individual characteristics (Model 1).

The higher the age, the less likely individuals are to participate in any type of adult learning. This result is in concordance with the human capital theory (Becker 1962), which states that younger individuals have a higher probability of participating in adult learning due to higher net returns over the remaining life course (Becker 1962; Ben-Porath 1967; Li et al. 2000; Fouarge and Schils 2009). The degree of urbanization matters only for formal adult learning without employer support. Thus, persons living in thinly populated areas have a lower probability of attending longer educational activities. This could be due to a lack of appropriate offers and to greater distances to the next educational institution (Hällsten 2011). Moreover, the results of the multilevel analysis indicate that the larger the firm is, the more likely individuals are to attend employer-sponsored adult learning activities. While this result has also been found in other studies (Pischke 2001; Almeida and Aterido 2008; Albert, García-Serrano and Hernanz 2010; Dieckhoff and Steiber 2011), it indicates that, on the one hand, larger firms have better opportunities to offer training to their workforce. On the other hand, this positive relationship might also mirror the fact that firms with a certain number of employees are obligated to offer adult learning in some countries.

Individuals with fixed-term working contracts have a lower probability of participating in non-formal employer-sponsored activities, yet they are more likely to attend formal employer-sponsored activities. This result suggests that in the case of non-formal adult learning, employers might invest more in persons with permanent job contracts in order to bring these individuals up to date.

It is worth mentioning that the described results are not found systematically in every country, but that some variation in the effect of different influencing factors exists among countries (see Tables 2.A1 and 2.A2 in the Appendix). Consequently, the country-specific situations of the welfare state, the labor market, and the economy are likely to influence participation patterns. For this reason, we include interaction effects in Models 2 and 3.

To arrive at our main research interest, the influence of education and gender on adult learning, our results strongly support the "*Matthew effect hypothesis*", which posits that better-educated persons participate more often in non-formal adult learning than their lower-educated counterparts. However, the same educational effect is also found for formal adult learning activities. The effect is very robust in both cases, and it seems as if education is the most important influencing factor for participation. This could be due to a complementary relationship between initial and adult learning and/or because of higher skill requirements and higher learning capacity of better-educated persons (Brunello 2001; Albert, García-Serrano and Hernanz 2010).

The multilevel analysis indicates that women are more likely to participate in all types of adult learning compared with men. While the "*gendered participation hypothesis*" suggests a higher probability for men to participate in employer-sponsored adult learning and a higher probability for women to attend non-employer-sponsored learning activities, the results only partly support this hypothesis.

To test our hypothesis regarding a differing influence of gender and education on participation in adult learning in different country groups, we examine interaction effects between country groups and the two individual level variables. Model 2 (Tables 2.2 and 2.3) shows the interaction effects between education and country group. Better-educated individuals are more likely to participate in all types of adult learning in all country groups. We find only weak support for the *"country-specific partial equalizing hypothesis"*, which posits that differences in the probability of participating in formal adult learning between lower- and higher-educated individuals are smaller in Nordic and liberal countries than in Central and Southern countries. Thus, as expected, the difference between higher- and lower-educated individuals is most pronounced in Southern countries. However, Nordic countries also show comparably high differences between lower- and higher-educated individuals in formal employer-sponsored adult learning, whereas liberal and Central European countries show less-pronounced differences. In formal non-employer-sponsored adult learning the differences between Nordic, Central, and liberal countries are very small regarding the difference in the probability of the participation of higher- and lower-educated individuals. Consequently, we do not find significant differences between Nordic and liberal countries, on the one hand, and Central countries, on the other hand. Rather, we find that Central countries are similar to Nordic and liberal countries, while Southern (and the remaining post-socialist countries) seem to form another group. Besides the structure of the educational system, welfare state support and active labor market policies are also likely to influence participation patterns between higher- and lower-educated individuals. Thus, the difference between Central and Southern European countries could be a result of lower-educated individuals' lack of (time and financial) resources to participate in formal adult learning in Southern countries. In turn, welfare state support and active labor market policies are higher in Central countries, and this might facilitate the participation of lower-educated individuals.

Model 3 (Tables 2.2 and 2.3) shows the interaction effects between gender and country group. The results reveal a general trend that women in Southern, Nordic, liberal, and post-socialist countries are more likely to participate in all types of adult learning. Interestingly, men in Central European countries have a higher probability of participating in employer-sponsored adult learning activities, while the probability of participating in formal non-employer-sponsored adult learning is slightly higher for women than for men, indicating an almost equal gender pattern. We do not find evidence for the *"country-specific gendered participation hypothesis"*, which posits that the differences between men's and women's participation in adult learning should be smaller in Nordic and liberal countries than in Southern and Central countries. On the contrary, we find differences between men and women to be most pronounced in liberal and post-socialist countries, indicating a strong female advantage. While Nordic and Southern countries show a moderate female advantage, Central countries indicate a male advantage or an almost-equal distribution between men and women depending on the adult learning activity. The

Table 2.2   Micro-level characteristics of participation in formal adult learning (multilevel logistic regression, log odds)

	Formal employer-sponsored			Formal non-employer-sponsored		
	Model 1	Model 2	Model 3	Model 1	Model 2	Model 3
Constant	−5.20**	−6.76**	−6.08	−5.13**	−5.80**	−5.45**
Female	0.15**	0.14**	0.07	0.31**	0.31**	0.30**
Age	−0.06**	−0.06**	−0.06**	−0.08**	−0.08**	−0.08**
Age squared	−0.00**	−0.00**	−0.00**	0.00**	0.00**	0.00**
Education (ref. below post-secondary)						
Post-sec. and tertiary	1.09**	1.46**	1.08**	0.84**	1.06**	0.84**
Urban (ref. non-urban)	−0.06	−0.06	−0.07	−0.06	0.31**	0.31**
Firm size (ref. 0–10)						
11–49	0.21**	0.20**	0.21**	–	–	–
50+	0.40**	0.39**	0.39**	–	–	–
Fixed-term contract (ref. permanent)	0.15*	0.17*	0.16**	–	–	–
Country group (ref. Southern)						
Nordic	–	−1.33**	−0.98	–	1.18**	1.83**
Central	–	0.74*	−0.47	–	0.51	0.38
Liberal	–	−1.88**	−1.00*	–	0.32	−0.28
Post-socialist	–	−0.57**	−0.34	–	0.16	0.06
*Country group * education*						
Nordic * higher ed.	–	−0.41**	–	–	−0.56**	–
Central * higher ed.	–	−0.75**	–	–	−0.53**	–
Liberal * higher ed.	–	−0.96**	–	–	−0.51**	–
Post-socialist * higher ed.	–	0.20	–	–	0.17*	–
*Country group * gender*						
Nordic * female	–	–	0.17	–	–	0.11
Central * female	–	–	−0.41**	–	–	−0.26**
Liberal * female	–	–	0.43**	–	–	0.45**
Post-socialist * female	–	–	0.20+	–	–	0.05
Individuals	75 156	75 156	75 156	184 702	184 702	184 702
Countries	23	23	23	25	25	25
Variance	0.344	0.226	0.219	0.317	0.231	0.224

Notes: **$p < 0.01$, *$p < 0.05$, +$p < 0.10$. Models control for the year in which the country surveys were conducted.

Source: Own calculations based on the Adult Education Survey 2007 (Eurostat).

Table 2.3   Micro-level characteristics of participation in non-formal adult learning (multilevel logistic regression, log odds)

	Non-formal employer-sponsored			Non-formal non-employer-sponsored		
	Model 1	Model 2	Model 3	Model 1	Model 2	Model 3
Constant	−2.18**	−3.24**	−3.22**	−4.55**	−5.01**	−4.41**
Female	0.06**	0.06**	0.07+	0.15**	0.15**	0.11**
Age	−0.01**	−0.01**	−0.01**	−0.03**	−0.03**	−0.03**
Age squared	−0.00**	−0.00**	−0.00**	−0.00**	−0.00**	−0.00**
Education (ref. below post-secondary)						
Post-sec. and tertiary	1.07**	1.05**	1.07**	0.97**	1.35**	0.97**
Urban (ref. non-urban)	−0.02	−0.02	−0.02	−0.02	0.00	−0.00
Firm size (ref. 0–10)						
11–49	0.29**	0.29**	0.29**	–	–	–
50+	0.46**	0.46**	0.45**	–	–	–
Fixed-term contract (ref. permanent)	−0.42**	−0.42**	−0.42**	–	–	–
Country group (ref. Southern)						
Nordic	–	2.44**	2.34**	–	0.93**	0.29
Central	–	1.77**	1.86**	–	1.21**	0.93**
Liberal	–	−0.64	0.42	–	0.25	0.46+
Post-socialist	–	0.02	0.06	–	−0.34*	−0.57**
*Country group * education*						
Nordic * higher ed.	–	−0.09	–	–	−1.12**	–
Central * higher ed.	–	0.04	–	–	−0.58**	–
Liberal * higher ed.	–	−0.16+	–	–	−0.96**	–
Post-socialist * higher ed.	–	0.37**	–	–	−0.28**	–
*Country group * gender*						
Nordic * female	–	–	0.11+	–	–	0.15+
Central * female	–	–	−0.24**	–	–	−0.00
Liberal * female	–	–	0.17+	–	–	0.31*
Post-socialist * female	–	–	0.28**	–	–	0.19*
Individuals	74 004	74 004	74 004	175 219	175 219	175 219
Countries	23	23	23	25	25	25
Variance	1.084	0.364	0.356	0.266	0.066	0.069

Notes: **p < 0.01, *p < 0.05, +p < 0.10. Models control for the year in which the country surveys were conducted.

Source: Own calculations based on the Adult Education Survey 2007 (Eurostat).

comparably long interruptions of women for childcare in Central European countries as well as the predominance of the male breadwinner model might explain why employers are more likely to invest in men's qualifications in these countries (Dieckhoff and Steiber 2011).

The Influence of Country-Level Characteristics on Participation in Adult Learning

Table 2.4 shows the influence of different country-level characteristics on participation in the four job-related adult learning activities. As expected, the adult learning framework that measures the countries' openness toward adult learning has a positive effect on all four types of adult learning. Thus, our findings are in line with the results of Groenez, Desmedt and Nicaise (2007).

Moreover, we find that the higher the expenditures in education in a country are, the more likely participation is in formal adult learning without

Table 2.4   The effect of country-level characteristics on participation in adult learning (multilevel logistic regression, log odds)

	Formal employer-sponsored	Formal non-employer-sponsored	Non-formal employer-sponsored	Non-formal non-employer-sponsored
Adult learning framework	0.08*	0.09**	0.26**	0.11**
Public expenditures in education	0.13	0.24*	0.80**	0.17
Expenditures on R&D	0.23	0.40**	1.01**	0.43**
Unemployment rate	−0.00	0.00	−0.15+	−0.04
Expenditures on social protection^	0.03	0.05**	0.10**	0.06**
Union density	0.00	–	0.02*	–
Individuals^	75 156	184 702	74 004	175 219
Countries^	23	25	23	25

Notes: **p < 0.01, *p < 0.05, +p < 0.10. ^ No information for Croatia on expenditures for social protection, which reduces the number of countries by one and the number of individuals by 1 202 (for employer-sponsored) or 3 089 (for non-employer-sponsored) in models with this variable. Each macro-variable is added separately to Model 1 (Tables 2.2 and 2.3), meaning that each multilevel model includes only one macro-variable.

Source: Own calculations based on the Adult Education Survey 2007 (Eurostat).

employer support and in non-formal activities with employer support. Higher expenditures in education in general could also indicate higher expenditures and support specific for adult learning, which might be one reason for the higher participation levels in formal adult learning. The positive influence of public expenditures in education on non-formal employer-sponsored learning activities could be a result of country-specific programs that promote non-formal learning activities and are co-sponsored by employers and states (e.g., France, see Behringer and Descamps 2009).

The higher public expenditures on R&D, the higher the probability of participation in both types of non-employer-sponsored and in non-formal employer-sponsored adult learning is. On the one hand, this positive effect indicates that an employee's probability of investing in adult learning increases if there is a greater orientation toward innovation and technology. The employees probably invest in their human capital to stay up to date and to not be replaced by younger or better-educated persons. Employers, on the other hand, might invest in the training of their workforce (non-formal employer-sponsored learning activities) to enhance their productivity and to stay competitive in a globalized world (Lee 2001).

Taken together, the results partly support our *"education and innovation hypotheses"*. The only exception is formal employer-sponsored adult learning activities. These learning activities show only a limited influence of the tested variables. The three other types of adult learning are indeed strongly influenced by the three country-level indicators, which indicates the importance of a general orientation toward education and innovations as well as the relevance of a knowledge-based society.

Regarding our *"labor market and welfare state hypotheses"*, we also test three different characteristics. The macro-economic context, measured via the unemployment rate, only influences participation in non-formal employer-sponsored learning activities. The higher the unemployment rate is, the lower the probability of attending non-formal employer-sponsored adult learning. This finding suggests that individuals and particularly employers are more likely to invest in adult learning in times of economic recovery, probably because by this time they have the necessary monetary resources (Bassanini et al. 2005).

As expected, the results suggest that the more states spend on social benefits for households and individuals to relieve them of the burden of a defined set of risks or needs, the higher the participation is in both types of non-employer-sponsored adult learning as well as in non-formal employer-sponsored learning activities. This positive relationship between participation in non-employer-sponsored learning activities and the expenditures on social protection could indicate that individuals are more willing to invest in adult learning when there is a guaranteed social security by the welfare state.

While unions bargain directly on job characteristics and adult learning opportunities with employers, higher union density in a country is likely to lead to higher participation rates for employed individuals (Booth, Francesconi and Zoega 2003). This result can be found for non-formal employer-sponsored learning activities, whereas the probability of participating in formal employer-sponsored adult learning is not influenced by this variable.

To sum up, our results partly support the *"labor market and welfare state hypotheses"*. Non-formal employer-sponsored learning activities are most sensitive to our country-level variables, while formal employer-sponsored activities are not influenced by these variables at all.

SUMMARY

In this chapter, we have examined characteristics at the individual and country level that influence participation in different types of job-related adult learning in up to 26 countries. By using the Adult Education Survey (2007), we distinguished between employer-sponsored formal and non-formal adult learning and formal and non-formal adult learning without employer support. We found the general trend that countries with high participation rates in formal adult learning also show high participation rates in non-formal adult learning and vice versa (only Belgium and the UK do not show this pattern). Moreover, non-formal learning activities with employer support are most frequently attended. While participation is highest in the Nordic countries, the Central European countries show moderate participation rates, whereas the participation rates of the Southern and of the majority of post-socialist countries are quite low.

Regarding the influence of individual characteristics on participation in the four job-related adult learning types, our results are in line with much of the existing literature. Younger individuals, individuals working in larger firms, better-educated individuals, and women are more likely to participate in different types of adult learning. Interestingly, interaction effects between country groups and gender demonstrate that differences between men and women are most pronounced in liberal and post-socialist countries, indicating a strong female advantage. While Nordic and Southern countries show a moderate female advantage, Central countries indicate a male advantage or an almost equal distribution between men and women. Regarding a country-group-specific influence of education on participation in adult learning, results demonstrate that higher-educated individuals are more likely to participate in adult learning than lower-educated individuals in all country groups. However, differences between lower- and higher-educated individuals are most pronounced in Southern European countries.

Beyond individual characteristics, we examined the influence of different country-specific characteristics on job-related adult learning. Indicators related to the emphasis of a country on education and innovation show a positive influence on adult learning, except for formal employer-sponsored learning activities, which were only influenced by the indicator referring to the adult learning framework. Regarding variables related to the labor market and welfare state, a lower unemployment rate and a higher union density increase the participation in non-formal employer-sponsored adult learning. The higher the expenditures on social protection are, the higher the probability of participating in all learning activities is, except for formal employer-sponsored adult learning.

In conclusion, job-related adult learning is influenced by different characteristics at the individual and the country level. The influence of characteristics varies depending on the type of adult learning, which suggests that it is important to distinguish between different types of job-related adult learning when analyzing factors that influence participation. Moreover, differences between countries regarding the influence of individual characteristics exist. Thus, country-specific characteristics lead to differences in the overall participation rates and in the participation rates of specific person groups within countries.

It is important to bear in mind that cross-national research is always susceptible to measurement issues, comparability, reliability, and validity of the data (Hoffmeyer-Zlotnik and Harkness 2005). Particularly in regard to our topic and our dataset, two points are important to take into consideration when interpreting the results. First, the AES 2007 is a pilot study. Second, although Eurostat has harmonized the questionnaire and given concrete definitions for the different adult learning activities, countries might differ in their interpretation of the different types of adult learning.

One promising way of extending this research would be to examine adult learning with longitudinal data and to include time-varying macro-factors. This type of data could be used to examine the influence of characteristics at the country level in a deeper way and over the course of time. Unfortunately, no longitudinal and comparative data on the topic of adult learning are available yet. The following country chapters in this volume, however, use the best available longitudinal data to conduct detailed country studies.

NOTES

1. The AES 2007 was collected between 2006 and 2009 as a pilot study. For convenience, we refer to it as "AES 2007"; Eurostat has no responsibility for the results and conclusions, which are solely those of the researcher(s).
2. For details on questionnaire and survey methods see Eurostat (2007) or consult the following web site (accessed 15.6.2012): http://epp.eurostat.ec.europa.eu/portal/page/ portal/ microdata/adult_education_survey.
3. Since some of our macro-variables show relatively high correlations, and since multilevel models with a limited number of level 2 cases are restricted by the number of independent variables, we opt to test the influence of every macro-variable individually.
4. Due to missing values and/or low participation rates in different countries, it is necessary to exclude some countries from the multilevel analysis. In formal employer-sponsored learning activities, we exclude France, Denmark and Italy; in formal non-employer-sponsored learning activities, we exclude France; in non-formal employer-sponsored learning activities, Denmark, Poland, and Italy are excluded; and in non-formal non-employer-sponsored learning activities, Poland is excluded.
5. Unfortunately, we cannot include the variables having children, country of birth, and job duration in the multilevel models because these variables have not been conducted in all countries. Moreover, we cannot use the labor force status in any model because of uncertainties about causality.

REFERENCES

Albert, C., C. García-Serrano and V. Hernanz (2010), 'On-the-job training in Europe: Determinants and wage returns', *International Labour Review*, **149** (3), 315–41.

Almeida, Rita K. and Reyes Aterido (2008), 'The incentives to invest in job training: Do strict labor codes influence this decision?', *Social Protection Discussion Papers*, No. 0832, World Bank, Washington, USA.

Arts, W. and J. Gelissen (2002), 'Three worlds of welfare capitalism or more? A state-of-the-art report', *Journal of European Social Policy*, **12** (2), 137–58.

Arulampalam, W. and A.L. Booth (1998), 'Training and labour market flexibility: is there a trade-off?', *British Journal of Industrial Relations*, **36** (4), 1–37.

Bassanini, Andrea, Alison Booth, Giorgio Brunello, Maria De Paola and Edwin Leuven (2005), 'Workplace training in Europe', *IZA Discussion Paper*, No. 1640, Institute for the Study of Labor, Bonn, Germany.

Becker, G. S. (1962), 'Investment in human capital: a theoretical analysis', *Journal of Political Economy*, **70** (5), 9–49.

Behringer, F. and R. Descamps (2009), 'Determinants of employer-provided training: a comparative analysis of Germany and France', *Zeitschrift für Berufs- und Wirtschaftspädagogik*, special issue, **22**, 93–123.

Bellmann, Lutz, Christian Hohendanner and Reinhard Hujer (2010), 'Determinants of employer-provided further training: a multi-level approach', *IZA Discussion Papers*, No. 5257, Institute for the Study of Labor, Bonn, Germany.

Ben-Porath, Y. (1967), 'The production of human capital and the life cycle of earnings',

Journal of Political Economy, **75** (4), 352–65.

Booth, A. L. and M. L. Bryan (2007), 'Who pays for general training in private sector Britain?', *Research in Labor Economics*, **26**, 85–123.

Booth, A., M. Francesconi and G. Zoega (2003), 'Unions, work-related training, and wages: evidence from British men', *Industrial and Labor Relations Review*, **57**, 68–91.

Brunello, Giorgio (2001), 'On the complementarity between education and training in Europe', *IZA Discussion Paper*, No. 309, Institute for the Study of Labor, Bonn, Germany.

Cai, Weiguo W. (2011), 'The determinants of adult participation in job-related education / training in Canada: Who gets access?', Dalhousie University, Canada.

Coulombe, S. and J. Tremblay (2007), 'Explaining cross-country differences in job-related training: Macroeconomic evidence from OECD countries', *Économie Internationale*, **110**, 5–29.

Cross, Patricia K. (ed.) (1981), *Adults as Learners: Increasing Participation and Facilitating Learning,* San Francisco, US: Jossey-Bass.

Cunha, Flavio, James J. Heckman, Lance Lochner and Dimitriy V. Masterov (2006), 'Interpreting the evidence on life cycle skill formation', in Eric A. Hanushek and Finis Welch (eds), *Handbook of the Economics of Education,* vol. I, Amsterdam: Elsevier B.V., pp. 698–812.

Dieckhoff, M. and N. Steiber (2011), 'A re-assessment of common theoretical approaches to explain gender differences in continuing training participation', *British Journal of Industrial Relations*, **49** (s1), 135–57.

Dieckhoff, Martina, Jean-Marie Jungblut and Philip J. O'Connell (2007), 'Job-related training in Europe: Do institutions matter?', in Duncan Gallie (ed.), *Employment Regimes and the Quality of Work*, Oxford: Oxford University Press, pp. 77–103.

Egerton, M. (2001), 'Mature Graduates I: Occupational attainment and the effect of labour market duration', *Oxford Review of Education*, **27** (1), 135–50.

Elman, C. and A. M. O'Rand (2002), 'Perceived job insecurity and entry into work-related education and training among adult workers', *Social Science Research*, **31** (1), 49–76.

Esping-Andersen, Gøsta (ed.) (1990), *The Three Worlds of Welfare Capitalism*, Princeton, NJ: Princeton University Press.

European Commission (2006), *Classification of Learning Activities – Manual*, Luxembourg: European Commission.

European Commission (2010), *Impact of ongoing Reforms in Education and Training on the Adult Learning Sector (2nd Phase). Final Report,* Zoetermeer, the Netherlands: Research voor Beleid.

Eurostat (2008), 'ESSPROS Manual. The European System of integrated Social PROtection Statistics (ESSPROS)', *Methodologies and Working Papers*, Luxembourg.

Evertsson, M. (2004), 'Formal on-the-job training: a gender-typed experience and wage-related advantage?', *European Sociological Review*, **20** (1), 79–94.

Fenger, M. (2007), 'Welfare regimes in Central and Eastern Europe: incorporating post- communist countries in a welfare regime typology', *Contemporary Issues and Ideas in Social Sciences*, **3** (2), 1–30.

Fouarge, D. and T. Schils (2009), 'The effect of early retirement incentives on the training participation of older workers', *Labour*, **23** (s1), 85–109.

Görlitz, Katja and Marcus Tamm (2012), 'Revisiting the complementarity between education and training: The role of personality, working tasks and firm effects', *IZA Discussion Papers*, No. 6278, Institute for the Study of Labor, Bonn, Germany.

Green, A. (2002), 'The many faces of lifelong learning: recent education policy trends in Europe', *Journal of Education Policy*, **17** (6), 611–26.

Gries, Jürgen, Matthias Lindenau, Kai Maaz, and Uta Waleschkowski (eds) (2005), *Bildungssysteme in Europa. Kurzdarstellungen* (Educational systems in Europe. Brief descriptions), Berlin: ISIS Berlin e.V.

Groenez, Steven, Ella Desmedt and Ides Nicaise (2007), 'Participation in lifelong learning in the EU-15: The role of macro-level determinants', *Paper for the ECER Conference*, Ghent, Belgium.

Hällsten, M. (2011), 'Late entry in Swedish tertiary education: Can the opportunity of lifelong learning promote equality over the life course?', *British Journal of Industrial Relations*, **49** (3), 537–59.

Heckman, J. J. (2000), 'Policies to foster human capital', *Research in Economics*, **54** (1), 3–56.

Hoffmeyer-Zlotnik, Jürgen and Janet A. Harkness (2005), 'Methodological aspects in cross-national research: Foreword', in Jürgen Hoffmeyer-Zlotnik and Janet A. Harkness (eds), *Methodological Aspects in Cross-National Research. Special issue 11*, Mannheim: ZUMA, pp. 5–10.

Holford, John and Agata Mleczko (2010), 'Lifelong learning: National policies in the European perspective', in Ellu Saar, Odd B. Ure and John Holford (eds), *Lifelong Learning in Europe: National Patterns and Challenges,* Cheltenham, UK and Northampton, MA, USA: Edward Elgar, pp. 25–45.

Hox, Joop J. (ed.) (1995), *Applied Multilevel Analysis*, Amsterdam: TT-Publikaties.

Hox, Joop J. (ed.) (1998), 'Multilevel modeling: when and why?', in Ingo Balderjahn, Rudolf Mathar and Martin Schader (eds), *Classification, Data Analysis and Data Highways*, New York: Springer, pp. 147–54.

Jenkins, A, A. Vignoles, A. Wolf, and F. Galindo-Rueda (2003), 'The determinants and labour market effects of lifelong learning', *Applied Economics*, **35** (16), 1711–21.

Kilpi-Jakonen, E., D. Vono de Vilhena, Y. Kosyakova, A. Stenberg and H.-P. Blossfeld (2012), 'The impact of formal adult education on the likelihood of being employed: a comparative overview', *Studies of Transition States and Societies*, **4** (1), 48–68.

Lee, J. W. (2001), 'Education for technology readiness: prospects for developing countries', *Journal of Human Development*, **2** (1), 115–151.

Li, H. J, M. König, M. Buchmann and S. Sacchi (2000), 'The influence of further education on occupational mobility in Switzerland', *European Sociological Review*, **16** (1), 43–65.

Macleod, F. and P. Lambe (2007), 'Patterns and trends in part-time adult education participation in relation to UK nation, class, place of participation, gender, age and disability, 1998–2003', *International Journal of Lifelong Education*, **26** (4), 399–418.

Markowitsch, Jörg and Günter Hefler (2007), 'To train or not to train. Explaining differences in average enterprise training performance in Europe – a framework

approach', *Working Paper CVTS*, No. 11, Vienna, Austria.
O'Connell, P. J. and D. Byrne (2010), 'The determinants and effects of training at work: bringing the workplace back', *European Sociological Review*, **28** (3), 283–300.
OECD (2007), *PISA 2006 Science Competencies for Tomorrow's World,* Paris: OECD publishing.
OECD (2012), *Education at a Glance 2012,* Paris: OECD publishing.
Pallas, Aaron M. (2002), 'Educational participation across the life-course. Do the rich get richer?', in Richard A. Settersen and Timothy Owens (eds), *New Frontiers in Socialization: Advances in Life Course Research*, Vol. 7, New York: Elsevier Science, pp. 327–54.
Pischke, J.-S. (2001), 'Continuous training in Germany', *Journal of Population Economics*, **14** (3), 523–48.
Rabe-Hesketh, Sophia and Anders S. Skrondal (2008), *Multilevel and Longitudinal Modeling Using Stata*, Texas: Stata Press.
Rillaers, A. (2001), 'Education and income inequality: The role of a social protection system', *Journal of Population Economics*, **14** (3), 425–43.
Rubenson, K. and R. Desjardins (2009), 'The impact of welfare state regimes on barriers to participation in adult education: a bounded agency model', *Adult Education Quarterly*, **59** (3), 187–207.
Snijders, Tom A. B. and Roel J. Bosker (1999), *Multilevel Analysis*, London: Sage Publications.
Stenberg, Anders, Xavier de Luna and Olle Westerlund (2011), 'Does formal education for older workers increase earnings? Analyzing annual data stretching over 25 years', *SOFI Working Paper* 8/2011, Swedish Institute for Social Research, Stockholm University, Sweden.
Von Rosenbladt, B. (2010), 'Adult education and training in comparative perspective – Indicators of participation and country profiles', *Statistics in Transition – new series*, **11** (3), 465–502.
Wolbers, M. H. J. (2005), 'Initial and further education: substitutes or complements? Differences in continuing education and training over the life-course of European workers', *International Review of Education*, **51** (5–6), 459–78.
Zhang, Xuelin and Boris Palameta (2006), 'Participation in adult schooling and its earnings impact in Canada', *Analytical Studies Branch Research Paper*, No. 276, Statistics Canada, Ottawa, Canada.

Table 2.A1 Multivariate logistic regression analysis, singular for each country (for formal adult learning with and without employer support)

		AT	BE	BG	CY	CZ	DE	DK	EE	ES	FI	GR	HR	HU	IT	LT	LV	NL	NO	PL	PT	RO	SE	SI	SK	UK
Female	act 1	−	n.s.	n.s.	−	n.s.	−	n.s.	+	n.s.	n.s.	n.s.	−	+	n.s.	n.s.	n.s.	n.s.	+	n.s.	n.s.	+	+	n.s.	+	+
	act 2	n.s.	+	n.s.	−	+	−	+	+	+	+	n.s.	n.s.	+	+	+	n.s.	n.s.	+	+	+	+	+	+	+	+
Age	act 1	n.s.	n.s.	+	n.s.	+	−	n.s.	n.s.	n.s.	+	n.s.	n.s.	n.s.	−	n.s.	n.s.	n.s.	n.s.	n.s.	n.s.	n.s.	+	n.s.	+	n.s.
	act 2	−	−	−	−	−	−	−	n.s.	−	−	n.s.	n.s.	−	−	−	n.s.	n.s.	−	−	−	n.s.	−	−	−	n.s.
Age squared	act 1	n.s.	n.s.	−	n.s.	−	+	n.s.	n.s.	n.s.	−	−	n.s.	n.s.	+	n.s.	n.s.	n.s.	n.s.	n.s.	n.s.	n.s.	−	−	−	n.s.
	act 2	+	+	+	n.s.	+	+	+	n.s.	+	+	n.s.	n.s.	n.s.	+	n.s.	n.s.	n.s.	+	n.s.	n.s.	n.s.	n.s.	n.s.	n.s.	n.s.
Education (ref. below post-secondary)																										
Post-secondary	act 1	+	+	+	+	+	+	+	+	+	+	+	+	+	+	n.s.	n.s.	n.s.	+	+	+	+	+	+	+	+
and tertiary	act 2	+	+	+	+	+	+	n.s.	+	+	n.s.	+	+	+	+	n.s.	+	n.s.	+	+	+	+	+	+	+	+
Children	act 1	n.s.	n.s.	n.s.	n.s.	n.s.	n.s.	n.s.	n.s.	−	n.s.	n.a.	n.s.	n.s.	n.a.	n.s.	n.a.	n.s.	n.s.	n.a.	n.s.	+	n.s.	n.s.	−	n.a.
(ref. no children)	act 2	−	−	−	−	−	−	n.s.	n.s.	−	−	n.a.	n.s.	n.s.	n.a.	n.s.	n.a.	n.s.	−	n.a.	−	−	−	n.s.	n.s.	n.a.
Birth country	act 1	n.s.	n.s.	n.a.	n.s.	n.s.	+	n.s.	+	+	n.a.	n.a.	n.s.	n.s.	n.a.	n.a.	n.a.	−	n.s.	n.s.	n.s.	n.a.	n.s.	+	n.s.	n.a.
(ref. born abroad)	act 2	n.s.	−	n.a.	n.s.	n.s.	n.s.	n.s.	n.s.	+	n.a.	n.a.	n.s.	n.s.	n.a.	n.s.	n.a.	−	−	n.s.	n.s.	n.s.	−	n.s.	n.s.	n.a.
Urban	act 1	+	n.s.	n.s.	n.s.	n.s.	n.s.	n.s.	−	n.s.	+	n.s.	n.s.	n.s.	n.s.	n.s.	−	n.s.	n.s.	n.s.	n.s.	n.s.	n.s.	n.s.	n.s.	n.a.
(ref. non-urban)	act 2	+	n.s.	n.s.	n.s.	+	+	+	n.s.	+	n.s.	n.s.	+	+	n.s.	+	n.s.	n.s.	n.s.	+	−	+	n.s.	n.s.	+	n.s.
Firm size (ref. 0–10)																										
11–49	act 1	n.s.	n.s.	n.s.	n.s.	n.s.	n.s.	n.s.	n.s.	+	n.s.	n.s.	n.s.	n.s.	n.a.	n.s.	n.s.	n.s.	n.s.	+	n.s.	n.s.	n.s.	+	n.s.	+
50+	act 1	n.s.	+	n.s.	n.s.	n.s.	n.s.	n.s.	n.s.	+	n.s.	+	+	n.s.	n.a.	+	n.s.	+	n.s.	+	+	n.s.	n.s.	n.s.	n.s.	n.s.
Fixed-term contract (ref. permanent)	act 1	+	n.s.	+	n.s.	n.s.	+	n.a.	+	+	+	n.s.	n.s.	n.s.	n.s.	+	n.s.	n.s.	−	n.s.	n.s.	n.s.	n.s.	n.s.	n.s.	n.a.
Part-time job (ref. full-time)	act 1	n.s.	−	n.a.	n.a.	n.s.	n.s.	+	n.s.	n.s.	−	n.s.	n.s.	n.s.	n.a.	+	+	n.s.	n.s.	n.s.	n.s.	n.a.	n.s.	n.a.	n.s.	−

54

Notes: act 1 = formal adult learning with employer support; act 2 = formal adult learning without employer support; + = positive effect; − = negative effect; n.s. = not significant; n.a. = not available.

Source: Own calculations based on the Adult Education Survey 2007 (Eurostat).

Table 2.A2 Multivariate logistic regression analysis, singular for each country (for non-formal adult learning with and without employer support)

		AT	BE	BG	CY	CZ	DE	DK	EE	ES	FI	FR	GR	HR	HU	IT	LT	LV	NL	NO	PT	RO	SE	SI	SK	UK
Female	act 3	n.s.	n.s.	+	n.s.	+	n.s.	n.s.	+	n.s.	+	−	n.s.	+	+	n.s.	+	n.s.	n.s.	n.s.	n.s.	+	+	n.s.	n.s.	n.s.
	act 4	+	n.s.	n.s.	−	+	n.s.	n.s.	+	+	+	n.s.	n.s.	+	n.s.	n.s.	+	n.s.	n.s.	n.s.	n.s.	+	n.s.	n.s.	n.s.	n.s.
Age	act 3	+	n.s.	n.s.	n.s.	n.s.	+	+	n.s.	+	n.s.	+	n.s.	n.s.	n.s.	+	n.s.	n.s.	n.s.	+	n.s.	n.s.	+	+	n.s.	n.s.
	act 4	+	n.s.	n.s.	n.s.	+	+	n.s.	+	+	n.s.	n.s.	n.s.	+	n.s.	+	n.s.	n.s.	n.s.	n.s.	+	+	n.s.	n.s.	n.s.	n.s.
Age squared	act 3	−	n.s.	n.s.	−	n.s.	−	−	n.s.	−	−	−	n.s.	n.s.	n.s.	−	n.s.	n.s.	n.s.	−	n.s.	n.s.	−	−	n.s.	n.s.
	act 4	−	n.s.	n.s.	n.s.	−	−	n.s.	−	−	−	−	n.s.	−	−	−	n.s.	n.s.	n.s.	n.s.	−	−	n.s.	n.s.	n.s.	n.s.
Education (ref. below post-secondary)																										
Post-secondary and tertiary	act 3	+	+	+	+	+	+	+	+	+	+	+	+	+	+	+	+	+	+	+	+	+	+	+	+	n.a.
	act 4	+	+	+	+	+	+	+	+	+	n.s.	+	+	+	+	+	+	n.s.	+	n.s.	+	+	+	+	+	n.s.
Children (ref. no children)	act 3	n.s.	n.s.	n.s.	n.s.	n.s.	n.s.	n.s.	n.s.	n.s.	−	n.s.	n.a.	−	n.s.	n.a.	n.s.	n.a.	n.s.	−	n.s.	n.s.	n.s.	−	n.s.	n.a.
	act 4	n.s.	−	n.s.	n.s.	n.s.	−	n.s.	n.s.	−	n.s.	−	n.a.	n.s.	n.s.	n.a.	n.s.	n.a.	n.s.	n.s.	−	n.s.	n.s.	n.s.	n.s.	n.a.
Birth country (ref. born abroad)	act 3	+	n.s.	n.a.	+	n.s.	+	n.s.	+	+	n.a.	+	n.a.	n.s.	n.s.	n.a.	n.s.	n.a.	n.s.	+	n.s.	n.a.	+	+	n.s.	n.a.
	act 4	n.s.	−	n.s.	+	−	+	−	n.s.	+	n.a.	n.s.	n.a.	+	n.a.	n.a.	n.s.	n.a.	n.s.	−	n.s.	n.a.	n.s.	n.s.	n.s.	n.a.
Urban (ref. non-urban)	act 3	+	n.s.	n.s.	+	+	−	n.s.	−	n.s.	+	n.s.	n.a.	+	n.s.	+	n.s.	−	n.s.	n.s.	n.s.	n.s.	n.s.	n.s.	n.s.	n.s.
	act 4	+	n.s.	n.s.	n.s.	n.s.	n.s.	n.s.	n.s.	n.s.	−	n.s.	n.a.	n.s.	n.s.	n.s.	+	n.s.	n.s.	n.s.	−	n.s.	n.s.	−	+	−
Firm size (ref. 0–10)																										
11–49	act 3	+	n.s.	n.s.	+	n.s.	+	+	+	+	+	+	+	n.s.	n.s.	n.a.	n.s.	n.s.	n.s.	+	+	n.s.	+	+	n.s.	n.s.
50+	act 3	+	+	n.s.	+	n.s.	+	+	+	+	+	+	n.s.	n.s.	n.s.	n.a.	n.s.	n.s.	n.s.	+	+	n.s.	+	+	n.s.	n.s.
Fixed-term contract (ref. permanent)	act 3	n.s.	n.s.	n.s.	n.s.	n.s.	−	n.a.	n.s.	−	−	−	n.a.	n.s.	n.s.	+	n.s.	+	n.s.	−	n.s.	n.s.	−	−	n.s.	n.s.
Part-time job (ref. full-time)	act 3	n.s.	−	−	−	n.s.	−	−	n.s.	−	−	−	n.a.	+	−	n.a.	−	+	n.s.	n.s.	n.s.	n.a.	−	n.a.	n.s.	−

Notes: act 3 = non-formal adult learning with employer support; act 4 = non-formal adult learning without employer support; + = positive effect; − = negative effect; n.s. = not significant; n.a. = not available.

Source: Own calculations based on the Adult Education Survey 2007 (Eurostat).

3. Returns to Adult Learning in Comparative Perspective

Moris Triventi and Carlo Barone

INTRODUCTION

This chapter develops a comparative analysis of wage returns to adult learning. Our analysis is guided by two main research questions. First, we assess whether different forms of adult learning ensure different economic rewards across 22 industrialized countries. Second, we are interested in testing whether the cross-national variability in returns to adult learning is systematically related to the institutional variation captured by the country groupings illustrated in the first chapter of this volume.

This chapter focuses on a cross-sectional analysis of wage returns to adult learning among employed persons, whereas the individual country chapters provide a wealth of information on the potential consequences of adult learning for access to employment, job mobility, and other career outcomes. Because we do not have access to longitudinal comparative data on adult learning, we must focus on wages at the time of the interview and on learning experiences undertaken over the 12 months prior to the interview. This means that we cannot trace the potential long-term economic consequences of participation in adult learning. Despite this limitation, our data allow for a large-scale analysis of wage returns to adult learning, thereby ensuring a high degree of standardization and comparability, an accurate measurement of adult learning, and detailed information to control for selection into adult learning.

PREVIOUS RESEARCH RESULTS

While a considerable number of studies have investigated the determinants of participation in adult learning, there is much less research on its occupational returns, especially in a comparative perspective (O'Connell and Byrne 2012). Furthermore, comparability across country studies is made difficult by the heterogeneity in the definition of adult learning and in the methods used to estimate its effect on occupational outcomes. Most economic research focuses only on employer-sponsored on-the-job training, and only a few studies use less-restrictive definitions.[1] Moreover, while several studies have used standard OLS regression models, others have made some attempts to control for endogeneity and unobserved heterogeneity using Heckman-type selection models (Lynch 1992), propensity score analyses (Muehler, Beckmann and Schauenberg 2007), instrumental variables (Abadie, Angrist and Imbens 2003), and fixed-effects models on panel data (Barron, Black and Loewenstein 1993; Booth 1993).

Most empirical studies using OLS regression models report that there are positive wage returns to employer-sponsored non-formal training, but when selection effects or ability are controlled for, the returns are frequently found to be smaller or even non-significant (OECD 2004; Bassanini et al. 2005; Dieckhoff, Jungblut and O'Connell 2007). Overall, research that assesses wage returns to non-formal training has reached very heterogeneous results (Dieckhoff, Jungblut and O'Connell 2007). Two recent literature reviews (Hansson 2008; Leuven and Oosterbeek 2008) indicate that after controlling for selection effects, wage returns to training are estimated at between 0 and 4.5 per cent in the United States, between 0 and 2 per cent in Germany, and around 2 per cent in Switzerland, while estimates vary considerably across studies in the United Kingdom (between 1 and 11 per cent). These studies provide interesting results, but they do not compare returns to different forms of adult learning and do not adopt a comparative approach, which is where our work differs.

THEORY AND HYPOTHESES

There are at least four reasons to expect adult learning to be positively rewarded in the labor market, which can be succinctly summarized as follows. First, from a human capital perspective, adult learning provides specific, ready-to-use skills that enhance workers' productivity, thus leading to higher wages (Becker 1962). Second, following Thurow's model (1975), education and training may offer opportunities to strengthen more general competencies and soft skills. Third, according to a signaling approach (Spence 1973), participation in adult learning signals employees' higher motivation and job involvement. Finally, a credentialist approach (Collins 1979) suggests that adult learning can provide certificates needed for promotion into higher-rank positions.

However, these basic mechanisms may operate differentially across different forms of adult learning and thus lead to different occupational outcomes (Loewenstein and Spletzer 1999). At one extreme, non-formal training organized by firms is more likely to be tailored to the specific skill and credential requirements of the firms, especially when sponsored by employers. Furthermore, employees investing in this form of adult learning show a clear signal of job involvement and attachment to their firms. Hence, we expect that non-formal training organized by firms should positively affect wages.

At the other extreme, when adult learning takes the form of participation in formal education, general competencies and soft skills are likely to be more important than the acquisition of specific, ready-to-use skills. These general competencies may be regarded by employers as less directly relevant for productivity, and they are more easily transferable to other firms, meaning that the signal of attachment to the firm is more ambiguous. Quite unsurprisingly, this form of training is less often sponsored by employers, and we expect that employers should also be less willing to reward it.

To be sure, this hypothesis does not imply that participation in formal education is irrelevant for labor market success. We simply argue that it is less often rewarded among employed persons by their current employers in the short term. At the same time, participation in formal education may afford individuals with more-transferable skills and more-widely recognized credentials that facilitate career advancement outside the firm. However, these potential positive consequences are more uncertain because they are contingent upon the success of between-firm mobility strategies and are less likely to show up in the short term.

There are, of course, intermediate and mixed forms of adult learning that lie between the two ideal types that we have just outlined. On the one hand, when formal adult education takes place in the vocational sector, it may also supply individuals with skills that are more directly relevant for productivity. On the other hand, when non-formal training takes place outside the firm, it does not need to be organized or sponsored by the firm. In this case, much depends on how the employers perceive the skill content and the quality of the training courses undertaken by their employees.

Moreover, institutional regulations can affect the characteristics of participation in adult learning and its economic implications, meaning that returns to different forms of adult learning can vary across countries. In general terms, we expect that institutional regulations are more likely to be consequential for formal adult education, which should lead to recognized certificates or diplomas. In this case, state regulations can establish the number, type, and content of learning courses that are given formal recognition, and they can also affect their economic value via wage policies and collective bargaining.

In particular, it is well documented that returns to education are low in Nordic countries because of the high degree of institutionalization and regulation of their labor markets. Solidaristic wage policies that aim at equal pay for equal work, regardless of the productivity of industries, firms, and workers, are more widely pursued in these countries, with the explicit purpose of reducing variation in wages (Badescu, D'Hombres and Villalba 2011). For similar reasons, it can be expected that formal adult education is also associated with less income variation in these countries. In post-socialist countries, we find the opposite pattern. Previous research has shown that returns to education have rapidly increased in these countries since the fall of the iron curtain, which is due not least to the sudden increase in wage inequality and to the shortages of highly educated workers (ibid.).

On the contrary, because non-formal training is more directly organized by firms and other private organizations, the influence of institutional regulations is more indirect, and structural characteristics of the economy should play a more prominent role. In the case of non-formal activities, the specific characteristics of industries and firms where training is offered drive the economic value of these activities more than the institutional environment. Wage policies may also compress returns to non-formal training, but when training is undertaken as a joint initiative between firms and employees, direct negotiation at the firm level on its wage or career consequences is likely to be far more relevant. Hence, we expect that the institutional variations captured by our country groupings should be more relevant for formal adult education.

RESEARCH DESIGN

Comparable cross-country longitudinal data for both European and non-European countries are currently unavailable; therefore, we are forced to use cross-sectional data. This is unfortunate because it is quite difficult to estimate the causal impact of adult learning on occupational outcomes with cross-sectional data for three reasons. First, potential endogeneity due to omitted-variable bias: adult learning experiences are not randomly assigned to workers since individuals self-select and/or firms select participants. Workers with higher wages might be more likely to participate in adult learning because of unobserved characteristics (e.g., work motivation) that also affect earnings. Since we do not have credible instrumental variables and cannot rely on a panel-data structure, we cannot make any causal claim and can only test whether adult learning is associated with higher earnings conditional on a set of covariates. Second, we must exclude reverse causality, which is quite a reasonable assumption once we consider that wages are measured in the month of the interview and information on training participation refers to the 12 months prior to the interview. Following Leuven and Oosterbeek (2008, p. 428), this implies that, on average, the time that elapses between training experiences and the measurement of wages is roughly six months. This time window is similar to that of most empirical training studies, but it limits the scope of our results, which refer to the short-term effects of adult learning.[2] Third and finally, sample selection bias could be an issue because employed individuals are likely to not be a random sample of the whole population. Hence, we do not make inferences on the whole population, and we interpret our results in terms of partial associations among employed individuals.

DATA, VARIABLES, AND METHODS

Data

We use data from the International Adult Literacy Survey (IALS), a large-scale comparative survey conducted under the auspices of the OECD and coordinated by the Canadian statistical office. The IALS includes representative samples of the non-institutionalized civilian population aged 16–65. It was carried out in 23 industrialized countries between 1994 and 1998 (NCES 1998). Despite the fact that it refers to the 1990s, we rely on the IALS because it is the only data source that provides detailed information on adult learning experiences together with background variables and test scores on general cognitive skills for a large number of countries.

We include in the analysis individuals who were employed at the time of the interview as well as those who were 22–64 years old if they had attained no more than upper secondary education (ISCED levels 3 and 4) and those who were 28–64 years old if they had attained tertiary education (ISCED levels 5 and 6). The sample size is thus reduced to 25 903 individuals living in 22 nations that cover the country groupings illustrated in Chapter 1.[3] The liberal countries include English-speaking (CA-En) and French-speaking (CA-Fr) Canada, Great Britain, Ireland, Northern Ireland, New Zealand, and the United States. The group of Central European countries is covered by Flemish-speaking Belgium (BE-Fl), three Swiss cantons (CH-Fr, CH-Ge, CH-It), Germany (DE), the Netherlands (NL), and Italy (IT).[4] The Nordic countries comprise Denmark (DK), Finland (FI), Norway (NO), and Sweden (SE). Finally, given the fact that we focus on the 1990s, we consider a fourth cluster of post-socialist countries,[5] which includes the Czech Republic (CZ), Hungary (HU), Poland (PL), and Slovenia (SI).

Variables

Our dependent variable is gross personal income from wages, salary, or self-employment and is available in quintiles of the national income distribution. To develop our main independent variable, we use information on the three most important adult learning experiences over the 12 months preceding the interview, considering: (1) whether the respondent had any adult learning experience, (2) if this experience was job-related or pursued for personal reasons, and (3) whether it led to a recognized certificate (university degree, college trade-vocational or apprenticeship certificate, elementary- or secondary-school diploma) or not (mainly for professional/career development). Our final variable is a typology of adult learning that classifies respondents in three categories: (1) no adult learning: no training experience, or course attended only for personal interest; (2) formal adult education: at least one experience that led to a recognized certificate; (3) non-formal training: at least one job-related experience without any certificate. If respondents had two or more training experiences of different types, formal adult education prevails over non-formal training.[6] Due to sample size constraints, we mainly rely on this parsimonious classification. However, in some additional analyses mentioned below, we further disaggregate non-formal training into internal and external training. The former refers to activities inside one's work organization, while external training refers to courses attended in schools, in private organizations, at home, etc.[7]

We introduce a number of control variables into our multivariate models that refer to socio-demographic characteristics and educational attainment, and we also introduce occupation-related variables and a proxy for cognitive skills. The first set includes gender, the highest level of education attained by the parents (primary, secondary, or tertiary education), area of residence (rural vs non-rural area), migration status (born in a foreign country or not), years of education attained upon leaving formal education, age, and age squared.[8] Occupation-related variables include total working time in hours, sector of employment (primary, secondary, social/personal services, wholesale, transportation, communication, and financing), occupational class (EGP schema: I-II, IIIa, IIIb, IV, V-VI-VII), and firm size.[9] Finally, we use an additive index of general cognitive skills, which combines information on respondents' literacy scores in three domains: prose, document, and quantitative literacy.[10]

Methods

The main purpose of our analyses is to assess whether adult learning experiences are related to wages and if so, how returns to adult learning vary across countries. To tackle these issues, we develop a two-stage strategy. In the first stage, we estimate regression models for each individual country; then, in the second stage, we use the estimated coefficients for returns to adult learning as dependent variables to assess whether they are related to a set of macro-variables.

Because our dependent variable is expressed in quintiles, OLS regression does not provide efficient estimates. Following Barone and van de Werfhorst (2011), we apply interval regression. This statistical model is appropriate when it can be assumed that an observed discrete response variable is derived from a continuous unobserved variable, as is the case in our model.[11] The assumptions concerning the distributional properties of the unobserved variable and error terms are very similar to the assumptions of standard OLS. This technique has three major advantages: (1) it produces more consistent estimates than OLS regression using the mid-points of the wage bands (Stewart 1983), (2) it does not require the strong assumptions of ordinal logistic regression (i.e., the proportional odds assumption), and (3) the interpretation of estimates is straightforward since the beta coefficients represent average changes in wages expressed on a percentile scale.[12]

We develop our micro-level models using four different specifications, all of which include adult learning as the main independent variable but differ with regard to the control variables included. Model 0 is the baseline model and does not include any control variable; Model 1 includes socio-demographic variables and educational attainment; Model 2 adds occupation-related variables; and finally, Model 3 also includes a measure for cognitive skills.[13]

In the second stage, we develop EDV (Estimated Dependent Variables) regression models in which the dependent variables are derived from estimates with known sampling error (Huber, Kernell and Leoni 2005; Lewis and Linzer 2005). Our dependent variables are the beta coefficients estimated from the country-specific interval regression models in the first stage, which represent the wage returns to adult learning taken from Model 3. Since the number of observations in each country is relatively large, under standard assumptions, each of the beta coefficients derived from the first stage is consistent and asymptotically normal. To assess whether returns to adult learning vary across our country groupings and other macro-variables, we use linear regression in the second stage, complemented by a suitable weighting matrix. Following Huber, Kernell and Leoni (2005), in the second-level regressions, we weight the coefficients from our first-level interval regressions by their precision (standard errors) using the weighting scheme described by Borjas and Sueyoshi (1994). These weights take into account two components of the error term. The first component comes from the individual-level regressions since each beta coefficient is estimated with error. The second component comes from the second-stage regressions because the macro-level variables do not entirely explain the cross-national variability in returns to adult learning. In short, this specification allows us to estimate multilevel models with interval regression techniques in the first stage while at the same time preserving two separate sources of estimate uncertainty in the second stage.

Table 3.1   Distribution of the typology of adult learning experiences in the preceding year (%)

Country	Code	No	Formal	Non-formal	Total	N
Belgium-Flanders	BE-Fl	77.9	4.1	17.9	100	826
Canada-Eng	CA-En	56.0	7.1	36.9	100	1 056
Canada-Fr	CA-Fr	70.9	8.0	21.0	100	486
Czech Republic	CZ	68.3	18.3	13.4	100	1 354
Denmark	DK	41.1	4.5	54.4	100	1 758
Finland	FI	35.0	6.2	58.9	100	1 458
Germany	DE	77.8	1.2	21.0	100	734
Great Britain	GB	45.6	8.5	45.9	100	2 078
Hungary	HU	79.1	3.6	17.3	100	885
Ireland	IE	73.3	6.8	19.9	100	845
Italy	IT	71.2	2.4	26.3	100	1 167
Netherlands	NL	62.2	7.4	30.4	100	1 485
New Zealand	NZ	49.4	9.9	40.8	100	1 809
Northern Ireland	IE-No	56.6	7.7	35.7	100	1 441
Norway	NO	47.4	3.3	49.4	100	1 751
Poland	PL	80.9	3.8	15.3	100	1 243
Slovenia	SI	58.8	5.4	35.9	100	954
Sweden	SE	41.8	4.0	54.2	100	1 364
Switzerland-Ge	CH-Ge	58.8	6.1	35.0	100	617
Switzerland-It	CH-It	59.3	4.5	36.2	100	584
Switzerland-Fr	CH-Fr	68.5	5.5	26.1	100	657
United States	US	47.7	8.3	44.0	100	1 351
Total		57.0	6.5	36.5	100	25 903

Source: Own calculations based on the IALS.

DESCRIPTIVES

We begin with a brief examination of the distribution of adult learning experiences across countries in the mid 1990s. Table 3.1 shows that there is substantial cross-national variation in the proportion of persons who did not undertake any adult learning. This share is larger in Poland, Hungary, Belgium, and Germany, where more than three-quarters of adult workers did not have any learning activity the year before the interview, while it is smaller in Finland, Sweden, and Norway, where less than half of workers had not been involved in any course. As already suggested in the previous chapter, this cross-national variation seems to at least partially reflect institutional differences among the groups of countries. In particular, the highest level of participation is found among the Nordic countries, while the lowest level is found among post-socialist countries. Within these two extremes, we find that the liberal countries are closer to the Nordic countries, whereas Central Europe comes closer to the post-socialist countries. Formal adult education and non-formal training are not equally widespread, and the latter is prevalent in almost all countries. On average in the 22 IALS countries under examination, 6.5 per cent of adult employees had at least one training experience that led to a recognized certificate, with Italy in last place (2.4 per cent) and the Czech Republic at the top (18 per cent). On average, 36.5 per cent of individuals attended at least one non-formal training course in the previous year, but this proportion amounts to 59 per cent in Finland and only to 13.4 per cent in the Czech Republic. Most of the non-formal training experiences were financed by the employer, while formal adult educational experiences were more often self-financed or received some support from the state.

Micro-Analysis

In this section, we examine wage returns to adult learning for adult employees across 22 industrialized countries. The results of our multivariate models are reported in graph form in order to make comparisons across countries and models more straightforward. The figures report point estimates of the beta coefficients and 95 per cent confidence intervals. The estimates represent the average differences in wage returns for individuals who attended various types of adult learning compared with those without any adult learning experience (the omitted reference category). The beta coefficients from interval regression models can be read as percentile differences in wages. The four graphs that constitute each figure report results from the four above-mentioned model specifications, which progressively include more controls. To save space, the estimates related to control variables are not reported, but they are available from the authors upon request. In each graph, countries are listed in descending order of the magnitude of the beta coefficients.

As can be seen in Figure 3.1, there is substantial variability in wage returns to formal adult education when looking at the bivariate relationships (Model 0). While there is a non-significant or even negative association in Nordic countries, we detect a positive, large, and significant bivariate association (around 10–20 percentile points) in post-socialist countries. However, returns to adult learning are mostly reduced and become non-significant once socio-demographic variables and previous educational attainment are introduced as control variables (Model 1). Nevertheless, the association remains significant and positive in some post-socialist (Hungary, Czech Republic) and Anglo-Saxon (Canada, Northern Ireland) countries. Finally, the introduction of additional controls related to the occupations and to the general cognitive skills of respondents (Models 2 and 3) does not change the main pattern of results, with the exception of Hungary, where the estimated effect becomes non-significant. Hence, formal adult education has a limited short-term impact on wages, particularly once we take into account the social selectivity of participation in this form of learning activity, which is mainly related to the social origins and education of individuals.

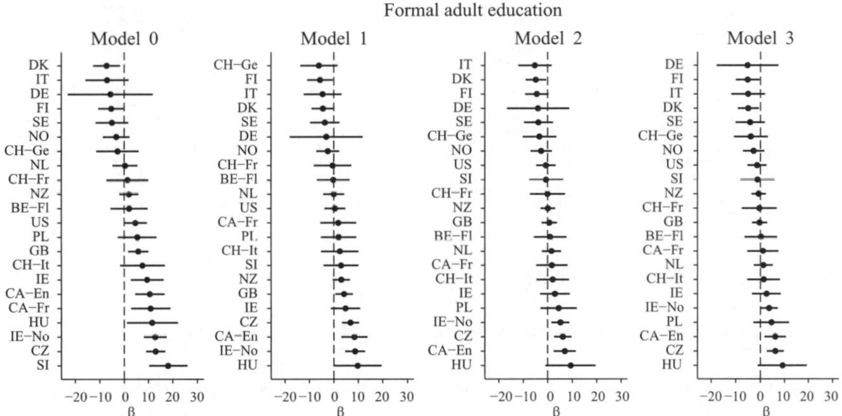

Note: Models 0–3 include different sets of control variables.

Source: Own calculations based on the IALS.

Figure 3.1 Interval regression models: average percentage differences (and 95 per cent confidence intervals) in wages between those with formal adult education experience and those without any experience

The overall pattern is rather different for returns to non-formal training (Figure 3.2). In all countries, the bivariate associations are positive, statistically significant, and much larger than those for formal adult education. The overall pattern of cross-country variation is only partially similar to that observed above. Returns to non-formal activities are smaller in the Nordic countries (around 5–7 per cent), at an intermediate level in Continental Europe, and larger in post-socialist and liberal countries (15–20 per cent). Interestingly, most estimates are only partially reduced when controlling for socio-demographic variables and educational attainment, while they are largely reduced – even if still significant for most countries – when controlling for occupational characteristics (around 5–8 per cent). Finally, controlling for cognitive skills in the Model 3 only slightly affects the estimated returns to non-formal adult learning.

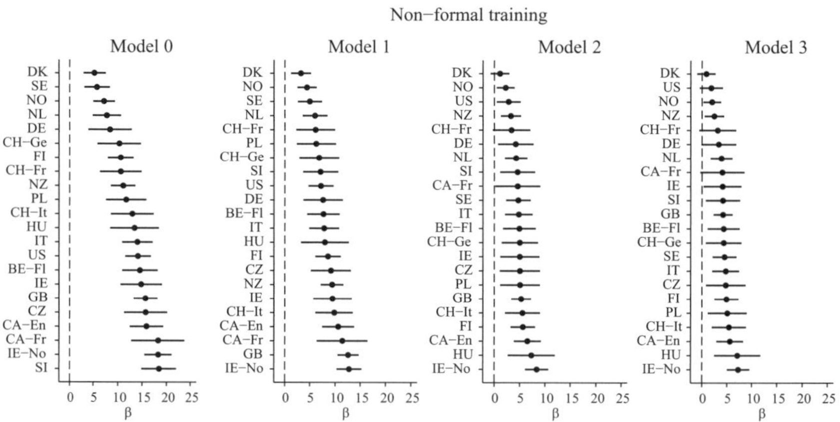

Note: Models 0–3 include different sets of control variables.

Source: Own calculations based on the IALS.

Figure 3.2   Interval regression models: average percentage differences (and 95 per cent confidence intervals) in wages between those with non-formal adult learning experience and those without any experience

This pattern of results across model specifications is in line with the results of the previous chapter and of previous research (Jenkins et al. 2003; Arulampalam, Bryan and Booth 2004), which have shown that access to on-the-job training is largely affected by occupationally-related characteristics, such as the sector of employment, the occupational level, firm size, and employers' willingness to fund employees' participation. On the contrary, participation in formal education among workers is more often an individual choice that is affected more by socio-demographic characteristics, such as gender, age, and the educational level attained. In line with these findings for participation in adult learning, the bivariate estimates for returns to formal adult education are affected more by socio-demographic factors (Model 1), while those for returns to non-formal training are affected more by occupation-related variables (Model 2). The latter are significantly higher than the former across all model specifications.

Interestingly, there is a positive relationship between wage returns to formal adult education and non-formal training, with the correlation coefficient amounting to 0.59. Indeed, several countries with high returns to formal adult education also have high returns to non-formal training experiences (Hungary, English-speaking Canada, Northern Ireland, the Italian Swiss canton, Poland, and the Czech Republic). On the contrary, Denmark, Norway, and the United States display relatively small returns to both forms of adult learning compared with the IALS average.

Given the high variability in non-formal training experiences, it could be useful to further distinguish these experiences at least into internal and external ones. Unfortunately, this distinction is unfeasible in the IALS data for Germany and Sweden, but a brief comment on the main pattern of results for the other countries is possible.[14] Both forms of non-formal training display a positive bivariate association with wages. Once all available control variables are controlled for, this association remains significant in 9 of 20 countries for internal training and in 12 of 20 countries for external training. At the macro-level, there is only a weak positive relationship between the returns to these two forms of non-formal training. The comparison of the beta coefficients suggests that, on the whole, there is not much difference between the returns to these two forms of non-formal training.

Returns to adult learning could vary by gender, although previous research has found mixed results on this point. The studies by Brunello (2001) and the OECD (2004) on ECHP data found lower wage returns to training for women, whereas some country studies found no difference, or even the opposite pattern (see the review in Hansson 2008). Our own explorative analyses on the IALS data (available upon request) confirm this heterogeneity across countries and types of adult learning, although our results should be interpreted with some caution because of the high estimate uncertainty. Returns to formal adult education look larger for women in most liberal countries, whereas we detect non-significant returns for women and negative returns for men for several countries in Northern and Central Europe. No major differences between the sexes are found among the post-socialist countries. Moreover, returns to non-formal activities are larger for women in all liberal countries and in most of the other countries, with only one exception in which the opposite holds (Belgium) and few exceptions in which estimates are very similar for both sexes (Germany, Finland, Sweden, and Hungary). On the whole, we may tentatively conclude that women benefit more than men from participation in adult learning activities.

Macro-Analysis

In this second part of the analysis, we aim to assess the extent to which cross-country differences in returns to formal adult education and non-formal training are systematically related to the institutional variation captured by our country groupings while controlling for some macro-economic variables. In this analysis, the dependent variables are the estimates for the wage returns to formal adult education and non-formal training presented in the previous section, while the main independent variable is formed by the country groupings illustrated in the "Variables" section.

Of course, cross-national differences in wage returns to adult learning may also reflect structural differences between the national economies (Dieckhoff 2007). Therefore, we include a set of control variables aimed at controlling for these structural features, as well as for the economic cycle. To our knowledge, this is the first attempt to directly assess which macro-variables affect returns to adult learning across countries.

We consider three main macro-economic indicators. The first is the unemployment rate, which may be taken as a proxy for the economic cycle. The second is an additive index of economic development, which is derived from three indicators: (1) the Gross Domestic Product (GDP) per capita, (2) expenditures in Research & Development (R&D) as a percentage of the GDP, and (3) the mean years of education attained in the population. The Cronbach's alpha for these three indicators is 0.69, suggesting that this index displays a relatively good internal consistency. The third macro-variable is the proportion of small firms (fewer than 20 employees) in each country. All these macro-variables – with the exception of mean years of education and firm size, which are derived from the IALS – have been extracted from the OECD online database (available at www.stats.oecd.org) and refer to the year before the IALS was conducted in each country.[15] All macro-variables have been standardized to have their means equal to zero and their standard deviations equal to one in order to harmonize their measurement scale.

In order to assess whether the groups of countries are characterized by systematically different returns to adult learning, we estimated two EDV

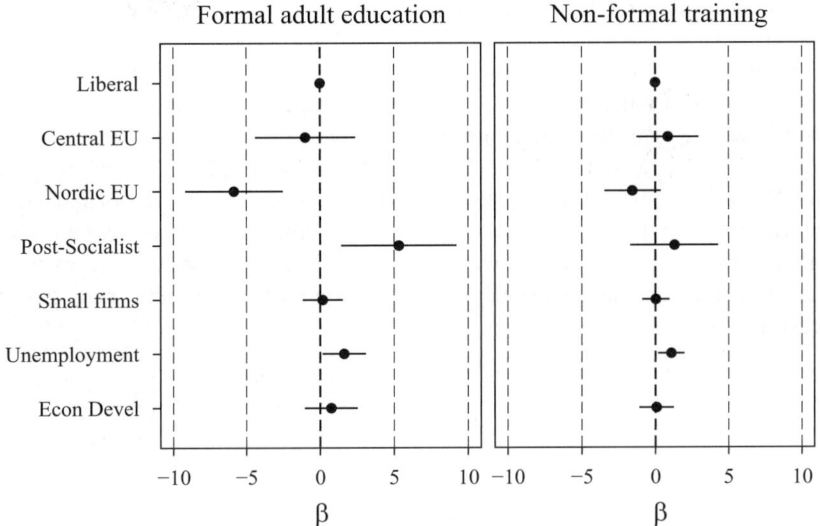

Source:　　Own calculations based on the IALS.

Figure 3.3　EDV (estimated dependent variable) regression models to analyze the effect of macro-variables on the cross-country variability in the wage returns to formal and non-formal adult learning: beta coefficients and 95 per cent confidence intervals

regression models at the macro-level for each outcome (wage returns to formal adult education and non-formal training). Results are reported in Figure 3.3.

Net of economic conditions, we find that Central European countries have, on average, similar wage returns to both forms of adult learning as do the liberal countries (reference category). The pattern is different for the other two comparisons. Interestingly, the Nordic countries demonstrate smaller returns to formal adult education compared with the liberal countries. This difference is quite relevant since it amounts to around 5–6 per cent. We do not detect any difference between these two groups in the case of returns to non-formal training. Moreover, post-socialist countries have systematically larger returns to formal adult education (5 per cent) compared with the other three groups from the mid-1990s, and they are characterized by similar returns to non-formal activities as the liberal and Central European countries. Finally, the effects of macro-economic variables appear small and with the exception of unemployment rates, they are not statistically significant. On the whole, we find that cross-national differences mainly involve formal adult education, with Nordic and Eastern European countries lying at opposite ends of the spectrum.

Figure 3.4 shows the predicted wage returns according to the country groupings. Both the liberal and Central European countries display non-significant returns to formal adult education, instead having positive and significant returns to non-formal training (around 4 per cent). On the contrary, the Nordic countries are characterized by negative returns to formal adult education and positive returns to non-formal training, much in line with the other countries (when not controlling for trade union density). Finally, post-socialist countries have similarly positive wage returns to both types of adult learning.

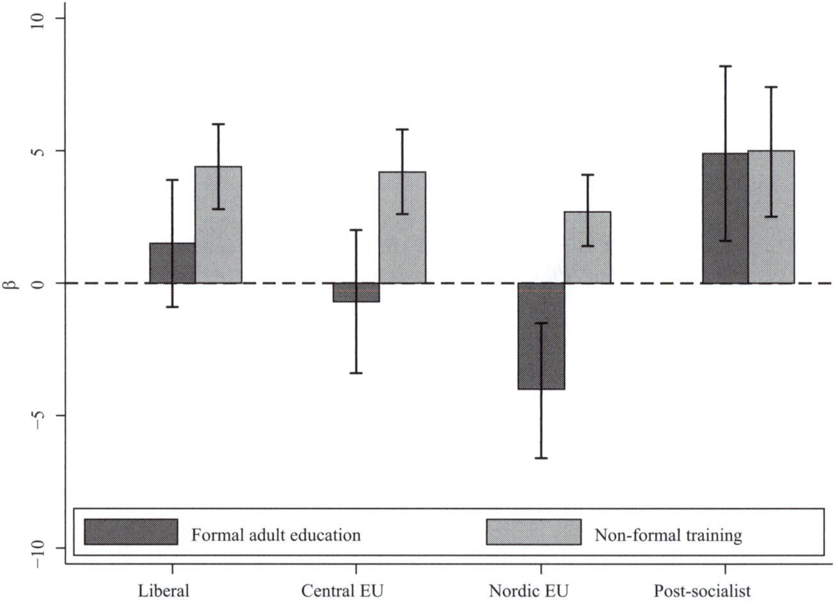

Source: Own calculations based on the IALS.

Figure 3.4 Predicted wage returns to various forms of adult learning according to the country groupings (%)

This pattern of results suggests that the institutional mechanisms driving cross-national differences in wage returns to formal adult education may be similar to the mechanisms driving differences in returns to formal standard education. Indeed, returns to years of education correlate more with returns

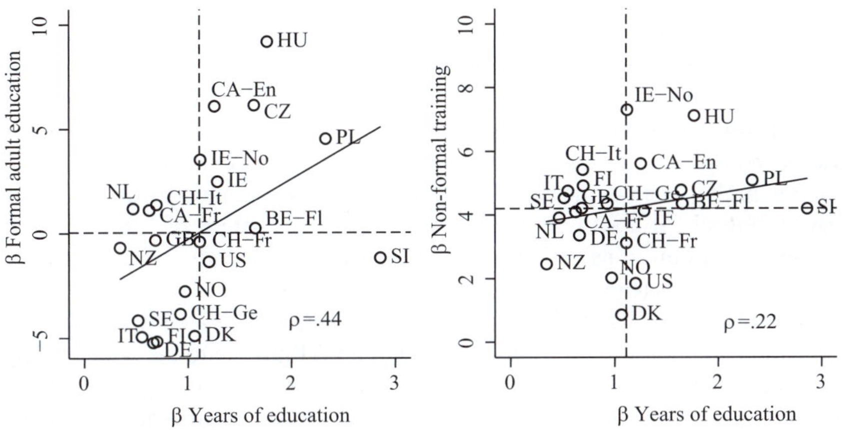

Note: Estimates from model 3.

Source: Own calculations based on the IALS.

Figure 3.5 Relationship between the returns to years of education, formal and non-formal adult learning: scatter-plots, correlation coefficients and linear regression lines

to formal adult education than with returns to non-formal training. Figure 3.5 shows the relevant scatter-plots, correlation coefficients, and regressions. There is a positive and strong correlation (0.44) between wage returns to years of education attained and returns to formal adult education. On the contrary, the correlation between returns to years of schooling and non-formal training is substantially weaker.

DISCUSSION

Our comparative analysis points to two main substantive conclusions. First, we find that adult learning experiences are positively rewarded in the labor market across a large set of industrialized countries and that, in line with our hypothesis, the magnitude of economic returns to non-formal training is systematically larger in the short term than are returns to formal adult education. As discussed above, it is not possible (at least with our data) to establish any causal interpretation of these empirical associations, but we would stress that the results are robust to the introduction of a rich set of controls relating to socio-demographic and occupational characteristics, as well as to a detailed measure of cognitive skills. In particular, the bivariate effect of formal adult education is substantially reduced when controlling for socio-demographic variables. It only remains significant in a few countries, yet even in these countries it appears quite small. On the contrary, the bivariate effect of non-formal training is reduced mainly by the introduction of occupation-related variables, but it remains systematically strong and statistically significant. Interestingly, when a measure of cognitive skills is added to the previous list of controls, it does not significantly affect this pattern of results, which suggests that ability selection into adult learning is already captured by the previous controls (e.g., education and type of occupation).

We wish to acknowledge that the distinction between formal adult education and non-formal training does not do full justice to the wide variety of lifelong learning activities. However, contrary to our expectations, a further distinction between training inside and outside the firm does not prove particularly informative. More than the location of the training itself, it is possible that what matters most for earnings is whether learning activities are undertaken as a joint strategy between employers and employees rather than as an individual initiative of employees.

Our second main conclusion is that, in line with our hypotheses, returns to adult learning vary considerably across industrialized countries and that the institutional differences characterizing the four clusters of countries under examination are relevant, at least in the case of formal adult education. In particular, in the second half of the 1990s, this type of learning activity was less rewarding in the Nordic countries and more rewarding in the post-socialist countries, with the liberal and Central European countries lying in between. We have suggested that the institutional mechanisms driving these differences may be similar to the mechanisms driving differences in returns to education. Indeed, wage returns to formal adult education display marked correlations across countries with wage returns to years of schooling, which were also low for the Nordic countries and high for post-socialist countries. Another possible explanation for these cross-national differences is that formal adult education is more widespread in Nordic countries and less common in post-socialist nations. In other words, the prevalence of adult learning may be inversely correlated with its economic returns. However, we have found that the share of participants in adult learning activities does not account for the differences among the clusters of countries. This work indicates that such differences do exist, but future research is needed to shed more light on the detailed institutional mechanisms that drive them.

NOTES

1. See Asplund (2004) and Hansson (2008) for comprehensive literature reviews.
2. We do not have information on the exact starting and ending dates of training episodes, which means that right-censoring may be an issue, at least for a minority of cases.
3. Among the 23 countries included in the IALS survey, we exclude Chile from our analysis. Some units of analysis at the macro-level include regions within nations (e.g., within Canada, Switzerland), which should not be regarded as independent units, but we ignore this complication.
4. Since Italy is the only Southern European country, we include it in the Central European group because it shares several important institutional characteristics with these countries.
5. These countries are likely to have been far more similar immediately after the fall of the Iron Curtain than now, which explains why we take a different choice than the previous chapter, that uses more recent data.
6. This decision is driven by the pragmatic concern that the formal adult education category has fewer cases, so we are urged to reduce the uncertainty of its multivariate estimates. This decision does not affect the main patterns of our results.
7. Individuals who reported both internal and external training experiences are assigned to the internal training category because it is likely that this activity is more valued by employers (Loewenstein and Spletzer 1999).
8. Parental occupation is not included because it is not available for all the countries and it has a relatively large number of missing values. Age could also be included among the occupation-related variables if considered as a proxy for job experience or tenure. This would not affect our main findings.
9. Unfortunately, we cannot include as a control variable employment in the public vs private sector, which is likely to affect both participation in adult learning and earnings, because this information is not available in the dataset. The type of contract is also excluded since it is not available for several countries and the share of fixed-term contracts was rather low in many countries in the mid-1990s.
10. Literacy is defined by the IALS team as the ability to "use printed and written information to function in society, to achieve one's goals and to develop one's knowledge and potential" (NCES 1998). The IALS administered a total of 114 open-ended literacy tasks, but each respondent answered only a subsample of this set of items. More details on the procedures of data collection, measurement, and scale construction can be found in the NCES (1998).
11. In our case, we attribute the following lower- and upper-bound values to the five original categories: I quintile = 0, 20; II quintile = 21, 40; III quintile = 41, 60; IV quintile = 61, 80; V quintile = 81, 100.
12. This model, as a standard OLS regression, focuses on mean outcomes and does not allow for the examination of whether the effect of training varies across the wage distribution. Nevertheless, Arulampalam, Booth and Bryan (2008) showed that for the majority of countries in their study, the association between training and hourly wages varies little across the conditional wage distribution, whereas there are considerable differences across countries in the average associations between training and wages.
13. It should be clear from this specification that we regard cognitive ability as the cumulative product of inherited talent, family socialization, education, and adult experiences in the work environment (and outside of it).
14. Due to space limitations, we do not report detailed estimates, which are available from the authors upon request.
15. When the appropriate information is missing, the information related to the closest year available is used. Information for sub-regions within countries is usually not available. In some cases, variability across sub-regions is achieved by imputing values for the whole country but in different years in relation to when the survey was administered. In other cases, when this strategy is not feasible, the sub-regions are assigned the same values on the macro-indicators.

REFERENCES

Abadie, A., J. Angrist and G. Imbens (2003), 'Instrumental variables estimates of the effect of subsidized training on the quantiles of trainee earnings', *Econometrica*, **70** (1), 91–117.
Arulampalam, W., M. L. Bryan and A. L. Booth (2004), 'Training in Europe', *Journal of the European Economic Association*, **2** (2–3), 246–360.
Arulampalam, W., A. L. Booth and M. L. Bryan (2008), 'Are there asymmetries in the effects of training on the conditional male wage distribution?', *Journal of Population Economics*, **23**, 251–72.
Asplund, Rita (2004), 'The provision and effects of company training: A brief review of the literature', *ETLA Discussion Paper*, No. 907, The Research Institute of the Finnish Economy (ETLA).
Badescu, Mircea, Béatrice D'Hombres and Ernesto Villalba (2011), 'Returns to education in European Countries. Evidence from the European Community Statistics on Income and Living Conditions (EU-SILC)', *JRC Scientific and Technical Reports*, Publications Office of the European Union, Luxembourg.
Barone, C. and H. van de Werfhorst (2011), 'Education, cognitive skills and earnings in comparative perspective', *International Sociology*, **26** (4), 483–502.
Barron, J. M., D. A. Black and M. A. Loewenstein (1993), 'Gender differences in training, capital, and wages', *Journal of Human Resources*, **28** (2), 343–64.
Bassanini, Andrea, Alison Booth, Giorgio Brunello, Maria De Paola and Edwin Leuven (2005), 'Workplace training in Europe', *IZA Discussion Paper*, No. 1640, Institute for the Study of Labour, Bonn.
Becker, G. S. (1962), 'Investment in human capital: a theoretical analysis', *Journal of Political Economy*, **70** (1), 9–49.
Booth, A. (1993), 'Private sector training and graduate earnings', *Review of Economics and Statistics*, **75** (1), 164–70.
Borjas, G. J. and G. T. Sueyoshi (1994), 'A two-stage estimator for probit models with structural group effects', *Journal of Econometrics*, **64**, 165–82.
Brunello, Giorgio (2001), 'On the complementarity between education and training in Europe', *IZA Discussion Paper*, No. 309, Institute for the Study of Labour, Bonn.
Collins, Randall (1979), *The Credential Society*, New York: Academic Press.
Dieckhoff, M. (2007), 'Does it work? The effect of continuing training on labour market outcomes: a comparative study of Germany, Denmark, and the United Kingdom', *European Sociological Review*, **23** (3), 295–308.
Dieckhoff, Martina, Jean-Marie Jungblut, and Philip J. O'Connell (2007), 'Job-related training in Europe. Do institutions matter?,' in Duncan Gallie (ed.), *Employment Regimes and the Quality of Work*, Oxford: Oxford University Press.
Hansson, Bo (2008), 'Job-related training and benefits for individuals: a review of evidence and explanations', *OECD Education Working Paper*, No. 19, OECD, Paris.
Huber, J. D., G. Kernell and E. L. Leoni (2005), 'Institutional context, cognitive resources and party attachments across democracies', *Political Analysis*, **13** (4), 365–86.
Jenkins, A., A. Vignoles, A. Wolf and F. Galindo-Rueda (2003), 'The determinants and labour market effects of lifelong learning', *Applied Economics*, **35** (16), 1711–21.

Leuven, E. and H. Oosterbeek (2008), 'An alternative approach to estimate the wage returns to private-sector training', *Journal of Applied Econometrics*, **23**, 423–34.

Lewis, J. B. and D. A. Linzer (2005), 'Estimating regression models in which the dependent variable is based on estimates', *Political Analysis*, **13** (4), 345–64.

Loewenstein, M. A. and J. R. Spletzer (1999), 'General and specific training: Evidence and implications', *The Journal of Human Resources*, **34** (4), 710–33.

Lynch, L. (1992), 'Private sector training and the earnings of young workers', *American Economic Review,* **82** (1), 299–312.

Muehler, G., M. Beckmann and B. Schauenberg (2007), 'The returns to continuous training in Germany: new evidence from propensity score matching estimators', *Review of Managerial Science*, **1**, 209–35.

NCES (1998), *Technical report on the first IALS*, Canada: National Center for Education Statistics.

O'Connell, P. and D. Byrne (2012), 'The determinants and effects of training at work: bringing the workplace back in', *European Sociological Review*, **28** (3), 283–300.

OECD (2004), *Co-financing Lifelong Learning: Towards a Systemic Approach*, Paris: OECD Publishing.

Spence, A. M. (1973), 'Job market signalling', *Quarterly Journal of Economics*, **87**, 355–74.

Stewart, M. (1983), 'On least squares estimation when the dependent variable is grouped', *Review of Economic Studies*, **14**, 737–53.

Thurow, Lester C. (1975), *Generating Inequality: Mechanisms of Distribution in the U.S. Economy*, New York: Basic Books.

PART III

Country-specific Contributions

4. Adult Educational Participation and Implications for Employment in the US Context

Cheryl Elman and Felix Weiss

INTRODUCTION

Much as other *edu*LIFE nations, the US has witnessed increasing life course (temporal) complexity in educational participation and skills training. Prior to 1970, only a small proportion of the US population pursued formal education beyond secondary school (Torche 2011), and most human capital gained in adulthood occurred on the job (Becker 1964). However, US adults over age 24 now routinely pursue formal education, especially at the postsecondary level (Elman and O'Rand 2004; Bozick and DeLuca 2005; O'Rand, Hamil-Luker and Elman 2009; Maralani 2011). Just what has motivated this shift in the US? Most adult education is work-related. Labor market demand-side arguments stress recent shifts in work arrangements and job skill requirements, e.g., workers (re)train to keep or regain employment as employment becomes increasingly competitive and insecure (Elman 2011). Employers offering "good jobs" with high wages and benefits increasingly expect workers to have the technological expertise and flexibility to change job tasks and work arrangements (Smith 1997; Kalleberg, Reynolds and Marsden 2003). In contrast, a larger and growing share of US employment involves "bad jobs", i.e., low-skilled work with limited wages and benefits (Kalleberg 2000) including limited access to on-the-job training in skills that might lead to better jobs and higher wages (Veum 1995; Loewenstein and Spletzer 1999). As on-the-job training has become selectively targeted to high-skilled workers over the last few decades (Brown 1990; Lynch 1991; Knoke and Ishio 1998; Yang 2006), marginally-skilled but low-status workers have turned to formal education or outside-of-firm skills-training, often vocational in nature (Lynch 1991; Veum 1999; Elman and O'Rand 2007).

Labor market supply-side factors also explain US adult schooling trends. Many adult participants have experienced discontinuity in their past educational careers due to life events such as early child-bearing or marriage, which limited their ability to complete degrees "on time" (Tanaguchi and Kaufman 2005; Maralani 2011). Labor market supply-side explanations are also supported by US findings that women and ethnic minorities, who, prior to the 1990s had not closed the gender and race/ethnic gaps in educational attainment (Buchmann and DiPrete 2006), have been especially likely to return to school at midlife (Elman and O'Rand 2004; Maralani 2011). However, both labor market demand- and supply-side theories neglect the unique US context (Kerckhoff 2003) that fuels adult education: a relatively age-blind secondary and postsecondary school system that, until recent retrenchments, provided much public funding as well as employer and national policy support for adult enrollment (Zemsky 1998). Given the relative ease of entry into the educational system, middle-aged adults have increased their rates of educational participation: More than one-third of high school equivalency credentials are earned after age 25 (Heckman and LaFontaine 2007). Since the 1990s, one-third of adults aged 45–54 and one-fourth aged 55–64 consistently enroll in one or more work-related courses in any given year (Levesque et al. 2008).

We address all of these issues in the first part of this chapter as we provide an overview of US patterns and trends in adult learning. We especially draw on the growing body of research that uses the National Longitudinal Survey of Youth (NLSY79) to elucidate recent attainment patterns. Another important issue we address involves the labor market consequences of adult learning when pursued as either formal schooling or as work-related training. Relatively few US studies have explored more than one type of human capital or the interconnections between different types, their life course timing, and their labor market outcomes. We therefore do not yet know the consequences of the growing complexity in the education and training careers of adults. For example, do later-life educational spells themselves and/or the types of training pursued significantly increase later-life wage attainment? Do they alter occupational attainment or employability? The second part of this chapter begins to fill these research gaps by empirically examining the labor market effects of two types of adult human capital gains (formal schooling and on-the-job training) by using the NLSY79-cohort followed longitudinally from the 1980s to 2010.

BACKGROUND

US Welfare State Regime and Employment System

Esping-Andersen's *Three Worlds of Welfare Capitalism* (1990) highlights nation-state differences in economy and society and reveals that the United States best fits a liberal state typology due to its comparatively weak regulation of capital and labor markets. While this point is generally accepted, the 20th century US regulatory climate varied considerably over time. It is important to begin by noting that the 1930s marked the emergence of a "critical period" of relatively strong state market regulation, which was designed to address the economic crisis of the Great Depression. These "New Deal" policies emerged in the context of a widespread adoption of Fordist production methods in which work arrangements across manufacturing and service industries involved a core of highly educated managers coordinating the routinized production activities of a large base of less-educated, less-skilled manufacturing- and/or service workers (Gordon, Edwards and Reich 1982).

Despite such a division, labor contracts for primary sector managers and floor workers alike under Fordism were linked to firm-based pensions via explicit or implicit contracts (O'Rand 1986) and to an expanding national pension structure. By the 1960s, national and firm-level policies were rooted in ways that promised long work careers and a reward of post-retirement income to eligible workers based on wage formulas, job tenure, and age rules (O'Rand and Henretta 1999). These state-capital-labor arrangements, referred to as the Fordist Accord (Kalleberg 2000), also promoted worker entry to firm and occupational job ladders that regulated job vesting, promotion through the ranks, bargaining power, and job security (O'Rand 1986; DiPrete, Goux and Maurin 2002). Career paths of advancement and rising wage profiles with seniority for covered workers (generally men of European/American background) reduced job quits and promoted labor productivity (Petersen, Spilerman and Dahl 1989).

This mid-century period was marked by great economic expansion and was also associated with a 1946–64 demographic baby boom. The US postsecondary educational system quickly expanded, partly in response to Fordist economic growth and the baby boom but also in response to national educational policies that promoted postsecondary schooling for adult military veterans (Torche 2011). Between 1950 and the 1970s, the number of US baccalaureate-level and community colleges doubled (Lazerson 1998), and the majority of mid-century educational enrollees and graduates were men (Buchmann and DiPrete 2006; Torche 2011).

A key issue in this context is the significance of postsecondary expansion for employment. The US "open market" model of job-matching (Kerckhoff 2003) allows individuals to decide whether and how much to invest in formal schooling based on estimates of future wage remuneration (Becker 1964). US employers, in turn, use educational attainment as an imperfect indicator of human capital or as a signal of future productivity (Spence 1973). Under the Fordist production regime, job exits (quits or firings) were part of the job-matching process and were most commonly a problem of young workers, who, inexperienced, also self-subsidized a good portion of their own on-the-job training costs in new employment as deferred wages (Becker 1964; Veum 1999). Once vested in career jobs, rising wage returns would reflect human capital as formal education and work training developed into experience/ job tenure (Mincer 1974). Thus, even during the Fordist period, there was little state intervention in job-matching or firm-specific training despite mid-century regulation and the facilitation of pre- and post-employment formal schooling, worker unionization, and employer-employee cooperation in the provision of worker benefits.

By the 1980s however, state policies had changed, allowing, if not actively promoting, the retrenchment of pension benefits and the elimination of employer-employee [union] contracts that had shaped wages, job security, and other benefits (e.g., health insurance). Alongside this change, the advent of flexible employment with "spot market" hiring practices led to hiring for short-term, contingent, and/or part-time employment (Smith 1997). Job-matching remained an "open-market" system yet became increasingly computerized and routed through private third-party match-makers and employment agencies (Smith 1997; Kalleberg, Reynolds and Marsden 2003). Greater automation of production, computer use, highly tailored design systems, and tightly managed supply chains required fewer but more technically skilled production workers (Bills 1995), leading to plant closures and a shedding of both blue-collar operative- and mid-level administrative and service (white-collar) jobs by the early 1990s (DiPrete 1993).

Thus, adult educational participation, especially at the postsecondary level, grew even more common as once-secure Fordist workers experienced precarious employment and perceived greater job insecurity (Elman and O'Rand 2002). In addition, the US adult life course became "restructured" as life expectancy increased while career job length significantly declined (Couch 1998). Labor market displacement rates rose for middle-aged workers who then joined the ranks of youth in educational participation and in seeking new job matches (Elman and O'Rand 2002; Elman 2011). Indeed, adult education may be especially important in the US context, for not only do midlife workers experience longer periods of job disruption when unemployed, but they also tend to replace lost jobs with jobs in new occupations and industries (Couch 1998). Older workers in the US are also less likely to receive on-the-job training (OJT) (Brown 1990).

The US Educational System and Recent Trends in Adult Educational Participation

Even at the height of the relatively regulated Fordist regime, the US maintained an educational preparation system only loosely connected to labor markets (Kerckhoff 1995). US primary grades continue to about grade 6 and are not tracked with regard to vocational or academic (college-oriented) preparation. Secondary (high school) level education, beginning in grade 8 or 9 and ending in grade 12, leads to the high school diploma and can be public or private. About 89 per cent of US public secondary schools are comprehensive schools, meaning that they can offer both academically-oriented and vocationally-oriented classes (Phelps et al. 2001). The remaining 11 per cent of public secondary schools focus on providing Career and Technical Education (CTE) and are hence classifiable as vocational schools (Phelps et al. 2001). Academically-oriented US high school students focus on earning diplomas and can take college preparation courses. In contrast, high school vocational programs in both comprehensive secondary and vocational secondary schools provide skills – often linked to occupational certifications – leading to occupations in business/marketing, health, consumer services, as well as to mechanical occupations and the trades. However, schools' selection of skills to teach and the methods of teaching them are often loosely linked to employer input in a great deal of secondary-level career and technical education (Phelps et al. 2001).

In addition to vocational vs academic program stratification in secondary school curricula, there are two different secondary school (high school) credentials based on different life course timing in high school completion. US high school students who complete requisite classroom work "on-time", and pass examinations in states that require them, earn high school *diplomas.* Students who exit the secondary school system prior to classwork completion and hence "drop out" for work, family formation, or other reasons might later earn a *GED,* passing a general educational development exam as an equivalent credential. How prevalent is each pathway? Tracking all NLSY cohorts from 1979 to 2002, Maralani (2011) found that the mean age for earning the high-school diploma was 17–19, with little sample variability. In contrast, the mean age of GED receipt is 21, and the conditional probability of obtaining the GED remained elevated for those aged 20–35. Yates's (2005) NLSY study tracked cohorts age 18 and under in 1979 until 2002 and discovered that 12 per cent initially dropped out of high school (12.6 per cent of men and 10.6 per cent of women). By 2002, when aged 38 to 41, about 53 per cent of these high-school dropouts had returned to school, 28 per cent had subsequently earned a GED, another 10 per cent had earned a GED and taken college courses, and 4 per cent had completed college after the GED (Yates 2005).

What differentiates these educational status groups? NLSY high school completers were more advantaged than GED recipients, having more highly-educated mothers (Yates 2005; Maralani 2011). In summary, the GED and diploma are very different high school credentials, and additional studies are necessary to decipher the differences in these credentials, especially due to the implication of life course timing and adult education. GED recipients appear to be more comparable to high-school dropouts than to graduates in their abilities and earnings (Heckman and LaFontaine 2007).

Beyond the realm of the secondary school lies a complex world of postsecondary education. The mid-20th century saw massive growth in the number of four-year institutions and two-year community college and vocational institutions of higher education (Zemsky 1998). Consistent with Esping-Andersen's liberal-state type, the 21st century US is witnessing explosive growth in market-based (for-profit) as opposed to public colleges and universities. From 1970 to early 2000, postsecondary enrollment in degree-granting institutions increased by 2.4-fold, whereas enrollment in for-profit institutions increased by over 100-fold (from 0.2 per cent to 9.1 per cent of total enrollments) (Deming, Katz and Goldin 2011). Based on these developments, the National Center for Education Statistics differentiates four postsecondary divisions, at least with regard to its funding policies: (1) public two-year colleges that generally lead to associate degrees; (2) public four-year colleges that generally lead to baccalaureate degrees; (3) private non-profit- and (4) private for-profit schools, colleges, and universities (Wei and Berkner 2008). The private schools and universities range from one-year vocationally-oriented schools (generally for-profit) to four-year elite universities (generally non-profit, but with overlaps). For-profit institutions only confer about 5 per cent of baccalaureate degrees but the shorter programs or vocational (or "career colleges") yield high rates of certificate completion and produce about 18 per cent of associate degrees, including 33 per cent of two-year degrees in business/management/marketing, 51 per cent in computer/information services, 23 per cent in health occupations, and 34 per cent in security and protective services (cited in Deming, Katz and Goldin 2011).

Adults of non-traditional age are increasingly entering postsecondary schools and thus constitute a growing share of these schools' student populations. Tracking NLSY white males who exited school for work for one year or more (degree status not reported) between 1979 and 1988, Light

(1995) found that about 35 per cent had returned to school by 1989 and 11 per cent returned more than one time. About 55 per cent of spells lasted more than six months and about 35 per cent lasted at least a year. Yates (2005) tracked male and female NLSY respondents under age 18 in 1979 until 2002 and found that, of the 55 per cent of students with a high school diploma who left school for work, 43 per cent returned; of the 22 per cent with some college experience who first exited for work, about 55 per cent returned; and of the 11 per cent whose first school exit for work was with a college degree, 41 per cent returned. More women than men returned to school in all educational categories save "some college", and more blacks than whites returned to school in all educational categories save "high school diploma" and "college degree". Unfortunately, these two studies do not account for the type of secondary credential that NLSY youths earned or the type of postsecondary school that they entered; respondents may have had GEDs or high school diplomas and may have entered two-year or four-year programs.

Maralani (2011) tracked all NLSY cohorts from 1979 to 2002, comparing entry into two-year and four-year schools for those with high school diplomas vs GEDs. She found that the timing of secondary school completion by credential type varied greatly by age, with age delays occurring (1) in high school completion and (2) in college entry after completion. Both types of delays contributed to the hazard of postsecondary entry, as did the type of high school credential earned. Controlling for social background, ability, age, and timing effects, Maralani (2011) found that GED recipients were more likely to enter two-year colleges from age 21 to well beyond age 30 and were also more likely to enter four-year colleges between ages 22–6 than "on-time" high school graduates. However, a critical issue is attainment, and Maralani's study does not address two- or four-year college completion. Alburg, McCall and Na (2002) modeled durations of NLSY adult college spells to dropout or completion, accounting for age, waiting time to enrollment, secondary credential type, and social background. They found that a GED (vs diploma) did not significantly reduce the probability of two-year college entry for adults, but that it did reduce the risk of four-year college entry and of both two- and four-year college completion.

Several patterns in these and additional US studies with other samples stand out. First, delayed timing and/or lack of continuity in early life-course school careers does not preclude formal college entry but rather pushes schooling forward into the adult life course – if further education occurs (Maralani 2011). Second, socioeconomic status during youth matters for estimating adult pathways to attainment: More status advantage in youth produces higher adult attainment. For example, for NLSY high-school dropouts, having an educated mother increased the likelihood of earning a GED by midlife net of other factors, including own ability (Murnane, Willett and Tyler 2000). Third, continuity in early formal schooling promotes later-life attainment. NLSY high school dropouts who returned to school as adults had completed more years of schooling than those who did not return (Light 1995; Murnane, Willett and Tyler 2000). More years of completed schooling even rendered insignificant the positive effect of delayed postsecondary entry on college dropout (Alburg, McCall and Na 2002). Fourth, adults who return to school adopt episodic patterns of schooling and their progress toward earning degrees is more blurred than "crisp" due to stop-outs across different semesters and/or enrollment in various types of schools (Goldrick-Rab 2006; Tanaguchi and Kaufman 2005). Fifth, a study of US adult education should not necessarily or primarily be focused on baccalaureate or higher-degree completion; relatively few adults obtain degrees due to institutional barriers, such as undertaking part-time vs full-time study (Jacobs and King 2002; Tanaguchi and Kaufman 2005) or entering two-year colleges which limits movement into four-year programs (Surette 2001; Elman and O'Rand 2007). They also face gender and life course barriers to attainment (Surette 2001; Jacobs and King 2002; Tanaguchi and Kaufman 2005) and do not necessarily aspire to the degree.

Recent Trends in Job Training

Employer-provided training is also theoretically important in labor market research, but its incidence and prevalence in employment were not well-studied until after the 1980s, when longitudinal databases became available (Altonji and Spletzer 1991). Employment-based job training is separate from formal schooling and general ability (Altonji and Spletzer 1991); it involves instruction offered by an employer or other trainer in off-production activities that lead to greater employee skill and productivity (Knoke and Ishio 1998). Becker (1964) differentiated formal schooling from job-related training and further differentiated job training as having two components, i.e., general training and specific training. The former, usually financed by a worker or through a non-employer source, increases worker productivity for all potential employers with wage remuneration accruing to the worker. Specific training, subsidized by both the worker and employer via a reduced starting wage (Veum 1999), only increases productivity and wages in the firm in which it is offered. Job training can be formal, taking place in classrooms at work or off-site, or informal, involving meetings, work groups, or other communication and learning.

The NLSY has asked questions about job-related human capital from the start, leaving us with a good sense of the NLSY cohorts' training. Lynch (1991) tracked respondents aged 18 and under in 1979 up to 1983, finding that about 17 per cent had employer-based formal training in a first job. Veum (1995) tracked employed men and women who began a job in or after 1992, from 1986 forward. He found that about 40 per cent received company-paid training (likely firm-specific) and about 19 per cent received training not paid for by employers (likely general). NLSY questions changed after 1986 to pick up more types of training. Lynch's (1991) lower estimate captured general and specific types of formal training (on-site and off-site) but missed informal training. Veum's (1995) higher estimates not only captured general and specific but also formal and informal training. In another study, Veum (1999) tracked NLSY respondents in a 1996 job from 1986 to 1996, or up until they were between 31–9 years old, finding that more than half of the sample (51 per cent) had received employer-financed training (firm-specific) and about 20 per cent had received non-employer-financed training (general) during this period. Most studies also find that the likelihood of training and the type of training are associated with the level of formal schooling. For example, Lynch (1991) found that NLSY college graduates had higher rates of employer training, often firm-specific, whereas high school graduates had lower rates, and the training was often general. Those with firm-specific training tended to stay with employers. Knoke and Ishio (1998) reported that NLSY men and women with college degrees were more likely to experience a transition into training, and net of this, women were less likely to make the transition than men. Both a larger firm size and managerial occupation also predicted training (Knoke and Ishio 1998; also see Brown 1990).

However, studies that examine the wage impacts of training find that these strict human capital theory assumptions may not hold across all settings. For example, firm-specific training does not always reduce starting wages or may do so only to a small degree (Veum 1999). Additionally, firm-specific training appears to be portable to other firms and hence partly general (Veum 1995). For example, Loewenstein and Spletzer (1999) examined responses to a one-time NLSY question in 1993 that asked whether recent employer-provided formal training could be "useful in doing the same kind of work for an employer DIFFERENT than [current employer]". Almost two-thirds of NLSY respondents thought skills learned would be useful to a different employer; only 11 per cent thought that less than half to none of the skills would be useful to another employer. Consistent with these self-reports, Loewenstein and Spletzer (1999) found that firm-specific skills gained in NLSY respondents' past jobs were rewarded in higher starting wages by current employers (see also Altonji and Spletzer 1991; Veum 1999). This raises concern: If employers are willing to pay comparable wages to newly hired workers with firm-specific skills ported from elsewhere, reducing their own need for training activities, then the employers might avoid hiring inexperienced workers including older adults with new certificates and degrees but little direct training.

In summary, job training is an important form of human capital. It has never been universal in US employment and now tends to be offered to the highest-value primary-sector workers (Yang 2006). Moreover, job training, especially the employer-sponsored firm-specific training thought until recently not to be portable, appears to accumulate over the adult life course as a *second stream of general human capital, which, like formal schooling, is portable to multiple employers*. To what degree is adult formal schooling interdependent with job-based training, and what are the labor market consequences of both forms of human capital over the adult life course? No existing labor market studies examine incremental gains in both forms of adult learning; studies focus on adult gains in one type of human capital and assume that the other type holds constant.

ANALYTIC PLAN OF THE CURRENT STUDY

Based on the above review, we develop and test hypotheses in two critical areas. A first area of interest involves differentiating and detailing patterns in two major forms of adult learning highlighted in *edu*LIFE and the NLSY, i.e., formal schooling and on-the-job training. Our study in this first area is largely descriptive. We expect to find that adults with a higher completed level of formal schooling by adulthood (educational advantage) have a higher likelihood of job training, which is concentrated in high human capital US workers (occupational advantage). Second, we test the effects of each type of adult human capital (net of the other) on wage, occupational attainment, and employability outcomes. Here, we explore the relative effects of high initial formal schooling and of job training and adult education on market rewards.

DATA AND VARIABLES

The US database used is the NLSY, which is a national probability sample of respondents between 14 and 21 years old in 1979. The respondents were re-interviewed annually until 1994, then biennially. Data pertaining to educational attainment and adult spells, labor market participation, and job-training is available on a monthly basis, as is information about life events (marriage, childbearing). The database has limitations in that job-training data is collected retrospectively in waves and the indicators used to measure job training shift over time. Moreover, we cannot link original occupations to specific adult learning activities, and the database alone is weak in detailing employers' characteristics and local and regional structural effects.

We thereby limit the sample to the representative portion of the study and omit minority, poor, and military subsamples. There are eight NLSY birth cohorts, but we limit our sample to respondents born between 1961 and 1964 for two reasons: First, older cohorts miss monthly information on educational attainment before age 18; second, the AFQT IQ-test was conducted with the older cohorts after the typical age of finishing high school. The final sample size is 2 164 cases. Response rates are high from year to year, although the use of a panel study over 31 years leads to panel attrition. Missing values for independent variables were filled by multiple imputation (Rubin 1987) using chained equations (adding 20 observations per imputation) when missing due to item-non-response, but not for panel dropouts. In a total of 293 cases, at least one variable had to be imputed.

We focus on three dependent variables: wages, occupational rank, and employability or labor market attachment. The first two dependent variables indicate economic work rewards and social standing in American society at midlife, respectively. The specific indicators used are the annual labor income in the last year (logged) and the socioeconomic index score (Hauser and Warren 1997). The third indicator, of integration in the labor market, is employment for at least 21 out of 24 months over the ages of 43 and 44 years old.

The NLSY provides a rich set of covariates on the determinants of educational and occupational attainment and adult education. Our central independent variables indicate adult timing patterns in the educational career. Initial education is operationalized as the educational level at the time the respondent leaves school for the first time for at least 12 consecutive months. Adult educational variables in this study indicate the enrollment in regular school over five-year periods after leaving initial schooling (up to age 25, 30, 35, and 40) measured in years. This enables us to differentiate the effects of schooling by the different age periods. Job training in this study is indicated by the number of times a respondent reported participation in job training of more than one month since his or her last interview.

Parental socioeconomic background is indicated by a five-class version of the EGP class-scheme (Erikson, Goldthorpe and Portocarero 1979) occupational class of the parents when their child was 14 years old. We distinguish among the service classes, the intermediate classes, the skilled and the unskilled working classes, and inactive parents. Based on both parents, the higher of these five categories is coded as the class of the family of origin. Models are run by sex and adjusted for race and cohort/birth year (varying between 1961 and 1964). We include percentiles of the AFQT (the armed forces qualification test), which is an indicator of IQ; the test was conducted for the entire sample in

1980. In order to model the interdependence of life course events, educational attainment, and labor market success, we include family formation in our model: childbirth or marriage before age 22 and childbirth before age 30. The age threshold of 22 years is chosen because in this case, family formation conflicts with regular education if college education is pursued.

RESULTS

Table 4.1 presents the results of a cross-tabulation between initial educational attainment, adult formal education (any school participation), and job training (any spell of training). The distributions of initial and adult formal schooling and job training show a clear pattern. Adult formal schooling and job training are highly correlated such that, in a Matthew effect based on initial school attainment, adult schooling and training opportunities are more likely for those with higher initial schooling. The low training rate for the lowest initial schooling groups is also illustrated by the median and mean number of training spells. We find that, for all groups, adult formal schooling is associated with

Table 4.1 Initial schooling, adult schooling and training

Initial schooling: level Frequency *row percentage*	Adult schooling:	Training: none	Training: any	Total	Median (mean) no. of trainings reported
Low: less than HS diploma	No	72	113	185	1 (1.1)
$[\chi^2(1)=10.5; p\leq0.001]$		*38.9*	*61.1*		
	Yes	22	91	113	2 (2.4)
		19.5	*80.5*		
Medium: $\geq$12 but <16 years	No	131	506	637	2 (2.5)
(HS-Diploma)		*20.6*	*79.4*		
$[\chi^2(1)=24.4; p\leq0.000]$	Yes	60	510	570	3 (3.6)
		10.5	*89.5*		
High: $\geq$16 Years, Bachelor	No	18	132	150	3 (4.0)
Degree or Higher		*12.0*	*88.0*		
$[\chi^2(1)=5.5; p\leq0.019]$	Yes	5	122	127	4 (4.0)
		3.9	*96.1*		
Total		308	1474	1782	

Notes: Overall $\chi^2(5)=102.7$; $p\leq0.000$ [χ^2 adult ed / training; within initial schooling level].

Source: Own calculations based on the NLSY.

having on-the-job training rates that resemble those of respondents in the next-higher initial educational level but without adult formal schooling.

Columns 1 and 2 of Table 4.2 present OLS regression results that predict logged annual wages at age 45 for men and women, respectively. For men, only initial school attainment of a college degree or higher, not formal adult schooling, increases earnings, which provides evidence of a Matthew effect, and the advantage of early timing. Furthermore, although higher AFQT scores predict high-school completion and GED receipt in many published studies (vs not having a high-school credential), we find that higher AFQT scores boost men's wages directly; earned GEDs actually reduce men's wages. For women, school timing matters less: Early life-course college attainment, GEDs earned after market entry, and formal schooling between ages 35–9 increase wages. For both men and women, net of formal schooling effects, work-related human capital such as career job length, work experience, and on-the-job training boosts wages. Later-life unemployment reduces men's but not women's wages, and life course variables are not significant for men or women net of other effects.

Columns 3 and 4 report the results of OLS regressions estimating the effects of the same variables on the prestige of the job held at age 45 for men and women, respectively. We find a similar initial education-related Matthew effect pattern for men as in the wage models: Early high attainment (indicated by a college degree or higher) leads to a higher occupational standing by age 45. (A high school diploma prior to market entry is associated with higher-status jobs for men, at $p<0.08$.) Advantaged career trajectories are important to men as well: Career job length (time in longest-held job), and not overall experience, increases occupational standing. For men and women, a higher initial AFQT, most formal schooling (with the exception of new GEDs), and job-training spells increase occupational status. Additionally, unemployment, its life course timing, and family-related life events do not affect occupational status. Net of these effects, non-white females have a significantly higher job status. Men from higher economic-status families (non-poor as youth) and women from higher socioeconomic-status families (more educated parents) also have a higher job status by midlife.

Columns 5 and 6 report the results of logistic regressions of "No Unemployment Spell of three months or more" (employability) (yes/no) on the same set of variables. Of importance is that the most significant predictors involve labor market activities for men and labor market and adult education activities for women. Employability for men reflects higher initial AFQT scores, longer career jobs, and more work experience with less unemployment (e.g., more stability in work pathways), especially at midlife. Women's employability also is enhanced by longer career jobs and more

Table 4.2 Labor market outcomes of adult learning: annual wage, occupational status and employability

	Logged wages age 45		SEI age 45		Employment – not out of work	
	1	2	3	4	5	6
	Male	Female	Male	Female	Male	Female
Ascription						
Non-White	−0.11	0.12	0.70	2.65*	0.12	−0.03
Social origins						
Poverty as child	−0.15*	0.05	−1.68+	−0.41	−0.02	0.27
Parents ed. 12+ yrs	0.10	0.11	1.31	1.75+	−0.05	−0.25
Parents' EGP-Class (ref. service class)						
Intermediate class	−0.12	−0.04	−0.08	−1.26	−0.20	−0.19
Working class	0.02	0.02	−0.78	−2.95**	0.39	−0.12
Inactive/unempl.	0.00	0.05	−0.21	0.62	0.41	−0.40
Human capital at labor market entry						
AFQT percentile†	0.04**	0.02	0.10**	0.81**	0.14*	−0.02
High-school dipl.	0.08	0.11	1.90+	1.20	0.45	0.20
Baccalaureate	0.52**	0.41**	11.87**	9.01**	0.32	−0.04
Labor market						
Longest work spell†	0.02**	0.03**	0.15**	0.09	0.14**	0.08**
Experience	0.33**	0.51**	−0.84	1.87	0.70**	1.69**
Exp. of unemp.: low	0.04	0.01	0.53	0.26	0.82+	−0.06
Youth: unempl.	−0.08	−0.11	−0.74	−0.93	−0.10	−0.19
Adult: unempl.	−0.36**	−0.11	−1.72	−1.70	−0.50+	−0.08
Life course						
Child prior to 22	0.09	−0.09	−0.15	−1.22	−0.80**	−0.13
Child 23–30	0.01	0.04	−1.03	−1.04	0.25	1.08**
Married prior to 22	0.09	0.10	0.22	−0.15	0.16	−0.57**
Adult learning						
Job training spells	0.03**	0.06**	0.37**	0.77**	0.04	0.09*
GED	−0.18+	0.20+	0.87	1.00	0.13	0.60*
Years in education:						
Age 25–9	0.05	0.07	2.04**	2.65**	0.08	−0.05
Age 30–4	0.07	0.07	3.08**	2.87**	−0.04	0.12
Age 35–9	−0.04	0.11*	1.96*	0.48	0.14	0.27
Age 40–4	0.02	0.09	0.94	1.47*	0.50	0.22
Constant	8.25**	6.42**	30.20**	17.47*	−4.15*	−8.95**
Individuals	987	907	1 082	907	1 082	1 082

Notes: **p < 0.01, *p < 0.05, +p < 0.10. † Coefficient has been multiplied by ten. All models adjust for NLSY cohort-year.

Source: Own calculations based on the NLSY.

work experience, but their labor force attachment at midlife is not impaired by experience of past unemployment. Furthermore, women's employability is increased by on-the-job training and new GEDs. Life events are significant for women: Later ages of marriage and childbearing are associated with market attachment. Overall, we do not see evidence of a school-related Matthew effect for men or women with regard to this outcome. Moreover, race/ethnicity and social origins do not strongly shape employability.

DISCUSSION

This study used the National Longitudinal Survey of Youth 1979–2010 to explore the domains of formal schooling and job-related training and the impact of both on the labor market outcome of earnings, occupational status, and employability. In addressing these issues, we find that adult human capital impacts are contingent on the type of labor market outcome considered and the characteristics of workers. For example, both the respondents' gender and their initial level of formal schooling are critically important in differentiating labor market outcomes that are often contingent on prior work trajectories such as wage and status attainment. In the case of men with regard to wages, upon leaving school and entering the labor market, wage gains are due to initial, high formal school attainment (college degree or higher), then followed by on-the-job training and longer durations of general work experience and career jobs. Men's later-life GEDs and postsecondary school spells add little to wage attainment, showing strong support of a Matthew effect. Men's occupational status by age 45 is somewhat similarly patterned: Initial high-attainment credentials of a college degree or secondary-level diploma followed by greater career job length but not general work experience confer a midlife status advantage. Men's occupational status increases with on-the-job training and some formal adult schooling (see below), but not with GEDs.

Women's wage- and status-attainment patterns do resemble men's in critical ways. For example, early college attainment and on-the-job training increase women's wage attainment and occupational status. However, significant gender differences are present: Women's wages rise if GEDs are obtained later in life although career job length and even work experience do not confer occupational status. This suggests that adult formal schooling spells convey less wage benefits to NLSY79 men than to NLSY79 women, but women's wage gains due to formal schooling may often occur in lower-skilled and lower-status jobs. Adult education does confer considerable status benefits to NLSY79 men and women, yet we hesitate to make strong claims about the causal direction since our models do not account for the sequencing of formal schooling, training, and status mobility. It is therefore possible that NLSY79 adults in upwardly mobile career job trajectories participated in formal schooling and job training at higher rates, rather than the reverse. But our findings are important, for they demonstrate that adult human capital and job advancement are strongly interdependent.

There is only weak evidence to suggest that adult education or a cumulative advantage in initial education shapes NLSY79 respondents' employability at midlife. What does predict employability are both labor market history (for men and women) and later life-course family-formation patterns with regard to marriage and childbearing (for women). "Marriage effects" may involve selectivity. Career-oriented women delay marriage and gain higher economic status; later in life, they have higher marriage probabilities and lower divorce rates. Thus, factors that promote women's selection into longer work pathways and delay marriage may also increase labor market security and attachment.

Of course, there is much left unaddressed in this study. A finer-grained analysis is needed to examine whether labor market returns reflect different types of education pursued later in life, such as remedial or technology-related courses, and how outcomes differ when respondents' schooling is continuous or erratic (part-time, multiple years, different schools, etc.) or in the private or public sector. Job training has strong effects on outcomes, but for this preliminary analysis, we combined all forms of job training: employer-sponsored (firm-specific) and other-sponsored (general) as well as formal and non-formal. Further study is needed to ascertain whether different training activities alter findings as well as to locate adult education in the context of dynamic labor market restructuring.

REFERENCES

Alburg, D. A., B. P. McCall and I. Na (2002), 'Time to dropout from college: a hazard model with endogenous waiting', *HHRI Working paper* 01–02, Industrial Relations Center, University of Minnesota.

Altonji G. and R. Spletzer (1991), 'Worker characteristics, job characteristics, and the receipt of on-the-job training', *Industrial and Labor Relations Review,* **45** (1), 58-79.

Becker, G. S. (1964), *Human Capital: A Theoretical and Empirical Analysis, with Special Reference to Education,* New York: Columbia University Press.

Bills, D. (1995), *The New Modern Times: Factors Reshaping the World of Work,* Albany: State University of New York Press.

Bozick, R. and S. DeLuca (2005), 'Better late than never? Delayed enrollment in the high school to college transition', *Social Forces,* **84** (1), 531–44.

Brown, C. (1990), 'Empirical evidence on private training', *Research in Labor*

Economics, **11**, 97–113.

Buchmann, C. and T. A. DiPrete (2006), 'The growing female advantage in college completion: the role of family background and academic achievement', *American Sociological Review*, **71** (4), 515–41.

Couch, K. A. (1998), 'Late life job displacement', *The Gerontologist*, **38** (1), 7–17.

Deming, D. J., C. Goldin and L. F. Katz (2011), 'The for-profit postsecondary school sector: nimble critters or agile predators?', *NBER Working Paper*, No. 17710.

DiPrete, T. A. (1993), 'Industrial restructuring and the mobility response', *American Sociological Review*, **58** (1), 74–96.

DiPrete, T. A., D. Goux and E. Maurin (2002), 'Internal labor markets and earnings trajectories in the post-Fordist economy: an analysis of recent trends', *Social Science Research*, **31** (2), 175–96.

Elman, C. (2011), 'The midlife years: human capital and job mobility', in Richard A. Settersten and Jacqueline L. Angel (eds), *Handbook of Sociology of Aging*, New York: Springer, pp. 245–61.

Elman, C. and A. M. O'Rand (2002), 'Perceived job insecurity and entry into work-related education and training among adult workers', *Social Science Research*, **31** (1), 49–76.

Elman, C. and A. M. O'Rand (2004), 'The race is to the swift: socioeconomic origins, adult education, and wage attainment', *American Journal of Sociology*, **110** (1), 123–60.

Elman, C. and A. M. O'Rand (2007), 'The effects of social origins, life events and institutional sorting on adults' school transitions', *Social Science Research*, **36** (3), 1276–99.

Erikson, R., J. H. Goldthorpe and L. Portocarero (1979), 'Intergenerational class mobility in three Western European societies: England, France and Sweden', *British Journal of Sociology*, **30** (4), 415–41.

Esping-Andersen, G. (1990), *The Three Worlds of Welfare Capitalism*, Cambridge: Polity Press.

Goldrick-Rab, S. (2006), 'Following their every move: An investigation of social-class differences in college pathways', *Sociology of Education,* **79** (1), 61–79.

Gordon, D. M., R. Edwards and M. Reich (1982), *Segmented Work, Divided Workers: the Historical Transformation of Labor in the United States,* New York: Cambridge University Press.

Hauser, R. M. and J. R. Warren (1997), 'Socioeconomic indexes for occupations: a review, update, and critique', *Sociological Methodology,* **27** (1), 177–298.

Heckman, J. J. and P. LaFontaine (2007), 'The American high school graduation rate: trends and levels', *IZA Discussion Paper*, No. 3216. Forschungsinstitut zur Zukunft der Arbeit.

Jacobs, J. A. and R. B. King (2002), 'Age and college completion: a life-history analysis of women aged 15–44', *Sociology of Education*, **75** (3), 211–30.

Kalleberg, A. L. (2000), 'Nonstandard employment relations: part-time, temporary and contract work', *Annual Review of Sociology*, **26**, 341–65.

Kalleberg, A. L., J. Reynolds and P. V. Marsden (2003), 'Externalizing employment: flexible staffing arrangements in US organizations', *Social Science Research*, **32** (4), 525–52.

Kerckhoff, A. C. (1995), 'Institutional arrangements and stratification processes in industrial societies', *Annual Review of Sociology*, **21**, 323–47.

Kerckhoff, A. C. (2003), 'From student to worker', in Jeylan T. Mortimer and Michael

J. Shanahan (eds), *Handbook of the Life Course,* New York: Kluwer Academic/ Plenum Publishers, pp. 251–67.

Knoke, D. and Y. Ishio (1998), 'The gender gap in company job training', *Work and Occupations,* **25** (2), 141–67.

Lazerson, M. (1998), 'The disappointments of success: higher education after World War II', *Annals of the American Academy of Political and Social Science,* **559**, 64–76.

Levesque, K., J. Laird, E. Hensley, S. P. Choy, E. F. Cataldi and L. Hudson (2008), 'Career and technical education in the United States: 1990 to 2005', *NCES* 2008–035, U.S. Dept. of Education, Washington, DC.

Light, A. (1995), 'The effect of interrupted schooling on wages', *Journal of Human Resources,* **30** (3), 472–502.

Loewenstein, M. A. and J. R. Spletzer (1997), 'Delayed formal on-the-job training', *Industrial and Labor Relations Review,* **51** (1), 82–99.

Loewenstein M. A. and J. R. Spletzer (1999), 'General and specific training: evidence and implications', *The Journal of Human Resources,* **34** (4), 710–33.

Lynch, L. M. (1991), 'The role of off-the-job vs. on-the-job training for the mobility of women workers', *American Economic Review,* **81** (2), 151–56.

Maralani, V. (2011), 'From GED to college: age trajectories of nontraditional educational paths', *American Educational Research Journal,* **48** (5), 1058–90.

Mincer, J.A. (1974), *Schooling, Experience, and Earnings,* New York: Columbia University Press.

Murnane, R. J., Willett, J. B., and J. H. Tyler. (2000), 'Who benefits from obtaining a GED? Evidence from high school and beyond', *Review of Economics and Statistics,* **82** (1), 23–37.

O'Rand, A. M. (1986), 'The hidden payroll: employee benefits and the structure of workplace inequality', *Sociological Forum,* **1** (4), 657–83.

O'Rand, Angela M. and John C. Henretta (1999), *Age and Inequality: Diverse Pathways through Later Life,* Boulder: Westview Press.

O'Rand, A. M., J. Hamil-Luker and C. Elman (2009), 'Childhood adversity, educational trajectories and self-reported health in later life among US women and men at the turn of the century', *Zeitschrift fürErziehungswissenschaft,* **12** (3), 409–36.

Petersen, T. Spilerman, S. and S. A. Dahl. (1989), 'The structure of employment terminations among clerical employees in a large bureaucracy', *Acta Sociologica,* **32** (4), 319–38.

Phelps, R.P., B. Parsad, E. Farris and L. Hudson (2001), 'Features of occupational programs at the secondary and postsecondary levels', *NCES* 2001–018, U.S. Department of Education, Washington, DC.

Rubin, D. B. (1987), *Multiple Imputation for Nonresponse in Surveys,* New York: Wiley.

Smith, V. (1997), 'New forms of work organization', *Annual Review of Sociology,* **23**, 315–39.

Spence, M. (1973), 'Job market signaling', *The Quarterly Journal of Economics,* **87** (3), 355–74.

Surette, B. J. (2001), 'Transfer from two-year to four-year college: an analysis of gender differences', *Economics of Education Review,* **20** (2), 151–63.

Tanaguchi, H. and G. Kaufman (2005), 'Degree completion among nontraditional college students', *Social Science Quarterly*, **86** (4), 912–27.

Torche, F. (2011), 'Is a college degree still the great equalizer? Intergenerational mobility across levels of schooling in the United States', *American Journal of Sociology*, **117** (3), 763–807.

Veum, J. R. (1995), 'Training, wages, and the human capital model', *Report NLS 96–31*, Washington, DC: Bureau of Labor Statistics.

Veum, J. R. (1999), 'Training, wages, and the human capital model', *Southern Economic Journal*, **65** (3), 526–38.

Wei, C. C. and L. Berkner (2008), 'Trends in undergraduate borrowing II: federal student loans in 1995–96, 1999–2000, and 2003–04', *NCES 2008–179*, National Center for Education Statistics, Washington, DC.

Yang, S. (2006), 'Organizational sectors and the institutionalization of job-training programs: evidence from a longitudinal national organizations survey', *Sociological Perspectives*, **49** (3), 325–42.

Yates, J. A. (2005), 'The transition from school to work: education and work experiences', *Monthly Labor Review*, **128** (2), 21–32.

Zemsky, R. (1998), 'Labor, markets, and educational restructuring', *Annals of the American Academy of Political and Social Science*, **559**, 77–90.

5. Adult Learning in Australia: Predictors and Outcomes

**Sandra Buchler, Jenny Chesters,
Angela Higginson, and Michele Haynes**

INTRODUCTION

Adult learning is often seen as an important component of promoting an adaptable and flexible workforce by enabling potential workers to stay in the labor market or improve their position. As outlined in the introductory chapter, globalization, demographic aging, and rapidly changing technology have increased the need for individuals to take part in adult learning in order to maintain or increase their human capital and remain competitive in the labor market. While it is often argued that adult learning can be used by policy-makers and individuals to compensate for earlier educational disadvantages, some research has found that educational disadvantages accumulate over the life course since the most advantaged individuals are the most likely to take part in adult learning (Pallas 2004; Dieckhoff, Jungblut and O'Connell 2007). Determining not only who participates in adult learning, but also whether this participation pays off in terms of employment outcomes, is important for understanding the role that adult learning plays in the ability of modern societies to keep the skill levels of their labor forces up-to-date. Australia is especially well-situated to be able to examine this association since a substantial proportion of the population completed additional formal education qualifications after spending some time in the labor force. Indeed, the OECD finds that Australia has one of the highest rates of participation in adult education among all OECD member countries (OECD 2010). Furthermore, Australia's institutional framework provides a unique context in which adults are able to return to education due to a flexible higher-education sector, a living allowance provided by the welfare state, and an interest-free income-contingent student loans scheme that pays for educational fees.

Using ten waves of the Household Income and Labour Dynamics in Australia (HILDA) Survey,[1] we examine the characteristics of those who participate in adult education[2] and the outcomes of completing an educational qualification as an adult on occupational status. Following a brief review of the welfare state and labor market in Australia, trends in lifelong learning and the links between educational attainment and employment status are outlined, followed by a presentation of the research questions and the methodology and results sections and a concluding discussion. Overall, we aim to explore how the unique institutional framework in Australia influences participation in and outcomes of adult education.

The Australian Welfare State

Using Esping-Andersen's typology, Australia is generally classified as a liberal welfare state and has traits similar to the other liberal welfare states included in this volume, i.e., the US, the UK, Russia, and Estonia. Welfare payments are provided on a universal basis and are targeted at those most in need, e.g., the unemployed, the disabled, the elderly, and those engaged in full-time study or training. The payments are means tested, whereby those judged as being able to provide for themselves are not eligible for all welfare payments. Full-time students, regardless of age, are eligible for welfare payments if they undertake a course at an approved institution, such as a secondary school, a Vocational Education and Training (VET) institution, or a university. Since the introduction of the Higher Education Contribution Scheme (HECS) in 1989, university students have been required to make a contribution toward the cost of their higher education through an income-contingent student loans scheme (Chapman 1997; Marks and McMillan 2007). Students receive an interest-free loan (although the balance is adjusted each year to take inflation into account) from the government, which they then repay via the taxation system once their income reaches a threshold that is roughly equivalent to the average graduate entry salary. Having access to these education-related welfare payments and this educational-fee loan scheme provides adult Australians with the means to return to study at any time.

Australia's Labor Market

Australia's labor market is characterized by high rates of part-time employment, a strong service sector, and increasing rates of non-standard employment (Campbell 2004). Between 1978 and 2011, the proportion of employed Australians working on a part-time basis rose from 15 per cent to 29 per cent (ABS 2011), largely due to the replacement of manufacturing-sector jobs with service-sector jobs and an influx of female workers. In the 1970s, the manufacturing-sector provided 28 per cent of all jobs, which were typically full-time and permanent (Woodward 2005), and in 2010, only 9 per cent of all jobs were in manufacturing (DEEWR 2011b). In 2010, the service sectors employed 75 per cent of the workforce (DEEWR 2011b). The recent increase in non-standard employment in Australia is dominated by a substantial level of growth in the incidence and spread of casual employment, in which an employee is paid one hour's wages for one hour's work and receives no further employment benefits (Buchler, Haynes and Baxter 2009). Casual employment in Australia increased from 16 per cent of the labor force in 1985 to 25 per cent in 2007 (Watson et al. 2003; ABS 2009). Gender segregation is well-established in the Australian workforce, with women dominating some industries and men dominating others. For example, almost 80 per cent of employees in the healthcare and social assistance industry and 70 per cent of employees in the education and training industry are female, whereas just 12 per cent of those employed in the construction industry and 16 per cent in the mining industry are female.

Lifelong Learning in Australia

The Australian educational system is divided into three sectors: school, VET, and Higher Education. Certificates I and II, which are offered through the VET sector and are equivalent to completing year 12, provide a gateway back into education for older workers seeking to retrain. They are the first step on the 'educational ladder of opportunity' (Moodie and Wheelahan 2009, p. 357), providing those returning to education with the opportunity to restart their educational career. The VET sector also provides students with the opportunity to undertake studies for certificates III and IV, diplomas, advanced diplomas, associate degrees, and in some cases, undergraduate degrees. Certificates III and IV are the entry-level qualifications for technical and trades occupations and may be undertaken in conjunction with an apprenticeship. Australian apprenticeships are not restricted by age or gender and in 2010, there were 57 500 apprentices aged 45 and above (DEEWR 2011b). Diplomas and Advanced Diplomas are often required for higher-level skilled occupations, such as management.

The VET sector is well-situated to provide Australians of working age with the opportunity to retrain and reenter the labor market. VET courses are available on campus, online, in the workplace, and in senior secondary schools, making them far more accessible than higher-education programs. The VET sector is also able to respond to changing economic, industrial, technological, and social conditions (O'Keefe and Dollery 2006) that have characterized Australia during the past three decades.

Between 1999 and 2009, the proportion of employed persons with a post-school qualification (either VET or higher education) increased from 51 per cent to 61 per cent (DEEWR 2010a). In 2010, 10 per cent of the population aged between 25 and 44 (equating to 644 000 students) and 6 per cent of the population aged between 45 and 64 (340 300 students) were enrolled in VET courses (DEEWR 2010b).

Although the majority of students undertaking university education transitioned directly from secondary school, around 25 per cent of domestic undergraduate students are aged 25 or older (DEEWR 2011a). Individuals who wish to enroll in a university after spending some time in the workforce may be enrolled on the basis of their previous VET coursework, their professional experience, or their age (Wheelahan 2009). The VET sector provides enabling courses for would-be university students, e.g., Preparation for Tertiary Education, which is the VET equivalent of Year 12.

Participation in Adult Education

As noted previously, the proportion of the Australian population that holds a post-school qualification has increased rapidly during the past two decades. As Figure 5.1 indicates, the percentage of those who held post-school qualifications increased for all age groups between 1991 and 2011. These increases were not entirely due to the aging of the cohorts: 51 per cent of those aged between 25 and 34 in 1991 held a post-school qualification. This figure increased to 55.5 per cent of those aged between 35 and 44 years in 2001. Similar increases are evident for other cohorts, indicating that as cohorts age, an increasing percentage of them hold post-school qualifications. Overall, this indicates that Australian adults are returning to education to increase their level of qualification.

While institutional settings in open societies allow persons from less-advantaged backgrounds to gain higher levels of educational attainment and move up through the social hierarchy (Pfeffer 2008), having a higher level of education does not automatically translate into higher levels of occupational prestige or higher earnings. As Goldthorpe (1996, p. 494) noted, it is the level of education that one has relative to one's 'competitors in the labour market' that counts. If the proportion of the workforce with high-level educational qualifications is greater than the proportion of jobs requiring high-level qualifications, then competition between highly educated workers will lead to credential inflation and the devaluation of qualifications (Van de Werfhorst and Andersen 2005). Despite these potential issues, the institutional setting in Australia is especially equipped to enable adults to return to education, leading to high rates of adult education among this group.

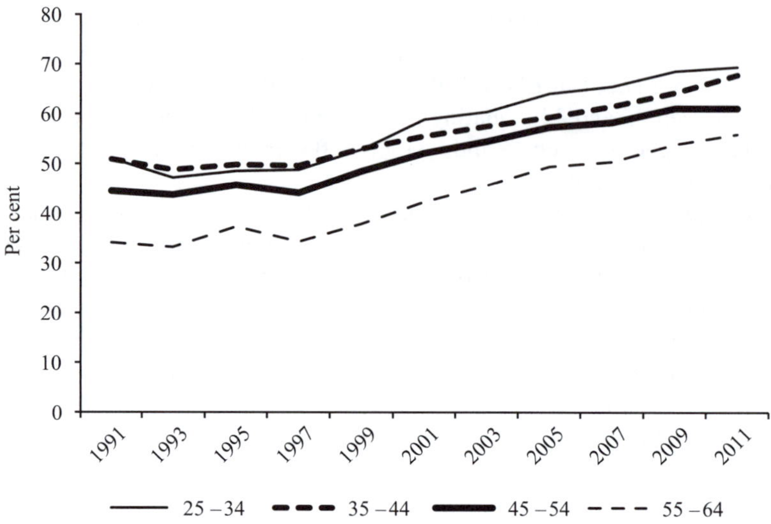

Source: Collated from figures published in ABS Education and Work 2001 & 2011.

Figure 5.1 Percentage of the population aged 25–64 with a post-school qualification, 1991–2011

RESEARCH AIMS

Given the restructuring of the labor market, the flexible pathways to tertiary education, the availability of welfare payments, and the interest-free student loans scheme available to those undertaking study, it is not surprising that a large proportion of the Australian population returns to education to upskill or reskill. The aim of the current investigation is to examine the following two questions: (1) What characteristics are associated with entry into education for adults in Australia between 2001 and 2010?; and (2) What are the outcomes of completing a course of adult education between 2001 and 2010 for occupational status? Together, these two research questions address the hypotheses presented in the conceptual framework (Chapter 1) and aim to examine both the predictors and outcomes of adult education in Australia. The following section outlines the methodology of the analysis.

DATA AND METHODS

Data

The current investigation uses the first 10 waves of the Household Income and Labour Dynamics in Australia (HILDA) Survey, collected between 2001 and 2010. The first wave is largely representative of Australian households (Goode and Watson 2007) and comprised of 13 969 individuals from 7 682 households (Watson and Wooden 2002). Since our primary interest is the effect of additional educational qualifications on job status, we selected a subsample of respondents aged between 20 and 54 in 2001 (aged 30 to 64 by wave 10). The lower age limit was chosen since entry into adult education is possible three years after the assumed standard age for entry. The upper age limit was chosen since those older than 54 in 2001 may have been retired or considering retirement in 2010.

Key variables

The outcome for the first research question is measured by a binary variable that indicates entry into adult education at any given wave, where 1 = 'started adult education'. Entry into adult education is determined as follows: postgraduate studies (doctorate) commenced after age 25, postgraduate coursework commenced after age 24, and all other forms of education are classified as adult education if they commenced after age 21. The number of respondents who began adult education is displayed by wave in the first column of Table 5.1. Please note that individuals who were age 20 in wave 1 are included in the sample since they may have entered adult education in wave 2 when they were 21 years old. To predict on-the-job training, we use a measure introduced into HILDA in wave 7, in which 1 = 'participated in any education or training scheme as part of employment in the last 12 months' and 0 = 'did not participate'.

The outcome variable for the second research question is measured using the AUSEI06 occupational status scale and is based on the respondents' current main job in any given year. This scale ranges from 0 to 100, where a higher value indicates a higher occupational status. Averaging across all waves in our sample, the mean is 40.2 and the standard deviation 29.6.

The primary independent variable of interest for research question two is the completion of an educational qualification as an adult. This is measured by a binary variable coded so that 1 = 'completed adult education in that wave' and 0 = 'did not complete adult education in that wave'. Completion of an adult educational qualification is defined as either completing a doctorate after 29; a master's degree after 26; a graduate diploma, graduate certificate, or honors degree after 25; a bachelor degree or advanced diploma after 24; a diploma, associate degree, or certificates III–IV after 23; or certificate level I or a diploma after 22. This variable has been lagged a number of times to create an indicator of time since completion. A second version of this variable carries the incidence of having completed adult education forward, so that 1 = 'has previously completed adult education' and 0 = 'has not completed adult education'. This variable allows us to examine trends in occupational status before and after completion of adult education in addition to examining change at the time of completion. The total numbers of respondents who completed adult education by wave are displayed in the second column of Table 5.1.

Table 5.1   *Number of respondents who begin and complete adult education by wave, N (%)*

Wave	Began adult education	Total sample RQ1	Completed adult education	Total sample RQ2
1	–	–	–	9 208
2	409 (5.46)	7 496	378 (4.45)	8 486
3	381 (5.40)	7 057	375 (4.57)	8 201
4	338 (4.93)	6 850	356 (4.53)	7 862
5	363 (5.93)	6 734	441 (5.56)	7 933
6	297 (4.45)	6 676	327 (4.16)	7 867
7	271 (4.06)	6 670	339 (4.43)	7 659
8	295 (4.58)	6 439	324 (4.29)	7 547
9	245 (3.90)	6 282	271 (3.51)	7 728
10	271 (4.20)	6 456	248 (3.22)	7 703
Total	2 870	60 660	3 059	80 194

Source: Own calculations based on the HILDA data.

Control variables

The control variables are divided into three groups and comprise demographic variables (gender, place of birth, age, and age-squared), socio-demographic and work-related variables (current level of education, income, occupation, employment contract, hours of paid work, tenure, and tenure squared), and contextual variables (marital status, household income, child(ren) under six present in the household, general health, and mental health). Both individual and household income have been included in the analysis because it is expected that both personal resources as well as resources available within the household are important when investigating entry into adult education.

Demographic variables

Gender is measured by a dummy variable for females. The variable measuring place of birth comprises three categories: born in Australia (reference category), born in a mainly English-speaking country (e.g., the United Kingdom, New Zealand, or Canada), and born in 'other' (a non-English-speaking country). Age is a continuous variable measured in years of age minus 20.

Work-related variables

The highest level of education achieved is measured by a variable with the categories postgraduate, bachelor degree, diploma or certificates III and IV (reference category), certificates I and II or year 12, and year 11 and below. Individual financial resources are measured by financial year gross wages and salary in Australian dollars (in thousands). The measure of occupation is derived from the Australian and New Zealand Standard Classification of Occupations (ABS 2006). The dummy categories comprise managers and professionals (reference category); technicians and trades workers; community, personal service, clerical, administration, and sales workers; and machinery operators and drivers as well as laborers. Employment contract is also measured using the dummy categories of fixed-term contract, casual contract, permanent contract (reference category), not an employee (e.g., self-employed persons and owner managers), and not in the labor force (for a discussion of employment status in Australia, see Campbell 2004). Hours of paid work, tenure, and tenure squared are continuous variables, where those who are not in the labor force are coded 0. Tenure is measured in years.

Contextual variables

Marital status is measured by a variable with categories comprising married (reference category), cohabiting, separated, divorced or widowed, and never married. Household income measures a household's current weekly gross wages and salary from all jobs in Australian dollars. The dummy variable for child(ren) under the age of six in the household is coded 1 when there is at least one child under six present in the household. Measures for general and mental health are measured by derived variables provided in HILDA based on the SF-38 for general health and the SF-36 for mental health, both of which are self-completion measures of health status. Both of these variables are measured on a scale of 0 to 100, with an increase representing a higher level of general or mental health. A number of these variables have been lagged or interacted based on the analysis performed. This procedure is discussed further in the analytical strategy section.

Analytic Strategy

The analytic strategy is divided into two sections, each dealing with one research question. To investigate the first research question, a multilevel logistic regression model predicting commencement of adult education was employed. The multilevel model contains a random error term for each individual to control for unobserved heterogeneity (Rabe-Hesketh and Skrondal 2008, p. 249). All independent variables are lagged by one year so that the characteristics that predict entry into adult education are measured in the wave before entry. This is particularly important since it can be expected that in the year an individual enters adult education, his or her socio-economic characteristics (e.g., income, employment contract, and hours of paid work) will already have changed from the time he or she made the decision to enter education. To examine the variations by gender, each of the independent variables was interacted with gender. Model 1 includes all of the independent variables, while Model 2 adds the gender interactions. A supplementary analysis has been included to investigate the characteristics associated with employment-related training and education. This analysis is based on wave seven and employs a logistic regression model that predicts participation in any education or training scheme as part of employment in the previous 12 months. The independent variables are lagged by one year, and the analysis only includes variables that were found to be significant.

A linear fixed-effects regression model predicting occupational status score is estimated to examine the second research question. This modeling technique accounts for the clustering of observations by individual by controlling for between-person variation (Singer and Willett 2003). The fixed-effects model controls for unobserved heterogeneity because it produces time-invariant estimates that are net of all observed and unobserved differences between individuals. While it is not possible to include time-invariant variables in a fixed-effects model, we are primarily interested in explaining the within-person associations, thereby making the fixed-effects model a preferred approach. It is also possible to include interactions with time-invariant variables (such as gender) in this model. The analysis consists of five models in which the independent variables are included in groups to enable the effects of different types of independent variables to be identified. Where relevant, differences between the dummy categories of the independent variables and between each interaction term and the main effect are tested for statistical significance using a linear combination of regression coefficients.

RESULTS

The results are divided into two sections, each dealing with one of the research questions.

Research Question One: What characteristics are associated with entry into education for adults in Australia between 2001 and 2010?

Table 5.2 displays the regression coefficients for the multilevel logistic model predicting the log-odds of commencement of adult education in the subsequent year. Model 1 indicates that compared with men, women are more likely to enter adult education. While the coefficient suggests that the likelihood of entering adult education increases with age, the age squared variable is also significant and negative, indicating that this is a quadratic relationship, with likelihood decreasing after age 27. There are no significant results for place of birth.

The results for education indicate that those who have a postgraduate or bachelor degree are the most likely to enter adult education, followed by those who hold a diploma or certificates III and IV and those who hold certificates I and II or year 12, while those with an educational achievement of year 11 and below are the least likely to participate. (There are significant differences between all categories, except between bachelor and postgraduate degree.) Overall, these results indicate an association of increasing strength between education level and the log-odds of entering adult education. Indeed, in a supplementary analysis using a measure of years of education and a dummy category for holding a degree (not shown), the likelihood of entering adult education increased with years of education, while holding a degree was not found to be significant.

The likelihood of commencing adult education decreases as personal income increases. Similarly, a higher level of household income is also associated with a lower chance of beginning adult education. Persons working in the clerical or service industries are more likely to enter adult education compared with all other groups (all associations are statistically significant at the p<0.01 level). Furthermore, as occupational status increases, so does the likelihood of beginning adult education.

Compared with those on a permanent contract, those who are fixed-term are more likely to enter adult education, while those who are not an employee are less likely. Furthermore, those who are not an employee are less likely to enter adult education than are both fixed-term and casual employees. Together, this indicates that individuals who are not

Table 5.2　Logistic multilevel model predicting commencement of adult education the following year

	Model 1	Model 2	Interactions (Female * Indep.)
Female (ref. male)	0.17**	−0.64	
Age (minus 20)†	0.23*	0.20	0.76**
Age squared†	−0.02**	−0.01*	−0.01**
Place of birth (ref. Australia)			
Mainly English-speaking	0.04	0.20+	−0.31*
NES	0.02	0.11	−0.15
Education (ref. dip. cert.III/IV)			
Postgraduate	0.17*	0.42**	−0.44**
Bachelor	0.14*	0.21*	−0.13
Certificates I/II and yr. 12	−0.16*	−0.07	−0.18
Yr. 11 and below	−0.64**	−0.62**	−0.07
Income†	−0.02*	−0.01	−0.03+
Household income†	−0.01**	−0.01**	0.01*
Occupation (ref. professionals)			
Technicians and trades	−0.08	−0.01	0.02
Clerical and service	0.29**	0.34**	−0.11
Production and transport	0.05	0.09	0.05
Occupational status scale	0.01**	0.01**	−0.00
Employment contract (ref. permanent)			
Fixed-term	0.219**	0.05	0.27+
Casual	0.07	0.06	0.02
Not employee	−0.36**	−0.46**	0.22
Not in the labor force	0.24	0.46	−0.23
Hours worked†	0.01	−0.01	0.06
Tenure†	−0.41**	−0.51**	0.28
Tenure squared†	0.01*	0.02**	−0.02*
Marital status (ref. married)			
Cohabiting	0.11+	−0.02	0.21+
Sep, div, or wid	0.31**	−0.10	0.60**
Never married	0.16*	−0.12	0.47**
Child under 6 in household	−0.13*	−0.09	−0.05
General health†	0.03*	0.06**	−0.04
General mental health†	−0.05**	−0.06**	0.03
Constant	−3.02**	−2.56**	
Observations	60 670	60 670	
Individuals	9 908	9 908	

Notes:　　**p < 0.01, *p < 0.05, +p < 0.10. † coefficient has been multiplied by ten.

Source:　　Own calculations based on the HILDA data.

employees, e.g., self-employed persons and owner managers, have a lower likelihood of entering adult education. Note that casual employees and those not in the labor force have the same likelihood of entering adult education as permanent employees. Hours worked is not significant. The results for tenure indicate that the likelihood of participating in adult education decreases as tenure increases. The squared term is significant and indicates that this is a negative quadratic relationship, with the calculated turning point suggesting that entering adult education becomes increasingly less likely leading up to tenure of 20.5 years.

All marital status groups are more likely to enter adult education compared with married persons (cohabiting is borderline significant at p=0.09). Both cohabiting and never married persons are less likely to enter adult education compared with separated, divorced, or widowed persons (never married is borderline significant at p=0.07). Persons with a resident child under the age of six are less likely to enter adult education. As general health increases, so does the likelihood of entering adult education. The inverse is true of mental health, with those who have lower mental health being more likely to commence adult education.

The findings for the gender interaction terms are displayed in Model 2 and show significant associations for gender interacted with age, age-squared, place of birth, education, income, household income, employment contract (borderline significant), tenure squared, and marital status. Interestingly, the main effects (which represent the coefficients for men) for age, income, and marital status are insignificant, indicating that there is no significant association between entering adult education and these characteristics for men. However, there are significant associations between these characteristics for women. The results for age and age squared indicate that there is a quadratic relationship between age and entering adult education for women, meaning that likelihood initially increases and then decreases. (For men, the significant quadratic main effect signifies that likelihood decreases with age.) For women, holding a postgraduate degree does not increase the likelihood of entering adult education, whereas it does for men. Interestingly, the influence of individual and household income differs for men and women. Compared with men, women are significantly more likely to participate in adult education as their household income increases and less likely to do so as their individual income increases (borderline significant at p=0.09). Men, on the other hand, are significantly less likely to participate as household income increases. This reflects the traditional role of men as the primary breadwinner of the household. There are no significant associations for gender and occupation or occupational status scale.

Women with a fixed-term contract are more likely to enter adult education than are those with a permanent contract (borderline significant at p=0.08), whereas this association is not significant for men. The results suggest that the quadratic relationship for tenure is weaker for women than it is for men. Married women are less likely to participate in adult education compared with women of all other marital statuses, whereas marital status does not matter for men. This, again, reflects the traditional role of wives as being primarily responsible for the private-sphere and not investing as heavily in labor market skills as unmarried women. There are no significant differences between men and women for health. While there is no significant difference between the genders regarding the presence of children under the age of six in the household, additional analyses (not shown) suggest that women with a child under the age of six are significantly less likely to enter adult education compared with women who do not have a child under age six.

The results for the supplementary analysis examining participation in employment-related training and education are presented in Table 5.3. Only the variables that were found to be significant have been included in the model. The results indicate that men and women are equally likely to participate in employment-related training. The likelihood of participating in training increases with age. Persons born in non-English-speaking countries are less likely to participate compared with both Australians and those from mainly English-speaking countries. Individuals who hold a postgraduate or bachelor degree are more likely to participate in employment-related training compared with those who hold a diploma or certificates III and IV, while those who hold certificates I / II or year 12 as well as year 11 and below are less likely. Individuals working in the clerical or service industries are more likely than those working as managers and professionals to participate in training. Individuals who have a higher occupational status and who work longer hours are also more likely to participate in training. Compared with those employed on a permanent contract, those who are on a casual contract or not employees are less likely to participate in employment-related training.

The gender interactions show a number of significant differences between men and women. Whereas place of birth does not have a significant effect for men, women born in non-English-speaking countries are less likely to take part in training than their Australian and mainly native English-speaking counterparts. Moreover, having children under six in the household has a stronger positive effect for women than for men.

Table 5.3   Logistic regression model predicting participation in any education or training scheme as part of employment

	Model 1	Model 2
Female (ref. male)	0.11	0.15+
Age (minus 20)†	0.08*	0.08*
Place of Birth (ref. Australia)		
Mainly English-speaking	0.05	−0.12
NES	−0.33**	−0.19
Education (ref. dip. cert.III/IV)		
Postgraduate	0.26*	0.26*
Bachelor	0.24**	0.24**
Certificates I/II and yr. 12	−0.22*	−0.22*
Yr. 11 and below	−0.45**	−0.45**
Occupation (ref. professionals)		
Technicians and trades	0.09	0.09
Clerical and service	0.26*	0.25*
Production and transport	0.22	0.23
Occupational status scale	0.01**	0.01**
Employment contract (ref. permanent)		
Fixed-term	−0.17	−0.18+
Casual	−0.44**	−0.44**
Not employee	−0.95**	−0.95**
Not in the labor force	0.14	0.13
Hours worked†	0.05*	0.05+
Child under 6 in household	0.08	0.19*
Interaction effects (female * independent variable)		
Place of birth (ref. Australia)		
Born mainly English-speaking		0.35+
Born NES		−0.29
Child under 6 in household		0.25+
Constant	−1.67**	−1.66**
Individuals	5 908	5 908

Notes: **p < 0.01, *p < 0.05, +p < 0.10. † coefficient has been multiplied by ten. Dependent variable from wave 7 (referring to the previous 12 months) and independent variables from wave 6.

Source: Own calculations based on the HILDA data.

Research Question Two: What are the outcomes of completing a course of adult education between 2001 and 2010 for occupational status?

Table 5.4 displays the results of the fixed-effects models predicting occupational status score. Model 1 indicates that an individual experiences a significant increase in his or her occupational status score by an average of 5.4 points (on a scale of 0–100) in the years after having completed adult education. Model 2 indicates that completing adult education leads to a significant increase in occupational status in the year of completion as well as in the following years. The magnitude of the coefficients suggests that the returns to adult education increase until about three years after completion, at which point they peak and thereafter decrease slightly.

There are significant differences, e.g., between occupational status in the year of completion and three years later, between one year and three years later, and between three years and seven years after completion.[3] Model 3 includes both the completed adult education variable and the carried-forward version. While the magnitude of the coefficients decreases for all of the lagged variables, they remain significant. This indicates that there are separate effects for having completed adult education and for time since completing adult education. When the control variables are included in Model 4, the coefficient for completing adult education (carried forward) decreases substantially yet remains significant (borderline at p=0.058). This indicates that completing adult education leads to an increase in occupational status when holding all other factors constant. In particular, as part of the effect of adult education is captured by the education control variables, the completed AE variable now captures increases in status that are not due to changes in educational level, i.e., when a person gets a qualification that is at the same (or a lower) level than the education that he or she previously had.

Model 5 includes the significant interaction terms for completed adult education (carried forward) in addition to the control variables. The results for the interaction effects indicate that place of birth, education, and employment contract have a differential impact on the association between completing adult education and occupational status above and beyond the average change in occupational status when completing adult education. The main effect of completing adult education is significant and positive, suggesting that persons who gain a new qualification but who do not change their level of education (since this is controlled) experience an increase in occupational status score. The results for place of birth indicate that persons born in non-English-speaking countries benefit more from completing adult education compared with those born in Australia or those born in mainly English-speaking countries.

Table 5.4   Linear fixed-effects model predicting occupational status score

	1	2	3	4^	5^
Completed AE carried forward	5.36**	–	2.43**	0.42+	1.24**
Completed AE		3.19**	1.45**		
Lagged 1 Year		4.39**	2.86**		
Lagged 2 Years		4.72**	3.29**		
Lagged 3 Years		4.79**	3.42**		
Lagged 4 Years		3.89**	2.56**		
Lagged 5 Years		3.14**	1.86**		
Lagged 6 Years		3.52**	2.33**		
Lagged 7 Years		3.03**	1.87*		
Lagged 8 Years		3.43**	2.30*		

Model 5 (selected variables):	Main effects	Interactions
Place of birth (ref. Australia)		
Mainly English-speaking	–	−0.90
NES	–	1.27*
Education (ref. dip. cert.III/IV)		
Postgraduate	13.69**	−1.06+
Bachelor	11.64**	0.74
Certificates I/II and yr. 12	−1.80**	0.17
Yr. 11 and below	−0.43	−0.16
Employment contract (ref. permanent)		
Fixed-term	1.76**	1.08*
Casual	−5.83**	0.03
Not employee	−0.85**	−1.41**
Not in the labor force	−44.37**	−5.10**

Notes: **$p < 0.01$, *$p < 0.05$, +$p < 0.10$. ^ Independent variables included. Coefficients not shown: age, age squared, education, employment contract, hours worked, marital status, and child(ren) under six in household. For all models: 80 194 observations and 12 028 individuals.

Source: Own calculations based on the HILDA data.

Education has been included in the model as an interaction to capture the effect of attaining a higher level of education as an adult (i.e., gaining a new qualification). The interactions between education and adult education indicate the differences in gaining these qualifications as an adult compared with the normal age range. In most cases, there are no significant differences between the two groups, the only exception being postgraduate degrees in which adult graduates have a slight disadvantage. The findings for employment contract indicate that fixed-term employees benefit significantly more from completing adult education compared with permanent and casual employees (p=0.07), those who are not employees (p=0.01), and those not in the labor force (p=0.001). Casual (and permanent) employees also benefit significantly more compared with those who are not employees (p=0.01) and those not in the labor force (p=0.001).

DISCUSSION AND CONCLUSION

The flexibility of the Australian educational and welfare systems and the propensity for older Australians to return to education and upskill or reskill provide an opportunity to examine the association between adult education and employment outcomes in a unique environment. As discussed earlier, a sizeable proportion of the Australian population completed additional educational qualifications after spending some time in the labor force, representing one of the highest rates of participation in adult education among all OECD member countries (OECD 2010). In this chapter, we have examined who participates in adult education and the effect of completing a new qualification on occupational status.

In regard to participation in formal adult education, the analyses suggest that the most privileged and the most disadvantaged in the labor market are less likely to participate. In particular, our analyses suggest that commencing formal adult education is more likely for women, individuals with a higher level of education, and those with lower income but a higher occupational status. Individuals who work in the clerical and service industries and who work on fixed-term contracts and have a shorter tenure are also more likely to participate. Formal adult education is also more common amongst those who are unmarried, have no children under the age of six in the household, and have a lower level of mental health but a higher level of physical health. These findings to some degree support the *"partial equalization hypothesis"* presented and discussed in Chapter 1, where it was hypothesized that individuals with a medium level of education as well as those in lower or less-stable employment positions would be the most likely to participate in formal adult education. Indeed, the findings for type of employment contract support this. While casual employees are in the most precarious employment position, individuals on fixed-term contracts have less employment security than do permanent employees (Campbell 2004).

In contrast, the results for employment-related training and education indicate that those in more privileged positions in the labor market (e.g., those who have a higher income, who have a higher occupational status, who are on permanent contracts, who are from English-speaking counties, and who work longer hours) are more likely to participate in training. This supports the "*Matthew effect hypothesis*", which predicted that more highly educated individuals and those in better occupational positions would be more likely to participate in non-formal adult education. The analyses also indicate that there are a number of important gender differences for both formal adult education and employment-related training. While women are more likely to participate in formal education, they have the same likelihood as men for participation in employment-related training and education. Older and unmarried women are more likely to participate in formal adult education, as are women on a fixed-term contract with a higher household income but a lower personal income. Compared with men, women who are born in mainly English-speaking countries and who have a child under the age of six in the household are more likely to participate in employer-related training.

Overall, the findings here are comparable with the findings of Coelli, Tabasso and Zakirova (2012), who investigated the decision of those over the age of 25 to enroll in education. While our findings support the "*gendered participation hypothesis*" in regard to formal adult education (in which it was expected that women would be more likely to participate in formal adult education), we do not support this hypothesis in regard to non-formal employer-sponsored adult education[4] (in which women are expected be more likely to participate in non-formal adult education if it is self-sponsored, but less likely to participate if it is employer-sponsored). While our analyses are not able to clearly specify what proportion of the training was paid for by the employer, the wording of the question in HILDA specified education or a training scheme as 'part of your employment', suggesting that it would be paid for by the employer. As such, our findings do not fully support the "*gendered participation hypothesis*" in regard to employer-sponsored adult education since we find women as likely to participate as men.

In regard to the outcomes of adult education, the analyses indicate a number of important findings. First, completing adult education is associated with an increase in occupational status, regardless of whether or not the completed qualification resulted in a higher level of qualification. Overall, the benefit appears to be greatest after roughly three years and to decrease thereafter. Importantly, when demographic, socio-demographic, work-related, and contextual factors are controlled, the benefits of adult education for occupational status remain significant. This supports the "*improved employment outcomes hypothesis*", which predicted that formal adult education would have a positive influence on employment outcomes when compared with non-participation. Examination of interaction effects between competing adult education and individual factors reveals that completing adult education benefits some groups more than others. These groups include persons born in non-English speaking countries, persons who do not hold a postgraduate degree, and fixed-term employees. As with participation, those who gain the most from adult education hold neither the weakest nor the strongest positions in the labor market.

In conclusion, our research finds that those who hold an intermediate position in the Australian labor market are the most likely to participate in adult education, and that participation leads to an increase in occupational status, with some groups benefiting more than others. Again, those who gain the most from completing formal education hold neither the most disadvantaged nor the most advantaged positions in the labor market. Thus, the institutional framework in Australia not only enables adults to return to education by providing a living allowance, an interest-free income-contingent student loans scheme, and a flexible higher-education sector, but it also provides an environment that is conducive to improvements in occupational status when these opportunities are taken advantage of.

ACKNOWLEDGEMENT

The authors wish to thank Mark Western for conceptual and methodological support.

NOTES

1. This paper uses unit record data from the Household, Income and Labour Dynamics in Australia (HILDA) Survey. The HILDA Project was initiated and is funded by the Australian Government Department of Social Services (DSS) and is managed by the Melbourne Institute of Applied Economic and Social Research (Melbourne Institute). The findings and views reported in this paper, however, are those of the authors and should not be attributed to either DSS or the Melbourne Institute.
2. This chapter primarily uses the term 'adult education' rather than 'adult learning' since the majority of our analyses focus on the commencement or completion of formal educational qualifications.
3. However, it should be noted that this may be due to period effects. For example, only those who graduated in 2002 or 2003 provided values for the lags of seven and eight years, and it is possible that graduating in the early 2000s may not have been as beneficial for occupational status as graduating in the mid- or late-2000s.
4. These findings may not be completely comparable to other country studies since we are not able to differentiate between formal and non-formal employer-sponsored adult learning.

REFERENCES

ABS (Australian Bureau of Statistics) (2001), *Education and Work, Australia, May 2001* Cat. No. 6227.0, available from: www.abs.gov.au.

ABS (2006), *Census Dictionary, 2006* (Reissue): Occupation. Cat. No. 1220.0, available from: www.abs.gov.au.

ABS (2009), 'Job flexibility of casual employees', *Australian Labour Market Statistics*, Cat. No. 6105.0, available from: www.abs.gov.au.

ABS (2011), *Education and Work, Australia, May 2011*. Cat. No. 6227.0, available from: www.abs.gov.au.

Buchler, S., M. Haynes and J. Baxter (2009), 'Casual employment in Australia: the influence of employment contract on financial well-being', *Journal of Sociology*, **45** (3), 271–89.

Campbell, I. (2004), 'Casual work and casualisation: How does Australia compare?' *Labour and Industry*, **15** (2), 85–111.

Chapman, B. (1997), 'Conceptual issues and the Australian experience with income contingent charges for higher education', *The Economic Journal*, **107**, 738–51.

Coelli, M., D. Tabasso and R. Zakirova (2012), 'Studying beyond age 25: who does it and what do they gain?' *Research Report,* Adelaide, Australia: NCVER.

DEEWR (Department of Education, Employment and Workplace Relations) (2010a), *Australian Jobs 2010*, available from: http://www.deewr.gov.au.

DEEWR (2010b), *Students & Courses: Australian Vocational Education and Training Statistics NCVER*, available from: http://www.deewr.gov.au.

DEEWR (2011a), *Table 2.1 Higher Education Statistics 2010 All students*, available from: http://www.deewr.gov.au.

DEEWR (2011b), *Australian Jobs 2011*, available from: http://www.deewr.gov.au.

Dieckhoff, M., J.-M. Jungblut, and P.J. O'Connell, (2007), 'Job-related training in Europe: Do institutions matter?', in D. Gallie (ed.), *Employment Regimes and the Quality of Work,* Oxford, UK: Oxford University Press, pp. 77–103.

Goldthorpe, J. H. (1996), 'Class analysis and the reorientation of class theory: The case of persisting differentials in educational attainment', *The British Journal of Sociology*, **47** (3), 481–505.

Goode, A. and N. Watson (eds) (2007), *HILDA User Manual – Release 5.0*, Melbourne, Australia: Melbourne Institute of Applied Economic and Social Research, University of Melbourne.

Marks, G.N. and J. McMillan (2007), 'Australia: changes in socioeconomic inequalities and university participation', in Yossi Shavit, Richard Arum and Adam Gamoran (eds), *Stratification in Higher Education: A Comparative Study*, Stanford, USA: Stanford University Press, pp. 351–73.

Moodie, G. and L. Wheelahan (2009), 'The significance of Australian vocational institutions in opening access to higher education', *Higher Education Quarterly*, **63** (4), 356–70.

OECD (Organisation for Economic Co-operation and Development) (2010), *Education at a Glance 2010*, Paris: OECD, available from: http://www.oecd.org.

O'Keefe, S. and B. Dollery (2006), 'Contemporary public policy perspectives on vocational education and training in Australia', *Journal of Economic and*

Social Policy, **10** (2), 95–113.

Pallas, A.M. (2004), 'Educational participation across the life-course. Do the rich get richer?', in Richard Settersen and Timothy Owens (eds), *Advances in Life-Course Research,* New York, USA: Elsevier Science, pp. 327–54.

Pfeffer, F. T. (2008), 'Persistent inequality in educational attainment and its institutional context', *European Sociological Review*, **24** (5), 543–65.

Rabe-Hesketh, S. and A. Skrondal (2008), *Multilevel and Longitudinal Modeling Using Stata,* (2nd ed.), College Station, Texas, USA: Stata Press.

Singer, J. D. and J.B. Willett (2003), *Applied Longitudinal Data Analysis: Modeling Change and Event Occurrence*, Oxford, UK: Oxford University Press.

Van de Werfhorst, H. G. and R. Andersen (2005), 'Social background, credential inflation and educational strategies', *Acta Sociologica*, **48** (4), 321–40.

Watson, I., J. Buchanan, I. Campbell and C. Briggs (2003), *Fragmented Futures: New Challenges in Working Life*, Sydney, Australia: Federation Press.

Watson, N. and M. Wooden (2002), *Assessing the Quality of the HILDA Survey Wave 1 Data*, Melbourne, Australia: Department of Family and Community Services, and The University of Melbourne.

Wheelahan, L. (2009), 'Do educational pathways contribute to equity in tertiary education in Australia', *Critical Studies in Education*, **50** (3), 261–75.

Woodward, D. (2005), *Australia Unsettled: The Legacy of 'Neo-liberalism',* Frenchs Forest, Australia: Pearson Education.

6. Cumulative (Dis)advantage? Patterns of Participation and Outcomes of Adult Learning in Great Britain

Patricia McMullin and Elina Kilpi-Jakonen

INTRODUCTION

Throughout Western societies, globalizing and demographic influences have placed additional pressure on policy makers to encourage investment in adult learning in order to maintain high levels of worker productivity and to promote equity between different socioeconomic groups. However, the conclusion of many previous studies on adult learning has been that educational opportunities follow a pattern of cumulative advantage, whereby the highly educated are more likely to participate (e.g., Elman and O'Rand 2004).

The British institutional setting promotes relatively high levels of participation in adult learning. In this chapter, we examine how participation opportunities are distributed within the population and across individuals' life courses. We also aim to analyze how adult learning influences labor market outcomes in a longitudinal manner. Our conclusions about the cumulative nature of advantages related to adult learning are based on the outcomes of these analyses.

Our study diverges from previous studies on adult learning in Britain and many of the other studies in this volume by taking into account a number of different types of adult learning and analyzing them separately. We are able to distinguish between formal and non-formal learning, and within non-formal learning, we distinguish between certified and non-certified learning as well as between employer-sponsored and self-sponsored learning. When analyzing labor market outcomes, we are also able to differentiate between qualifications of different levels. Overall, we are able to paint a comprehensive picture of adult learning in Great Britain.

ADULT LEARNING AND THE BRITISH INSTITUTIONAL CONTEXT

It is important to consider how the British institutional context influences adult learning. In the following section, we discuss how adult learning is structured in Britain and outline our expectations on patterns of participation in adult learning and its possible effects in the labor market.

Adult Learning in Great Britain

Most formal adult education takes place in colleges of further education and in universities. The educational system is relatively open when it comes to adult learning. Boundaries between secondary- and tertiary-level studies are blurred due to the fact that study at the two levels can take place in the same institution, and entry requirements have been widened in order to accommodate those who do not meet the traditional entry conditions (see Eurydice 2003).

The British educational system can generally be characterized as relatively unstratified and unstandardized (Shavit and Müller 1998). Efforts to increase standardization include the development of a centralized National Qualifications Framework (NQF), through which all types of qualifications can be approved and classified (see Eurydice 2003 for more information about the NQF). For the purpose of our study, whether or not a qualification can be classified within the NQF represents the dividing line between formal and non-formal adult learning.[1]

Certified training that is not included in the NQF tends to be of relatively short duration and is often sponsored by employers (own analyses from the BHPS). Overall, employers are a major provider and sponsor of adult learning in Britain. One of the reasons for this is the low vocational specificity of the British educational system, which means that employers need to invest in the training of new employees, particularly if these employees have recently left the educational system (Scherer 2005). Moreover, there have been multiple interventions on the part of the state aimed at encouraging employers to invest further in the skills of their employees. These interventions include the "New Deal" programs introduced under New Labour as well as regulations that give young workers the right to take time off to participate in adult learning under the "Teaching and Higher Education Act 1998" (Eurydice 2003).

On the other hand, the low level of employment protection in Britain means that labor market turnover is high (Sørensen and Tuma 1981). This means that employers may be put off from investing heavily in their employees due to their fear of poaching from competing firms (Soskice 1999).

At the individual level, low employment protection and relatively low levels of welfare benefits give individuals incentives to invest in their own job-related skills in order to remain competitive in the labor market.

Patterns of Participation in Different Forms of Adult Learning

Despite the various institutional reasons that lead us to expect relatively high levels of adult learning in Britain, we also expect that there are likely to be differences in which groups find participation the easiest and most beneficial.

The unstratified nature of general education as well as the openness of higher-level institutions to individuals who do not fulfill traditional entry requirements would lead us to expect that educational differentials in entry to formal education should be relatively small. This suspicion is also supported by the generally higher opportunity costs for the higher educated to take part in time-intensive formal education. On the other hand, we also recognize that the lower educated may face dispositional barriers to reentering formal education institutions (Rubenson and Desjardins 2009). Moreover, although opportunity costs may be lower for the lower educated, the absolute costs of formal courses may also be a barrier to entry.

The costs of formal education may also make it more attractive to employees who can get their employers to pay their fees and support them during their (part-time) studies. Employers, on the other hand, are likely to have greater incentives to sponsor the studies of those employees from whom they can expect greater productivity increases, which in general applies to those who are already medium to highly skilled.

Numerous studies have observed a positive relationship between educational attainment and the probability of participating in work-related training programs and in training sponsored by employers (Pallas 2002; Dieckhoff, Jungblut and O'Connell 2007). Therefore, employers' preferences to train the highly skilled in the British context are expected to affect the educational stratification not only of employer-sponsored non-formal learning but also of formal education.

Employers' incentives to invest in the training of their employees are also higher for younger employees due to the low level of vocational specificity in the educational system. This can also be the case when individuals begin a new job (Cheung and McKay 2010) and after an employment interruption, e.g., women when they return to work after childbearing. Gendered perceptions of parenthood have been found to give rise to a "motherhood penalty". It is additionally possible that these perceptions similarly influence the willingness of employers to invest in training opportunities for women (Dieckhoff and Steiber 2011).

Due to the generally high incentives for individuals to invest in adult learning in Britain, we can expect that the groups that are most overlooked by employers have higher probabilities of taking part in other types of adult learning – most notably non-formal learning that is non-employer-sponsored as well as formal education (to some extent). These groups include women, the non-employed, older individuals, and the lower educated.

Previous research has found that those with already high levels of education are more likely to earn new qualifications as adults (Jenkins et al. 2003) and to participate in work-related training (Cheung and McKay 2010). Research using the BHPS has found that individuals with no qualifications in 1991 were significantly less likely to take on additional training in the future (Blanden et al. 2009).

Additionally, research using the NCDS has found that men have a substantially higher probability than women of undertaking both employer-sponsored training and work-related training leading to a formal vocational qualification (Blundell, Dearden and Meghir 1996).

Adult Learning and Career Progress

There are two major institutional factors that lead us to expect relatively small effects of formal adult education on career progression: open employment structures and the low signaling power of qualifications. Open employment structures have to do with the fact that labor market mobility in Britain is high and happens as a consequence of a variety of factors, thus downplaying the role of education. This is further strengthened by the low signaling power of qualifications, which is largely due to the low level of educational stratification and the waves of reforms in the educational system (see Brauns, Müller and Steinmann 1997).

Previous studies on formal education have found contrasting results. On the one hand, studies using the NCDS have not found that new qualifications increase wages (Jenkins et al. 2003; Silles 2007). On the other hand, a study using the BHPS found that new qualifications increase earnings and prestige (Blanden, Buscha and Sturgis 2010). Positive results from formal education, particularly at the tertiary level, have also been found for employment opportunities (Jenkins et al. 2003; Woodfield 2011; Kilpi-Jakonen et al. 2012).

The productivity-enhancing effects of employer-sponsored non-formal learning should also improve the employment outcomes of adult learners. However, since a substantial amount of this type of learning is likely to take place upon hiring new employees, it is likely that in many cases improvements take place simultaneously with, rather than following, training. In the long run, it is expected that those who invest in their own skills, and those whose skills employers invest in, have better labor market chances than those who do not. Without appropriate controls for selectivity, some of the beneficial effects of training may be overestimated since they also capture unmeasured individual productivity differentials.

Previous literature has found positive wage returns to work-related training, even after controlling for selectivity (Arulampalam and Booth 1998; Cheung and McKay 2010). Other studies have also found positive returns to obtaining a new qualification or "other" education and training on upward intra-generational mobility, with results moderated by gender and appearing over time (Blanden et al. 2009).

DATA AND METHODS

The dataset used in this study is the nationally representative sample of 5 505 British households collected as the original sample of the British Household Panel Study (BHPS). The BHPS is a longitudinal panel study consisting of 18 waves that began in 1991 and ended in 2008/09.[2] We focus on data collected over the years 1998–2008 (waves 8–18 of the BHPS) since the inclusion of additional questions on training from wave 8 onward makes it possible to distinguish between employer-sponsored and unsponsored non-formal training. The first stage of this analysis is to examine the factors influencing participation in adult learning. We use random-effects logistic regression models for panel data in which observations are nested within individuals.

We differentiate between formal adult education and non-formal adult learning. For formal adult education, we examine enrollment patterns rather than educational attainment. This gives us a better idea of the factors that lead adults to begin formal education and (particularly with regard to labor force participation) gives us a more accurate picture than looking at the situation immediately before graduation would do.

Our specification of non-formal adult learning includes receiving a new qualification that is not on the standard list of qualifications covered in the BHPS questionnaire. These other professional, technical, or higher-level qualifications cannot be classified under the National Qualifications Framework. We refer to this type of qualification as certified non-formal adult learning. Based on our descriptive analyses, certified non-formal adult learning is often employer sponsored, with a substantial amount also taking place in private training centers and in colleges of higher or further education (particularly if the respondent is unemployed). Training for these qualifications is typically of quite short duration, often lasting less than one week when converted into working weeks.

An additional type of non-formal adult learning analyzed here is training that does not lead to a qualification. We further break down this category by distinguishing between learning that takes place internally (employer sponsored and/or located at the workplace or employer's training center) and externally (not sponsored by the employer but with the purpose of improving job skills either for current or future positions).

We model men and women separately, and independent variables include age, age squared, previous educational attainment (highest level of educational attainment), marital status, age of youngest child in the household, household income, year (wave) labor force status, occupational class, firm size, full-time vs part-time job, permanent vs short-term contract, job experience, and branch of industry (based on a modified version of Singelmann's 1978 classification) collapsing transformative and distributive industries, personal service and producer service industries, and transport and communicative industries (Schmelzer 2008). Employed individuals are those who did paid work the previous week, including those who had a job in the previous week despite being away from it. Unemployment is based on an individual's self-definition and not being in paid work the previous week.

In order to ensure that we only capture learning events that take place after the completion of initial education, we exclude from our sample individuals studying for qualifications within the "normal age range". We define this using OECD statistics on the normal age at which specific levels of qualifications are obtained (OECD 2002) and allow for an additional two years of studying. For example, the age at which first degrees are normally obtained in Britain is 21. Therefore, individuals who gain these qualifications up to the age of 23 are excluded from the sample until they have graduated. In addition, we use the retirement age as the cut-off at the other end, excluding women from age 60 and men from age 65. In some analyses, the sample is further restricted to include only those in employment.

The second stage in this study is the examination of returns to adult learning using both discrete time event history analysis for repeated events (multilevel random-effects logistic regression models) and fixed-effects linear regression models. Our outcomes are upward and downward prestige mobility for the first analysis and the absolute level of prestige for the second analysis. For formal adult education, we distinguish between obtaining a new degree, a new tertiary diploma, a qualification equivalent to an A-level, and lower secondary qualifications. For these analyses, we can also extend our data to include waves 1–7. We use the CAMSIS scores available in the BHPS as our measure of prestige and define upward mobility as an increase of at least 5 points on the CAMSIS scale, whereas downward mobility is defined as a decrease of at least 1 point or exit from employment. Depending on the model, we use either a measure of "ever having completed adult learning" (as observed during the survey) or a set of yearly lags for the adult learning variables. We also control for missing information in the lags, taking into account missing waves and item non-response for the adult-learning variables.

RESULTS

In this section, we present the results of our investigation of the factors influencing participation in formal adult education and non-formal training. We also present our findings with regard to the impact of adult learning on the probability of prestige mobility (controlling for duration spent in the current job) and on change in prestige.

Descriptive Analysis: Participation Rates in Formal and Non-Formal Adult Learning

Figure 6.1 illustrates patterns of participation in adult learning by age group and gender. Both men and women participate more in non-formal internal training that does not lead to a qualification than in either formal adult education or certified non-formal adult learning.

While female participation in non-formal internal adult learning is greater than male participation in the early and late stages of the life course, women participate less in non-formal internal adult learning than men during their main childbearing years.

In addition, while female participation in formal adult education sharply drops off after the age of 25, women between the ages of 25–45 still participate in formal adult education significantly more than men. After 45, women participate less in formal adult education and more in employer-sponsored internal training. These patterns suggest that both employer-sponsored adult learning and formal adult education are moderated by gender and reflect the interrupted career pattern of females.

For certified non-formal adult learning, we find that male participation increases until it peaks at age 25, steadily declining thereafter. Female participation in certified non-formal learning is lower and the curve gentler until the age of approximately 32, at which point female participation matches that of males. The curve for non-formal external adult training is relatively flat at approximately 2 per cent for both women and men (not shown).

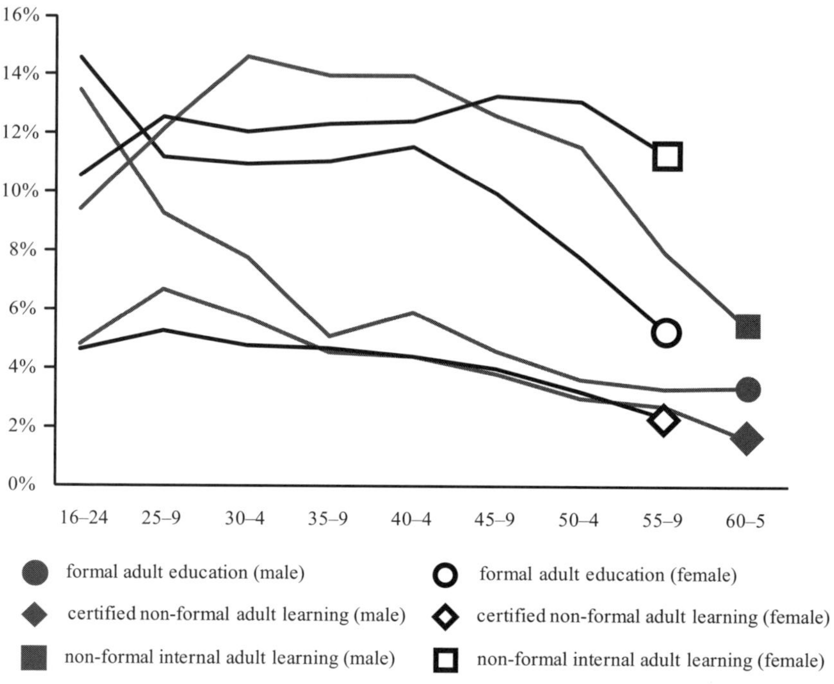

Source: Own calculations based on the BHPS.

Figure 6.1   Proportion of adult learners within age range in Britain by type of adult learning

Patterns of Participation in Adult Learning

We present our results of enrollment in formal adult learning and participation in non-formal adult learning separately for the general and employed populations (Tables 6.1 and 6.2, respectively). Moreover, we only focus on certified non-formal adult learning and internal training for the employed since these are the most relevant types of adult learning for both groups.

Gender and labor force status shape the type of learning that individuals participate in since they have differential effects on the different types of adult learning. Women are more likely to enter formal adult education and to participate in external training, whereas among the employed there is no gender difference for certified non-formal learning and internal training.

We find that the non-employed are more likely to enroll in formal adult education and undertake external training than the employed. In comparison with other groups, unemployed men are particularly likely to participate in external training. This supports the expectation that groups that may be overlooked by employers should have higher probabilities of taking part in other types of adult learning.

On the other hand, the effect of educational level is surprisingly similar across the different types of adult learning. The more-highly educated are more likely to participate in all models, with possibly slightly stronger differences in internal and external training than in the two certified types of learning. In this sense, a "Matthew effect" (Merton 1968) is evident in all types of adult learning. This effect is further enhanced for internal training by the unequal distribution of participation by occupational class since manual workers are less likely to participate than non-manual employees. There is also a separation for women within non-manual employees. For certified non-formal learning, the groups least likely to participate are the routine non-manual and personal service employees.

The effect of age varies by gender and type of learning. In some cases, age does not have a statistically significant effect, whereas in others, the effect is curvilinear (first increasing and then decreasing). The latter is the case for entry into formal education for women and internal and external training for men.

Having children in the household does not seem to affect men, but this variable has a strong effect on women's enrollment in formal and non-formal qualifications. Higher household income increases internal training for both men and women but reduces enrollment in formal education. For the employed, having children in the household under the age of one increases the probability of participation in certified non-formal learning for men and decreases the probability of participation for women, whereas there is no effect on internal training.

With regard to other employment characteristics, larger firms are more likely to train persons internally than smaller firms. Holding a fixed-term contract reduces the probability of internal training for men. Working part-time reduces the probability of internal training for both genders and of participation in certified non-formal adult learning for women, whereas higher levels of job experience reduce women's participation in both certified non-formal adult learning and internal training.

Returns to Adult Learning: Career Progress

We present the results of the effect of adult learning on upward and downward prestige mobility and on absolute levels of prestige separately for formal and non-formal adult learning (Tables 6.3 and 6.4 for formal and Table 6.5 for

Table 6.1   Enrollment in formal adult learning and participation in non-formal adult learning (results as log odds ratios)

	Enrollment in formal education		Certified non-formal learning		Internal training		External training	
	Women	Men	Women	Men	Women	Men	Women	Men
Female (from model with both genders)	0.51**	–	−0.03	–	0.19**	–	0.19*	–
Age (minus 16)	0.04**	−0.03+	0.01	−0.014	−0.01	0.04**	0.04	0.05*
Age squared	−0.00**	−0.00	−0.00**	−0.00	0.00	−0.00**	−0.00	−0.00*
Labor force status (ref. employed, incl. self-employed)								
Unemployed	0.28+	0.28	−0.31+	−0.34**	−0.83**	−1.24**	−0.08	1.24**
Outside	0.31**	0.77**	−0.34**	−0.60**	−2.33**	−2.23**	−0.64**	−0.42
Age of youngest child in household (ref. no children)								
Under one	−0.56**	−0.16	−0.74**	0.17	−0.25*	0.14	0.10	−0.23
Between one and three	−0.17+	−0.18	−0.22**	0.01	−0.02	−0.02	0.00	−0.05
Four and over	0.21**	−0.03	0.01	−0.09	−0.06	0.04	0.07	−0.12

Table 6.1 Continued

	Enrollment in formal education		Certified non-formal learning		Internal training		External training	
	Women	Men	Women	Men	Women	Men	Women	Men
Highest education (ref. first degree)								
Postgraduate degree	0.33*	−0.29	−0.11	−0.27	−0.01	−0.33+	−0.07	−0.17
Teaching qualification	0.25	−0.09	0.22	0.38+	0.37+	−0.40	0.60*	−0.30
Other tertiary qualification	−0.21*	−0.55**	−0.10	0.02	−0.38**	−0.53**	−0.40*	−0.57**
A-level and equivalent	−0.45**	−0.51**	−0.51**	−0.32**	−0.70**	−0.67**	−0.83**	−0.89**
GCSE and equivalent	−0.69**	−0.72**	−0.79**	−0.64**	−0.79**	−0.97**	−1.08**	−0.81**
Other secondary	−1.09**	−1.18**	−1.15**	−0.78**	−1.11**	−1.55**	−1.34**	−1.52**
Other	−1.78**	−0.19	−1.59**	−1.27*	−2.08**	−2.03**	−1.59	−0.17
None	−1.63**	−1.71**	−1.40**	−1.08**	−1.67**	−1.89**	−1.34**	−1.65**
Log household income	−0.08*	−0.01	0.02	−0.06+	0.36**	0.35**	0.13	0.06
Observations	27 471	27 774	50 036	47 533	31 188	29 290	31 186	29 286
Individuals	4 688	4 655	5 479	5 482	4 418	4 254	4 417	4 250

Table 6.2   Participation in non-formal adult learning for the employed population only (results as log odds ratios)

	Certified non-formal learning		Internal training	
	Women	Men	Women	Men
Female	−0.08	–	−0.06	–
(from model with both genders)				
Age (minus 16)	0.00	−0.03*	−0.03*	0.04*
Age squared	−0.00	−0.00	0.00**	−0.00**
Age of youngest child in household (ref. no children)				
Under one	−0.82**	0.23*	−0.17	0.14
Between one and three	−0.17	−0.00	0.14	−0.02
Four and over	0.02	−0.08	0.04	0.03
Social class (ref. higher professionals)				
Lower professionals	−0.13	−0.03	−0.10	0.03
Routine non-manual employees	−0.39**	−0.37**	−0.28**	0.06
Personal service employees	−0.23+	−0.75**	−0.43**	0.25
Self-employed	−17.64	−14.73	−15.26	−14.99
Farmers	−17.58	−0.67	−0.46	−1.13
Foremen and technicians	−0.01	0.27**	−0.71**	−0.20+
Skilled manual workers	−0.32	−0.04	−0.65**	−0.48**
Semi- and unskilled manual workers	−0.11	−0.05	−0.84**	−0.74**
Firm size (ref. 50 and fewer)				
50–250	0.01	0.04	0.15*	0.32**
250+	−0.15+	0.07	0.41**	0.44**
Part-time (ref. full-time 30 h and more)	−0.16*	−0.03	−0.25**	−0.27+
Fixed-term contract (ref. permanent)	0.08	0.20	−0.10	−0.45**
Log of job experience	−0.08*	−0.03	−0.09**	−0.02
Observations	33 043	32 181	21 113	20 608
Individuals	4 516	4 403	3 603	3 417

Notes: **p < 0.01, *p < 0.05, +p < 0.10. All models control for highest education, marital status, household income, and industry.

Source: Own calculations based on the BHPS (waves 7–18 for internal training and waves 1–18 for certified non-formal learning).

non-formal). More specifically, Table 6.3 examines returns to ever having completed adult learning, Table 6.4 examines the relationship between formal qualifications and career progress lagged over the following three years, and Table 6.5 presents the results of non-formal adult learning on career progress with lagged effects included.

Overall, we find positive returns to formal adult education and few but mainly positive returns to non-formal adult learning. One possible explanation as to why we find less returns to non-formal adult learning is that both prestige mobility and non-formal training occur simultaneously (for reasons outlined above).[3] In addition, the fixed-effects models show more positive returns than the event history models. We interpret this as suggesting that adult learning does not necessarily increase the chances of making large "mobility jumps" but that it does tend to increase occupational prestige at the individual level.

In Table 6.3, our results indicate a positive impact on upward mobility for women and a positive impact on prestige score for both genders with regard to ever having obtained a new qualification as an adult. When we differentiate between qualification levels, we find that all levels of qualification obtained as an adult learner have a positive impact on prestige scores, with the possible exception of men who obtain an A-level or equivalent. However, analyzing duration until mobility jumps gives a different picture, with men experiencing upward mobility after obtaining a university degree or an A-level/equivalent and women benefiting from an A-level or lower. A tertiary diploma does not have an effect on upward or downward mobility but does have an effect on prestige scores.

In Table 6.4, we find that a university degree as an adult learner has a quick impact, and the benefits are long term. A tertiary diploma as an adult learner pays off in the first year, weakens in the second, and only benefits men in subsequent years. An A-level or equivalent has a stronger effect for women, yielding them returns in the second year and returns to men in subsequent years. A lower secondary qualification as an adult learner benefits women in the first year, with benefits disappearing in the second year and returning later. A lower secondary qualification benefits men after a lag of two years.

In Table 6.5, we find positive returns for men with regard to upward mobility and downward mobility in the following year for non-formal certified training. However, this advantage with regard to downward mobility turns into a disadvantage after a lag of two years. We find a positive effect on prestige scores for both men and women after a lag of two years.

For non-formal internal training that does not lead to a qualification, only after a lag of two years do we find positive returns to upward mobility for women and an insulating effect from downward mobility for men. In terms of

Table 6.3   Returns to formal adult learning in the form of downward and upward mobility and prestige

	Upward mobility		Downward mobility		Prestige	
	Women	Men	Women	Men	Women	Men
Adult learning carried forward (ref. no adult learning)						
Any new qualification	0.12**	0.06	0.01	−0.01	2.17**	1.52*
Adult learning carried forward (ref. no adult learning)						
University degree	−0.05	0.24**	0.02	0.04	7.34**	4.00**
Tertiary diploma	−0.11	0.03	−0.09	−0.05	1.73**	1.71**
A-level and equivalent	0.16*	0.16*	0.10	0.03	1.70**	0.65
Lower secondary	0.17**	−0.03	0.02	−0.03	1.08**	0.75*
Observations	39 137	42 855	39 177	42 861	41 642	45 885
Individuals	4 842	5 069	4 843	5 070	4 945	5 273

Notes: **p < 0.01, *p < 0.05, +p < 0.10. Models for mobility use discrete time event history analysis for repeated events and those for prestige use panel fixed-effects linear regression. All models control for age, age squared, period, marital status, age of youngest child in household, firm size, industry, and working full-time. Models of mobility additionally control for duration in job, educational level, non-response for adult learning, and missing information in lags.

Source: Own calculations based on the BHPS (waves 1–18).

Table 6.4   Returns to formal adult learning in terms of absolute prestige (panel fixed-effects linear regression models)

	Prestige	
	Women	Men
University degree as adult learner		
In previous wave	4.44**	2.30**
Lag of 2 waves	6.00**	3.32**
Lag of 3 waves and carried forward	6.12**	4.77**
Tertiary diploma as adult learner		
In previous wave	1.73**	1.67*
Lag of 2 waves	1.06+	1.45+
Lag of 3 waves and carried forward	0.09	1.90**
A-level and equivalent as adult learner		
In previous wave	0.57	−0.10
Lag of 2 waves	1.88**	0.24
Lag of 3 waves and carried forward	2.51**	0.86+
Lower secondary qualification as adult learner		
In previous wave	0.92**	0.27
Lag of 2 waves	0.50	0.10
Lag of 3 waves and carried forward	1.64**	1.49**
Observations	41 642	45 885
Individuals	4 945	5 273

Notes: **$p < 0.01$, *$p < 0.05$, +$p < 0.10$. All models control for age, age squared, period, marital status, age of youngest child in household, firm size, industry, and working full-time.

Source: Own calculations based on the BHPS (waves 1–18).

Table 6.5   *Returns to non-formal adult learning in the form of downward and upward mobility and prestige*

	Upward mobility		Downward mobility			Prestige	
	Women	Men	Women	Men		Women	Men
Certified non-formal learning							
In current wave	−0.08	−0.06	0.09	0.11	In previous wave	0.19	−0.17
In previous wave	0.14	0.17+	−0.03	−0.18*	Lag of 2 waves	0.78**	0.59*
Lag of 2 waves	0.09	−0.06	0.08	0.17*	Lag of 3 waves and carried forward	0.38	0.77**
Non-formal internal training (not leading to a qualification)							
In current wave	−0.08	0.04	−0.08	0.04	In previous wave	0.02	0.41*
In previous wave	0.02	−0.06	−0.03	0.00	Lag of 2 waves	0.03	−0.13
Lag of 2 waves	0.16*	0.05	0.04	0.20**	Lag of 3 waves and carried forward	−0.25	−0.40+
Non-formal external training (not leading to a qualification)							
In current wave	−0.14	−0.04	−0.33*	−0.31*	In previous wave	0.83+	1.02+
In previous wave	−0.45*	0.03	−0.12	−0.09	Lag of 2 waves	−0.04	0.71
Lag of 2 waves	0.25	−0.02	−0.27	−0.12	Lag of 3 waves and carried forward	0.46	0.65
Observations	22 862	24 773	22 889	24 779		25 241	27 530
Individuals	3 754	3 780	3 755	3 781		3 846	3 936

Notes: **p < 0.01, *p < 0.05, +p < 0.10. Models for mobility use discrete time event history analysis for repeated events and those for prestige use panel fixed-effects linear regression. All models control for age, age squared, period, marital status, age of youngest child in household, firm size, industry, and working full-time. Models of mobility additionally control for duration in job, educational level, non-response for adult learning, and missing information in lags.

Source: Own calculations based on the BHPS (waves 8–18).

134

prestige scores, we find positive returns to men from the training reported in the previous wave.

For non-formal external training that does not lead to a qualification, we find the strongest impact for both men and women to be an insulating effect on downward mobility that occurs in the wave after training has been reported. We also find weak positive returns in the form of prestige scores in the following year. Moreover, there seems to be a negative effect on upward mobility for women two years after training has been reported.

CONCLUSION

In conclusion, we find that the most prevalent form of adult learning in Britain is non-formal employer-sponsored training, confirming the role of investment by employers as the main factor that influences adult learning in Britain. However, there is also a sizeable share of individuals participating in other types of adult learning, in particular formal adult education, suggesting that individuals are compelled to invest in their own skills in order to remain competitive in the labor market. This observation is substantiated by the finding that the non-employed are more likely to enroll in formal adult education and external training than the employed.

Besides employment, another key factor influencing participation in different types of adult learning is level of education. The higher educated are more likely to participate in both formal and non-formal adult learning, which supports previous findings of a cumulative advantage in educational attainment in the adult life stage. This effect is slightly stronger for uncertified work-related training, reflecting employers' propensity to maximize the efficiency of training by investing in employees with the highest levels of education and skill. Within the employed population, this is compounded for both men and women by occupational level.

The findings of the British chapter therefore support the hypothesis outlined in Chapter 1, which stated that more-highly-educated individuals and those in better occupational positions are more likely to participate in non-formal adult learning (*"Matthew effect hypothesis"*). This chapter does not support the hypothesis that those with medium levels of education are more likely to participate in formal adult education, but we did find that those not employed are more likely to participate (*"partial equalization hypothesis"*).

Regarding gender, this chapter partially supports the *"gendered participation hypothesis"*, with women more likely to participate in formal adult education and unsponsored external training. Contrary to our expectations, men are generally not more likely to participate in internal training than women.

When the relationship is explored in more detail, we find that women participate in non-formal internal training more than men both before and after their peak childbearing years, which suggests that employers are not necessarily unwilling to invest in the training of women. It is more likely that employers are incentivized to invest in their most productive employees as well as in new employees.[4] Therefore, since women typically enter the labor market with higher levels of education than men, they may have an initial advantage in internal training before they reach childbearing age, after which point their productivity level potentially drops. During this time, men receive more internal training.

With regard to labor market returns, we found that formal adult education has strong positive effects on prestige mobility, thus supporting the *"improved employment outcomes hypothesis"* outlined in Chapter 1. However, a more complex picture emerges when the level of qualification and the timing of returns are taken into consideration. We found stronger positive returns in the fixed-effects models than in the event history models, suggesting that adult learning does not necessarily play a large role with regard to large mobility increases or in reducing the risk of downward mobility.

The highest returns were found for tertiary degrees, which produce the largest increases in prestige scores for both men and women. Relatively stable and high returns were also found for A-level and equivalent qualifications. One possible reason why lower qualifications produce weaker increases in prestige is that these qualifications do not serve as educational upgrades for those obtaining them as often as new tertiary qualifications do. This means that there are likely to be more career sidesteppers within the group obtaining lower qualifications, thus driving down average returns to these qualifications. Nevertheless, the differential returns produce more cumulative advantage patterns since individuals who are able to invest in higher levels of education also reap larger benefits from their investments.

We found fewer returns for non-formal internal training, which might be explained by the fact that the key benefits to non-formal adult learning may happen instantaneously with the direction of causality uncertain. In other words, we cannot establish whether training leads to a new job immediately after having taken place or whether new employees receive training immediately after being hired. We assume that both of these processes happen. Moreover, as seen in our participation models, women tend to receive the most training when they have been in their job for a short duration. Therefore, Great Britain can be said to support the *"indeterminate employment outcomes hypothesis"* with regard to the impact of non-formal adult learning on prestige mobility.

Overall, our expectation that groups that may be overlooked by employers should have higher probabilities of taking part in other types of adult learning is supported since both the non-employed and women are more likely to enroll in formal adult education and external training. However, we also found evidence of cumulative disadvantage since those with the lowest levels of qualification are the least likely to participate in adult learning of any kind.

Furthermore, labor market chances are improved by investments in skills. This means that investment in adult learning has the potential to compensate for earlier educational disadvantages if the least advantaged are able to overcome barriers to participation.

Further research in this area could explore how dispositional and institutional barriers to participation in formal adult education change over the life course. Another interesting avenue for future research would be further exploration of the relationship between adult learning and the movement of individuals between (as well as within) firms and across sectors. This would be of particular use in exploring the career mobility of women who have more discontinuous career trajectories. Furthermore, in order to increase employability, adult learning could be used to lead to sectoral moves for workers in declining industries.

NOTES

1. This also means that the dividing line between formal and non-formal adult learning in our study differs slightly from that of other studies, e.g., those using the Adult Education Survey.
2. The BHPS was incorporated into the UK Household Longitudinal Study (Understanding Society) from the second wave of interviews onward. For more information, see: https://www.understandingsociety.ac.uk.
3. We found an instantaneous effect when examining the impact of non-formal training on upward and downward mobility, but because causality cannot be determined, we do not include the results here. Full results are available from the authors upon request.
4. However, we also have evidence to suggest that employers invest more in training of a greater duration for men, even directly after labor market entry. Full results are available from the authors upon request.

REFERENCES

Arulampalam, W. and A. Booth (1998), 'Labour market flexibility and skills acquisition: Is there a trade-off?', *British Journal of Industrial Relations*, **36** (4), 521–36.

Blanden, Jo, Patrick Sturgis, Franz Buscha and Peter Unwin (2009), 'The effect of lifelong learning on intra-generational social mobility: evidence from longitudinal data in the United Kingdom', *DIUS Research Report*, Department for Innovation, Universities and Skills, London, UK.

Blanden, Jo, Franz Buscha and Patrick Sturgis (2010), 'Measuring the returns to lifelong learning', *CEE Discussion Paper*, No. 110, Centre for the Economics of Education, London School of Economics, London, UK.

Blundell, Richard, Lorraine Dearden and Costas Meghir (1996), *The determinants and effects of work-related training in Britain*, London: Institute for Fiscal Studies.

Brauns, Hildegard, Walter Müller and Susanne Steinmann (1997), 'Educational expansion and returns to education. A comparative study on Germany, France, the UK, and Hungary', *Arbeitsbereich I*, No. 23, University of Mannheim, Germany.

Cheung, Sin Y. and Stephen McKay (2010), 'Training and progression in the labour market', *DWP Research Report*, No. 680, University of Birmingham, UK.

Dieckhoff, M. and N. Steiber (2011), 'A re-assessment of common theoretical approaches to explain gender differences in continuing training participation', *British Journal of Industrial Relations*, **49** (s1), 135–57.

Dieckhoff, Martina, Jean-Marie Jungblut and Philip J. O'Connell (2007), 'Job-related training in Europe: Do institutions matter?', in Duncan Gallie (ed.), *Employment Regimes and the Quality of Work*, Oxford: Oxford University Press, pp. 77–103.

Elman, C. and A. M. O'Rand (2004), 'The race is to the swift: socioeconomic origins, adult education, and wage attainment', *American Journal of Sociology*, **110** (1), 123–60.

Eurydice (2003), *Structures of education, vocational training and adult education systems in Europe: United Kingdom*, Brussels: Eurydice European Unit.

Jenkins, A., A. Vignoles, A. Wolf and F. Galindo-Rueda (2003), 'The determinants and labour market effects of lifelong learning', *Applied Economics*, **35** (16), 1711–21.

Kilpi-Jakonen, E., D. Vono De Vilhena, Y. Kosyakova, A. Stenberg and H.-P. Blossfeld (2012), 'The impact of formal adult education on the likelihood of being employed: A comparative overview', *Studies of Transition States and Societies*, **4** (1), 48–68.

Merton, R. K. (1968), 'The Matthew effect in science', *Science*, **159** (3810), 56–63.

OECD (2002), *Education at a Glance 2002: OECD Indicators*, Paris: OECD Publishing.

Pallas, A. M. (2002), 'Educational participation across the life course Do the rich get richer?', *Advances in Life Course Research*, **7**, 327–54.

Rubenson, K. and R. Desjardins (2009), 'The impact of welfare state regimes on barriers to participation in adult education: A bounded agency model', *Adult Education Quarterly*, **59** (3), 187–207.

Scherer, S. (2005), 'Patterns of labour market entry – Long wait or career instability? An empirical comparison of Italy, Great Britain and West Germany', *European Sociological Review*, **21** (5), 427–40.

Schmelzer, Paul (2008), 'Increasing employment instability among young people? Labor market entries and early careers in Great Britain since the 1980s', in Hans-Peter Blossfeld, Sandra Buchholz, Erzsébet Bukodi and Karin Kurz (eds), *Young Workers, Globalization and the Labor Market: Comparing Early Working Life in Eleven Countries*, Cheltenham, UK and Northampton, MA, USA: Edward Elgar, pp. 181–205.

Shavit, Yossi and Walter Müller (eds) (1998), *From School to Work: A Comparative Study of Educational Qualifications and Occupational Destinations*, Oxford:

Clarendon Press.
Silles, M. (2007), 'Adult education and earnings: evidence from Britain', *Bulletin of Economic Research*, **59** (4), 313–26.
Singelmann, Joachim (1978), *From Agriculture to Services. The Transformation of Industrial Employment*, Beverly Hills, CA: Sage Publications.
Sørensen, A. B. and N. B. Tuma (1981), 'Labor market structures and job mobility', *Research in Social Stratification and Mobility*, **1**, 67–94.
Soskice, David (1999), 'Divergent production regimes: coordinated and uncoordinated market economies in the 1980s and 1990s', in Herbert Kitschelt, Peter Lange, Gary Marks and John D. Stephens (eds), *Continuity and Change in Contemporary Capitalism*, New York: Cambridge University Press, pp. 101–34.
Woodfield, R. (2011), 'Age and first destination employment from UK universities: Are mature students disadvantaged?', *Studies in Higher Education*, **36** (4) 409–25.

7. Job-Related Adult Learning in the Russian Federation: More Educational Opportunities without an Equalization Effect

Yuliya Kosyakova

INTRODUCTION

The adjustment of adults' human capital in Russia is an important factor for successful integration into the labor market against the country's background of transformation processes that have led to a labor market economy and to Russia's integration into a globalizing world. Since the collapse of the Soviet Union in 1991 and the consequent liberalization of the labor system, adult learning has become a very important mechanism for coping with the inequalities that have developed. However, this issue has not received much attention in Russia from empirical researchers in recent years. In this sense, the current study aims to shed some light on adult learning in Russia since the fall of the Iron Curtain.

Specifically, I investigate whether adult learning can compensate for previous inequalities in educational attainment and if it can thereby contribute to economic and societal equalization. More precisely, I examine (1) the participation patterns of different groups in adult learning in Russia in the last decade and (2) whether participation in different types of adult learning contributes to employment and career progress. Previous research in adult learning demonstrates that both participation rates and payoffs are country specific and associated with institutional settings, such as the organization of the educational system and the welfare regime (for an extended literature review, see Chapter 1). Accordingly, I use the specific institutional settings in Russia to shape my expectations based on the global hypotheses outlined in Chapter 1 and to discuss the obtained results.

NATIONAL INSTITUTIONAL SETTINGS

Adult Learning Framework

Before the collapse of the Soviet Union, adult learning was an established system (Kljucharev 1997) with a significant network of participating educational institutions (Popova 2008) and included obligatory compulsory education and improvement of qualifications (Zajda 2003). After the breakdown of the Soviet Union, a series of official acts concerned with adult learning were adopted. However, despite various important presidential decrees, free access, and guaranteed funding, the adult learning sector suffered from a lack of adequate financing (Zajda 2003; Berger, Earle and Sabirianova 2001).

In the late 20th century, Russia implemented new policies that emphasized lifelong learning in accordance with UNESCO proclamations (Ministry of Education 2009). Despite this implementation, only one in four adults in Russia currently participates in some form of adult learning, including learning not related to work, whereas the rate in the EU-25 is one in two adults (GU VShE 2010).

There are two main types of adult learning in Russia: (1) formal, which includes all forms of initial education, post-tertiary professional education, and supplementary professional education (SPE), and (2) non-formal, including vocationally oriented and general cultural courses in the "People's Universities", centers of lifelong learning, and adult education; lectures of the public non-governmental organization "Znanie" ("knowledge"); television lectures; and various intensive courses (Ministry of Education 2009; see also Zajda 2003). Additionally, non-formal adult learning includes a growing sector of corporate education.

Nevertheless, due to the poor legislative basis, the weak normative legal base (Popova 2008), and the high level of corruption in Russia, there is a large amount of different certified and non-certified educational establishments (Gorshkov and Kljucharev 2011; Veits, Khokhlova and Kozlovskiy 2011). This creates a low level of transparency and high informational asymmetry. Moreover, the proportion of public expenditures on training and retraining is less than 1 per cent of all public expenditures on education and contributes to only 0.03 per cent of the GDP (GU VShE 2010).

The Role of Certificates in Russia

In formal education, Russia has one of the highest levels of accumulated human capital in the world (with slightly more than half of the population achieving tertiary degrees[1]) and an average educational duration above the

OECD level (Barro and Lee 2001; OECD 2011b). However, Russia's public expenditure on education is one of the lowest in the world. Additionally, empirical research has shown that the monetary returns to vocational and higher education are smaller in Russia than in other countries (for a literature review, see Kapeliushnikov 2008).

The structure of the modern educational system in Russia, which resembles that of Germany, was inherited from the Soviet Union. In 1992, the Federal Law on Education was adopted, eliminating the state monopoly on education. Education remains highly standardized (Ministry of Education 2012) and stratified, especially regarding access to high-quality education (Konstantinovskiy et al. 2006). Therefore, certificates should theoretically function as strong signals for employers (Allmendinger 1989). However, this might not be the case in Russia. The educational expansion between 1995 and 2001 has led to a situation in which having a certificate (especially a tertiary degree) is a "social norm" (Larionova and Meshkova 2007). Moreover, public expenditure on education is very low, which might result in its being of low quality. As a result of these developments, certificates lose their differentiating function and become weaker as signals. For employers, a certificate is therefore more of a standard criterion than a selection criterion and does not guarantee a place in the labor market (Krasil'nikova and Bondarenko 2007a, 2007b).

Russia's educational system is still based on old institutions and educational standards, which might prove inappropriate for modern labor market demands (Gimpelson et al. 2009). The growing sector of private institutions and paid services in vocational education is more oriented toward the demands of students than the demands of the labor market (Larionova and Meshkova 2007). These trends yield a weak link between the labor market and the educational system, resulting in a delayed transition from school to work and in higher unemployment risks for graduates (Gerber 2003).

Support for Vulnerable Groups

As discussed in Chapter 1, the supply of lifelong learning in a country also depends on the welfare state and the national market economy model. These specific institutional settings play a significant role in determining how responsibilities to offer and implement adult learning are distributed between state, market, and civil society, which influences who participates in adult learning and the extent to which adult learning pays off.

An important feature of the Russian labor market is its volatility, which leads to high levels of labor turnover with high hiring and separation rates (Gimpelson, Kapeliushnikov and Lukiyanova 2010; OECD 2011a). Additionally, the Russian labor market can be characterized by low and stable unemployment rates, which are mostly unaffected by economic fluctuations. Instead, firms adapt to the economic situation through the reduction of real wages, wage arrears, unpaid leave, or reduced working hours (Gimpelson and Kapeliushnikov 2011; OECD 2011a). Therefore, it may be that workers in Russia are less likely to be permanently excluded from the labor market, yet they might be at greater risk of under-employment. This characteristic could potentially influence participation opportunities in adult learning for vulnerable groups in Russia.

The state supports adult learning by interventions through the Labor Codex (2012) and the Tax Codex (2012).[2] The Labor Codex protects employers' investments in their workers' education with a special (educational) employment contract that binds the employee with the employer for a defined period after training. The Labor Codex also supports workers by obligating employers to provide both additional training at least once every five years of an employee's tenure as well as the necessary conditions to combine study and work. Nonetheless, the level of employment protection is characterized by low enforcement rates with significant variation across regions in Russia (Gimpelson, Kapeliushnikov and Lukiyanova 2010; OECD 2011a). The Tax Codex encourages firms to invest in employee training by subtracting these expenditures from the firms' revenue. However, employee training must correspond to special strict requirements and take place in an establishment with state accreditation and a license for education (Tax Codex 2012), which might constrain any incentives for firms to invest in non-formal adult learning not supported by the state.

Several studies have attempted to classify the welfare regime in Russia by using different analytic techniques (e.g. Fenger 2007; Davidova and Manning 2009). Despite different cluster compositions, the various researchers all characterize Russia as a country with low social protection, low spending on employment policies, high poverty rates, a wide income distribution, and high income inequality. In general, the Russian welfare state resembles more liberal countries that only provide minimal standards and minimal support for disadvantaged groups. This resemblance might also be reflected in the state's role of supporting adult learning for vulnerable groups, which is usually seen as a part of active labor market policies directed toward the non- or under-employed (Chapter 1). In Russia, labor market policy is mostly transfer-based, which might reduce incentives to participate in adult learning for some groups (DiPrete and McManus 2000). Active labor market programs have very limited budgets, and the personal assistance system for jobseekers is poor and inefficient (OECD 2011a).

LINKING INSTITUTIONAL SETTINGS AND ADULT LEARNING

Having discussed the educational system, the infrastructure of lifelong learning, and the Russian labor market, I conclude that education in Russia is necessary but not sufficient to guarantee individuals' labor market success. Education is characterized by a high level of standardization and stratification, which theoretically should result in strong signaling power of certificates and rather smooth school-to-work transition (Allmendinger 1989). However, more than half of the Russian population has a tertiary degree. This, in turn, leads to the low differentiating power of certificates and increases the importance of occupational training and on-the-job skill development (Blossfeld and Stockmann 1999). In summary, I expect non-formal training to be both widespread and the most important strategy available for adapting the workforce to the new demands of the labor market.

Due to low state support and insufficient incentives for firms to invest in worker training, investment in adult learning seems to mostly be a private decision. This characteristic, in turn, should create financial barriers for individuals with lower income to participate in adult education, independent of their competencies and skills. Accordingly, participation in adult learning is probably strongly dependent on individuals' labor market status as well as on opportunities offered by employers (Kilpi-Jakonen et al. 2012). Considering previous discussions about the importance of occupational training in Russia as well as the incentives imposed by labor policies, higher participation rates by the employed in non-formal training can be expected. Additionally, it is reasonable to assume that employers are more likely to invest in individuals with more skills since their training might consume less time and expenditures and lead to higher post-training productivity (Becker 1962; Elman and O'Rand 2004). This might, in turn, lead to the so-called "Matthew effect", in which individuals with higher educational attainment are more likely to obtain further education (Elman and O'Rand 2004). Therefore, I expect *the most advantaged in Russia in terms of both occupational status and educational attainment to have the highest probability of participating in non-formal adult learning ("Matthew effect hypothesis").*

Liberal welfare regimes create additional strong incentives for updating current qualifications or gaining new ones in order to increase individuals' labor market chances (Dieckhoener and Peichl 2009). Additionally, low unemployment benefits supplement this effect by functioning as an insufficient outside option and creating stronger incentives for different societal groups to participate in adult learning even without employers' support. As outlined in Chapter 1, those in good employment positions are less likely to participate in formal adult education due to the high opportunity costs. Moreover, having a formal certificate (preferably from tertiary education) is quite common in Russia and should place higher pressure on individuals with lower levels of education to upgrade their skills to a tertiary degree, leading to a "catching up effect". Thus, I also expect *the lesser or medium educated and those in lower or less-stable employment positions in Russia to be the most likely to obtain formal adult education ("Partial equalization hypothesis").*

I have competing expectations regarding the gender differences in adult learning participation. On the one hand, traditional gender roles could have a positive effect on the adult learning incidence of women since they might use adult learning to compensate for higher rates of employment interruptions (Dieckhoff and Steiber 2011). Furthermore, due to women's higher life expectancy – 74 as compared with 62 for men (OECD 2011a) – they have a longer time horizon for returns to adult education.[3] This might also increase employers' incentives to invest in occupational training since longer life expectancy might lead to longer post-graduation returns. Therefore, it is reasonable to assume *higher participation rates for women in both formal and non-formal adult learning (an assumption that partly contradicts the global "gendered participation hypothesis").*

On the other hand, poor state support for formal childcare in Russia is likely to discourage mothers with small children from participating in adult learning and especially in (time- and finance-consuming) formal adult education. This discouragement is further intensified by employers' lower motivation to invest in training for female workers in societies with traditional gender roles (Dieckhoff and Steiber 2011). However, in this male breadwinner model, married men and men who anticipate parenthood might be more motivated to participate in adult learning in order to gain better labor market positions to better be able to cope with family responsibilities. Thus, I expect *family characteristics such as being in a partnership or having small children to increase participation rates for men and to decrease them for women ("Family responsibilities hypothesis").*

Overall, I expect formal adult education to have a positive impact on employment outcomes. In contrast to the discussion in Chapter 1, it is not the case that employers in Russia value formal certificates, but rather that certificates seem to serve as a standard prerequisite for employers. However, in an uncoordinated market economy, success in the labor market is determined more by individual resources, such as performance and previous work history (DiPrete et al. 1997). In this case, a formal diploma at a mature age might be used as a signaling device to show high motivation and productivity levels to employers (Spence 1973), thereby increasing labor market chances. Additionally, empirical findings for Russia indicate positive returns to a formal upgrade later in life for the employed population (Kilpi-Jakonen et al. 2012). This finding might be interpreted as demonstrating that employed individuals have more economic resources to access higher-quality education and thus profit more. As result, I expect *formal adult education to have a positive influence on employment outcomes when compared with non-participants ("Improved employment outcomes hypothesis").*

I further expect positive labor market returns to non-formal adult learning. As discussed in Chapter 1, employers are more likely to invest in individuals for whom they expect higher post-training productivity. As a result, returns to non-formal adult learning may be caused not by learning but rather by participants' characteristics. Moreover, employers tend to invest in their workers' training, particularly just after hiring or promotion. This tendency might distort the interpretation of the causal inference between non-formal training and employment outcomes. Therefore, and in concordance with the *"Indeterminate employment outcomes hypothesis"*, I expect *non-formal adult learning and employment outcomes to be positively related, yet I remain cautious about commenting on their causality.*

Overall, considering that women in Russia are generally more educated and display higher returns to educational attainment (Kapeliushnikov 2011), I expect *adult learning effects to be greater for women than for men ("Gendered outcomes hypothesis").*

DATA AND METHODS

The current research is based on the nationally representative household panel survey of the Russia Longitudinal Monitoring Survey (RLMS-HSE).[4] The RLMS-HSE contains detailed information on educational behavior, including various forms of adult learning. The analysis might be slightly biased due to the lower response rates of disadvantaged groups and low response rates overall in Moscow and St. Petersburg (Mu 2006).

In the regression analysis, I restrict the data to the years 2000–10, mainly due to the lack of important information for my analysis in the earlier panel waves. Furthermore, the sample is restricted to "adults", i.e., those at risk of participating in adult learning. I exclude respondents reported as being in full-time study for an age-appropriate qualification, which is defined as being less than three years older than the national median upon completion of a specific level of education. I also exclude all respondents above retirement age (55 for women and 60 for men). Regression modeling is built separately for men and women because they are often guided by gender-specific motivations in their decisions to participate in adult learning (Kilpi-Jakonen et al. 2012).

As outlined previously, my first specific research question concerns the patterns of obtaining (1) formal and (2) non-formal adult learning. In the first case, I look at the duration until the next formal degree is obtained as an adult, estimating a discrete-time model for repeated events (Steele, Goldstein and Browne 2004; Steele 2005). The data are interval-censored, meaning that only the year of obtaining a degree is identified. In the second case, I analyze the patterns of participating in self-reported non-formal (1) employer-sponsored and (2) non-employer-sponsored training with the help of random effects logistic regressions. In the former case, training includes non-formal training that may or may not be related to the current profession or occupation, whereas in the latter case, non-formal training activities that are not related to the current profession or occupation are excluded since these training activities might not be related to the labor market. The main predictor variables in the participation models used to analyze inequality patterns are educational attainment before obtaining formal adult learning and the labor market status of the respondent. I further include age, partnership, children under three years old, an indicator of whether a person lives in a rural area, desire to find a (new) job, and a control for the period. In the analysis of the employed, I add labor market related variables such as occupational status, an indicator for working in the public sector and for having a precarious job (see below), tenure, and firm size.

In order to analyze the effect of adult learning on occupational class mobility, I employ event-history analysis techniques that model upward and downward mobility in separate binary response models (Steele, Goldstein and Browne 2004; Steele 2005). To define my dependent variable, I use a change in self-reported occupational class based on the ESeC class scheme (Bessudnov 2011). In the analysis of upward mobility, any positive change is considered an upward move, whereas all other moves are treated as censored. To deal with left-censored data, I use the respondents' self-reported starting year for their current job and use this to control for the length of the job spell. The same approach is employed for the analysis of downward mobility, for which an event is defined as any negative change in occupational class status, including becoming unemployed or having a casual job.

Finally, I ask whether adult learning can increase the chances of those in precarious labor market positions of exiting into a good job. A precarious labor market position is defined as either being unemployed or having a job with precarious characteristics, such as a part-time job, a casual job, an unwritten contract, a job with low security, being a member of the working poor, or being self-employed without employees. I restrict the sample to the precarious labor market position spells observed in the survey period, taking the year of last employment or the reported year of starting a job into account in order to define the start of the spell for left-censored cases and to control for spell duration.

In the models related to labor market outcomes, the key explanatory variables are adult learning variables in the year prior to the transition. With regard to formal adult education, I distinguish between tertiary (postgraduate, university, and special secondary) and non-tertiary (upper and lower secondary with/without some vocational training) degrees obtained in the year of the interview. Non-formal adult learning includes employer-sponsored and non-employer-sponsored training. I also include the lagged effect of adult learning and controls for missing information in the lags for adult learning variables (round and item non-response).[5]

RESULTS

Participation Rates in Adult Learning

Figure 7.1 depicts patterns of participation in adult learning in the previous 12 months by age group and gender. Overall, the figure shows that adults participate in both formal and non-formal learning activities at mature ages. As expected, non-formal employer-sponsored training is by far the most likely type of training to be obtained. This might be explained by the lower signaling power of initial education that leads to a situation in which non-formal training becomes a more useful strategy to adapt the labor force to the new demands of the job market.

Another interesting fact is that women generally participate more in any type of adult learning than men (with the exception of non-tertiary formal adult education), which is in concordance with my expectations regarding traditional gender roles in Russia. Moreover, the curves for women are shifted to the right regarding age, and this shift might, in turn, support the assumption of a longer time horizon for returns to adult learning investment due to women's longer life expectancy.

Patterns of Obtaining Adult Learning in Russia

Tables 7.1 and 7.2 illustrate the influencing factors for obtaining formal and non-formal adult learning in Russia between 2000 and 2010. Overall, the results indicate that formal adult education has a weak equalizing effect, whereas non-formal training reproduces the Matthew effect.

Accordingly, individuals with low educational attainment and higher occupational status have the highest probability of obtaining a formal degree

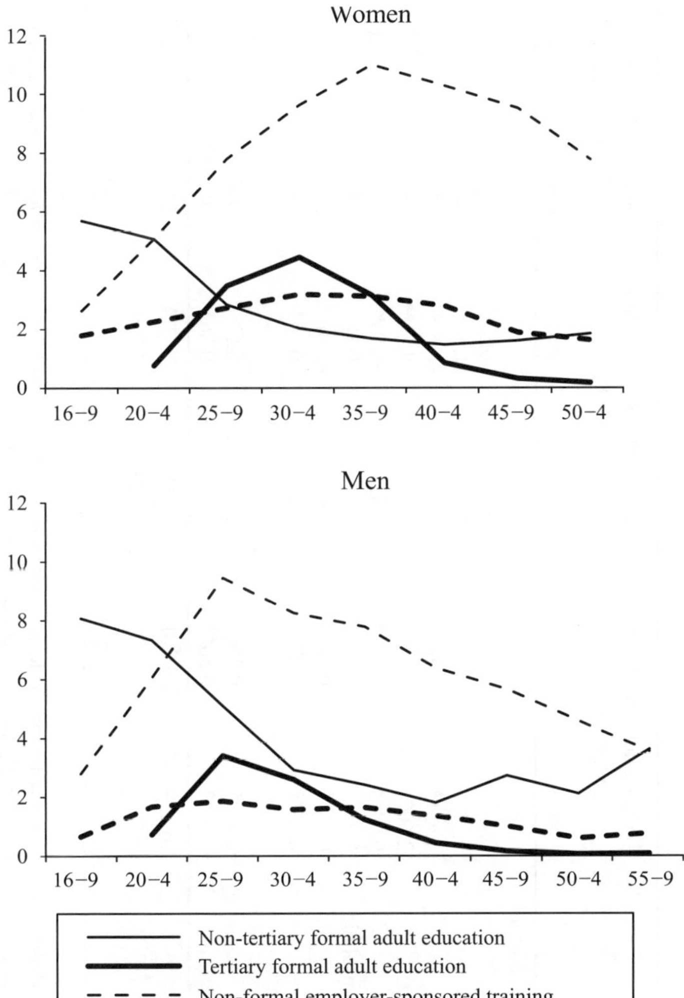

Source: Own calculation based on the RLMS-HSE (2000–10).

Figure 7.1 Proportion of adult learning participants within age range in Russia, by type of adult learning obtained, in %, 2000–11

Table 7.1 Patterns of obtaining formal and non-formal adult learning by the employed in Russia (dependent variable: obtaining adult learning in the next round; results as log odds ratios)

	Formal adult education (Model 1.1)		Employer-sponsored training (Model 1.2)		Non-employer-sponsored training (Model 1.3)	
	Women	Men	Women	Men	Women	Men
Highest qualification (ref. university degree)						
Postgraduate degree	−0.44	−0.75	0.47+	−0.82+	−0.57	1.16
Special secondary degree	0.21	0.80**	−0.40**	−0.54**	−0.28	−0.16
Upper secondary degree	1.45**	0.96**	−0.73**	−0.51**	−0.92**	−0.34
Lower secondary degree or below	2.60**	2.35**	−1.49**	−1.31**	−0.88	−1.23+
Age	−0.04**	−0.04**	−0.02**	−0.03**	−0.03**	−0.04**
Children under three years old in household	0.21	0.30**	−0.25**	−0.11	0.15	−0.10
Lives in partnership	0.05	0.24	−0.08	−0.01	−0.11	0.28
Would like to find a (new) job	0.35**	0.07	0.09	0.39**	−0.06	0.46**
Occupational status (ref. salariat)						
Intermediate class	−0.44**	−0.30	−1.24**	−0.62**	−0.47**	−0.62
Working class	−0.96**	−0.50**	−1.32**	−0.86**	−0.65**	−0.15
Number of observations	26 824	25 010	22 226	20 214	22 225	20 213
Number of individuals	5 734	5 527	5 293	5 080	5 293	5 080
Number of events	360	384	1 123	780	242	127

Notes: ** p<0.01, * p<0.05, + p<0.1. Model 1.1 uses a discrete-time model for repeated events. Models 1.2 and 1.3 use random effects logistic regression models. All models control for residence area, health status, employment characteristics (public sector, precarious job, tenure, and firm size), and period. Model 1.1 further controls for duration.

Source: Own calculations based on the RLMS-HSE (2000–10).

later in life (Table 7.1). As discussed above, the prevalence of workers with tertiary degrees might create a strong incentive for those with lower degrees to catch up. In contrast to my expectations, I find higher rates of formal adult education for those in higher positions. It is possible that individuals in higher positions in Russia are more motivated to upgrade their educational level in order to match their occupational position. This is also in line with previously discussed literature that reveals that certificates in Russia do not provide a differentiating signal in terms of an employees' skills, but rather function more as a social norm. Participants in non-formal training generally have higher educational attainment as well as a higher occupational status, which is in concordance with my expectations. Thus, despite some state interventions in the labor market, the advantaged (in terms of being employed) seem to be even more advantaged and enjoy better access to any type of adult learning.

With regard to labor force status (Table 7.2), the findings indicate that women in precarious jobs as well as unemployed women have the lowest probability of obtaining a formal degree later in life. A plausible explanation for this could be that women might not see formal adult education as a path to improving their labor market position (Jenkins et al. 2003). Moreover, these results might also be explained through poor transfer-based state support in Russia that might discourage individuals from participating in time- and finance-consuming formal adult education. For men, I find no significant results regarding labor force status. This is possibly due to the more-or-less equal access to formal adult education for advantaged and disadvantaged groups. Non-formal employer-sponsored training is mostly available for individuals in good jobs. This is in concordance with the human capital approach (Becker 1962), which states that employers tend to invest in individuals with higher skills since these individuals demonstrate higher post-training productivity. In contrast, non-employer-sponsored non-formal training shows no significant difference between the employed and the unemployed. This observation indicates that the unemployed have equal access to non-formal training and might use it to increase their chances of employment. Taking into account the fact that the unemployed (especially unemployed women) have the lowest probability of undertaking formal adult education, it can be assumed that the insufficient active labor market programs in Russia support mainly non-formal learning for the unemployed.

With regard to gender differences, I do not find any significant differences in the participation rates in adult learning between employed men and women (results are not presented). Only in the case of non-employer-sponsored training do the results suggest higher probabilities for women than for men. Having small children increases the probability of obtaining a new degree for men and decreases the chances of employer-sponsored training for women

Table 7.2   *Patterns of obtaining formal and non-formal adult learning by employment status at a mature age in Russia (dependent variables: formal and non-formal adult learning in the next round; results as log odds ratios)*

	Formal adult education (Model 2.1)		Employer-sponsored training (Model 2.2)		Non-employer-sponsored training (Model 2.3)	
	Women	Men	Women	Men	Women	Men
Labor force status (ref. good job)						
Precarious job	−0.21+	−0.09	−0.49**	−0.42**	−0.26+	0.30
Unemployed (ILO)	−0.70**	−0.20	−1.08**	−1.00**	−0.04	−0.59
Not in labor force	−0.20	−0.15	−2.73**	−2.53**	−0.52**	−0.54
Number of observations	35 682	32 564	29 573	26 333	29 572	26 332
Number of individuals	6 687	6 280	6 280	5 865	6 280	5 865
Number of events	505	492	1 169	825	291	145

Notes: ** p<0.01, * p<0.05, + p<0.1. Model 2.1 uses a discrete-time model for repeated events. Models 2.2 and 2.3 use random effects logistic regression models. All models control for age, partnership, having children under three years old in the household, the desire to find a (new) job, health status, and period. Model 2.1 further controls for duration.

Source: Own calculations based on the RLMS-HSE (2000–10).

(Table 7.1). This implies that becoming a father might motivate men to gain a better occupational position in order to succeed in the labor market. For women, having small children has no statistically significant impact on the probability of undertaking formal adult education, suggesting that mothers are equally likely to obtain a formal degree later in life. However, as expected, employers are less likely to invest in mothers' non-formal training, which is perhaps due to their interrupted career patterns.

Further results in Table 7.1 imply that particularly women consider formal adult education an adequate instrument for finding a (new) job; men looking for job changes are more likely to participate in non-formal adult learning.

Adult Learning Outcomes: Occupational Class Mobility and Exiting Precarious Labor Market Positions

Table 7.3 outlines the effects of adult learning on workers' (up- and downward) occupational mobility and on the probability of those in a precarious labor market position (i.e., those in precarious jobs or the unemployed) to enter a good job (separately for men and women).

Overall, participants in formal adult education have a higher probability of succeeding in the labor market compared with non-participants. However, only a formal tertiary degree pays off significantly if acquired later in life. Accordingly, obtaining a tertiary diploma at a mature age increases the chances of an upward move, reduces the risks of occupational class downward mobility, and helps in exiting a precarious labor market position. Moreover, tertiary diplomas seem to have a long-term positive effect. Considering the lower signaling function of the formal certificate itself, it could be concluded that formal tertiary degrees acquired later in life in Russia are valued in the labor market, but perhaps only as an instrument to signal higher worker motivation. This hypothesis might be further supported by the fact that having a lower level of education is penalized in the Russian labor market: The lower educated are less likely to move upward and more likely to move downward as well as have a lower chance of exiting precarious labor market positions. Thus, considering the fact that the lower educated have the highest probability of obtaining a formal degree, it seems that upgrading to a tertiary degree can help them avoid labor market failure.

Further findings suggest that obtaining employer-sponsored training is a good strategy for career progress and also helps reduce the risk of a downward occupational move. Considering the higher probabilities for the employed to obtain employer-sponsored training, this result might also support a selection hypothesis for this type of training. However, it generally has a short-term effect, suggesting that if employer-sponsored training does not pay off

Table 7.3   *Returns to different forms of adult learning in the form of downward and upward occupational class mobility and exit from a precarious labor market position to a good job in Russia (dependent variable: transition in the next round; discrete-time model for repeated events; results as log odds ratios)*

	Upward occupational mobility (Model 3.1)		Downward occupational mobility (Model 3.2)		Precarious labor market position exit (Model 3.3)	
	Women	Men	Women	Men	Women	Men
Unemployed	–	–	–	–	−0.67**	−0.67**
Highest qualification before adult learning (ref. university degree)						
Postgraduate degree	1.03**	−0.12	−0.98**	−0.50**	0.12	0.07
Special secondary degree	−0.64**	−0.62**	0.17**	0.46**	−0.53**	−0.31**
Upper secondary degree	−0.82**	−0.99**	0.40**	0.54**	−0.87**	−0.48**
Lower secondary degree or below	−1.31**	−1.03**	0.38**	0.63**	−1.52**	−0.69**
Adult education: tertiary degree	0.67**	0.74**	0.05	−0.72**	0.54**	0.64+
AE: tertiary degree, lagged 1	0.63**	0.68**	−0.07	−0.43	0.66**	0.90**
AE: tertiary degree, lagged 2	0.72**	0.34	−0.66**	−0.68**	0.67**	0.34
AE: tertiary degree, lagged 3	0.28	0.17	−0.01	0.42	1.34**	0.43
AE: tertiary degree, lagged 4 and more	0.39+	0.20	−0.13	−0.13	0.26	0.22
Adult education: vocational degree	−0.04	−0.06	0.14	0.11	−0.12	−0.26
AE: vocational degree, lagged 1	0.24	0.18	−0.31	0.13	−0.01	−0.31
AE: vocational degree, lagged 2	0.27	−0.05	0.18	−0.02	−0.28	0.20
AE: vocational degree, lagged 3	0.03	−0.11	−0.05	0.06	−0.18	−0.28
AE: vocational degree, lagged 4 and more	0.14	0.13	0.07	−0.05	0.28	0.02

Table 7.3   Continued

	Upward occupational mobility (Model 3.1)		Downward occupational mobility (Model 3.2)		Precarious labor market position exit (Model 3.3)	
	Women	Men	Women	Men	Women	Men
Employer-sponsored training	0.43**	0.30**	−0.27**	−0.20**	0.58**	0.57**
Employer-sponsored training, lagged 1	−0.09	0.14	−0.13	0.08	0.31**	0.71**
Employer-sponsored training, lagged 2	0.06	0.21	−0.08	−0.17	0.16	0.68**
Employer-sponsored training, lagged 3	0.26+	0.22	−0.02	0.22+	0.28+	0.39+
Non-employer-sponsored training	−0.03	−0.21	−0.05	−0.27	0.27	0.09
Non-employer-sponsored training, lagged 1	0.09	0.33	−0.04	0.26	0.39+	0.01
Non-employer-sponsored training, lagged 2	0.05	−0.13	−0.08	−0.75**	0.24	0.03
Non-employer-sponsored training, lagged 3	0.01	0.01	−0.31	−0.28	0.24	−0.91+
Number of observations	24 071	23 507	27 839	26 002	16 309	12 906
Number of individuals	5 364	5 284	5 774	5 567	4 846	4 363
Number of events	2 375	2 571	2 876	3 557	3 287	3 109

Notes: ** p<0.01, * p<0.05, + p<0.1. All models control for the duration of the spell, non-response rounds, missing information in lags for non-formal adult learning, age, partnership, and having children under three years old in the household. Models 3.1 and 3.2 additionally control for occupational class status, employment characteristics (public sector, precarious job, and firm size), and period.

Source: Own calculations based on the RLMS-HSE (2000–10).

immediately, it does not pay off at all. Nevertheless, both men and women experience a strong positive effect from this type of training on their probability of exiting a precarious labor market position. Moreover, it seems to have a long-term positive effect. Employer-sponsored training therefore appears to be an efficient instrument for improving one's labor market situation.

In contrast to employer-sponsored training, non-formal training without employer investments does not pay off significantly. Taking into account the fact that unemployed women have the highest probability of undertaking this type of training, it does not seem to be a good way for them to exit unemployment.

In sum, adult learning generally has a positive impact on the probability of succeeding in the labor market, with formal adult education being more effective for women and employer-sponsored adult learning benefiting both genders. However, in the analysis of the exit from a precarious labor market position, these positive effects are counteracted by being unemployed. Moreover, the results indicate a negative effect of the experience of longer spells in a precarious labor market position on exit probability (these results are not presented). Apparently, a record of unemployment might provide employers with a strong negative signal. This might indicate a type of internal labor market in Russia in which labor market insiders have better access to almost all types of adult learning and have better chances of succeeding than outsiders. Additionally, low expenditures on active labor market policies and the inefficiency of existing programs (partly found by Akhmedov, Denisova and Kartseva 2003 and by Benus et al. 2004 for Russia) do not contribute much to employment probabilities. Finally, poor state support for the unemployed might reduce their access to high-quality formal education and might explain why they do not benefit much from it.

With regard to the gender differences, the results indicate that for men, the signals of experience of unemployment are more important determinants for labor market success than are educational signals, suggesting men's marginalized position in the labor market (Theunissen et al. 2009).

CONCLUSION

The aim of this chapter was to study the importance and meaning of adult learning in Russia in the last decade as well as whether (and to what extent) adult learning can affect labor market success. Using applied techniques of longitudinal and event history analysis on the RLMS-HSE data, I analyzed which factors influence the undertaking of formal and non-formal adult learning and their payoffs in the labor market. A thorough analysis of different institutional settings is used to interpret the obtained results.

To sum up, formal adult education in Russia has an equalization effect with regard to educational attainment, and this effect only applies to men with regard to labor market status, which partly supports the *"partial equalization hypothesis"*. Moreover, formal adult education seems to pay off for the employed and for those in precarious labor market positions (as expected by the *"improved employment outcomes hypothesis"*), but only when one obtains tertiary adult education. Due to the high proportion of individuals in Russia with tertiary education, certificates might not have strong differentiating signals for employers, and a tertiary degree appears to be regarded as a social norm and a prerequisite for labor market success. Acquiring a tertiary certificate later in life, therefore, seems to be more of a catching-up effect for the lower educated, who are strongly penalized on the labor market.

These conditions are further intensified by the uncoordinated labor market economy in Russia, in which individual resources are crucial for labor market success. In this sense, earning a tertiary degree at a mature age might mostly serve as a signaling instrument to employers of an individual's higher motivation, resulting in positive effects on labor market outcomes. This effect is further supported by the stronger negative effect of an unemployment spell, which also suggests that individuals' working histories might be more crucial for their employment outcomes than are their qualifications. Hence, it seems that formal adult education is profitable only for the working population, and it therefore does not seem to contribute much to the equalization effect.

Overall, employer-sponsored non-formal training proves to be a good alternative to formal adult education in order to be successful in the labor market. However, generally only the most advantaged (in terms of educational and occupational attainment) participate in it, which might contribute to a Matthew effect and increase inequality (*"Matthew effect hypothesis"*). Thus, it could be concluded that employer-sponsored non-formal learning and employment outcomes are positively related (*"indeterminate employment outcomes hypothesis"*). Moreover, although non-formal training without employer support is equally available for all labor market participants, it does not pay off significantly in the labor market. As a result, non-formal adult learning is likely to facilitate inequality in Russia even more.

Finally, I have shown that institutional settings such as the educational system and the welfare regime do matter and have an important effect on adult learning patterns and returns. While the results suggest positive effects of adult learning, many disadvantaged individuals are effectively excluded from the positive outcomes of education and training later in life. Therefore, if policymakers wish to reduce inequality, policies should focus more on supporting the education, training, and work-placement activities of the disadvantaged segments of society in order to improve their labor market success.

NOTES

1. Tertiary degrees in Russia, particularly those at the non-university level (officially called special secondary education in Russia), might not be entirely comparable to degrees obtained in western societies (Kapeliushnikov 2008).
2. The references are related to the latest legislation, but the law has essentially remained the same for the last decade.
3. Although the statutory retirement age is low, pensions are independent of salary and current labor market status. Due to the low level of public pensions, pensioners are often forced to remain in the labor market (Kolev and Pascal 2002).
4. The Russia Longitudinal Monitoring survey (RLMS-HSE) is conducted by the National Research University Higher School of Economics and ZAO "Demoscope" together with the Carolina Population Center, University of North Carolina at Chapel Hill, and the Institute of Sociology RAS. I only use data from round 5 onward, at which point the entire sample was replaced.
5. More detailed information about additional variables included in the model as well as information about the construction of dependent and independent variables is available from the author upon the request.

REFERENCES

Akhmedov, Akhmed, Irina Denisova and Marina Kartseva (2003), 'Active labor market policies in Russia: regional interpretation determines effectiveness', *CEFIR working paper*, Center for Economic and Financial Research and New Economic School, Moscow.

Allmendinger, J. (1989), 'Educational systems and labor market outcomes', *European Sociological Review,* **5** (3), 231–50.

Barro, R. J. and J.-W. Lee (2001), 'International data on educational attainment: updates and implications', *Oxford Economic Papers*, **53** (3), 541–63.

Becker, G. S. (1962), 'Investment in human capital: a theoretical analysis', *Journal of Political Economy*, **70** (5), 9–49.

Benus, Jacob, Raluca Catrinel Brinza, Vasilica Cuica, Irina Denisova and Marina Kartseva (2004), 'Re-training programs in Russia and Romania: impact evaluation study', *CEFIR Policy Paper,* No. 17, Center for Economic and Financial Research and New Economic School, Moscow.

Berger, Mark C., John S. Earle and Klara Z. Sabirianova (2001), 'Worker training in a restructuring economy: evidence from the Russian transition', *IZA Discussion Paper,* No. 361, Institute for the Study of Labor, Bonn, Germany.

Bessudnov, Alexey (2011), 'Social class, employment contracts and economic security in the Russian labour market', *EUI Working Paper MWP 2011/13*, European University Institute.

Blossfeld, H.-P. and R. Stockmann (1999), 'Guest editor's introduction. The German dual system in comparative perspective', *International Journal of Sociology*, **28** (4), 3–28.

Davidova, Nadia and Nick Manning (2009), 'Russia: state socialism to marketized welfare', in Pete Alcock and Gary Craig (eds), *International Social Policy: Welfare Regimes in the Developed World*, Houndmills, UK and New York, US: Palgrave Macmillan, pp. 190–209.

Dieckhoener, Caroline and Andreas Peichl (2009), 'Financing social security: simulating different welfare state systems for Germany', *EUROMOD Working Paper,* No. EM 3/09, Institute for Social and Economic Research, University of Essex.

Dieckhoff, M. and N. Steiber (2011), 'A re-assessment of common theoretical approaches to explain gender differences in continuing training participation', *British Journal of Industrial Relations,* **49** (s1), 135–57.

DiPrete, T. A. and P. A. McManus (2000), 'Family change, employment transitions, and the welfare state: a comparison of household income dynamics in the US and Germany', *American Sociological Review*, **65** (3), 343–70.

DiPrete, T. A., P. M. De Graaf, R. Luijkx, M. Tahlin and H.-P. Blossfeld (1997), 'Collectivist versus individualist mobility regimes? Structural change and job mobility in four countries', *American Journal of Sociology*, **103** (2), 318–58.

Elman, C. and A. M. O'Rand (2004), 'The race is to the swift: socioeconomic origins, adult education, and wage attainment', *American Journal of Sociology*, **110** (1), 123–60.

Fenger, H. J. M. (2007), 'Welfare regimes in Central and Eastern Europe: incorporating post-communist countries in a welfare regime typology', *Contemporary Issues and Ideas in Social Sciences*, **3** (2), 1–30.

Gerber, T. P. (2003), 'Loosening links? School-to-work transitions and institutional change in Russia since 1970', *Social Forces*, **82** (1), 241–76.

Gimpelson, Vladimir and Rostislav Kapeliushnikov (2011), 'Labor market adjustment: is Russia different?', *IZA Discussion Paper,* No. 5588, Institute for the Study of Labor, Bonn, Germany.

Gimpelson, Vladimir, Rostislav Kapeliushnikov, Tatiana Karabchuk, Zinaida Ryzhikova and Tatiana Biljak, (2009), 'Выбор профессии: чему учились и где пригодились?' (Choice of Occupation: Where Have We Studied and Where Are We Working?), *Working paper Preprint WP3/2009/03,* Higher School of Economics, Moscow.

Gimpelson, V., R. Kapeliushnikov and A. Lukiyanova (2010), 'Employment protection legislation in Russia: regional enforcement and labor market outcomes', *Comparative Economic Studies*, **52** (4), 611–36.

Gorshkov, Mihail and Grigorij Kljucharev (2011), *Непрерывное образование в котексте модернизации* (Continuing Education in the Context of Modernization), Moscow: IS RAN, FGNU CSI.

GU VShE (2010), *Образование в Российской Федерации: Статистический сборник* (Education in the Russian Federation: Statistical Collection), Moscow: GU VShE.

Jenkins, A. A. Vignoles, A. Wolf and F. Galindo-Rueda (2003), 'The determinants and labour market effects of lifelong learning', *Applied Economics*, **35** (16), 1711–21.

Kapeliushnikov, Rostislav (2008), 'Записка об отечественном человеческом капитале' (Russia's human capital: an assessment), *Working paper Preprint WP3/2008/01*, Higher School of Economics, Moscow.

Kapeliushnikov, Rostislav (2011), 'Спрос и предложение высококвалифицированной рабочей силы в России: кто бежал быстрее?' (The race between demand and supply of skilled labor in Russia: who is a winner?), *Working paper Preprint WP3/2011/09*, Higher School of Economics, Moscow.

Kilpi-Jakonen, E., D. Vono de Vilhena, Y. Kosyakova, A. Stenberg, and H.-P. Blossfeld (2012), 'The impact of formal adult education on the likelihood of being employed: a comparative overview', *Studies of Transition States and Societies*, **4** (1), 48–68.

Kljucharev, G. A. (1997), 'Observing adult education in contemporary Russia', *Community Development Journal*, **32** (3), 280–6.

Kolev, A. and A. Pascal (2002), 'What keeps pensioners at work in Russia? Evidence from household panel data', *Economics of Transition*, **10** (1), 29–53.

Konstantinovskiy, D., V. S. Vahshtajn, D. J. Kurakin and J. M. Roshchina (2006), 'Доступность качественного общего образования в России: возможности и ограничения' (The accessibility of quality education in Russia: opportunities and restrictions), *Voprosy obrazovanija*, **2**, 186–202.

Krasil'nikova, M. D. and N. V. Bondarenko (2007a), '*Спрос на рабочую силы – мнение работодателей*' (The demand for labor – the view of employers), Информационный бюллетень (Newsletter), Moscow: GU-VShJe.

Krasil'nikova, M. D. and N. V. Bondarenko (2007b), 'Рынок труда и профессиональное образование – каков механизм сотрудничества' (Labour market and vocational education – what is the mechanism of cooperation?), Информационный бюллетень (Newsletter), Moscow: GU-VShJe.

Labor Codex (2012), 'Chapter 31, 32; Articles 196–197, 198–208', available at http://www.trkodeks.ru/glava/tk-glava-31/ (accessed 12.4.2012).

Larionova, Marina and Tatiana Meshkova (eds) (2007), *Аналитический доклад по высшему образованию в Российской Федерации* (Analytical Report on Higher Education in the Russian Federation), Moscow: GU-VShE.

Ministry of Education. (2009), '*The development and present state of adult education in Russia: national report of the Russian Federation*', CONFINTEA VI, Belém, Brazil.

Ministry of Education (2012), 'Website of the National Information Centre on Academic Recognition and Mobility', available at http://www.russianenic.ru/english/rus/index.html (accessed 1.4.2012).

Mu, R. (2006), 'Income shocks, consumption, wealth, and human capital: evidence from Russia', *Economic Development and Cultural Change*, **54** (4), 857–92.

OECD (2011a), *OECD Reviews of Labour Market and Social Policies: Russian Federation*, Paris: OECD Publishing.

OECD (2011b), *Education at a Glance 2011: OECD Indicators,* Paris: OECD Publishing.

Popova, I. P. (2008), 'Дополнительное профессиональное образование в стратегиях работающих специалистов (1995–2005)' (Additional vocational training in the strategies of employed professionals (1995–2005)), *Sociologicheskie issledovanija*, **3**, 79–91.

Spence, M. (1973), 'Job market signaling', *The Quarterly Journal of Economics*, **87** (3), 355–74.

Steele, Fiona (2005), 'Event history analysis', *NCRM Methods Review Papers,* No. NCRM/004, ESRC National Centre for Research Methods, University of Bristol.

Steele, F., H. Goldstein and W. Browne (2004), 'A general multilevel multistate competing risks model for event history data, with an application to a study of contraceptive use dynamics', *Journal of Statistical Modelling*, **4** (2), 145–59.

Tax Codex (2012), 'Chapter 25; Articles 252, 264 etc.', available at http://www.rnk. ru/journal/archives/2003/19/nalogi_i_sbory/nalogovyy_i_bukhgalterskiy_ uchet/102556.phtml (accessed 12.4.2012).

Theunissen, G., M. Verbruggen, A. Forrier and L. Sels (2009), 'Career sidestep, wage setback? The impact of different types of employment interruptions on wages', *Gender, Work & Organization*, **18** (s1), 100–31.

Veits, Maria, Anisya Khokhlova and Vladimir Kozlovskiy (2011), 'Participation of adults in lifelong learning in Russia: possibilities and barriers', *LLL2010 Working Paper,* No. 73, Institute for International and Social Studies, Tallinn University.

Zajda, J. (2003), 'Lifelong learning and adult education: Russia meets the West', *International Review of Education*, **49** (1–2), 111–32.

8. Cumulative Inequality Effects of Adult Learning in Estonia

Ellu Saar, Marge Unt, and Eve-Liis Roosmaa

INTRODUCTION

Fragoulis, Masson and Klenha (2004) indicate that educational reform initiatives in the 1990s and 2000s were mainly limited to the initial formal educational system in most transition countries in Europe. While this system of initial education seems to operate quite efficiently (at least in quantitative terms) and reveals superior performance (compared with the EU-15), there is a lack of educational and training provisions for adults in Estonia. All in all, one of the key problems in Estonia (just as in other transition economies) is not the low educational level of the population; rather, it is the orientation toward preparing the workforce, which often specializes in a narrow technical field and is employed in the contracting sectors and professions (Eamets 2008). An OECD report (2012) also indicates that 32 per cent of the Estonian workforce has no professional (vocational or tertiary) education and that the share of under-skilled and under-qualified persons is one of the highest among OECD countries. The availability of further education is thereby of great importance.

Developments in adult learning tend to be path dependent and shaped by history. In the Estonian context (as with many other post-socialist countries), this means that there has been a need to reconcile the Soviet past with the requirements of the new regime. Due to the lack of perceived legitimacy of the old regime and scarce resources, the previously well-established institutional systems of adult learning have been discontinued.

However, in addition to path dependence, the specific character of transformation in transition countries is also important (Saar et al. 2013). The Estonian case is special in terms of the radical character of market reform, which has been deep, profound, and swift in nature. Estonia might thus be recognized as advanced in terms of marketization. However, given the high speed of market reform and the fact that institutional solutions have often been 'imported',[1] it is of critical importance to study how these solutions work and what impact they have on adult participation in lifelong learning as well as on returns to additional education in the labor market.

We begin the chapter with an overview of the institutional and ideological changes to Estonia during its transition from the Soviet Union to the European Union. Thereafter, we take a closer look at adult learning provision in post-communist Estonia. Some descriptive as well as logistic models of participation in formal and non-formal learning are then presented in order to enable the study of participation patterns in adult education. Competing risks piecewise constant exponential models are presented to answer the following research question: Does participation in adult learning influence occupational class mobility?

INSTITUTIONAL AND IDEOLOGICAL CONTEXT

In its later stages, the Soviet educational system was prone to supporting and encouraging persons to find a purpose in contributing to (not necessarily materialistic) common social goals. Through this effort, education could and did become a tool with which to achieve social integration and development rather than mere economic progress.

The collapse of the communist regime in Estonia was reflected in a strong liberal discourse in education curricula, with neoliberalism clearly evident through attempts to introduce the notions of decentralization, deregulation, market rules and values, the rhetoric of choice, and an ideology of service provision (Aava 2009). Much as other post-communist countries, Estonia tends to see adult learning as a method of enhancing economic development (see Holford et al. 2007). Its neoliberal policy choices, incorporating an instrumental approach to schooling, narrow the aim of schooling to work-related goals and self-actualization through increased labor market competitiveness. This shift is also reflected in the views and practices of adult learners themselves (Roosalu and Roosmaa 2010; Tamm and Kazjulja 2010).

The peculiarities of the Soviet system of skills formation are still important in Estonia, both at the institutional level and at the individual level (see Saar et al. 2013).

First, the pre-transition Estonian economy was characterized as a 'Soviet-style low-production-quality and extensive development-oriented economic structure' (Ennuste et al. 2004). In this economy, the pressure on the skill formation system to secure flexible upgrading of skills was rather weak.

Second, the logic of coordination between economic actors is bureaucratic in a command economy as opposed to the market or corporate types. Pre-transition Estonia was so profoundly involved with the formation of skills that there was no need for proactive training policies managed by enterprises.

Third, the command economy operated under a chronic shortage of primarily blue-collar labor. Because of the stable demand for blue-collar workers with different levels of qualification, it was not workers but rather the managers of enterprises who needed to adapt to rare (e.g., bureaucratically imposed) changes in the enterprise environment. There was neither pressure on nor strong motive for blue-collar workers to continue their education. However, white-collar workers were obligated to upgrade their qualifications after normatively defined periods (e.g., once every five years).

Fourth, non-job-related adult learning for personal development was relatively well developed. It was promoted and subsidized by the state due to its connection with socialist ideology.

Regarding market reforms, the process that is often called the 'return to the market economy' began after the restoration of independence in 1991. The difficult economic situation of enterprises pushed employee training and development aside, and priority was given to short-term goals related to survival in the market. The move toward the market economy in the first half of the 1990s was characterized by significant change in the sectoral structure of the economy (the contribution of industry declined both in relative and absolute value, while the significance of services increased) as well as in the geographical structure of foreign trade (from Eastern to Western markets) (Terk 1999). However, these changes were frequently accompanied by a transition from more complex production to less complicated work, usually involving subcontracting to foreign companies (mainly from Scandinavia). This means that Estonia integrated itself into the global economy mainly through both labor-intensive traditional industries controlled by highly mobile transnational corporations and through resource-based exports and related services (Paas and Sepp 2008), which have high diversity in their human-resource development strategies and practices.

According to Nölke and Vliegenthart (2009), a special type of capitalism is emerging in Hungary, Poland, the Czech Republic, and the Slovak Republic – a dependent market economy (DME). Estonia seems to be a drastic and liberal example of a DME because its export is based on labor-intensive traditional industries and services that are controlled by highly mobile transnational corporations. Some of these corporations usually subcontract production, which eliminates the need to train employees, rather than investing significantly in local facilities. However, some corporations enter the market with direct investments. By offering higher wage levels, these companies hire the best-qualified workforce and provide them with international training in order to ensure a stable high production quality. By doing so, the goal of training becomes higher efficiency. In cases where the local executive management was trained abroad, the aim is to also train local managers to become more convenient business partners and to improve the multinational corporations.

Provision of Non-Formal and Formal Adult Learning

Participation in adult learning has greatly increased in Estonia, from 4.3 per cent in 1997 to 12 per cent in 2011 (Eurostat 2013a). This percentage is already above the EU average. However, the participation rate has only increased for younger age groups (age groups 25–34 and 35–44). Older age groups participate quite rarely. More than half of the total increase in participation is due to participation in professional conferences and hobby-related training (OECD 2012). However, adult learning spells are short and do not result in certification (NAO 2010). Funding for adult learning is also a source of concern. The proportion of employer-financed training in the private sector is agreed upon in individual contracts or collective agreements. Due to low coverage by collective agreements, the majority of employees in Estonia rely on individual employment contracts. The role of collective bargaining in continuing vocational training is low (Nurmela and Roosaar 2009). During cycles of labor shortages, the employers' association has often tackled the issue of skill formation. Nevertheless, just as with management in the command economy, some employers do not consider themselves responsible for skill formation and even feel free to follow a poaching strategy in which they hire employees from other companies who have already received the relevant training.[2] These employers take the proactive role of the state for granted. According to their claims, the educational system should be reoriented toward a better provision of vocational education. The costs for all kinds of personnel education and training by the employer in Estonia used to be taxed (until January 2012) to the same extent as wages, as if these costs had been intended to be regarded as direct income support to the employee, and this taxation clearly discouraged employers from training their employees. However, a recent reform that excludes employers' spending on employees' work-related studies from the fringe benefit tax is likely to stimulate spending. Participation in training activities is significantly lower in small and medium-sized enterprises than in large firms. Among large firms, 77 per cent dedicate a specific budget to training (but only 16 per cent of small enterprises) (OECD 2012, p. 66). In conclusion, pressure to upgrade skills is rather low in the private sector. Moreover, this low pressure does not motivate employers to invest in human capital. In short, the transition to the market economy has not brought about an increase in the demand for qualified labor or in the demand for the flexible upgrading of skills.

Regarding the public sector, the responsibilities of the state have decreased since the pre-transition period. Ongoing training financed by the state is currently mainly intended for civil servants and teachers in state and municipal schools, as well as for the unemployed. Given the monopoly of the former socialist state and its institutions over the provision and financing of the whole range of institutionalized educational activities and a stable economic structure and secure material conditions for the population, the patterns of participation in lifelong learning during the transition were (and continue to be) primarily dependent on how the state abandoned this monopoly. These patterns depended on what the new institutional settings had been in the event that they replaced the previous ones, as well as on how (in which way, to what extent, at what speed) market mechanisms were allowed to work.

According to the typology of diversity in educational supply for adults (Hefler 2011), the formal adult educational system in Estonia has a low level of diversification because the variety of institutions providing formal adult education is restricted to the very same institutions that also provide initial education. A poorly diversified formal adult educational system worked quite well when the role of the state was crucial in the process of lifelong learning. Later, this low diversification (combined with marketization and liberalization in education) brought about a sharp increase in inequality of participation because individuals were now mainly responsible for their own education. However, compared with the educational system during the period immediately following the social change, the education offered at this time had already become more flexible and diverse during the transition period, e.g., through the introduction of special shorter formal training programs and of programs designed in cooperation with certain enterprises or regional industrial clusters (Roosmaa and Tamm 2010).

Special schools for adults have been retained only at the general educational level. Those who acquire basic education (grade 9) or continue education beyond the age of compulsory school attendance (age 17) can acquire basic and general upper secondary education in adult gymnasiums, and study is free of charge for students. However, adult secondary school students receive no study allowance, which means that they either have to work or be supported by family members. The number of adolescents without basic education increased in Estonia during the 1990s (Eurostat 2013b); therefore, the continuation of studies in adult gymnasiums is increasing in popularity among younger age groups. The age profile of students in adult gymnasiums and in initial education gymnasiums does not differ considerably. In 2008, most of the students (67 per cent) in adult gymnasiums were between 15 and 20 years of age (the normal age for completing upper secondary education). A significant proportion (24 per cent) of students enrolled part-time were 21–5 years of age.

A large share of students at adult secondary schools come from disadvantaged backgrounds (either family or social reasons) (Tamm and Saar 2010).

Based on a 2006 amendment to the law, vocational education institutions, which were previously only engaged in formal education, may now offer several flexible opportunities to participate in vocational training. Vocational education is provided free of charge except for some post-secondary programs that are not included in state-commissioned education. Vocational schools pay a study allowance if students' academic achievement and behavior are satisfactory. Some vocational schools receive support from their local government to cover the accommodation and catering costs of students from economically disadvantaged backgrounds. The share of older learners in vocational schools has increased somewhat in recent years. In the 2009–10 academic year, the share of students aged 25 and older was 15 per cent.

In addition, universities and professional higher education institutions enable adults to study part-time. However, part-time students have to pay fees (an exception being the fee for teachers' training). In the 2008–09 academic year, 71 per cent of adult students paid for their studies themselves (52 per cent of all students paid themselves) (Tõnisson 2011). In general, study allowances and study loans are granted only to students who study full time, meaning that these allowances are not available to most adult learners. Adults studying part-time do not have student health insurance. During the middle of the 1990s, 21 per cent of those participating in part-time higher education were over 30. The age distribution of students has now changed: 40 per cent of part-time students and 33 per cent of full-time students are older than 30. The percentage of older students is higher in professional higher education institutions.

Two reasons for the increase of older age groups in formal education deserve mentioning: First, new qualification requirements have been imposed on some occupations (e.g., nursing, pre-school teaching). Second, many students postpone graduation or only choose to acquire tertiary education at a later age after having entered the labor market. Adult access to basic, secondary, and vocational education in Estonia is more flexible compared with higher education. A survey of adult education providers indicates that more than half of adult basic and secondary schools and 90 per cent of vocational schools actively recruit students from disadvantaged groups (Saar et al. 2013).

EXPECTATIONS

It is generally known that persons with higher levels of formal education as well as those in occupational categories located higher in the social hierarchy participate on average more frequently in training (see Brunello and Medio 2001; Bassanini et al. 2007; Dieckhoff, Jungblut and O'Connell 2007). Previous analyses in Estonia also indicate the same pattern (Helemäe, Roosmaa and Saar 2008; Tamm and Kazjulja 2010). Estonia stands out as a country with one of Europe's highest rates of participation in training by managers and professionals and is outperformed only by Sweden and Finland in this area (Roosmaa and Saar 2010, p. 89). However, the same cannot be said for the participation of those in elementary occupations, which is instead at an average level compared with the rest of Europe. A comparison of data from 1997 and 2007 indicates that the gap in adult learning participation between the different occupational groups has actually widened (Tamm and Kazjulja 2010).

A comprehensive educational system means that the role of employers in offering occupation-specific skills should be quite important. Participation in adult learning is therefore strongly dependent on an individual's labor market status. Once again, previous analyses indicate that the difference between the participation of employed respondents and that of the unemployed and non-active persons is indeed significant (Helemäe, Roosmaa and Saar 2008). European funds might foster the participation of the unemployed in training. These patterns of participation in adult learning suggest that current allocation principles do not respond to the needs of training and therefore are more likely to increase rather than to mitigate existing inequalities.

With age, both career development and promotion become less significant. Participation in trainings may turn out to be more expensive, too. Older persons have fewer remaining years of working life than do younger persons, which means that the benefit older persons can gain from training can be enjoyed for a shorter period of time (Fouarge and Schils 2009). An employee's age thereby exerts influence upon an employer's decision of whether or not to invest in the employee. Readiness to study also decreases with older age. For instance, in Estonia, more than two-fifths of persons 46–50 years old and more than three-fifths of persons 51–65 years old consider themselves too old to study (Saar and Roosmaa 2011). The reason for this may lie in the small number of trainings and programs that meet older persons' needs.

As a result, we expect to find that younger age groups, persons with a higher level of formal education, workers in highly skilled positions, and employed persons enjoy greater training opportunities.

Human capital theory connects gender differences in training attendance with differences in their labor force participation. The breaks that occur in women's working lives and their shorter periods of employment relative to men also reduce the time span in which they can profit from training. Thus, in theory, women who plan to have children should have a smaller probability of participating in training because the knowledge gained just before going on childcare leave is not necessarily relevant when they return to work in some years' time. Employers who offer training follow the same logic. Since employers do not have information about women's plans to have children, they are less willing to invest in the training of women of reproductive age (Dieckhoff and Steiber 2011).

A long childcare leave may have an effect on a particular woman's future training possibilities. The effect may be negative since a long-term withdrawal from the labor market reduces ties with the labor market. As a result, the probability of an employer's wish to invest in a woman's human capital and offer her training decreases. At the same time, the opposite effect may be revealed: In order to make up for the lost human capital, the employer may increase the number of trainings (Puhani and Sonderhof 2008). However, we assume that women participate more in both non-formal and formal adult learning in Estonia because women are motivated to increase their level of education as much as possible, which is necessary in order to compete with both men and other women in the labor market (Veldre 2007). It seems that women need to participate in adult learning to equalize their labor market opportunities with those of men.

Firms' specific characteristics are also influential in their employees' participation in training. Small and micro-firms, which are particularly prevalent in Estonia, face more obstacles when investing in training, including a lack of financial resources, a lack of resources to replace missing workers, and a lack of customized training. Participation in training may also depend on the economic activity of the enterprise. We expect that participation is higher in the tertiary sector, especially in education and public administration, because the state finances the training of civil servants and teachers. The role of private enterprises is smaller.

Based on human capital theory, an increase in individual knowledge and skills and thus productivity (participation in adult learning) should result in upward occupational mobility. Several studies indicate that training does result in higher wages (Albert, Garcia-Serrano and Hernanz 2010; O'Connell and Byrne 2010). Economists have found that women tend to profit more from training compared with men since their salaries are more likely to increase following a training incidence (Ashenfelter and Card 1985). However, there is also a reason to assume the opposite since several studies demonstrate that men profit more from training (Evertsson 2004; Gosling 2009). In this case, employers provide training to an employee who is more likely to stay with the company, which in turn results in the employee's promotion and increased wages (Lazear and Rosen 1990). Women are usually considered more likely to leave the company, even if only on a temporary basis. Several studies indicate that men tend to be promoted more often than women with the same qualifications (Kalleberg and Reskin 1995) or alternatively, that the probability of promotion is the same for both sexes, yet women receive lower monetary returns for their career advancement (Booth, Francesconi and Frank 2003).

According to Evertsson (2004), employees working in the education and healthcare sectors participate less in training that could result in occupational advancement, and these sectors employ mostly women. However, results also reveal that even though women receive lower returns for participation, adult learning still pays off – women who train receive higher wages compared with those who do not train (Evertsson 2004).

DATA AND METHODS

To examine the factors that influence formal and non-formal adult learning participation, we use the Estonian Adult Education Survey 2007 (AES 2007), which provides detailed information on education and training over the previous 12 months. This survey is part of the EU Statistics on lifelong learning and is coordinated by Eurostat. The target population in the Estonian survey was persons aged 20–64 (Eurostat applied the age gap of 25–64), and 3 968 face-to-face interviews were conducted.

In order to analyze the effects of adult formal education on occupational mobility, we use the Estonian Family and Fertility Survey 2004–05 (FFS 2004). This survey was conducted in the framework of UNECE's (United Nations Economic Commission for Europe) Gender and Generation Program. The FFS applies the life-course approach and contains retrospective event histories on major life careers, including family formation, childbearing, education, work, and residential mobility. The FFS covers the population aged 20–79, and the dataset includes 7 855 face-to-face interviews.

To analyze factors influencing participation in adult formal and non-formal learning, we apply logistic regression analysis (with repeated events in the case of the latter). The AES 2007 collected detailed information on up to three of the most important non-formal education incidences. Our dependent variables are participation in formal and non-formal education during the 12 months preceding the survey. As a control, we include gender, age, age-squared, marital status, labor market position, level of education, occupational position, economic sector, and firm size in the regression models.

In the occupational mobility analysis, the dependent variable is defined as mobility between first and second job after completing the highest educational level. In order to measure upward and downward mobility, we studied the difference between two consecutive work episodes measured by the International Socio-Economic Index (ISEI) scale (Ganzeboom et al. 1992). An upward change of more than 6.5 points in the ISEI counts as upward mobility, whereas any change downwards counts as downward mobility. Since mobility event episodes from second to third job are very infrequent, repeated events are not taken into account. In this context, we use the competing risks piecewise constant exponential model.

Our main independent variable in the mobility models measures the attainment of highest education in adulthood (three years beyond median completion age at each level of education). As controls, we use time period, gender, age, age-squared, level of education, and economic sector.

RESULTS

Participation in Adult Education

Figure 8.1 displays the proportions of respondents aged 25–64 who participated in formal and non-formal learning during the year preceding the survey. As we expected, women participate more in formal as well as non-formal education, the only exceptions being for age groups 25–9, 30–4, and 60–4, for whom we did not find gender differences in participation in non-formal learning.

The gender gap is greatest in the acquisition of formal education, for which the share of participating women is almost twice as large as that of men. The difference between men and women is mainly caused by the attainment of education among age groups 25–9 and 30–4. Men's educational path is disrupted earlier and is terminated at lower levels of education. The enrollment in formal education rapidly declines with age, and formal educational activity in the previous 12 months was reported by less than 2 per cent of the respondents in the age group 50+.

Age influences the participation of women in non-formal learning to a lesser extent than that of men. Up to the age of 50, women actively participate in studying, nearly half of them having taken part in training. The participation rate of men begins to decline from the age of 35. In the case of those older than 35, a gender gap emerges and widens to the disadvantage of men. Older individuals are less likely to participate in non-formal training, but the decrease in participation is not as steep as is that for formal learning.

Results modeling the factors influencing participation in formal adult education are presented in Table 8.1. Women have a higher probability of participating in formal adult education compared with men. Age has a strong negative effect on the acquisition of formal education, and the effect is stronger for males. Non-married individuals seem to have more opportunities

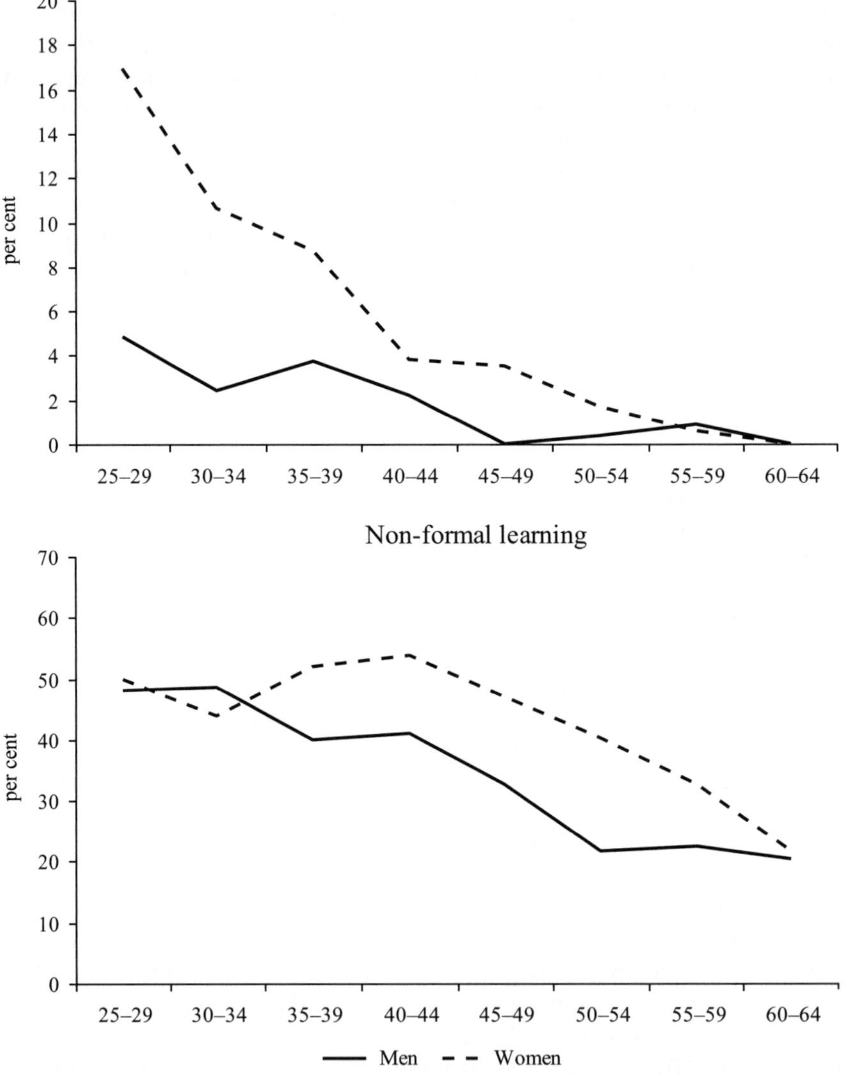

Source: Own calculations based on the Adult Education Survey (2007).

Figure 8.1 Participation in adult learning (%) by gender and age group, 2007

Table 8.1　Factors influencing participation in formal adult learning activities (logistic regression models)

	All men	All women	Working men	Working women
Gender (ref. women) from model with all				
Men	−0.78 **	–	−0.41 **	–
Age	−0.32 **	−0.18 **	−0.34 **	−0.16 **
Age squared †	0.02 **	0.01 **	0.03 **	0.00 **
Marital status (ref. married)				
Non-married	0.55 **	0.41 **	0.32 **	0.19 **
Labor market position (ref. working)				
Unemployed	−1.12 **	−1.23 **	–	–
Pensioner	−18.63	−0.25 *	–	–
Housewife/husband	−17.48	−2.84 **	–	–
Other non-active	−17.00	−1.68 **	–	–
Education (ref. higher)				
Primary or basic	−4.43 **	−1.35 **	−1.25 **	−0.23 **
Vocational	−2.95 **	−1.01 **	−0.93 **	−0.06 +
General secondary	−1.33 **	−0.01	−0.31 **	0.71 **
Post-secondary	−2.29 **	−0.05 **	−1.54 **	0.23 **
Occupational position (ref. blue collars)				
Managers, professionals			2.64 **	1.46 **
Lower white collars			1.50 **	1.38 **
Economic sector (ref. agriculture)				
Manufacturing			0.45 **	0.05
Construction			−0.23 **	0.86 **
Transportation, communication			1.44 **	0.38 **
Trade, service			0.89 **	0.10
Business service			1.87 **	0.85 **
Education, art			1.90 **	1.19 **
Healthcare			1.68 **	0.82 **
Public administration			1.78 **	1.28 **
Firm size (ref. 250 and more)				
1–10			−0.66 **	−0.51 **
11–19			−0.68 **	−0.38 **
20–49			−0.60 **	−0.64 **
50–249			−0.43 **	−0.46 **
Individuals	1 278	2 680	1 029	1 977

Notes:　**p < 0.01, *p < 0.05, +p < 0.10. † Coefficient has been multiplied by ten.

Source:　Own calculations based on the Adult Education Survey (2007).

to continue their educational path, regardless of gender. Individuals with higher levels of education appear to participate more in formal adult education. However, the effect of the previously attained educational level is stronger for men, for men with vocational, general secondary, and lower levels of education very rarely continue their formal education. Due to the fact that there are fewer men than women with at least secondary education in the population, these men are in a much better situation than women with secondary education in terms of competition in the labor market. It is easier for them to distinguish themselves from other candidates (who are mostly women), meaning that there is no need for these men to attain a higher level of education. Employed persons participate in formal adult education more than those not engaged in work.

A number of workplace-related factors also influence participation in formal adult education. Occupational group is one of these factors, and employees in higher occupational positions are more likely to participate. Blue-collar workers, on the other hand, attend formal education the least. The effect of the occupational position is stronger in the case of men. Additionally, there is a higher probability that persons working in the tertiary sector participate in adult formal education. Once again, the effect seems to be stronger for men. Firm size is also a good predictor of formal education: The probability of acquiring formal adult education is greater in larger enterprises.

Table 8.2 summarizes the factors influencing participation in adult non-formal learning from the logistic regressions separately for women and men. As we expected, women are more likely to participate in non-formal training activities. Age seems to have a curvilinear effect, especially for women: At first, participation increases somewhat, but after the age of 45, it begins to decrease. Non-married persons have lower participation rates. More-highly educated persons participate more in non-formal adult learning than their lesser-educated counterparts.

It seems that education is a very important factor in influencing participation in adult education. The impact of education is somewhat stronger for women. Descriptive analysis indicates that men with primary or basic education participate in training more than women with similar levels of education. The greater activeness of men with a low level of education in attending training may be conditioned by the fact that the employment rate of men with less than upper secondary education is higher than is that of women, and a large proportion of training is job-related. In addition, more men than women work in positions requiring a higher level of education than they actually have (Randoja 2008). Looking at labor market status, we find that employed individuals are the most likely to get trained, and the model does not indicate that further learning would be a typical pathway out of unemployment. Participation in adult non-formal learning is especially low among unemployed men.

Table 8.2   Factors influencing participation in non-formal adult learning activities (logistic regression models)

	All men	All women	Working men	Working women
Gender (ref. women) from model with all				
Men	−0.33 **	−	−0.22 **	−
Age	−0.04 **	0.06 **	−0.02 **	0.12 **
Age squared †	0.00	−0.01 **	0.00 **	−0.02 **
Marital status (ref. married)				
Not married	−0.36 **	−0.16 **	−0.33 **	−0.13 **
Labor market position (ref. working)				
Unemployed	−1.25 **	−0.91 **	−	−
Pensioner	−1.66 **	−2.14 **	−	−
Housewife/husband	−1.56 **	−1.47 **	−	−
Other non-active	0.58 **	−1.40 **	−	−
Education (ref. higher)				
Primary or basic	−1.39 **	−2.08 **	−0.26 **	−1.23 **
Vocational	−0.75 **	−1.08 **	0.10 **	−0.44 **
General secondary	−1.24 **	−1.34 **	−0.62 **	0.58 **
Post-secondary	−0.43 **	−0.32 **	0.13 **	−0.18 **
Occupational position (ref. blue collars)				
Managers, professionals			0.86 **	1.37 **
Lower white collars			0.85 **	0.63 **
Economic sector (ref. agriculture)				
Manufacturing			0.75 **	0.04
Construction			0.71 **	0.15 **
Transportation, communication			1.22 **	0.67 **
Trade, service			0.91 **	0.62 **
Business service			1.27 **	0.21 **
Education, art			1.60 **	0.73 **
Healthcare			2.07 **	1.17 **
Public administration			2.20 **	1.32 **
Firm size (ref. 250 and more)				
1–10			−0.47 **	−1.24 **
11–19			0.19 **	−0.72 **
20–49			0.27 **	−0.54 **
50–249			0.49 **	−0.16 **
Individuals	422	1 048	402	946

Notes: **$p < 0.01$, *$p < 0.05$, +$p < 0.10$. † Coefficient has been multiplied by ten.

Source: Own calculations based on the Adult Education Survey (2007).

Firm size seems to have a different impact on female and male non-formal learning participation. Large companies tend to invest more in the training of their female workforce. The effect on male participation is not so obvious: Participation is highest among men working in medium-sized enterprises (with 50–249 workers). Current occupational position has a strong impact on participation – employees in higher occupational positions are more likely to participate in training. Although this pattern applies to both men and women, the effect of occupational position is larger in the case of women, which is in contrast to the results of formal education. Participation in training also depends on the economic sector: It is higher for employees working in the tertiary sector, especially in public administration, healthcare, and education.

We do not find an equalizing effect for either type of adult learning. Instead, a cumulative advantage exists for both better-educated individuals as well as for higher occupational groups.

The Effect of Participation in Adult Education on Occupational Mobility

Table 8.3 shows the effects of participation in adult education on workers' upward and downward occupational mobility for both men and women (separately). Regarding upward moves, we observe that workers are generally more mobile at the beginning of their career, after having completed their highest level of education (men during the first three years and women during the first two years) and that their chances of upward mobility decrease sharply year by year thereafter. We find no gender differences in regard to upward occupational mobility. With increasing age, the probability of upward mobility decreases, but again there are no gender differences. Participation in formal adult education has a positive effect on upward mobility, yet only women seem to benefit from upgrading their level of education in adulthood. Persons who have attained higher education are more likely to be upwardly mobile in comparison with workers with primary (or basic), vocational, or general secondary education (although the latter effect is considerably weaker). In addition, it appears that the negative effect of vocational education on upward mobility is significant only for women.

Results indicate that the probability of downward mobility is high during the beginning of one's career, after attainment of the highest level of education (first two years) for both men and women, and subsequently decreases. Yet after time, the risk of downward mobility increases again for men (in the fourth year after completion of the highest education).

In general, men are somewhat less likely to experience downward occupational mobility than women. However, attainment of formal education

Table 8.3   *Outcome of participation in adult formal education on occupational mobility (competing risk models)*

	Upward mobility		Downward mobility	
	Men	Women	Men	Women
Time period (ref. five or more years)				
One year	4.15 **	2.81 **	3.25 **	2.58 **
Two years	3.01 **	1.99 **	2.51 **	1.10 *
Three years	2.60 **	0.88	1.49 +	0.55
Four years	1.30	0.47	1.69 *	−1.36
Age	−0.19	−0.27	−0.69 **	−0.40 **
Age squared	0.00	0.00	0.00 **	0.00 **
Education obtained as an adult	0.12	1.10 *	0.08	0.14
Education (ref. higher)				
Primary or basic	−1.15	−1.55	−0.98	−0.88
Vocational	−0.36	−1.23 +	−0.47	−0.36
General secondary	−0.19	−0.64	−0.87	−1.13 *
Post-secondary	0.63	−0.13	−0.36	0.11
Economic sector (ref. agriculture)				
Manufacturing	−1.27 *	−0.16	2.96	−0.48
Construction	−1.93 **	−0.24	1.70	0.43
Transportation, communication	−1.42 +	−0.28	2.01	0.13
Trade, service	−1.94 **	−0.46	2.78	0.26
Business service	−1.90 **	−0.76	2.91	−0.12
Education, art	−1.65 *	−1.10	2.82	0.13
Healthcare	−14.80	−0.74	3.96 +	−0.49
Public administration	−2.84 *	−1.40	2.92	0.14
Individuals	393	636	393	636

Notes: **p < 0.01, *p < 0.05, +p < 0.10.

Source: Own calculations based on the Family and Fertility Survey (2004–05).

in adulthood does not offer security against downward mobility for either men or women (when age and age squared are excluded from the analysis, education obtained as an adult does reduce downward mobility for men). Persons with higher levels of education are less likely to be downwardly mobile in comparison with those with primary (or basic) and general secondary education. However, if we examine the results for men and women separately, only women with general secondary education are worse off.

These results demonstrate that formal education attained later in life increases the chances of upward occupational mobility for women, whereas there is no effect on downward mobility for either sex. The level of education also has a significant role: Higher levels of education offer security against downward mobility in comparison with some lower levels of education, and they increase the probability of upward moves. According to the OECD Economic Survey (2012), the return to higher education in Estonia is low in international comparison of wage differences, which might explain why the effect of higher education on upward moves is not more straightforward.

CONCLUSION

The aim of this chapter was to provide an overview of adult learning in Estonia, to study the impact of different individual and meso-level factors on participation in formal and non-formal adult learning, and to analyze adult learning's effect on individuals' labor market outcomes.

Our analysis reveals that although participation in adult learning is quite high in Estonia, the participation pattern seems to increase inequalities. Lesser-educated individuals, persons not engaged in the labor market, lower occupational groups, and small and micro-firms' employees (i.e., persons who need further training and education the most) have a smaller chance of participating. Therefore, adult learning has a cumulative effect and increases inequality.

Results regarding labor market outcomes indicate that women are more likely to experience upward occupational mobility after participation in adult formal education, which contradicts the results of most previous studies. In the Estonian labor market, women feel pressure to increase their level of education as much as possible in order to be competitive (Veldre 2007), whereas men in higher occupational positions might get ahead even without higher education.

At first glance, it seems that Estonia might have a lifelong learning regime which is characteristic of liberal countries. However, there are both similarities to and differences from the typical liberal countries. Looking at the small level of the government's total expenditures in Estonia compared with the EU-15 and the rather small role of trade unions, we can conclude that the social protection system in Estonia is liberal. Labor market policy in Estonia is insufficiently funded (Helemäe and Saar 2011). Moreover, the proportion of active measures is low in both expenditure and participation rates. The limited amount of resources spent on active labor market measures is reflected in the small proportion of unemployed with access to these measures. Nevertheless, expenditures on active labor market measures have increased in recent years due to the implementation of the European Social Fund.

Labor market success is substantially determined by individuals' previous work history and social networks (Kazjulja and Roosalu 2011). However, due to the expansion of higher education, higher education degrees seem to be regarded as a social norm and a prerequisite for access to higher occupational groups, especially for women (Unt et al. 2013). In the structure of secondary education, general secondary education dominates. This means that many persons enter employment directly after general education (Saar and Lindemann 2008).

Unlike most liberal countries, Estonia does not provide good opportunities to participate in formal education later in life. The educational system has limited diversity, which means that adults who are interested in participating in formal education have few choices in terms of both different educational institutions that offer formal adult education as well as in finding programs that meet their needs in terms of the intensity and duration of studies. Quite high participation rates among women in formal adult education are caused by new qualification requirements imposed on some typical female occupations.

Although the role of the state has decreased compared with that of the pre-transition period, its role is larger in Estonia than in most liberal countries because the state finances the training of civil servants and teachers – occupational groups that have higher participation rates.

There are also some clear signs of the existence of the lifelong learning regime characteristics of Southern European countries in Estonia. As mentioned above, activation strategies for the unemployed are quite restricted. Our analysis indicates that adult learning opportunities are rare for outsiders to the labor market. This means that the adult learning system is not structurally open.

Estonia therefore seems to have a lifelong learning regime that combines elements of two different regimes typical of liberal and Southern European countries. The end result is that adult learning has a strong cumulative effect that differentiates the opportunities of labor market insiders and outsiders, different occupational groups, and individuals with different educational levels.

ACKNOWLEDGEMENT

Preparation of this chapter was supported by the European Social Fund Program PRIMUS within the project 'Labor market challenges to higher education institutions: Estonia in the context of European Union'.

NOTES

1. Bohle, Radice and Shields (2007) emphasize the role of international political and economic bodies in the establishment of different transition strategies. The impact of neoliberal ideology through external advisors and the conditionality of the internal financial institutions are considered very important (see Kennedy 2002). However, in the context of Estonia, the radical

liberalization of society is also the clear option of the elite (Lagerspetz 2001), enabling the Estonian elite to be part of the global neoliberal 'community'.
2. The mentality prevalent in business circles is oriented only toward an individualist competition ideology. Research has shown that the idea of cooperation with competitors is strongly rejected (Terk 1999, p. 62).

REFERENCES

Aava, K. (2009), 'Haridusalaste tekstide võrdlev diskursusanalüüs' (Comparative discourse analysis of educational texts), *Eesti Rakenduslingvistika Ühingu Aastaraamat (Estonian Papers in Applied Linguistics)*, **5**, 7–17.

Albert, C., C. Garcia-Serrano and V. Hernanz (2010), 'On-the-job training in Europe: determinants and wage returns', *International Labor Review*, **149** (3), 315–41.

Ashenfelter, O. and D. Card (1985), 'Using the longitudinal structure of earnings to estimate the effect of training programs', *Review of Economics and Statistics*, **67** (4), 648–60.

Bassanini, Andrea, Alison Booth, Giorgio Brunello, Maria DePaola and Edwin Leuven (2007), 'Workplace training in Europe', in Giorgio Brunello, Pietro Garibaldi and Etienne Wasmer (eds), *Education and Training in Europe*, Oxford: Oxford University Press, pp. 143–309.

Bohle, D., H. Radice and S. Shields (2007), 'Introduction', *Competition & Change*, **11** (2), 81–7.

Booth, A. L., M. Francesconi and J. Frank (2003), 'A sticky floors model of promotion, pay and gender', *European Economic Review*, **47** (2), 295–322.

Brunello, G. and A. Medio (2001), 'An explanation of international differences in education and workplace training', *European Economic Review*, **45** (2), 307–22.

Dieckhoff, M. and N. Steiber (2011), 'A re-assessment of common theoretical approaches to explain gender differences in continuing training participation', *British Journal of Industrial Relations*, **49** (s1), 135–57.

Dieckhoff, Martina, Jean-Marie Jungblut and Philip J. O'Connell (2007), 'Job-related training in Europe: Do institutions matter?', in Duncan Gallie (ed.), *Employment Regimes and the Quality of Work*, Oxford: Oxford University Press, pp. 77–104.

Eamets, Raul (2008), 'Economic structure, labor market and education', in Mati Heidmets (ed.), *Estonian Human Development Report 2007*, Tallinn: Eesti Koostöö Kogu, pp. 97–101.

Ennuste, Ülo, Kalev Kukk, Tiia Püss and Mare Viies (2004), 'A political economics narrative analysis of Estonian 1987-2006 capitalist market reform process', available at: http://www.gdnet.org/pdf2/gdn_library/global_research_projects/ understanding_reform/Estonia_third_draft.pdf (accessed 3.5.2011).

Eurostat (2013a), 'Life-long learning', available at: http://epp.eurostat.ec.europa.eu/ tgm/table.do;jsessionid=9ea7d07d30e703ad3d029d134f36ba3294b4c6eede98. e34OaN8PchaTby0Lc3aNchuMc30Re0?tab=table&plugin=1&language=en&

pcode=tsdsc440 (accessed 21.3.2013).

Eurostat (2013b), 'Early leavers from education and training', available at: http://epp.eurostat.ec.europa.eu/tgm/table.do?tab=table&init=1&language=en &pcode=tsdsc410&plugin=1 (accessed 21.3.2013).

Evertsson, M. (2004), 'A gender-typed experience and wage-related advantage?' *European Sociological Review*, **20** (1), 79–94.

Fouarge, D. and T. Schils (2009), 'The effect of early retirement incentives on the training participation of older workers', *Labor*, **23** (s1), 85–109.

Fragoulis, H., J.-R. Masson and V. Klenha (2004), 'Improving opportunities for adult learning in the acceding and candidate countries of Central and Eastern Europe', *European Journal of Education*, **39** (1), 9–30.

Ganzeboom, H. B. G., P. De Graaf and D. J. Treiman (with J. De Leeuw) (1992), 'A Standard International Socio-Economic Index of Occupational Status', *Social Science Research*, **21** (1), 1–56.

Gosling, Matilda (2009), 'Gender and skills: a long way to go', *Positioning paper*, No. 3, City & Guilds, Centre for Skills Development, London.

Hefler, Günter (2011), 'The qualification-supporting company – the significance of formal adult education in small and medium organizations', *LLL2010 SP4 Comparative Report, Working Paper,* No. 34, available at: http://LLL2010.tlu.ee.

Helemäe, Jelena and Ellu Saar (2011), 'An introduction to post-socialist transition in Estonia', in Ellu Saar (ed.), *Towards a Normal Stratification Order. Actual and Perceived Social Stratification in Post-Socialist Estonia*, Frankfurt: Peter Lang, pp. 13–32.

Helemäe, Jelena, Eve-Liis Roosmaa and Ellu Saar (2008), 'Institutional preconditions for work-related training: Estonia on the backdrop of European Union countries', in Mati Heidmets (ed.), *Estonian Human Development Report 2007*, Tallinn: Eesti Koostöö Kogu, pp. 16–20.

Holford, John, Sheila Riddell, Elisabet Weedon, Judit Litjens, Guy Hannan, Vida A. MohorčičŠpolar, Peter Beltram, Angela Ivančič and Jasmina Mirečeva (2007), 'Lifelong learning: patterns of policy in thirteen European countries LLL2010 SP 1 comparative report', *LLL2010 Project Reports*, No. 1, available at: http://www.gdnet.org/pdf2/gdn_library/global_research_projects/understanding_ refom/Estonia_first_draft.pdf.

Kalleberg, A. L. and B. F. Reskin (1995), 'Gender differences in promotion in the United States and Norway', *Research in Social Stratification and Mobility*, **14**, 237–64.

Kazjulja, Margarita and Triin Roosalu (2011), 'Achieving high level occupational status: the relevance of social network capital', in Ellu Saar (ed.), *Towards a Normal Stratification Order: Actual and Perceived Social Stratification in Post-Socialist Estonia*. Frankfurt: Peter Lang, pp. 219–52.

Kennedy, Michael D. (2002), *Cultural Formations of Post-Communism: Emancipation, Transition, Nation and War.* Minneapolis/London: University of Minnesota Press.

Lagerspetz, M. (2001), 'Consolidation as hegemonization: the case of Estonia', *Journal of Baltic Studies,* **32** (4), 402–20.

Lazear, E. P. and S. Rosen (1990), 'Male-female wage differentials in job ladders', *Journal of Labor Economics,* **8** (1), 106–23.

NAO (2010), 'In-service training and retraining of adults', *Report of the National Audit Office to the Riigikogu,* Tallinn.

Nölke, A. and A. Vliegenthart (2009), 'Enlarging the varieties of capitalism: the emergence of dependent market economies in East Central Europe', *World Politics,* **61** (4), 670–702.

Nurmela, Kristi and Liis Roosaar (2009), 'Estonia: collective bargaining and continuous vocational training', available at: http://www.eurofound.europa.eu/eiro/studies/tn0804048s/ee0804049q.htm.

O'Connell, P. J. and D. Byrne (2010), 'The determinants and effects of training at work: bringing the workplace back', *European Sociological Review,* **28** (3), 283–300.

OECD (2012), *Economic Surveys. Estonia. Overview,* available at: http://www.oecd.org/eco/surveys/estonia2012.htm.

Paas, Tiiu and Jüri Sepp (2008), 'Structure of the Estonian economy', in Mati Heidmets and Erik Terk (eds), *Estonian Human Development Report 2007,* Tallinn: Eesti Koostöö Kogu, pp. 92–7.

Puhani, Patrick A. and Katja Sonderhof (2008), 'The effects of maternity leave extension on training for young women', *IZA Discussion Papers,* No 3820, Institute for the Study of Labor, Bern, Bonn.

Randoja, Marin (2008), 'Soolised palgaerinevused' (Gender wage gap), in Raul Eamets (ed.), *Pilk tööellu* (*A Glimpse into the Working Life*), Tallinn: Statistics Estonia, pp. 116–33.

Roosalu, Triin and Eve-Liis Roosmaa (2010), 'Back at school: do they really have nothing else to do? Lifelong learning ideologies', in Vladimir Kozlovskiy, Rein Vöörmann and Triin Roosalu (eds), *Learning in Transition: Policies and Practicies of Lifelong Learning in Post Socialist Countries,* St Petersburg: Nauka, pp. 41–65.

Roosalu, Triin and Auni Tamm (2010), 'Human resource managers as agencies of lifelong learning: the case of Estonia', in Vladimir Kozlovskiy, Rein Vöörmann and Triin Roosalu (eds), *Learning in Transition: Policies and Practicies of Lifelong Learning in Post Socialist Countries,* St Petersburg: Nauka, pp. 221–33.

Roosmaa, Eve-Liis and Auni Tamm (2010). 'Täiskasvanutel hariduse omandamist võimaldavad koolid ja õppetöö korraldus' (Schools and organisation of learning which enable adult education attainment), in Triin Roosalu (ed), *Kolmekesi elukestvas õppes: õppija, kool ja tööandja* (Three parties in lifelong learning: learner, school and employer), Tallinn: Tallinna Raamatutrükikoda pp. 38–43.

Roosmaa, Eve-Liis and Ellu Saar (2010). 'Employees' participation in training', in Marju Lauristin (ed), *Estonian Human Development Report 2009,* Tallinn:

Eesti Koostöö Kogu, pp. 88–92.

Saar, Ellu and Kristina Lindemann (2008), 'Estonia', in Irena Kogan, Michael Gebel and Clemens Noelke (eds), *Europe Enlarged: A Handbook of Education, Labor and Welfare Regimes in Central and Eastern Europe*, Bristol: Policy Press, pp. 151–81.

Saar, Ellu and Eve-Liis Roosmaa (2011), 'Barriers to participation in adult education: Comparison of European countries', Presentation at ECER Conference, Berlin.

Saar, Ellu, Triin Roosalu, Eve-Liis Roosmaa, Auni Tamm and Rein Vöörmann (2013), 'Developing human capital in post-socialist capitalism: Estonian experience', in Ellu Saar, Odd Bjorn Ure and John Holford (eds), *Lifelong Learning in Europe: National Patterns and Challenges*, Cheltenham, UK and Northampton, USA: Edward Elgar Publishing.

Tamm, Auni and Margarita Kazjulja (2010), 'Who learns what: the different experiences of professional groups in further education in Estonia', in Vladimir Kozlovskiy, Rein Vöörmann and Triin Roosalu (eds), *Learning in Transition: Policies and Practicies of Lifelong Learning in Post Socialist Countries*, St Petersburg: Nauka, pp. 155–70.

Tamm, Auni and Ellu Saar (2010), *LLL2010 Subproject 5 Estonia Country Report*. Tallinn: Institute of International and Social Studies / Tallinn University.

Terk, Erik (1999), 'Estonia's economic development: achievements, conflicts, prospects', in Raivo Vetik (ed.), *Estonian Human Development Report 1999*, Tallinn: UNDP, pp. 60–6.

Tõnisson, Eve (2011), *Kõrghariduse valdkonna statistiline ülevaade 2011* (Statistical overview of higher education 2011), Tartu: Estonian Ministry of Education and Research.

Unt, Marge, Kadri Täht, Ellu Saar and Jelena Helemäe (2013), 'The expansion of higher education: devaluation or differentiation? The Estonian case', in Ellu Saar and Rene Mõttus (eds), *Higher Education at a Crossroad: the Case of Estonia*, Frankfurt: Peter Lang.

Veldre, V. (2007), 'Hariduslik kihistumine soolisest aspektist' (Educational differentiation according to gender), *Eesti Statistika Kuukiri*, **6**, 5–16.

9. Adult Learning, Labor Market Outcomes, and Inequality: The Case of Sweden

Elina Kilpi-Jakonen and Anders Stenberg

INTRODUCTION

In this chapter, we examine formal adult education in Sweden, i.e., adult re-enrollment in secondary and tertiary education. We focus on formal adult education because this type of adult learning is relatively common in Sweden and benefits from strong institutional support. As a result, adult reentry into schools is not associated with stigmatizing effects.

It should be noted that what we consider to be adult education in this chapter is narrower than international definitions of adult education and learning, which include on-the-job training among other things. The distinction is important to make since re-enrollment in schools often involves a substantial time investment (one year or more), whereas on-the-job-training typically requires modest time investments of around one week. However, we later provide some descriptive analyses using a broader definition of adult learning.

In terms of the institutional setup of formal adult education in Sweden, municipalities are legally obligated to provide adult education at the basic (compulsory) and upper secondary levels. Komvux is the institute that provides this service. Tertiary-level institutions are also primarily public and financed to a large extent on the basis of the number of students registered, which also enables older students to attend. To stimulate the demand for education, students at all levels are eligible for study allowances of about €1 000 per month (2010 value and of which about two-thirds is a loan) to cover modest living expenses. Importantly, employees also have a legal right to be on study leave and be reinstated with similar conditions after the completion of their studies.

Adult education provided by municipalities (*Komvux*) was particularly widespread in the late 1990s. The government's "Adult Education Initiative" (in effect from autumn 1997 until 2002) entitled participants to attend a year of full-time studies in Komvux and receive a Special Grant for Education and Training (UBS) equal to a maintained unemployment insurance benefit. The public expenditures in Komvux then amounted to one-fourth of that for regular upper secondary education, and the numbers enrolled were at one stage comparable to the 300 000 youths in regular upper secondary school each year (see Figure 9.1). This high enrollment existed against the backdrop of very high unemployment levels following a recession in the early 1990s, which saw unemployment rates increase from 2 per cent in 1990 to 11 per cent in 1993 (for details on the Swedish downturn, see Englund 1999). In order to cope with unemployment, the government began to financially assist study places in Komvux for the unemployed in autumn 1993. These assisted study places represented around 10 per cent of the total seats in 1994 and 1995 (Stenberg 2011, p. 1265).

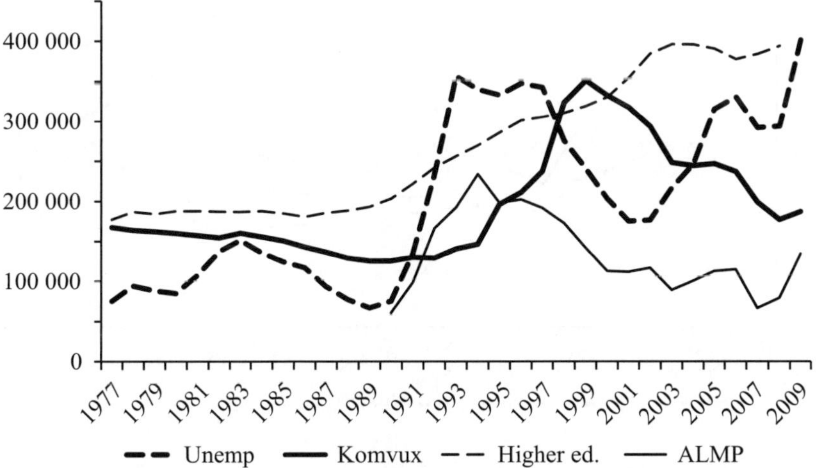

Source: Own calculations based on Statistics Sweden.

Figure 9.1   Numbers in unemployment, active labor market programs, Komvux, and higher education, 1977–2009

Figure 9.1 also shows that the supply of tertiary education increased steadily during this period, which facilitated access to most study programs. It is plausible that the recession increased the demand for education since the opportunity costs in terms of average foregone earnings decreased. In contrast to Komvux, the expansion of tertiary education continued in the latter part of the 1990s. In terms of Komvux registrations, the period of 1997–2002 was most likely a historical exception. Since the mid 1990s, youths have been much more likely to be eligible for tertiary education after secondary school completion and the need to upgrade at the secondary level in order to access tertiary education has therefore decreased (see, e.g., Stenberg 2012).

Figure 9.2 gives an overall picture of participation patterns in formal adult education by age, period, and cohort. This figure also highlights the strong period effect of the 1990s. In addition, we can see that participation declines according to age. Cohort differences do not seem to be particularly strong, although the period effects make it rather difficult to assess them.

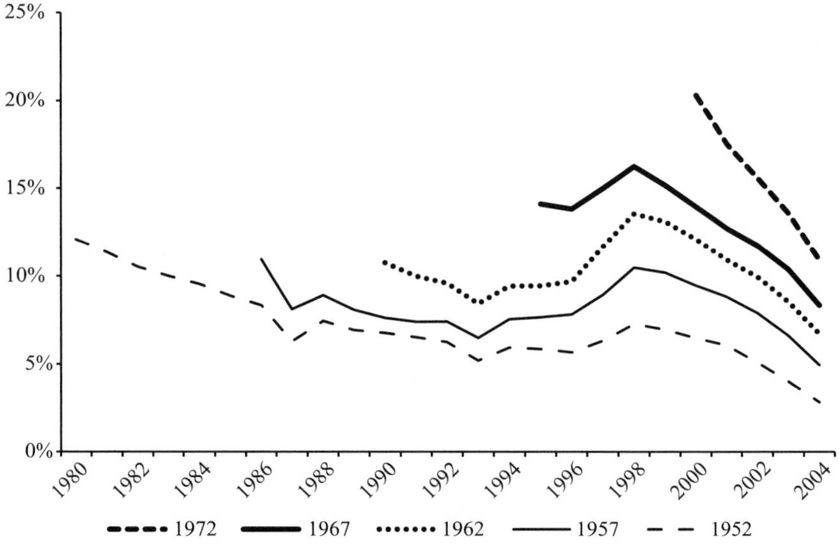

Source: Own calculations based on Statistics Sweden.

Figure 9.2 Registration in Komvux or higher education, 1980–2004, by cohort (from age 28)

The institutional context of Sweden in terms of educational provision for adults, employment protection, and active labor market policies should promote high levels of participation in adult learning in general as well as formal adult education in particular. Moreover, high state support for adult learners should also promote relatively equal participation rates among different socioeconomic groups. Given the relatively high levels of mobility in the Swedish labor market (DiPrete et al. 1997), there should also be possibilities for adult learners to benefit from new educational qualifications, even if they are obtained later in life.

Our main aims in this chapter are to analyze the predictors of enrollment in formal adult education and of upgrading following enrollment, as well as to analyze labor market success following educational upgrading and the extent to which the results of such upgrading are sensitive to model specification and the time frame used. To summarize our main results on labor market success, we find that adult education improves both employment probabilities (by about 2 per cent) as well as log annual earnings (by between 2 and 5 per cent). We later also demonstrate that the positive effects on earnings may be grossly underestimated if one relies on cross-sectional data, which ignore the timing of enrollment. Estimates of the impact of formal education also appear underestimated if the time frame is too short since about 7–10 years are required before earnings increases fully emerge.

ADULT LEARNERS IN SWEDEN AND HYPOTHESES

Sweden has very high participation rates in adult learning compared with other European countries. Participation rates in non-formal employer-sponsored learning are particularly high (see Table 2.1 in Chapter 2). In addition, participation in formal education is also among the highest in Europe, particularly when it is not employer sponsored. Figure 9.3 shows a general picture of who takes part in adult learning using the EU Labour Force Survey from 2011 and contrasting Sweden with the EU as a whole.[1]

In general, women participate in adult learning to a greater extent than men. This pattern is relatively strong in Sweden and may partly be explained by the fact that two-thirds of participants in formal education are female. Regarding the level of education, we see the well-known pattern that the more highly educated are more likely to participate in adult learning than the lesser educated. The provision of education by the private sector is typically directed more at the highly skilled, though public-sector provision could mitigate this tendency. The EU average indicates participation rates that are four times higher for the category with the highest educational level compared with those with the lowest educational level. The corresponding ratio in Sweden is "only" two. Regarding labor force status and employment characteristics, the unemployed are the most likely to participate in adult learning in Sweden, whereas in the EU as a whole, they are slightly less likely than employees to participate. Using employees as a point of reference, the participation rate of the inactive population is also relatively high in Sweden. Those in temporary and part-time employment are more likely to participate in both Sweden and

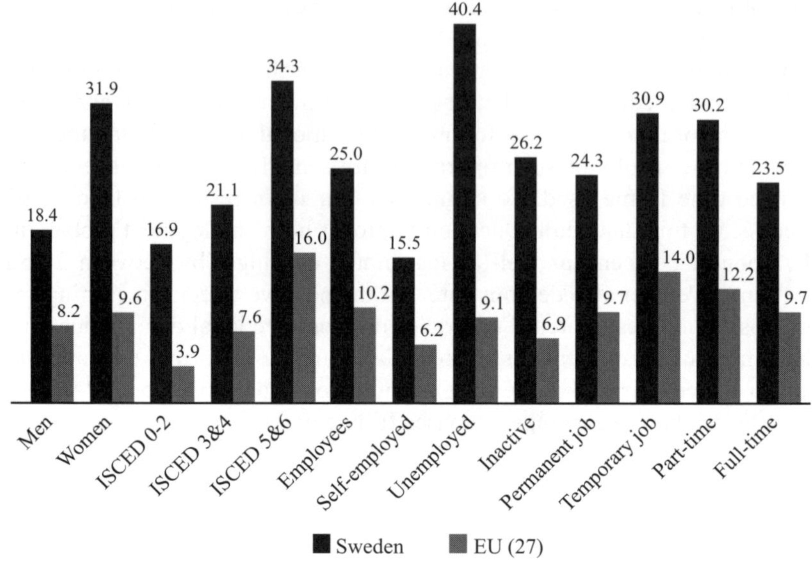

Source: Labor Force Surveys (Eurostat).

Figure 9.3   Participation rates in adult learning in Sweden and the European Union (27) by educational level, labor force status, and employment characteristics in 2011 (ages 25–64)

the EU (see multivariate results in Chapter 2). However, among women in Sweden, employment characteristics hardly have an effect (not displayed).

Evertsson (2004) studied on-the-job training in more detail by using pooled cross-sectional data from the years 1994–98 and focusing on training that lasted longer than one week (full time) and took place in the preceding three years. She reported a disadvantage in participation rates for females as well as for those working part time. In addition, socioeconomic status has a clear positive gradient for participation, whereas educational level does not influence participation when socioeconomic status is controlled for. Women also tend to receive more specific training than men, which is largely due to gender segregation in industries.

With regard to formal adult education, Hällsten (2011) examined mature applicants to tertiary education and Stenberg (2011) reported results on enrollment in Komvux. Hällsten (2011) conditioned his sample on those with upper secondary education and demonstrated that low earnings and unemployment experiences increase the likelihood of application. Moreover, individuals with previous registration in tertiary education are more likely to apply. Stenberg (2011) conditioned his sample on those with less-than-full upper secondary education and showed similar results with regard to earnings and unemployment.

We analyze prior levels of education together. Our expectations of enrollment and upgrading build on previous findings as well as the hypotheses presented in Chapter 1. However, we analyze a step that is not included in the prior research, i.e., upgrading following enrollment. The more highly educated may be more likely to have the educational resources necessary to complete a new level of education, although they may at the same time be more likely to be drawn back to the labor market before upgrading. The same ambiguity is likely to be present in the relationship between earnings and upgrading. When controlling for both prior education and earnings, we may assume educational level to be a measure of educational resources, whereas earnings prior to enrollment can be assumed to be a measure of opportunity costs. Contingent on enrollment, it is unclear whether opportunity costs would exert a further influence, yet educational resources may still do so. Overall, our expectations are that

Individuals with medium levels of education should be more likely to enroll in adult education than those with lower or higher education. Individuals with lower earnings (controlling for education) should be more likely to enroll in adult education than those with higher earnings. We expect women to be more likely to enroll than men. Following enrollment, we expect the higher educated to be more likely to upgrade.

In general, all kinds of adult learning have been found to have a positive influence on earnings in Sweden. Evertsson (2004) reported this effect for on-the-job training lasting over one week, and the effect was found to be larger for men than for women. Stenberg (2011) reported this for enrollment in Komvux among 24–43-year-olds, with larger point estimates for women than for men. Stenberg, de Luna and Westerlund (2011) found no significant effect for older men aged 42–55, although there was a significant effect for older women. Hällsten (2012) reported positive effects of education at the tertiary level on both employment probabilities and earnings. The effects tend to be larger for women than for men, and he did not find systematic variation according to age or cohort.

The partial exception to this effect is training in terms of active labor market programs. An influential literature review by Calmfors, Forslund and Hemström (2002) found these programs to have rather weak effects. However, the studies they reviewed mainly concerned programs in the first half of the 1990s, at which time unemployment was exceptionally high, many of the courses had only recently been set up and were introductory in nature, and completion of courses gave individuals an extension in unemployment benefits. Moreover, the follow-up period in the studies was often relatively short. More recent studies have reported beneficial effects of these types of training (Stenberg and Westerlund 2004; Axelsson and Westerlund 2005; de Luna, Forslund and Liljeberg 2008).

Our expectations with regard to employment outcomes follow the results of previous studies and the hypothesis in Chapter 1:

Formal adult education is expected to increase employment probabilities and annual earnings when compared with non-participation. Women are expected to have higher returns than men.

In addition, we examine whether the effects differ by level of education. The results reported in the above-mentioned studies suggest that earnings effects are higher from tertiary than secondary adult education. This is in line with the "job polarization" hypothesis, which suggests that the demand for the medium skilled to perform routine tasks has dropped in the last decades (Goos and Manning 2007; Autor, Katz and Kearney 2008). The implications for returns to schooling would be that low-skilled individuals who upgrade to medium-skilled receive lower returns compared with individuals going from medium to high-skilled.

DATA

We use population register data to study formal adult education, focusing on enrollment in 1994 and 1995, and exclude from our analyses all individuals who were registered in adult education in the period from 1977 (the earliest year in which data were available to us) to 1993. We focus on four cohorts: those born in 1952, 1957, 1962, and 1967. We chose the years 1994 and 1995 for enrollment in order to have as long a follow-up period as possible to be able to assess the effects of adult education, which can take some time to materialize. Using these years also enables us to control for a number of relevant factors that precede participation (available to us from 1990 onward). In total, we analyze approximately 150 000 men and 120 000 women.

We define "upgrading" as having completed enough schooling so that the record "years of completed schooling" increases by at least one year between our observations in 1994 and 2010 (i.e., we can observe an educational upgrading).[2] For our models of upgrading, we limit the sample to persons enrolled (we call this "upgrading following enrollment"). Table 9.1 shows the proportion of enrollees and upgraders among enrollees for two specific cohorts (those born in 1952 and 1962) and two educational levels (lower secondary and full upper secondary). Within these groups, the proportion enrolling for

Table 9.1   *Proportions of enrollees and upgraders for selected cohorts and educational levels*

Educational level in 1994	Cohort	Enrolled in AE 1994/95 for the first time	Upgraded by 2010 (out of those enrolled)
Lower secondary (or less)			
Men	1952	1.3	33.3
	1962	2.9	48.5
Women	1952	2.9	42.2
	1962	5.1	49.8
Full upper secondary			
Men	1952	2.1	37.3
	1962	6.6	50.7
Women	1952	5.1	43.9
	1962	8.5	60.6

Source: Own calculations based on Statistics Sweden.

the first time in 1994 and 1995 varies between a low of 1.3 per cent (men born in 1952 with only lower secondary education) and a high of 8.5 per cent (women born in 1962 with full upper secondary education). Concerning the proportions of educational upgraders, in general, only approximately half of those who began studies in 1994/95 had upgraded by 2010, with proportions varying from 33.3 per cent to 60.6 per cent.

In our regression analyses, when adult education is an independent variable, we estimate the linear relationship between years of added schooling and the incidence of employment as well as the annual labor earnings, both measured in 2010.[3] For example, if a person enrolled in a university in 1994 after having completed upper secondary education (academic track) and received a (lower) university degree in 2002, his or her value for the adult education variable is 3 (having increased from 12 to 15 years of schooling).

The independent variables that we use for both the enrollment/upgrading and labor market outcome models come from the years 1990–93 and include cohort (4 categories), prior education (6), marital status (2), number of children at home (6), age of children (6), employment sector (7), rural or metropolitan area (3), pre-treatment annual earnings, labor market transitions in the years immediately prior to enrollment, and five different kinds of social insurance benefits related to unemployment insurance, parental leave, sick-leave, early retirement pensions, and social welfare (for the social insurance benefits, we apply both dummy variables to measure the incidence of the various benefits and continuous measures of amounts). We also explore changes in these transfers in the year prior to enrollment. Annual earnings is inherently a composite variable that encompasses both productivity and probability of employment since it reflects hourly wage levels multiplied by the number of hours worked.

When studying labor market outcomes, we use two dependent variables, measured for the most part in 2010. The first is being employed, which is defined as having annual labor earnings of at least SEK 100 000 (approximately €11 000). The second is the natural logarithm of annual earnings for those who are employed. We only study earnings of the employed (and thus exclude those with earnings below SEK 100 000) to avoid having results that are driven by exaggerated log increases (or decreases) associated with low earnings levels.

The payoff of adult education is an issue closely related to that of inequality. Figure 9.4 reveals the earnings trajectories from 1982 to 2010 of men and women born in 1962 separately by both educational level and participation in adult education. The figure demonstrates that individuals who choose to participate in adult education are those who, for a long period of time, have fallen behind others with the same level of education (though this is not the case for females with 12 years of schooling). Although the time taken to study also holds individuals back, after they finish studying, their earnings begin to rise again. However, as can be seen in the figure, this is less clear for low-skilled men than for other groups. In our multivariate analyses, we examine the extent to which this is a general finding that holds after other controls have been introduced.

RESULTS

Participation in Formal Adult Education

Descriptive statistics of those who enrolled in adult education in 1994/95 for the first time and those who did not (Table 9.2) reveal that, on average, enrollees are younger and tend to have higher levels of education prior to enrollment than non-enrollees. However, enrollees are not a typically positively selected sample. In the case of males, they rather tend to be negatively selected, as reflected in substantially lower earnings, a higher proportion receiving social welfare benefits, a higher proportion being foreign born, and a lower proportion being married among enrolled men in comparison with those who do not enroll. For women, these differences are rather small. Moreover, among both men and women, those who enroll are more likely to have been outside

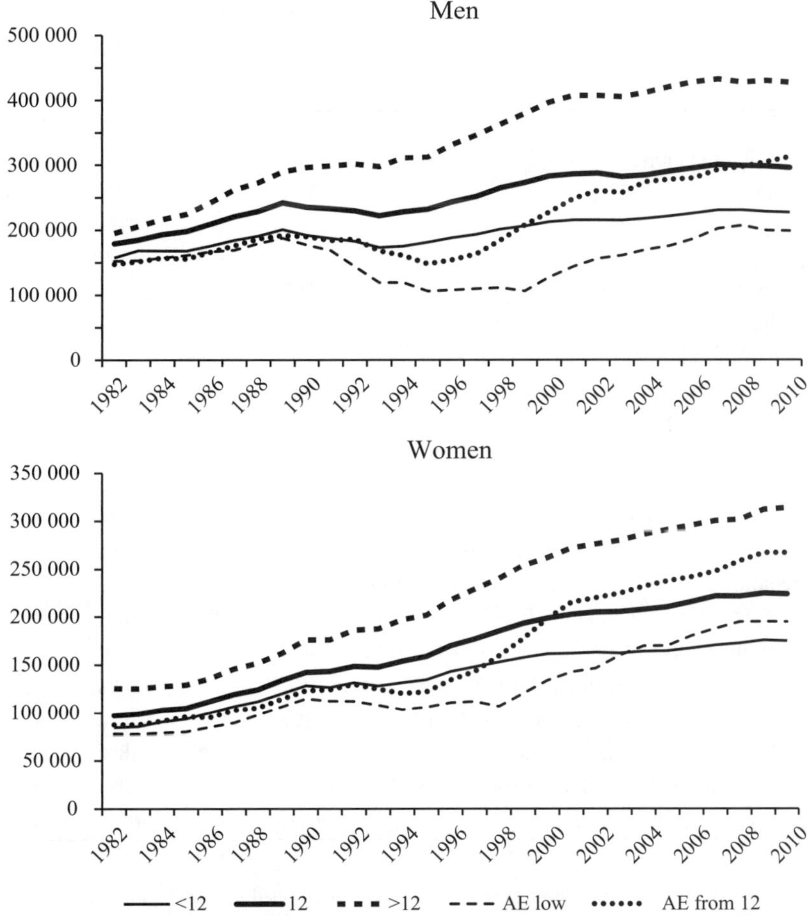

Note: The first three entries of the legend refer to whether less than, exactly, or more than 12 years of schooling had been completed by 1994. The last two refer to participants in adult education (enrolled in 1994–95), who had below ("low") or exactly ("from") 12 years of schooling in 1994.

Source: Own calculations based on Statistics Sweden.

Figure 9.4 Average annual labor earnings, 1982–2010, cohort born 1962

Table 9.2   *Characteristics of enrollees (1994/95) and non-enrollees*

	Men		Women	
	Enroll	Not	Enroll	Not
Age	31.9	34.7	33.3	34.7
Years of education	11.9	10.3	11.8	10.2
Married	31%	37%	48%	46%
Foreign-born	31%	21%	27%	24%
Age at immigration	8.8	6.2	*7.4*	*7.2*
Earnings in 1990 (thousand SEK)	153	192	109	119
Earnings in 1993 (thousand SEK)	126	175	103	114
Number of children	0.88	1.08	1.35	1.38
Received parental benefits in 1992	*18%*	*18%*	36%	37%
Received unemployment benefits in 1992	25%	22%	21%	22%
Received active labor market benefits in 1992	24%	18%	16%	17%
Received sickness benefits in 1992	31%	30%	36%	39%
Received social benefits in 1992	26%	16%	21%	19%
Unemployed in 1992, employed in 1993	18%	19%	15%	19%
Unemployed in 1992, out of labor force in 1993	6%	2%	5%	2%
Unemployed in 1992 and in 1993	19%	20%	16%	20%
Out of labor force in 1992, unemployed in 1993	*0%*	*0%*	2%	1%
Out of labor force in 1992 and 1993	9%	8%	10%	9%
Out of labor force in 1992, employed in1993	2%	1%	4%	4%
Employed in 1992, unemployed in 1993	*22%*	*22%*	18%	21%
Employed in1992, out of labor force in 1993	7%	2%	7%	5%
Employed in 1992 and 1993	67%	81%	67%	76%

Note: All differences between the enrolled and the not enrolled are significant at the 5% level, except those in italics (t-tests of difference in means).

Source: Own calculations based on Statistics Sweden.

the labor force in 1993 (regardless of their situation in 1992) and less likely to have been employed in both 1992 and 1993 than those who did not enroll.

Moving on to multivariate analyses of participation, our full model shows that the pre-enrollment level of education affects both enrollment and the probability of upgrading one's educational level given enrollment (Figure 9.5). There is a relatively strong educational gradient for enrollment and a slightly weaker gradient for upgrading. These results refer to models in which all other control variables have already been introduced.[4] We can see

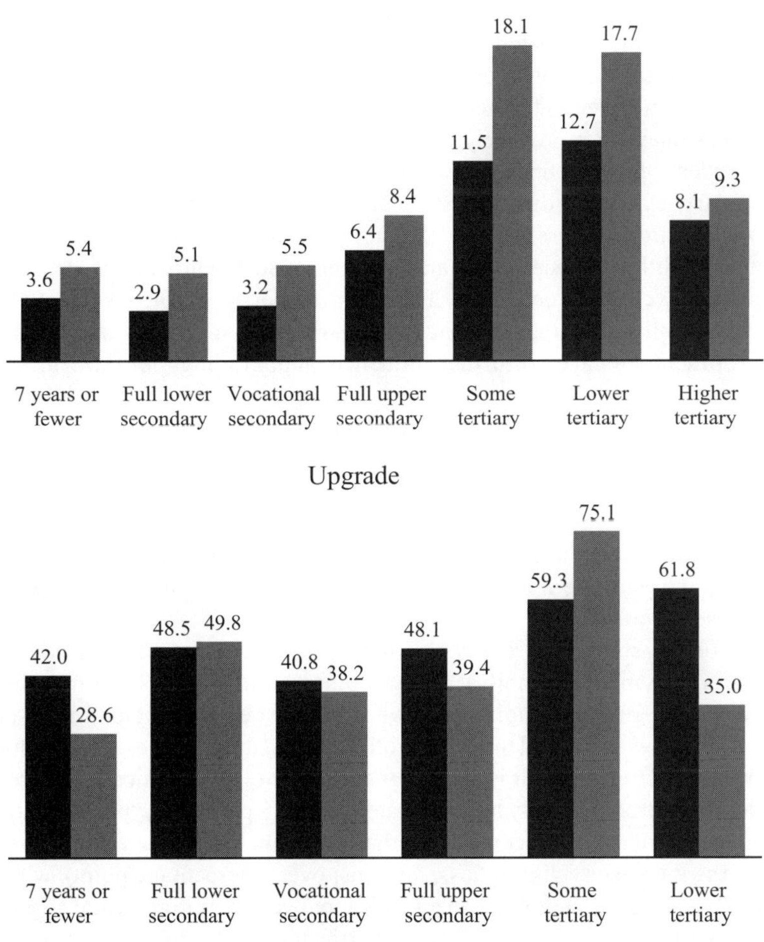

Source: Own calculations based on Statistics Sweden.

Figure 9.5   Effect of educational level on enrollment and upgrading (following enrollment), models with all other independent variables included (set at 0), baseline 1962 cohort with lower secondary education

particularly high enrollment rates among those who have already participated in tertiary education (including up to having earned a degree), and this group of participants also tends to be the most likely to upgrade following enrollment (with the exception of women who already have a degree). Those who only completed lower secondary education are the least likely to enroll, but this group is somewhat more likely to upgrade compared with groups with either some or less upper secondary education. The higher upgrading probability is particularly evident at the two extremes of the educational distribution.

With regard to the results for the other control variables, the two that we want to highlight concern age and earnings. Both confirm the descriptive results that we presented earlier. The older the person is, the less likely he or she is to enroll and to upgrade; and lower earnings lead to a higher probability of enrollment but have no further influence on upgrading (not shown).

The Effect of Formal Adult Education on Labor Market Outcomes

To analyze labor market outcomes, we begin with the effects of adult education on the probability of being employed before we move on to the effects of adult education on annual labor earnings. All results presented in this section are from multivariate models that include all independent variables (unless otherwise specified).

Figure 9.6 shows the results of how a one-year increase in education affects employment probability after all other controls have been introduced. The reference group is individuals who did not begin participating in adult education in 1994–95, and the pre-enrollment educational level that the models control for is from 1994. It is clear that each year of adult education increases employment probability by approximately 2 to 2.5 percentage points (with the exception of men who start with less than full upper secondary education, for whom the increase is slightly less, only just over 1 percentage point), which is relatively similar to the return on an additional year of initial formal schooling (not shown). Many of the upgrades within the low adult education group are of only one year, which is a relatively marginal employment increase, though the increase is slightly higher for women. Upgraders in the high adult education group often upgrade from upper secondary to a university degree, which is an upgrade of three years. The employment effect from this type of adult education is approximately 7.5 percentage points for men and 6 percentage points for women.

Before going into depth in our analyses of the effect on log annual labor earnings, we first look at how the earnings effect develops over time. Figure 9.7 shows the results of models run separately for each year from 1996 to 2010, combining all cohorts and adult educational levels but run separately for men

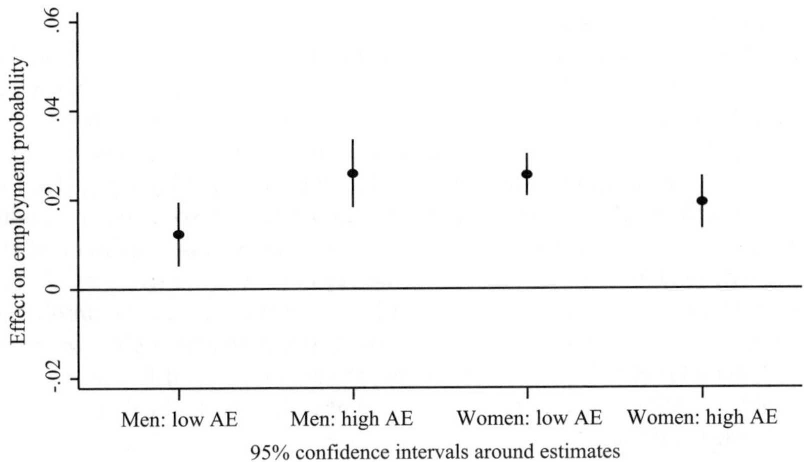

Source: Own calculations based on Statistics Sweden.

Figure 9.6 Effect of one year of adult education (upgrade) on employment in 2010 (linear probability model)

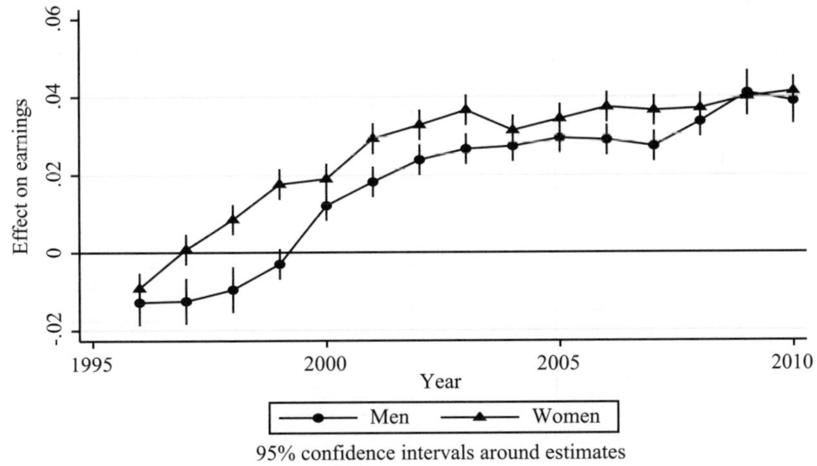

Source: Own calculations based on Statistics Sweden.

Figure 9.7 Effect of one year of adult education (upgrade) on (log) earnings in 1996–2010

and women. The results show that the earnings effect begins by being negative but turns significantly positive for women in 1998 and for men in 2000. For women, the earnings effect continues to increase until 2002/03, after which time it becomes relatively stable. For men, there was also relative stability from 2002–07, but with an ensuing increase that makes estimates similar to those for women in 2008–10. It is possible that this catching up is due to a selection effect, whereby those men who do not benefit so much from adult education (i.e., the older cohorts, as discussed below) exit employment and those who benefit more remain (since earnings are conditioned to be above a threshold value). Overall, we see that at least 5–6 years following enrollment are necessary to see positive earnings effects (for men and slightly fewer for women), and preferably two or three more years are needed for these effects to reach a relatively stable level. The initial negative effects likely reflect time that is spent studying.

We further separate our population into the "old" (born 1952 or 1957) and the "young" (1962, 1967) and analyze earnings in 2010. Figure 9.8 again shows the results of how a one-year increase in education affects the log annual earnings after all other controls have been introduced. The largest

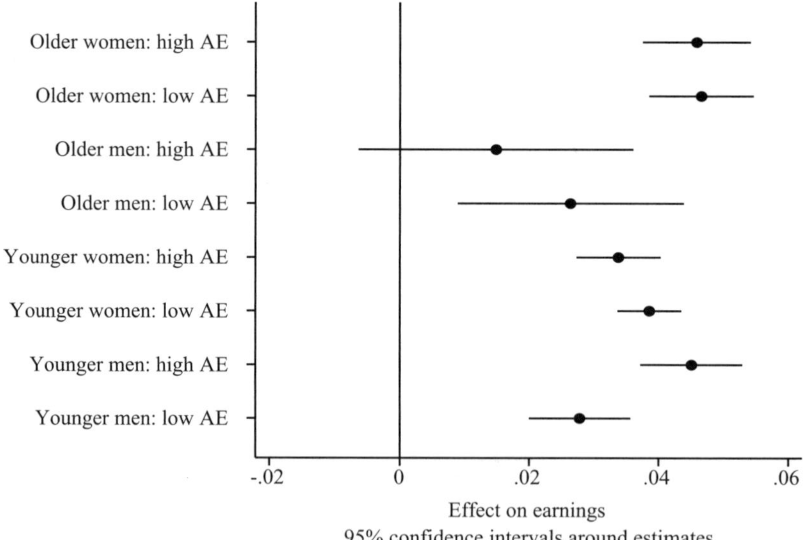

Source: Own calculations based on Statistics Sweden.

Figure 9.8 Effect of one year of adult education (upgrade) on (log) earnings in 2010

increase can be seen for older women, for whom one year of (any type of) adult education increases earnings by almost 4.5 log points (approximately 4.5 per cent). This is also the case for young men taking part in tertiary-level adult education. Slightly below this level are young women, for whom one year of adult education increases earnings by approximately 3.5 log points, whereas low adult education increases the earnings of both old and young men by approximately 2.5–3 log points. Finally, the estimated increase in earnings for older men upgrading at the tertiary level is about 2 log points but it is statistically insignificant.

We also check which of our controls matter for the results. For women, the earnings effects that we have seen are relatively stable across model specifications. Even when only controlling for cohort and educational level in 1994, we see results that are similar to those in the full model (3.2 per cent with age and educational dummies compared with 4.1 per cent in the full model, not shown). This is not the case for men. Figure 9.9 shows the effect of one year of adult education on men's log earnings with different model specifications. We see a positive effect of adult education in all models, but the effect is significantly smaller if we do not control for earnings prior to enrollment. Indeed, after controlling for earnings, the addition of other controls does not make much difference for the estimated effect.

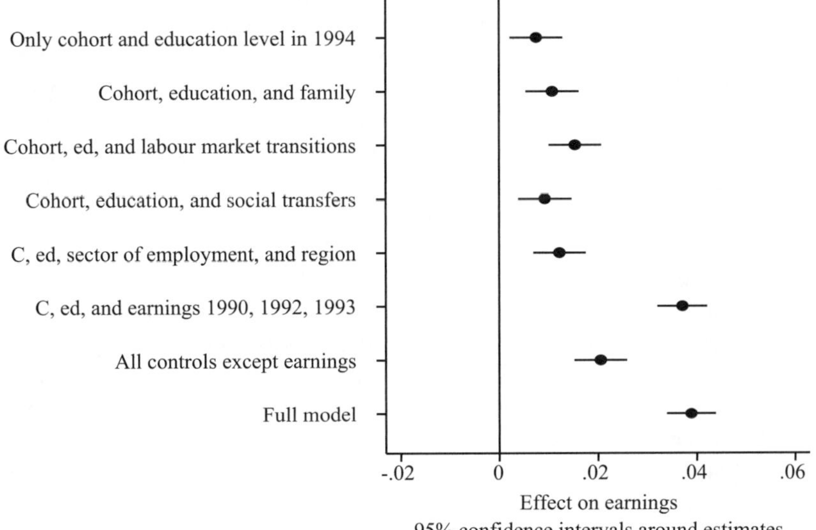

Source: Own calculations based on Statistics Sweden.

Figure 9.9 Effect of one year of adult education (upgrade) on (log) earnings in 2010, results from models with different control variables, only men

The strong effect of earnings is not completely surprising since we have seen that low earnings predict the enrollment of men in particular. Given that fertility decisions are less influential on average earnings for men compared with women, earnings may also function as a relatively accurate control for inherent ability for men, but less so for women. Thus, in models without earnings prior to enrollment, the positive impact that adult education has for these relatively negatively selected men is at risk of being underestimated. This may be an important finding for other country-specific analyses if they are based on cross-sectional data and/or data in which pre-enrollment earnings (or wages) are not available.

SUMMARY AND CONCLUSION

In this chapter, we examined formal adult education, particularly in the form of educational upgrading. We found that overall, a higher level of education leads to a greater probability of entering adult education and to a slightly greater probability of educational upgrading following enrollment. This is to some extent in line with our expectations that the medium educated would be more likely to enroll and the higher educated more likely to upgrade following enrollment. These results are interesting since low education may imply a greater need for further education, whereas high education may signal ability, i.e., the so-called "Matthew effect". The findings here indicate that the Matthew effect dominates, although not in a linear fashion since it is the groups with some tertiary education (but not a degree) that seem most likely to enroll. In this regard, our results go somewhat against the expectation that strong institutional support for adult education should lead to relative equality in participation patterns.

On the other hand, marginalization in the labor market also leads to an increased probability of adult education, especially among men. This finding supports our expectation and the *"partial equalization hypothesis"* put forward in the introductory chapter, which expected those in worse labor market positions to be more likely to participate in formal adult education. Moreover, it is possible that the equalization that we expected with regard to educational level is transferred to participation based on (a lack of) prior labor market success. In this regard, it may be particularly important to highlight the effect of prior earnings since this effect demonstrates that there is enough financial support from the state and that participation is not the prerogative of the wealthy in Sweden.

We did not focus on gender differences in participation in our results section. Nevertheless, our analyses show that women are more likely to enroll and to have upgraded, thus supporting our expectations (see also Kilpi-Jakonen et al. 2012). However, the gender difference in upgrading following enrollment depends very much on the educational level studied.

With regard to labor market outcomes, we found increased employment probabilities as well as increased earnings as a consequence of educational upgrading. Older men tend to be the least likely to benefit from adult education. Moreover, the benefits for younger men are greater from tertiary rather than secondary-level adult education, which supports the job-polarization hypothesis for this group (Goos and Manning 2007; Autor, Katz and Kearney 2008). In general, benefits are most consistent for women and tend to appear sooner for them than for men.

The results from this section also confirm the expectations that we had at the beginning of the chapter and support the *"improved employment outcomes hypothesis"* from Chapter 1. The finding that job-polarization seems to affect men but not women may be due to horizontal gender segregation in the labor market, whereby men are concentrated in production jobs and women in service jobs.

In comparison with the other Nordic countries, our results are largely consistent with those from Finland and Denmark (to the extent that they can be compared). The main difference is that we tend to find adult education to be more beneficial for women than for men, whereas the opposite is the case in Finland and there is generally gender equality in Denmark. In this regard, the results for formal adult education in Sweden are also different than those for non-formal employer-sponsored adult learning(Evertsson 2004). Moreover, the effect of (prior) education is slightly smaller for women than for men in Sweden (results not shown), which makes the findings from formal adult education all the more surprising. The one group for which higher male returns are evident is adult learners from younger age groups who take part in tertiary-level adult education.

Our analyses highlight the need for a long follow-up period in order to see the full benefits of adult education. Moreover, we also showed how the effects might be underestimated when we do not take into account the starting position of adult learners. This effect was found to be important for men and their earnings prior to enrollment. If we do not take this aspect into account, we are left with a much more pessimistic picture concerning the benefits that men receive from participating in adult education.

Overall, our results suggest that formal adult education can contribute to limiting the growth of social inequality within cohorts by allowing those who have fallen behind in wage progression to catch up. Nevertheless, this may be partly due to the institutional setup in Sweden that strongly supports participation in (formal) adult learning on the one hand and maintains a relative openness in the labor market by allowing occupational mobility over the life course on the other hand.

NOTES

1. The Labor Force Surveys ask about participation in adult learning during the preceding four weeks.
2. Some of the upgrading that we see is due to changes in the educational classification system in 2000. This leads to a slight overestimation of the proportion of individuals who upgrade and is also likely to lead to some downward bias for our estimates of labor market outcomes. In robustness checks, where we try to exclude individuals for whom reclassification is the only reason for observing an educational upgrade, we find relatively similar results to the ones reported here.
3. Years of schooling are based on the Swedish classification, which includes six categories. The lowest categories are assigned 9 years of schooling, then 11 years of schooling if categorized with a completed two-year upper secondary school, 12 years if categorized with three years of upper secondary school, 13 years if "less than three years of higher education" are completed, 15 years if "at least three years of higher education" are completed, and 18 years if some postgraduate degree is completed (including licentiates, which are degrees approximately halfway between a Master's and a PhD, as well as PhDs).
4. The results presented here are roughly confirmed if, instead of concentrating only on enrollment in 1994/95, we analyze duration until enrollment from age 27 (starting in 1989 for cohorts born in 1962 and in 1994 for those born in 1976, and ending in 2004 for both).

REFERENCES

Autor, D. H., L. F. Katz and M. Kearney (2008), 'Trends in US wage inequality: revising the revisionists', *Review of Economics and Statistics*, **90** (2), 300–23.

Axelsson, Roger and Olle Westerlund (2005), 'Kunskapslyftets effekter på årsarbetsinkomster – Nybörjare höstterminen 1997' (Adult education effects on annual earnings), *Umeå Economic Studies*, No. 647.

Calmfors, Lars, Anders Forslund and Maria Hemström (2002), 'Does active labor market policy work? Lessons from the Swedish experiences', *IFAU Working Paper* 2002:4, Uppsala.

de Luna, Xavier, Anders Forslund and Linus Liljeberg (2008), 'Effekter av yrkesinriktad arbetsmarknadsutbildning för deltagare under perioden 2002–04' (Effects of vocational training for participants in the period 2002–04), *IFAU Rapport* 2008:1, Uppsala.

DiPrete, T. A., P. M. De Graaf, R. Luijkx, M. Tåhlin and H.-P. Blossfeld (1997), 'Collectivist versus individualist mobility regimes? Structural change and job mobility in four countries', *American Journal of Sociology*, **103** (2), 318–58.

Englund, P. (1999), 'The Swedish banking crisis – roots and consequences', *Oxford Review of Economic Policy*, **15** (3), 80–97.

Evertsson, M. (2004), 'Formal on-the-job training: a gender-typed experience and wage-related advantage?', *European Sociological Review*, **20** (1), 79–94.

Goos, M. and A. Manning (2007), 'Lousy and lovely jobs: the rising polarization of work in Britain', *Review of Economics and Statistics*, **89** (1), 118–33.

Hällsten, M. (2011), 'Late entry in Swedish tertiary education: can the opportunity of lifelong learning promote equality over the life course?', *British Journal of Industrial Relations*, **49** (3), 537–59.

Hällsten, M. (2012), 'Is it ever too late to study? The economic returns on late tertiary degrees in Sweden', *Economics of Education Review*, **31** (1), 179–94.

Kilpi-Jakonen, E., D. Vono de Vilhena, Y. Kosyakova, A. Stenberg and H.-P. Blossfeld (2012), 'The impact of formal adult education on the likelihood of being employed: a comparative overview', *Studies of Transition States and Societies*, **4** (1), 48–68.

Stenberg, A. (2011), 'Using longitudinal data to evaluate publicly provided formal education for low skilled', *Economics of Education Review*, **30** (6), 1262–80.

Stenberg, Anders (2012), 'Access to education over the working life in Sweden – priorities, institutions and efficiency', *OECD Education Working Papers*, No. 62, Paris.

Stenberg, Anders and Olle Westerlund (2004), 'Does comprehensive education work for the long-term unemployed?', *Umeå Economic Studies*, No. 641.

Stenberg, Anders, Xavier de Luna and Olle Westerlund (2011), 'Does formal education for older workers increase earnings? Analyzing annual data stretching over 25 years', *SOFI working paper* 8/2011, Stockholm University.

10. Adult Learners in Finland: Formal Adult Education as an Opportunity for Reducing Inequality?

Elina Kilpi-Jakonen, Outi Sirniö, and Pekka Martikainen

INTRODUCTION

Finland experienced radical social changes in the second half of the 20th century. For the purposes of this study, two transformations stand out. First, there was a rapid rise in the educational level of the population that took place alongside Finland's shift from a rural agricultural society to an urban service society. Second, there was a deep recession in the first half of the 1990s that led to increasing social inequality, particularly between the employed and the non-employed. Both of these large-scale societal changes led to specific population sub-groups being left behind either educationally or in the labor market. Our interest lies in whether these groups can catch up by attending formal adult education.

Our particular focus is on adults gaining a new qualification, be it an educational upgrade or a qualification in a new field. We examine what leads adults to embark upon such a course of study and how their labor market chances evolve before and after graduation. We also show how these chances evolve for young graduates. Our analysis focuses on formal adult education due to its possible role in reducing social inequalities; non-formal learning, on the other hand, tends to increase existing educational inequalities.

We begin by describing the Finnish context in more detail, including both the historical changes relevant to our study as well as the current institutional context. We then lay out the main aims of our study in more detail, followed by a description of the data and methods used and then our results. We end with a discussion of the results with reference to both the expectations that we laid out as well as those of this volume as a whole (see Chapter 1), focusing in particular on the implications of adult education for social inequality.

THE HISTORICAL AND INSTITUTIONAL CONTEXT

The social change that took place in Finnish society between the Second World War and the early 1970s is known as the "Great Move", a name that refers in particular to the population's move from rural to urban areas.[1] Industrialization occurred relatively late in Finland and even then, the shift to a service economy took place at essentially the same time. These changes were contemporaneous with and partly related to the creation of the welfare state, which began in the 1960s and continued to expand until the recession of the 1990s.

The Educational System and Adult Learning

There were both major changes in the Finnish educational system in the second half of the 20th century and substantial growth in the educational level of the population. The proportion of the population (aged 15 and over) with at least secondary education rose from 10 per cent in 1950 to 25 per cent by 1970, 50 per cent by 1990, and up to 67 per cent by 2007 (Pekkala Kerr 2012). The main characteristics of the current Finnish educational system are a nine-year comprehensive school and a dual system of education at the secondary and tertiary levels. The main changes that occurred in the educational system in the 1990s were the establishment of polytechnics (universities of applied sciences) at the tertiary level and the introduction of competence-based qualifications at the secondary level. The latter are primarily aimed at employed adults.

Adult education has been an important feature of Finnish society for over a century, and the first institutions specifically for adult learners were established in the late 19th century (Ahonen 2011). The 1960s was an important decade for labor market oriented adult learning, at which point active labor market policies were established despite the fact that training courses for the unemployed had been around since the 1920s (Ahonen 2011, 2012). Adult learners make up a substantial proportion of students at both secondary and tertiary levels these days. Approximately a quarter of new students in vocational secondary institutions, in polytechnics, and in universities were aged 25 and above in 2002 (Ministry of Education 2004). In absolute terms, vocational studies at the secondary level are the most popular (ibid.). There is also a substantial amount of adult learning taking place in universities that does not lead to a qualification. Open universities are important providers of these courses. They are strongly tied to the curriculum of the regular universities and in the 2000s, they boasted student numbers that were almost as high as the number studying for lower-level university degrees (Kantasalmi 2012).

In most cases, there are no tuition fees for education leading to qualifications since this type of education is publicly funded. Moreover, full-time students are given a monthly study grant and a housing supplement, and the possibility of withdrawing government-guaranteed student loans also exists. The Finnish Education Fund provides funding for further education for employees who have been working for at least eight years (previously five years). Their grant is higher than the regular study grant but is only available for a maximum of 18 months.

Changes in the Labor Market

The recession of the early 1990s resulted in the loss of half a million jobs in a country of 5 million persons (Statistics Finland 2007). Jobs held by individuals aged 55–9 were particularly vulnerable since over half of these jobs vanished (Huovinen and Piekkola 2001, p. 254). The recession resulted in mass lay-offs rather than adjustments through lower wages. Real wages as well as average real wage dispersion remained constant throughout the recession (Kyyrä 2001, p. 275). The increasing economic inequality introduced by the recession, in particular between the employed and the unemployed, was persistent despite the rapid growth of the economy in the late 1990s. Recent studies show that particularly those individuals who entered the labor market during the recession have had lower chances of finding employment and of attaining high incomes (Kiander 2004; Korkeamäki 2012; Loukkola 2012).

One of the methods of dealing with the unemployment problem has been the use of active labor market programs (ALMP), including labor market training and subsidized jobs. The use of these measures increased during the recession, and the proportion of the labor force participating in ALMPs during the year rose from 5 per cent in 1990 to 10 per cent in 1996 (Lehtonen et al. 2001, p. 109). However, the effectiveness of this type of training was hampered by the low skill levels of most participants and the structurally low demand for low-skilled labor (Lehtonen et al. 2001). This demand shrank further during the 1990s with the dramatic rise in the proportion of the workforce using information technology as part of their job (Blom, Melin and Pyöriä 2001). In recent years, the labor market structure has continued to change, which has caused the share of jobs that do not require any educational qualifications to decrease distinctly, resulting in greater difficulties in finding employment for those without qualifications (Järvinen and Vanttaja 2001; Sipilä, Kestilä and Martikainen 2011).

Returns to education showed contradictory trends during the early 1990s. On the one hand, educational differentials in wages were reduced, but at the same time, unemployment differentials grew (Kyyrä 2001). Previous research on new qualifications obtained by adults has found positive rates of return, particularly for individuals who upgrade to higher-level tertiary education (Kruhse-Lehtonen 2007).

The main characteristics of the Finnish labor market are relatively high employment protection together with comparatively generous unemployment benefits. Finland also displays high labor market participation rates for women, with particularly high numbers of women in full-time employment. Continued education is seen as important, and employees have the right to two-year study leaves without pay if they have been working for the same employer for at least one year.

Although it might be beneficial for the unemployed to return to formal education in order to improve their labor market opportunities, they may be dissuaded from doing so due to the fact that study grants are lower than unemployment benefits. Moreover, the unemployed used to be unable to take part in (full-time) education without losing their unemployment benefits, although this changed in 2010. On the other hand, labor market training can also be organized within the auspices of formal education since most of this type of training aims at vocational qualifications or parts of them (Duell, Grubb and Singh 2009).

Participation in Non-Formal Adult Learning

Given that the focus of our analyses is on formal adult education, it is important at this stage to make a few comments about adult learning more broadly. Participation in all types of adult learning is relatively high in Finland (see Chapter 2). Employers are a major provider of job-related training: Approximately 95 per cent of job-related training episodes reported in the Finnish Adult Education Studies of 1990 and 1995 were on-the-job training (Laukkanen 2010, p. 43). There is relatively little age differentiation for all other forms of adult learning except for on-the-job training. Analyses of the wage returns to job-related training show relatively large positive effects, especially when on-the-job training lasts for at least ten days and wage returns are measured one or two years after training (Laukkanen 2010).

AIMS OF THE STUDY

Formal adult education is meant to provide opportunities for reducing educational and labor market differences between population sub-groups, but it is not clear whether it actually does so. Based on our review of the historical and institutional context, we identify a number of groups whose participation in adult education would be beneficial in terms of reducing social inequality: older age groups, the long-term unemployed, and the lesser educated. These three groups also represent somewhat overlapping categories due to the rapid educational expansion and the increasing educational differentials in unemployment risks, including the probability of being unemployed long-term (Suikkanen, Linnakangas and Martti 2002). Our first aim is thus to study whether these three groups are more likely than others to gain new qualifications as adults.

We expect that some equalization – in the form of higher propensities of the disadvantaged to participate in adult education – has already taken place due to the strong emphasis on adult learning in Finnish society and the openness of educational institutions to adult learners at both the secondary and tertiary levels. Moreover, the time period under study coincides to some extent with a government-subsidized program to increase the educational level of adults with only basic education, which took place in 2002–09 (Ministry of Education and Culture 2010). Given the high participation rates of women in all types of education as well as in the labor market, we also expect women to be more likely to be adult learners in our study population.

In addition to participation, we are additionally interested in the effects of adult education on labor market outcomes. Our expectation is that a new qualification is related to both reduced unemployment risks as well as increased income. However, we should note that our analyses combine adults who upgrade their educational level with those who gain a new qualification at the same level but in a new field, and it is likely that improvements are more pronounced in the former case as compared with the latter. The relative openness of the Finnish employment system is likely to favor adult learners. Nevertheless, we can also assume that the income growth of those graduating at older ages may not be as high as that of their younger counterparts due to employers' incentives to invest in the training and career progression of younger employees. In order to study these questions, we look at labor market trajectories before and after graduation for both adult and young graduates. Furthermore, given that returns to education are generally lower for women than for men (Kivinen, Hedman and Kaipainen 2007), we also expect that this effect may be the case for adult learners.

DATA AND METHODS

The data used in this study comes from a unique longitudinal register dataset obtained from Statistics Finland and drawn from administrative registers. Annual individual-level information from sources including censuses, employment registers, and tax registers is combined by using personal identification numbers. The data is a representative 11 per cent sample of the whole population that resided in Finland for at least one year during the period from 1987 to 2007.

Subjects born between 1931 and 1981 were selected for this study. In the first part of the study (the analyses of participation patterns), subjects were followed from 1996 to 2007. The follow-up began in 1996 or at the age of 24 and ended in 2007 or upon death, retirement, or reaching age 65. In this first part of the study, an adult learner is defined as a subject who enrolls in an educational institution at the minimum age of 25 and graduates during the follow-up with a qualification at a higher level or in a different field compared with the previous highest educational qualification. This sample includes 3 167 644 person-years, 389 523 subjects, and 16 754 adult learners.

In the second part of the study (the analyses of labor market outcomes of adult education), subjects were followed from 1987 to 2007, and the sample was restricted to those who graduated at the minimum age of 31 during the follow-up period between 1993 and 1995 (during the recession) or 1999 and 2001 (after the recession). Our sample is relatively evenly balanced in terms of numbers graduating in the two periods, with slightly more observations from the period during the recession than after it. The follow-up began 10 years before graduation (in 1987 or at the age of 18) and ended 10 years after graduation (in 2007 or upon death, retirement, or reaching age 65). Individuals with only one observation during the follow-up were excluded (0.2 per cent). This sample includes 707 189 person-years and 51 916 subjects, of whom 13 190 were adult learners (4 862 men and 8 328 women). Among male and female adult learners, 59 and 54 per cent of qualifications, respectively, were at the tertiary level. The rest were at the secondary level and most of these were vocational qualifications.

Methods

The analyses for the first part of the study were conducted using random-effects logistic regressions suitable for a longitudinal study design in which measurements are clustered within individuals. The dependent variable was enrollment in adult education (at the minimum age of 25) in the following year. We focused on enrollment that led to eventual graduation during the follow-up. Analyses were performed separately for men and women.

In terms of the independent variables used for the enrollment models, we included individual and household-level information derived from administrative registers. The variables that we used are age group (divided into seven categories), highest educational qualification (6), unemployment experience during the year based on the number of months with more than 14 days of unemployment (5), individual taxable income (in quintiles), household taxable income (in quintiles), social class based on occupation and economic activity (7), household structure (4), type of municipality based on the proportion of the population living in urban settlements or the size of the largest urban settlement in the municipality (3), and country of birth (2). All variables were included as time-varying covariates.

In the second part of the study, the year of graduation was taken as the reference point. If a person graduated more than once during the follow-up, the last graduation was chosen as the reference. We estimated two labor market outcomes: the average number of months of unemployment per year and annual income. The number of months refers to the sum of months during the year with more than 14 days of unemployment. Only those months in which the subject was registered as unemployed were taken into account; in other words, months outside the labor force (e.g., months spent as a student) were not considered unemployment. Second, we estimated the annual income level relative to others. The income level of the study population was divided into deciles by calendar year for all males and females aged 18 to 64 between 1987 and 2007. This measurement, obtained from the official registers of the tax authorities, incorporated all forms of taxable income including wages, capital income, and taxable income transfers.

Since graduation can influence both the level and the temporal trend of unemployment and income, we conducted our analyses using repeated measures linear regression and implemented the method of generalized estimation equations with an exchangeable correlation structure. This method estimated population-averaged effects while taking into account within-subject correlation. We accordingly measured the annual average number of months of unemployment and the annual income level for 10 years before and after graduation, controlling for year of birth. Analyses were conducted separately for males and females, for those who graduated during or after the deep economic recession of the 1990s, and for different educational levels.

RESULTS

We begin with a descriptive figure of how adult learning is distributed over the life course (Figure 10.1). This figure includes all years in which an individual is registered in an educational institution. In their early thirties, approximately 15 per cent of Finns are registered as students, and this percentage drops relatively slowly, dipping below 5 per cent only in individuals' late fifties. Overall, women are slightly more likely to be students than men, and this difference is relatively pronounced at ages 35–45.

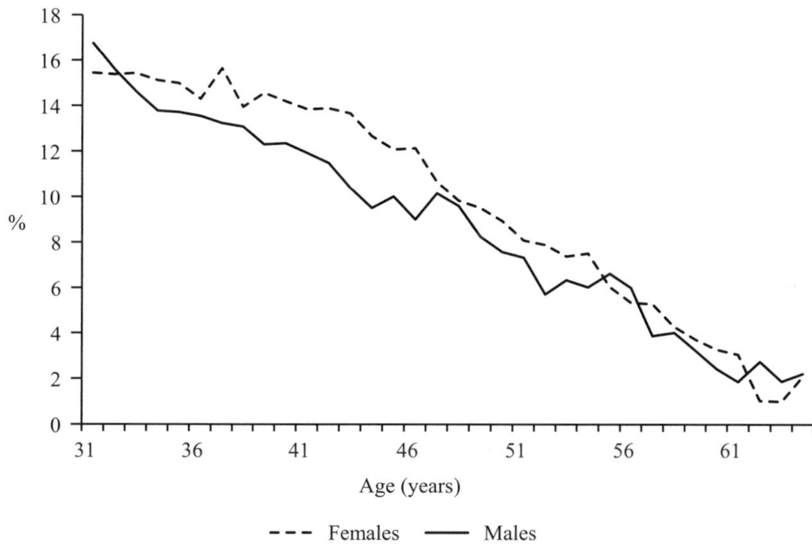

Source: Own calculations based on unpublished linked registration data from the Statistics Finland Labor Market data file 1987–2007 and the Longitudinal Population Census data file 1970–2005.

Figure 10.1 Registration in an educational institution (%) by gender and age

The first descriptive results of adult learners are presented in Table 10.1. This table shows characteristics of adult learners from the year before enrollment and includes "graduating" adult learners and all adult learners as well as the whole population for reference. The difference between all adult learners and the ones for whom we observe graduation may stem from differential dropout rates or from the fact that we are only able to observe graduation when it leads to an upgrade or a change of educational field. The largest group of graduating adult learners is those who enter with a vocational upper secondary degree. However, in terms of odds, individuals with an academic upper secondary degree are most likely to become adult learners. Finally, it seems that unemployment experiences increase the likelihood of enrollment and graduation. Women are slightly more likely to enroll than men and substantially more likely to be adult graduates.[2]

Table 10.1 *Distribution (%) of age, education, and unemployment in the study population (Pop.), among all adult learners (All), and graduating adult learners (Gr.). Odds ratios among graduating adult learners (OR)*

	Men				Women			
	Pop.	All	Gr.	OR	Pop.	All	Gr.	OR
Age								
25–9	11.0	14.2	24.9	1.00	11.5	14.3	17.8	1.00
30–4	14.8	11.2	25.1	0.81**	15.0	13.1	21.9	1.01
35–9	16.3	10.3	19.2	0.52**	16.2	13.5	21.4	0.86**
40–4	16.6	10.4	14.1	0.34**	16.2	13.1	18.3	0.67**
45–9	15.5	12.2	9.4	0.21**	15.0	12.1	12.5	0.43**
50–4	13.6	15.4	5.3	0.12**	13.3	12.3	6.2	0.21**
55+	12.3	26.3	2.0	0.05**	12.8	21.7	1.8	0.07**
Education (highest completed qualification)								
Basic or unknown	28.7	39.2	21.9	1.00	23.4	33.4	18.7	1.00
Vocational upper sec.	36.3	30.6	33.4	0.85**	59.3	27.8	33.1	1.14**
Academic upper sec.	6.5	5.7	18.1	5.96**	9.7	9.0	20.2	3.33**
Lowest lev. tertiary	12.5	11.1	15.6	1.58**	21.1	16.4	18.4	1.02
Lower level tertiary	7.2	6.4	7.8	0.55**	7.1	6.4	7.1	0.61**
Higher lev. tertiary	8.8	7.1	3.3	0.21**	9.4	7.0	2.5	0.18**
Unemployment during the previous year								
None	80.2	62.9	67.4	1.00	83.1	66.9	65.2	1.00
< 1 month	2.2	3.4	5.3	2.01**	2.5	4.0	6.5	2.17**
1–6 months	7.0	11.9	13.7	2.14**	6.7	11.3	16.3	2.28**
7–11 months	5.9	13.5	10.2	2.14**	4.7	11.0	9.6	2.09**
Whole year	4.7	8.8	3.5	0.93**	2.9	6.8	2.4	0.83**

Notes: **p<0.01, *p<0.05, +p<0.10.

Source: As in Figure 10.1.

Multivariate Results of Enrollment

Table 10.2 shows the results for all our explanatory variables, beginning with only the results of each social indicator adjusted for demographic variables and then displaying results from the full model. On the whole, the descriptive results for educational level and unemployment are confirmed in the adjusted models as well as in the full models. In the full model, individuals with academic upper secondary education are most likely to be adult learners, followed by those with lowest-level tertiary education (for men) and basic education (for women). Experiences of unemployment lead to a greater likelihood of adult learning, albeit not for the long-term unemployed. Age has a negative effect on enrollment, albeit a relatively weak one until the mid-30s for men and the late 30s for women.

Initially, both individual and household incomes indicate that the higher the income is, the less likely adult learning is. However, in the full model, household income reverses direction: When we control for individual income, higher household income leads to a greater probability of adult learning, particularly for women. The effect of social class is complex. In general, employees tend to demonstrate a greater likelihood of adult learning than the self-employed, farmers, and those outside the labor force. Within employees, the greatest likelihood of adult learning is seen in upper non-manual workers and the lowest in skilled manual workers.

Except for the differences discussed above, the effects tend to be in the same direction for both genders, although their magnitude may differ. For example, individual income potentially has a stronger effect for men, whereas unemployment experiences seem to have a stronger effect for women. In the full model, with men and women analyzed together, women are found to be significantly more likely to become adult learners than men (odds ratio 2.46, results not shown).

Results from Analyses of Labor Market Outcomes

We begin by analyzing unemployment months before and after graduation. Our analyses are complicated by the substantial increase in unemployment levels that occurred due to the recession of the 1990s. This can also be seen in Figure 10.2 when comparing the average number of months in which individuals were unemployed approximately five years before graduation for those who graduated during the recession and those who graduated after. The large fluctuations in years immediately before and after graduation reflect time as a student and during a job search after graduation. For long-term trends, it is better to analyze the levels approximately 5–7 years before and after graduation. These comparisons show that adult learners graduating during the recession experienced more unemployment after graduation on average, whereas those graduating after the recession experienced less. However, the difference in unemployment experiences after graduation among the two graduation periods is not statistically significant in the long term.

Given the clear impact of the timing of the recession on unemployment, it may be more instructive here to compare adult learners to young graduates. This comparison shows that the differences in unemployment experiences after graduation were not significantly different for those graduating during the recession, but adult learners were slightly disadvantaged compared with young graduates after the recession.

Table 10.2 Adjusted odds ratios and full model of enrollment leading to graduation during the follow-up, by gender

	Men		Women	
	Adjusted effects	Full model	Adjusted effects	Full model
Highest completed qualification (ref. basic or unknown)				
Vocational upper secondary	0.72**	0.79**	0.88**	0.92**
Academic upper secondary	3.06**	3.07**	1.77**	1.89**
Lowest level tertiary	1.31**	1.24**	0.65**	0.66**
Lower-degree level tertiary	0.53**	0.54**	0.44**	0.47**
Higher-degree level tertiary	0.21**	0.21**	0.13**	0.12**
Unemployment during the previous year (ref. none)				
< 1 month	1.70**	1.57**	1.83**	1.82**
1–6 months	1.88**	1.68**	1.98**	1.89**
7–11 months	2.04**	1.72**	2.02**	1.81**
Whole year	1.22**	0.98	1.26**	1.08+
Individual income quintile (ref. lowest)				
2nd	1.11*	1.01	1.19**	1.05*
3rd	0.99	0.92+	0.95	0.91**
4th	0.73**	0.73**	0.74**	0.81**
Highest	0.58**	0.61**	0.63**	0.87**
Household income quintile (ref. lowest)				
2nd	0.84**	1.09*	0.80**	1.05
3rd	0.70**	1.07	0.84**	1.16**
4th	0.69**	1.19**	0.74**	1.18**
Highest	0.56**	1.06	0.66**	1.29**
Social class (ref. upper non-manual)				
Lower non-manual	1.31**	0.79**	1.16**	0.65**
Skilled manual	0.77**	0.49**	1.12**	0.53**
Unskilled manual	1.09*	0.64**	1.39**	0.66**
Farmer	0.50**	0.29**	0.92	0.48**
Self-employed	0.64**	0.38**	1.02	0.55**
Other	0.67**	0.41**	0.65**	0.38**
Age (ref. 25–9)				
30–4		0.92**		1.05*
35–9		0.64**		0.90**
40–4		0.43**		0.71**
45–9		0.27**		0.45**
50–4		0.15**		0.22**
55+		0.07**		0.07**
Household structure (ref. living alone)				
Married/cohabiting, no children		1.16**		0.82**
Married/cohabiting, children		1.15**		0.90**
Single parent		0.79**		1.04

Table 10.2 Continued

	Men		Women	
	Adjusted effects	Full model	Adjusted effects	Full model
Type of municipality (ref. urban)				
Semi-urban		0.86**		0.93**
Rural		0.83**		0.97
Country of birth (ref. Finland)				
Other		1.33**		0.96

Notes: **p<0.01, *p<0.05, +p<0.10. Adjusted effects control for age, family structure, type of municipality, and state of birth for each indicator separately. 3 167 644 person years altogether; 389 523 individuals; 16 754 age 25+ mature students with graduation / change of field.

Source: As in Figure 10.1.

Figure 10.3 breaks down graduates by their achieved educational level. The first thing of note is the higher unemployment levels of secondary graduates compared with tertiary graduates. Although it seems that most adult learners (particularly men at the secondary level) benefit in terms of reduced unemployment in the long run, the standard errors for these estimates are so large that the differences in unemployment levels before and after graduation are not statistically significant (not shown). There are also no significant differences compared with young graduates. Overall, the beneficial effects of graduation on unemployment appear to be quite similar for adult and young graduates at all educational levels.

The recession had less of an effect on trends in income deciles, and we therefore do not present the analyses before and after the recession here. Figure 10.4 presents income levels before and after graduation by achieved educational level. Beginning with adult learners at the tertiary level, we see a significant increase in income after graduation for both women and men. Although men earn more after graduation, the increase is relatively similar for both. Looking at adult learners at the secondary level, we see no increase for men and only a very slight one for women. It should be noted that this result of no change is the case when looking at incomes approximately 3–5 years before graduation rather than immediately before graduation since there is a slight dip in earnings before graduation, which is probably due to lower income while studying.[3] We can also compare adult learners with younger graduates and we see that among men, the former tend to be disadvantaged compared with the latter, but this is not the case among women. In particular,

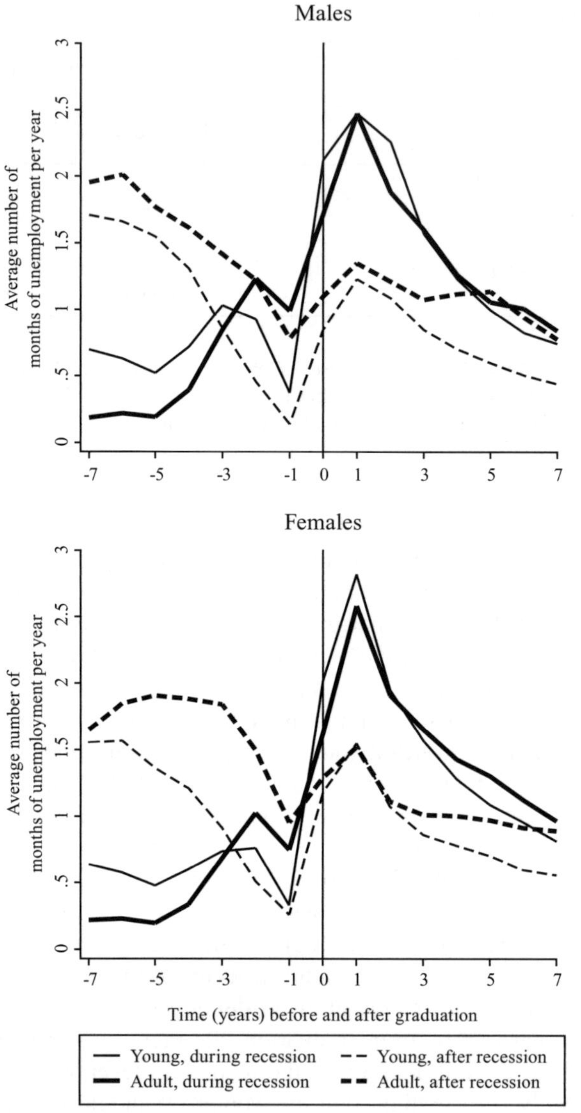

Source: As in Figure 10.1.

Figure 10.2 Average number of months unemployed per year among Finnish males and females graduating from any educational institution between 1993–95 (during the recession) or 1999–2001 (after the recession)

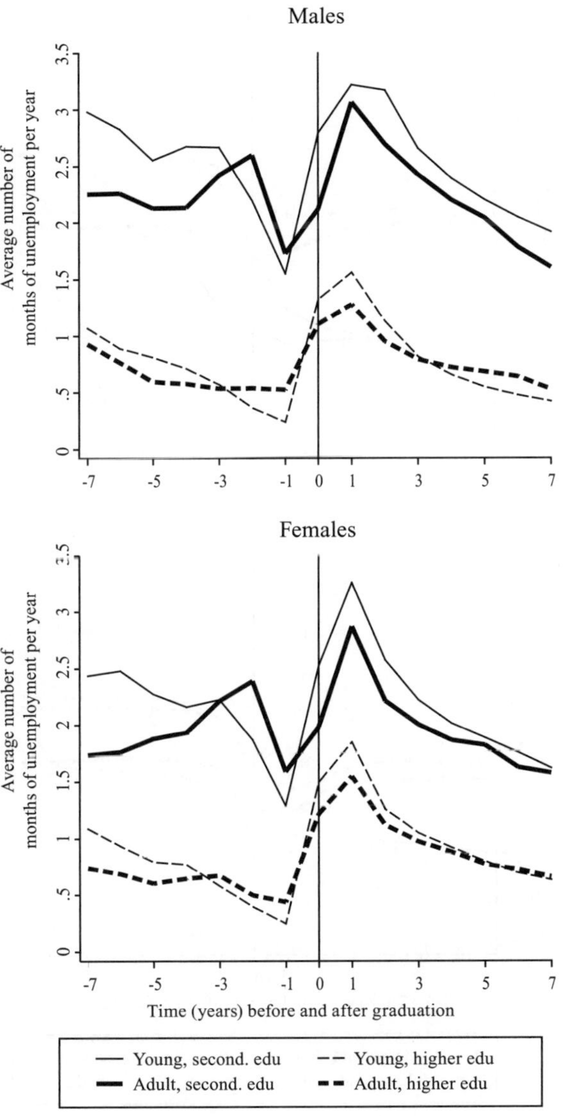

Source: As in Figure 10.1.

Figure 10.3 Average number of months unemployed per year among Finnish males and females graduating from any educational institution between 1993–95 or 1999–2001 by level of completed qualification

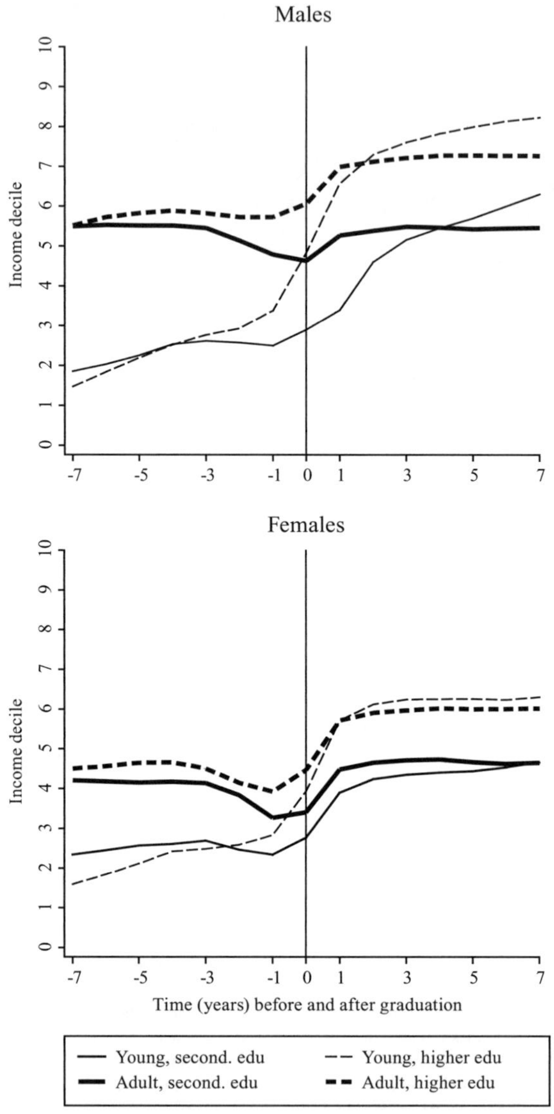

Source: As in Figure 10.1.

Figure 10.4 Achieved income level (decile by year) among Finnish males and females graduating from any educational institution between 1993–95 or 1999–2001 by level of completed qualification

younger male graduates tend to see sustained growth in their incomes, whereas this is not the case for the other groups, for whom graduation only leads to a step change (if anything) but not to sustained growth. Overall, both men and women benefit from new qualifications as adults at the tertiary level but not as much as do young graduates.

DISCUSSION AND CONCLUSION

Our aim was to analyze whether formal adult education leads to reductions in social inequality. In particular, we asked whether older age groups, the long-term unemployed, and the lesser educated were more likely to become adult learners since these are the groups that should find it most beneficial. Our results suggest that inequality along these lines was reduced to some extent during the time period under study, but not fully. Overall, the oldest have the lowest likelihood of being adult learners leading to graduation (even though they are highly likely to enroll in adult education), and the medium educated as well as those with some experience of unemployment (but not the long-term unemployed) have the highest likelihood. In other words, our results support the *"partial equalization hypothesis"* that was set out in the introductory chapter and posited that medium-educated individuals and those in lower or less-stable employment positions should be most likely to participate in formal adult education. Moreover, the gender pattern of more female participation also supports the *"gender hypothesis"* of the introductory chapter, which expected that women should be more likely to participate in formal adult education compared with men.

Our second aim was to analyze labor market outcomes of adult learning. Our analyses of unemployment are greatly affected by the large changes in unemployment levels before, during, and after the recession. Overall, our conclusion from these results is that adult learning slightly reduces the experience of unemployment when measured by average unemployment months. However, these results are not strong enough to show up as statistically significant when divided by educational level. Regarding income, it is mainly graduation at the tertiary level that improves adult learners' income trajectories, whereas those graduating at the secondary level maintain steady income levels in the long run. Nevertheless, there is a slight disadvantage compared with younger graduates at the tertiary level.

From a gender point of view, female adult learners do not attain the same income levels as their male counterparts, and this finding supports our expectation of lower returns for women. Nevertheless, it should also be noted that the income gap between adult learners and younger graduates is smaller

     Adult learning in modern societies

for women than for men. The female disadvantage in income may also reflect childbearing and household work at these relatively young ages. There do not seem to be significant gender differences in unemployment months.

It is possible that the different results for income for the two educational levels are due to the fact that tertiary education is more likely to lead to an educational upgrade than secondary education and that it also involves more years of study than does secondary education. Moreover, it may be that there are a substantial number of adult learners at the secondary level who earn credentials for a job that they already have. This is particularly likely to have been the case in the later period, when competence-based qualifications began to become more numerous.

Qualitative results based on the government's *Noste* program, which aimed at increasing the educational level of individuals with only basic education, report increases in professional expertise, work motivation, self-confidence, and perceived employment security (Ministry of Education and Culture 2010), all of which are outcomes that we have not been able to measure in our study. Despite these positive outcomes, new qualifications do not always lead to increased employment positions or wages (ibid.).

It seems that formal adult education contributes to some extent to reducing inequality, but mainly within generations rather than between generations. Moreover, inequalities seem to be reduced to a greater extent among women than among men. However, many of the reductions come from changes between the medium and the top rather than from improving the situation of those at the bottom relative to others. Previous qualitative and survey evidence also suggests that formal adult education can only have limited success in reducing social inequalities because those who would need it the most are also the ones least likely to be interested in pursuing official qualifications (Stenström et al. 2002).

Overall, the sheer volume of formal adult education in Finland, its relatively equal distribution, and several positive labor market effects are a signal of Finnish society's relative openness. Further improving the employment opportunities of adult learners would likely be beneficial for society as a whole due to increased tax revenues, which would off-set the substantial costs that go into supporting adult learning. Nevertheless, we should also note that adult learning is likely to enable horizontal career moves, which may not show up as increased incomes but are likely to lengthen employment careers by giving persons who are no longer interested in being (or able to be) employed in their current job a chance to continue in employment. These horizontal moves are likely to become increasingly important in order to cope with an aging labor force.

ACKNOWLEDGEMENTS

Outi Sirniö and Pekka Martikainen are supported by the Academy of Finland. The authors wish to thank Janne Uusivirta for his research assistance and Heta Moustgaard for her methodological support.

NOTES

1. The share of the rural population fell by over 25 percentage points, with a similar drop in the share of employment in agriculture (see, for example, Miettinen 2011).
2. The proportion of women is 50.9 per cent among enrollees and 69.2 per cent among adult learners; in both cases, the gender difference is statistically significant ($p<0.01$).
3. It is also possible that this dip in earnings is part of the reason for enrollment in adult education, which is also known in the literature as Ashenfelter's dip. However, given that the dip mainly comes one or two years prior to graduation, it is more likely that it reflects lower income during (full-time) studies rather than a drop prior to enrollment.

REFERENCES

Ahonen, Kirsi (2011), 'Aikuiset opintiellä' (Adults in education), in Anja Heikkinen and Pirkko Leino-Kaukiainen (eds), *Valistus ja koulunpenkki* (Education and Schooling), Helsinki: Suomalaisen Kirjallisuuden Seura, pp. 430–54.

Ahonen, Kirsi (2012), 'Ammatillinen aikuiskoulutus' (Vocational adult education), in Pauli Kettunen and Hannu Simola (eds), *Tiedon ja osaamisen Suomi* (Finland of Information and Skills), Helsinki: Suomalaisen Kirjallisuuden Seura, pp. 249–260.

Blom, Raimo, Harri Melin and Pasi Pyöriä (2001), *Tietotyö ja työelämän muutos. Palkkatyön arki tietoyhteiskunnassa* (Knowledge Work and Changing Working Life), Helsinki: Gaudeamus.

Duell, Nicola, David Grubb and Shruti Singh (2009), 'Activation policies in Finland', *OECD Social, Employment and Migration Working Papers*, No. 98, OECD, Paris.

Huovinen, Pasi and Hannu Piekkola (2001), 'Unemployment and early retirements of the Finnish aged workers in 1989–1996', in Jorma Kalela, Jaakko Kiander, Ullamaija Kivikuru, Heikki A. Loikkanen and Jussi Simpura (eds), *Down from the Heavens, Up from the Ashes. The Finnish Economic Crisis of the 1990s in the Light of Social and Economic Research*, Helsinki: Government Institute for Economic Research, pp. 247–74.

Järvinen, T. and M. Vanttaja (2001), 'Young people, education and work: trends and changes in Finland in the 1990s', *Journal of Youth Studies*, **4** (2), 195–207.

Kantasalmi, Kari (2012), 'Yliopistot ja aikuiskoulutus' (Universities and adult education), in Pauli Kettunen and Hannu Simola (eds), *Tiedon ja osaamisen Suomi* (Finland of Information and Skills), Helsinki: Suomalaisen Kirjallisuuden Seura, pp. 261–71.

Kiander, Jaakko (2004), 'The evolution of the Finnish model in the 1990s: from depression to high-tech boom', *VATT Discussion Paper*, No. 344, Helsinki.

Kivinen, O., J. Hedman and P. Kaipainen (2007), 'From elite university to mass higher education: educational expansion, equality of opportunity and returns to university education', *Acta Sociologica*, **50** (3), 231–47.

Korkeamäki, Ossi (2012), *Essays on Labour Demand and Wage Formation*, Helsinki: Government Institute for Economic Research.

Kruhse-Lehtonen, Ulla (2007), *Empirical Studies on the Returns to Education in Finland*, Helsinki: Helsinki School of Economics.

Kyyrä, Tomi (2001), 'Evolution of inequality in the Finnish labour market, 1988–1996', in Jorma Kalela, Jaakko Kiander, Ullamaija Kivikuru, Heikki A. Loikkanen and Jussi Simpura (eds), *Down from the Heavens, Up from the Ashes. The Finnish Economic Crisis of the 1990s in the Light of Social and Economic Research*, Helsinki: Government Institute for Economic Research, pp. 275–302.

Laukkanen, Erkki (2010), *Wage Returns to Training: Evidence from Finland*, Helsinki: Labour Institute for Economic Research.

Lehtonen, Heikki, Simo Aho, Jarmo Peltola and Mika Renvall (2001), 'Did the crisis change the welfare state in Finland?', in Jorma Kalela, Jaakko Kiander, Ullamaija Kivikuru, Heikki A. Loikkanen and Jussi Simpura (eds), *Down from the Heavens, Up from the Ashes. The Finnish Economic Crisis of the 1990s in the Light of Social and Economic Research*, Helsinki: Government Institute for Economic Research, pp. 100–25.

Loukkola, A. (2012), 'Lamavuonna 1992 tutkinnon suorittaneet työllistyivät huonosti' (Graduates of the recession year 1992 have difficulties in finding employment), *Hyvinvointikatsaus* (Periodical of Statistics Finland), **23** (1), 40–2.

Miettinen, A. (2011), 'Population data on Finland 1900–2010', *Finnish Yearbook of Population Research*, **XLVI**, 163–72.

Ministry of Education (2004), *Aikuiskoulutuksen vuosikirja. Tilastotietoja aikuisten opiskelusta 2002* (Yearbook of Adult Education), Helsinki: Opetusministeriö.

Ministry of Education and Culture (2010), *Noste-ohjelma 2003–2009. Loppuraportti* (The Noste Program 2003–09), Helsinki: Opetus- ja kulttuuriministeriö.

Pekkala Kerr, Sari (2012), 'Koulutusmenot ja väestön koulutustaso' (Educational expenditures and the level of education of the population), in Pauli Kettunen and Hannu Simola (eds), *Tiedon ja osaamisen Suomi* (Finland of Information and Skills), Helsinki: Suomalaisen Kirjallisuuden Seura, pp. 295–320.

Sipilä, N., L. Kestilä and P. Martikainen (2011), 'Koulutuksen yhteys nuorten työttömyyteen. Mihin peruskoulututkinto riittää 2000-luvun alussa?' (The association between education and youths' unemployment), *Yhteiskuntapolitiikka*, **76** (2), 121–34.

Statistics Finland (2007), 'From slash-and-burn fields to post-industrial society – 90 years of change in industrial structure', available at http://tilastokeskus.fi/tup/suomi90/helmikuu_en.html (accessed 11.2.2013).

Stenström, Marja-Leena, Pirjo Linnakylä, Antero Malin, Pentti Nikkanen, Ellen Piesanen and Sakari Valkonen (2002), *Yli 40-vuotiaat aikuiskoulutuksessa: "Kyllä sieltä aina jotakin reppuun jää!"* (Over 40s in Adult Education), Helsinki: Opetusministeriö.

Suikkanen, A., R. Linnakangas and S. Martti (2002), 'Työllisyyden muutos ja koulutuksen merkitys' (The change of employment and the meaning of education), *Aikuiskasvatus*, **2002** (2), 114–23.

11. Adult Learning in Denmark: Patterns of Participation in Adult Learning and Its Impact on Individuals' Labor Market Outcomes

Susanne Wahler, Sandra Buchholz,
Vibeke Myrup Jensen, and Julia Unfried

INTRODUCTION

Education has become a major topic of public and scientific discourse in modern societies since the first PISA evaluation in 2000. Though there has been a long-standing interest in the education of children and youths in Denmark, awareness of educational opportunities later in life has increased, especially in the more recent past (Sprogoe 2003). This increasing interest in adult learning is linked with accelerated structural and technological changes in the labor market of globalized societies. For the workforce, the need for adult learning creates two new main challenges. First, as the demand for new skills arises, workers need to manage these skills after having left the educational system. Second, the labor market requires a high level of adaptability to these new skills in order for a worker to maintain employment (Jørgensen 2007; Georgiadis and Zisimos 2010). Moreover, the increased focus on adult learning brings along other important aspects for society since it is considered an essential instrument for enhancing socioeconomic equality within the European Union (Dieckhoff 2007). Adult learning has hence become a prominent issue in policies on education, economy, and welfare at both the national and international level and is therefore also being firmly embedded into the European agenda (Georgiadis and Zisimos 2010). For example, one of the five EU-benchmarks for 2020 defined in the "New strategic framework for European cooperation in education and training" (known as ET 2020) has as its goal that 15 per cent of all adults aged 25–64 participate in adult learning by 2020 (measured by the European Labour Force Survey). In 2009, adult participation in lifelong learning remained at 9.3

per cent, exhibiting large variation among the member states (Commission of the European Communities 2011). Denmark has one of the highest levels of participation in adult learning within the European Union, reflecting a framework of activation and reemployment measures as well as the social-democratic ideology that everyone should engage in lifelong learning (Cort 2002; Grunow and Leth-Sørensen 2004; Jørgensen 2007; UNESCO Institute for Lifelong Learning 2009).

Although Denmark is characterized by a well-elaborated system of adult learning, little research is available to shed light on the patterns of participation in adult learning for Denmark, the various implications for adults in the Danish job market and on the ability of adult learning to counterbalance inequality patterns later in life (Jørgensen 2007). This chapter thereby contributes to the literature in two ways. First, it provides an overview of participation in the different forms of adult learning in Denmark and investigates the participants' age distribution as well as examines the factors that determine enrollment. Second, the chapter analyzes how participation in adult learning affects the following three labor market trajectories: (1) becoming unemployed, (2) leaving unemployment, and (3) direct career mobility. In order to answer our research questions, we use population register data by employing the Integrated Database for Labor Market Research (IDA).

The chapter proceeds as follows: First, we portray the Danish institutional setting, including the welfare state and the labor market model as well as the mainstream and adult learning systems. Second, on the basis of this institutional description, we derive the general hypotheses of our empirical analyses. Third, we describe our data, the research design, and methods. Fourth, we present our empirical findings regarding the research interests mentioned above. Fifth and last, we provide a short summary and conclusion.

INSTITUTIONAL SETTING

Welfare State and Labor Market Model

The Danish welfare system can be characterized as a so-called social-democratic welfare regime because it comprises a number of constituent elements, such as a universalistic and egalitarian welfare provision by the state, generous cash benefits, a large supply of public services, and an emphasis on the equality of opportunity (Powel and Barrientos 2004; Andersen and Svarer 2007; Kvist and Greve 2011). The high level of public services is financed by a progressive income tax system in which it is not uncommon for employees to pay an income tax of 40–50 per cent. The fact that the welfare system is tax-based also means that a large proportion of the population must be in employment for the model to be financially sustainable (Andersen and Svarer 2007). Consequently, an additional characteristic of the Danish welfare state is the close relationship between the institutions of welfare and work and therefore the goal of maximizing economic participation, thereby striving for "full employment" (Kildal 2001; Powel and Barrientos 2004). In order to create a well-functioning labor market and to keep unemployment low, the Danish labor market policy is thus based on the "Golden Triangle of Flexicurity" (Plougmann and Madsen 2002).

The first element of this model is a flexible labor market, which is a consequence of slightly restrictive rules on dismissal ("hire and fire") and ensures that Danish companies (mostly smaller in size) can easily adjust their labor input (Andersen and Svarer 2006). As a result, the individual mobility of workers between jobs and the job turnover (job creation and job destruction) are at a relatively high level. A large number of employees are confronted with joblessness every year, but most of them are able to return to the labor market after a short episode of unemployment. Moreover, due to the Danish industrial structure with the predominance of small and medium-sized firms in the private sector, internal labor markets are of minor importance, which makes it easier to shift from one enterprise to another as a result of lower entry barriers at the company level (Madsen 2002; Andersen and Svarer 2007). Nevertheless, there is also a substantial share of workers in long-term employment relationships who acquire workplaces in which they remain much of their lives (Eriksson and Westergaard-Nielsen 2008). Since the employers' need for flexibility is satisfied by appropriate dismissal rules, the Danish labor market contains a relatively low and stable proportion of atypical employment relationships, such as fixed-term contracts and part-time employment (Bredgaard et al. 2009). Despite the low level of employment protection, Denmark can be termed a coordinated market economy whose main regulatory mechanism is the agreements between trade unions and employers (Eriksson and Westergaard-Nielsen 2008).

The second element of the triangle is a generous social security system that offers permissive and long-lasting unemployment benefits. This element is important in order to balance out the social risks resulting from the flexible hiring and firing rules (Andersen and Svarer 2006, 2007). The combination of these two elements is often referred to as the "flexicurity model", which unites firms' needed flexibility with workers' quest for income security.

The third element of the model is the active labor market policies. Since the social safety net placed under those who fall outside of employment serves to protect income but not to bring unemployed persons (back into) employment, this final element provides incentives and support schemes for (re)entering employment (Cox 1998; Andersen and Svarer 2007). Annual spending on active labor market policies that aim at (re)integrating unemployed persons (back) into employment by means of upskilling or reskilling them through adult learning constitute 1.5 per cent of the GDP (UNESCO Institute for Lifelong Learning 2009).

Hence, the present Danish labor market policy represents a new way of thinking about the balance between rights and duties, namely that the unemployed have a right to receive assistance when they are without a job, but in return, they have the duty of searching for work, participating in skills upgrading activities, and accepting job offers (Cox 1998; Andersen and Svarer 2006). With this shift from a more passive to a more active labor market policy in the 1990s, unemployment in Denmark was reduced by 50 per cent and is thus labeled the Danish "Employment Miracle" (Andersen and Svarer 2007). However, this significant decline in unemployment must also be seen in light of both an economic up-turn that also began in the mid-1990s as well as the inflow in early retirement schemes, leave schemes, and active labor market programs (Madsen 2002; Ebralidze with Leth-Sørensen 2008). Moreover, it was mainly the public sector that provided jobs for the unemployed within the new framework of activation and that today accounts for approximately 31 per cent of total employment (Madsen 1999; Grunow and Leth-Sørensen 2004). Nevertheless, Denmark enjoys the highest rate of employment among comparable welfare states and includes an exceptionally high activity level among women with around three quarters being in work. This remarkable female employment rate is made possible through the provision of publicly financed childcare (Cox 1998; Kildal 2001). As a result, there is only little difference regarding participation in the labor market between women with and without children. Moreover, the activity rate and the working hours are almost the same between men and women. Denmark therefore represents a dual-earner model within an egalitarian gender regime, but there is still an earnings gap between men and women, a gender-specific labor market segregation (with a larger proportion of women in low-paid jobs), and a gender division of labor in the private sphere (with women being mainly responsible for the family and domestic duties) (Kulawik 2005; Hoheisel 2007).

The Danish Educational System

In Denmark, adult learning is not solely targeted at the unemployed, but also at the workforce in general (Plougmann and Madsen 2002; Andersen and Svarer 2006). In order to meet the needs and changes within the labor market, the aim of adult learning in Denmark is to give adults the possibility of upgrading their competences and to ensure a skilled and flexible workforce. The educational system in Denmark can therefore be divided into two parts, namely (1) the mainstream educational system and (2) the adult learning and continuing training system. Together, these two types of educational systems provide the framework for lifelong learning (Plougmann and Madsen 2002; Cort 2002).

The Mainstream Educational System

The typical path through the mainstream educational system is to attend a comprehensive, ten-year primary and lower secondary school without tracking and then to make a choice between the academically oriented courses of general upper secondary education and the practically oriented vocational upper secondary education and training courses. While the former comprise mainly a preliminary stage of higher education, the latter prepare trainees for working in a specific trade or industry in the form of dual training by combining theoretical and practical education (Ebralidze with Leth-Sørensen 2008; Danish Agency for Universities and Internationalisation 2011). In spite of this structure, the various pathways within the Danish educational system are cross-connected so that it is still possible to change tracks. Moreover, since at least 10 per cent of Danish students are older than 25 when they leave upper secondary education, it is relatively easy to exit the educational system and reenter at a later time. Regarding the maximum educational attainment achieved among the population, the expansion of education in Denmark within the last decades is related to the fact that younger people tend to reach higher educational levels. For instance, the percentage of first-time graduates from university-level education rose from 25 in 1995 to 48 in 2009, whereas women surpassed men with a ratio of 60 per cent to 35 per cent, respectively, in 2009 (OECD 2011).

The Adult Learning and Continuing Training System

Though the Danish adult learning and continuing training system is specifically designed for adults and is hence a "parallel system" to the mainstream educational system, it provides qualifications that are well-recognized in the Danish labor market. Denmark has a long-standing tradition of lifelong learning. Adult learning is offered by various institutions and is composed of a wide range of programs within the formal and non-formal area that are embedded in a coherent and transparent adult educational system (Cort 2002). On the one hand, formal adult learning consists of general adult education, including preparatory adult education, general adult education, and higher preparatory single subject courses. On the other hand, it is composed of vocationally oriented adult education comprising adult vocational training courses, basic adult education, and formal educational degrees equivalent to degrees at short-cycle, medium-cycle, and long-cycle higher educational levels. All of these courses lead to nationally accredited formal qualifications that qualify graduates for further education or for the labor market (Danish Agency for Universities and Internationalisation 2011). As in the mainstream educational system, adult learning is mainly organized and financed by the state. Thus, adult learning is a public good and reflects a high degree of state involvement and responsibility (Cort 2002; Keogh 2009; UNESCO Institute for Lifelong Learning 2009). Non-formal adult learning (e.g., Danish as a second language, study circles, or home economics) is usually offered by non-governmental actors, such as folk high schools, evening schools, university extension services, or study associations, and for the most part does not result in generally recognized formal qualifications that are valuable to the labor market (Danish Agency for Universities and Internationalisation 2011).

HYPOTHESES

Based on the Danish institutional context, we derive the following general hypotheses for our empirical analyses:

1. We expect to find a comparatively high participation rate in adult learning since it is so deeply rooted in Denmark and because of the existence of appropriate lifelong learning opportunities. Indeed, we anticipate that most of the individuals in our sample will take part in additional learning activities in their adult lives. In particular, our expectation is that formal adult learning and returning to the mainstream educational system should be the most common forms of adult learning, the latter being more prevalent with younger individuals.
2. Regarding social inequalities, we hypothesize that Denmark should be able to reduce inequalities by means of its adult learning system. Concretely, we expect that women have better chances of taking part in adult learning because of their higher need to (re)train as a result of their higher risk of employment interruption and their exceptionally high labor force participation rate ("*gendered participation hypothesis*"). Moreover, we expect that Denmark is able to provide additional learning, particularly to lesser-qualified individuals ("*partial equalization hypothesis*").
3. Concerning labor market outcomes, attending adult learning should generally have a positive impact on individuals' labor market chances, though non-formal learning activities should pay off less than the other existing options. In contrast, gains from formal adult learning and returning to the educational system are expected to be high since these activities equip participants with skills that are of relevance for the job market and lead to valuable labor market signals.

DATA, RESEARCH DESIGN, AND METHODS

We use various sources of administrative data maintained by Statistics Denmark. Among our data sources, we use information from the Integrated Database for Labor Market Research (IDA). The IDA is a register dataset that includes the whole population of Denmark and whose information comes from various statistical registers. For employees, the IDA additionally includes employers' information. The link between persons and establishments is identified at the end of November because it is close to the end of the year and therefore expected to not be influenced by seasonal effects. With the exception of education variables, which are collected in October, personal variables are mainly collected at the end of the year. Altogether, more than 200 variables are listed in the database, which provides data on the population, the population's attachment to the labor market, and on establishments and firms. The IDA obtains data once per year and in our study, we include persons in birth cohorts from 1955 to 1980, thereby covering the period from 1981 to 2009. All in all, the IDA is particularly well-suited for following persons and companies over time and carrying out longitudinal analyses.

For the purpose of our empirical study, we proceeded as follows: Adult learning is understood as participation in *adult learning programs* particularly designed for adults (in the form of formal and/or non-formal adult learning activities) as well as a return to the mainstream educational system (*mainstream educational programs*) after labor market entry. In practice, we observe whether persons in our sample have participated in the following types of adult learning: (1) any kind of adult learning (defined as attending at least one of the subsequent kinds of adult learning), (2) formal adult learning, (3) non-formal adult learning, (4) tertiary education, (5) vocational upper secondary education, and (6) general upper secondary education. However, in order to define this risk-set, we make different sample restrictions for the younger (born 1965–80) and older cohorts (born 1955–64) because a large part of our population entered the labor market before the beginning of the IDA database (1980). As a result, for younger cohorts, we use information from the time when they finished their mainstream education for the first time (meaning that the first uninterrupted educational episode has ended). For older cohorts, we use all full episodes between 1980 and 2009, and activities that began before 1980 are excluded from the sample (left-censoring). Based on these definitions, our data includes a total of 1 949 781 individuals, equivalent to 35 per cent of the Danish population.

As mentioned in the introductory section, our empirical study consists of two main steps. To test our first two research hypotheses, the first step of our study investigates whether persons in our sample participated in adult learning and if so, in which forms of adult learning. Moreover, we are interested in the participants' age distribution in different types of adult learning and the persons' likelihood of attendance in relation to gender and their initial educational degree. Regarding the latter, we differentiate between the following levels of qualification: no educational qualification, lower secondary degree, upper secondary degree, A-level, and tertiary degree. Our baseline level of education is always lower secondary education. To provide an overview of participation and to explore the participants' age pattern in the above-mentioned types of adult learning, we created a corresponding cross-sectional dataset and performed frequency analyses and calculated cross tables. To study the chances of entering adult learning, we applied logistic regression models. In our multivariate models, we controlled for persons' gender and their originally obtained level of education. Though the effects are not displayed (to maintain simplicity), we additionally controlled for birth cohort and migrant status.

To address the third of our research hypotheses, the second step of our analyses focuses on labor market returns to different forms of adult learning in Denmark. Specifically, we examine (1) individuals' risk of becoming unemployed, (2) their chances of exiting unemployment, and (3) their chances of direct career mobility. The latter is studied by examining individuals' significant gains and losses in salary as measured by inflation-adjusted gross wages. Annual income increases of at least 10 per cent are classified as upward career mobility, whereas downward mobility is identified as a loss of income of 5 per cent or more. In our longitudinal analyses, we applied multivariate event history methods by using logistic regression models with robust standard errors and clustered by the individual. Moreover, we ran separate models for men and women to take gendered career trajectories into account. In our longitudinal analyses, we proceeded as follows: In Model 1, we calculated the effects of participating in different kinds of adult learning on our three labor market outcomes (i.e., risks of unemployment, chances of leaving unemployment, and career mobility). In Model 2, we additionally included the persons' initial educational level. Though we also controlled for birth cohort, age, age squared, and migrant status in our models, in the interest of simplification, we only display the effects for the following covariates in our tables: participation in different forms of adult learning and individuals' initial level of education. In our analyses on the risks of becoming (full-year) unemployed, we additionally present the effect of part-year unemployment (in order to investigate if a vulnerable labor market position in one year significantly increases individuals' risk of becoming full-year unemployed in the subsequent year).

RESULTS

Participation in Various Forms of Adult Learning

In the first step of our empirical study, we (1) describe how Danes attend various forms of adult learning, (2) offer a glance at the participants' age distribution among these types of adult learning, and (3) analyze a person's likelihood of attending adult learning.

Figure 11.1 displays the share of persons in our sample who actually participated in adult learning after labor market entry as well as the share of persons attending different kinds of adult learning. In line with our expectations, adult learning activities prove to be a widespread phenomenon in Denmark. The majority of the persons of our sample, namely 77 per cent, have attended some kind of adult learning. Moreover, and as anticipated, only about 6 per cent participated in non-formal adult learning, whereas formal adult learning programs constitute the most common learning activity with a share of about 62 per cent. Furthermore, the figure shows that persons often upgrade their initial educational degree by returning to the mainstream educational system after a period of time in the labor market. Concretely, 27 per cent of the persons in our sample entered tertiary education. A smaller percentage of our sample attended general upper secondary education (7 per cent). All in all, our results confirm our first hypothesis that adult learning is of particular significance in Denmark and is undertaken mainly in the form of formal adult learning and by reentering the mainstream educational system. Only about 23 per cent of our sample never participated in any kind of adult learning after entering the labor market.

Figure 11.2 shows the age distribution of participants in the various adult learning opportunities. Though adult learning is widespread in Denmark, the results of Figure 11.2 indicate that participation in adult learning is strongly dependent on individuals' age and that especially persons above the age of 40 show low participation rates in adult learning. In general, adult learning is mostly pursued by persons aged 26–40. However, when we investigate the age distribution among the different types of programs, young adults up to the age of 25 are overrepresented among non-formal adult learning, vocational upper secondary education, tertiary education, and particularly among upper secondary education. In contrast, formal adult learning programs (which are the dominant form of adult learning in Denmark; see Figure 11.1) are by far most pursued by individuals aged 26–40. All in all, our findings show that as persons get older, the proportion of them participating in adult learning decreases. However, the Danish system cannot be described as very youth-oriented since the most dominant form of adult learning (i.e., formal adult learning) clearly focuses on middle-aged persons who participate most in such trainings.

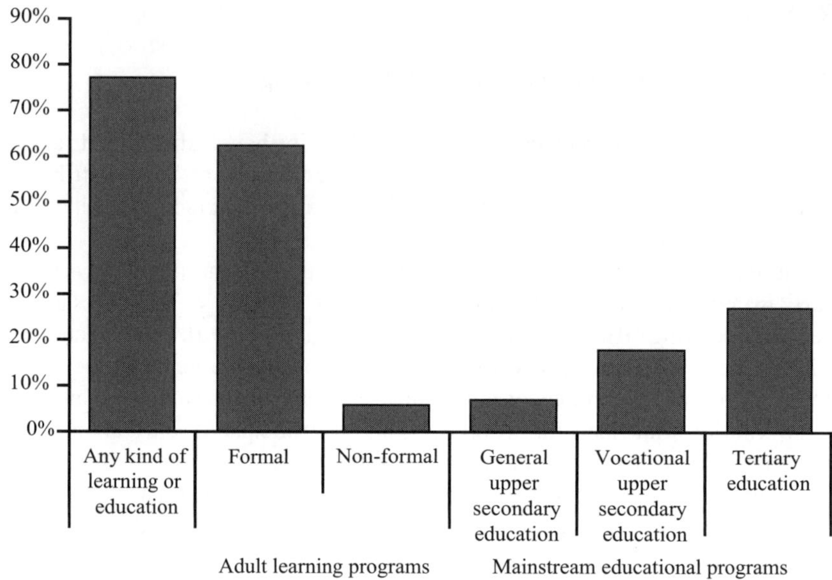

Notes: Figure 11.1 displays persons who reentered education at least once in their lives after labor market entry. Persons may have entered more than one form of adult education after their labor market entry and they may have participated in programs more than once.

Source: Own calculations based on the IDA.

Figure 11.1 Participation in different forms of adult learning and training after labor market entry

In light of this descriptive overview, Table 11.1 presents our multivariate findings for persons' likelihood of participating in adult learning in general and in different forms of adult learning activities after labor market entry. We first investigate gender differences and find that women are more likely to participate in adult learning than men. This result confirms our expectation that the Danish system tries to support the integration of women into the labor market (in this case, by supporting their (re)training), which is in accordance with our second hypothesis, which postulated a gendered participation in adult learning. Second, we examine a person's likelihood of participating in adult learning given his or her initial level of education. Our baseline level of education is lower secondary education and compared with this group, all other educational groups are less likely to participate in adult learning, with one exception, i.e., persons with an A-level, for whom we find a positive and significant effect on

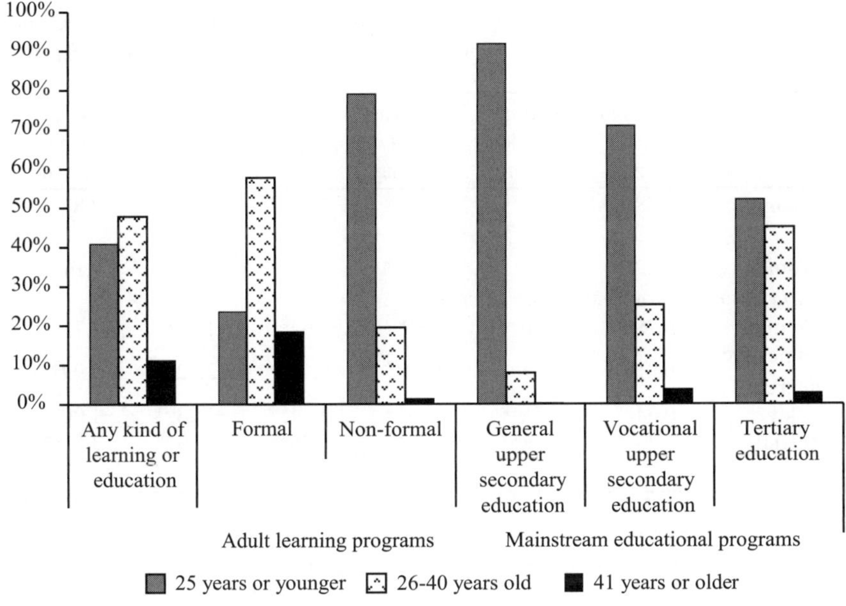

Source: Own calculations based on the IDA.

Figure 11.2 Participants' age distribution in different forms of adult learning and training

the likelihood of entering any type of adult training. Examining the different types of adult learning, we observe similar results as in the investigation of attending adult learning in general. It is a general trend that mainly persons holding a lower secondary degree are most likely to take part in adult learning (except for persons with an A-level). These persons are most likely to participate in a tertiary degree program and non-formal adult learning.

Of course, it must be noted that the chances of participating in mainstream educational programs are dependent on a person's initial level of education. For example, an individual needs an A-level to enter tertiary education. However, upon measuring individuals' level of education at the time of labor market entry in our analyses and observing all later educational activities of the persons in our sample, it becomes clear that individuals with a lower educational level at the time of labor market entry could theoretically also qualify for tertiary education afterwards (e.g., persons with a lower secondary degree at labor market entry could attain an A-level first and attend university afterward). All in all, the findings support our second hypothesis, which posited that

Table 11.1   *Chances of participating in different forms of adult learning and training after labor market entry (logistic regression models)*

	Any kind of adult learning	Formal adult learning	Non-formal adult learning	Tertiary ed.	Vocational upper sec. ed.	General upper sec. ed.
Constant	0.58**	0.15**	−4.37**	−3.06**	−1.82**	−2.87**
Gender (ref. men)						
Women	0.02**	0.01*	0.34**	0.15**	0.13**	0.16**
Qualification (ref. lower secondary degree)						
No qual.	−0.75**	−0.20**	−0.31**	−1.64**	−1.18**	−1.73**
Upper sec. degree	−0.81**	−0.19**	−1.07**	−0.48**	−2.02**	−1.99**
A-level	0.64**	−0.71**	0.43**	2.34**	−1.23**	−1.00**
Tertiary degree	−1.76**	−1.19**	−1.73**	−0.36**	−3.39**	−3.61**

Notes: ** $p < 0.01$; * $p < 0.05$; + $p < 0.10$. N for all models 1 949 781. In our models, we additionally control for birth cohort and migrant status.

Source: Own calculations based on the IDA.

adult learning in Denmark contributes to reducing previously experienced educational inequalities because comparatively low-educated persons (holding only a lower secondary degree) are in general most likely to receive adult learning. However, there is also a group of "losers" in the Danish system. While lesser-educated individuals indeed have higher chances of receiving valuable adult training, those adults with no education are not successfully integrated into adult learning. However, it must be noted that this group is rather small in Denmark.

Labor Market Outcomes of Various Forms of Adult Learning

In the second step of our empirical study, we investigate the labor market returns to different kinds of adult learning in Denmark. This comprises (1) the risks of unemployment, (2) the employment chances of the unemployed, and (3) direct career mobility.

Risks of unemployment

The results of our longitudinal analyses for individuals' risk of becoming unemployed and how this risk is affected by attending adult learning are presented in the left panel of Table 11.2. The table reveals that persons who have been part-year unemployed (indicating that persons have been employed for less than half of the year) exhibit an increased risk of facing full-year unemployment in the following year. In other words, being part-year unemployed paves the way to full-year unemployment and to being fully excluded from employment. Turning to the influence of adult learning, the results reveal that with the exception of non-formal adult learning, all forms of adult learning substantially decrease the risk of becoming unemployed. This is true for both men and women. Concerning persons' initial level of qualification, our findings indicate that those with no education and those with only a lower secondary degree are most susceptible to unemployment. A lower risk of becoming unemployed can be observed for all other educational levels. All in all, our analyses support our third research hypothesis, which postulated that participating in formal adult learning and upgrading the initial level of education in the form of mainstream educational programs should prove helpful in protecting individuals against unemployment. The same applies to having a higher level of initial education. Therefore, investing in education and adult learning clearly pays off in Denmark by enhancing individuals' employment stability.

Employment chances of the unemployed
The right panel of Table 11.2 displays the findings of our longitudinal analyses concerning full-year unemployed persons' chances of becoming employed.

As observed with the risks of unemployment, we find that participating in adult learning during unemployment also positively affects individuals' chances of (re)entering the labor market. Taking part in formal adult learning, tertiary education, or vocational upper secondary schooling significantly improves full-year unemployed persons' chances of becoming employed. Participating in non-formal adult learning, however, does not raise persons' chances of becoming employed. As a result, non-formal adult learning neither protects individuals from becoming unemployed nor enhances the chances of the unemployed to become employed. Obviously (and in accordance with our third hypothesis), non-formal adult learning is not able to equip individuals with valuable signals for the labor market. In contrast to our results on the risks of becoming unemployed, participating in general upper secondary schooling does not increase individuals' labor market chances. Apparently, general upper secondary schooling is only valuable for individuals if they are employed but not if they are unemployed, whereas vocational upper secondary schooling (which is more practically oriented) is helpful for both, i.e., it protects individuals against unemployment if they are employed and increases their chances of becoming employed if they are unemployed. Regarding individuals' level of qualification, we again find that a high(er)

Table 11.2   Unemployment risks and employment chances of the unemployed (logistic regression models)

| | Unemployment risks | | | | Employment chances of the unemployed | | | |
| | Men | | Women | | Men | | Women | |
	1	2	1	2	1	2	1	2
Constant	−10.85**	−11.8**	−8.32**	−9.98**	0.5**	0.88**	−1.22**	−0.68**
Part-year unemployment	1.42**	1.37**	1.1**	1.02**	–	–	–	–
Adult learning								
Formal adult learning	−0.39**	−0.4**	−0.18**	−0.25**	0.16**	0.12**	0.11**	0.09**
Non-formal adult learning	0.29	0.31	−0.29+	−0.18	−0.02	−0.10	0.21**	0.09
Tertiary education	−0.4**	−0.25**	−1.38**	−1.04**	0.19**	0.11+	0.28**	0.13+
Vocational upper sec.	−0.58**	−0.84**	−0.47**	−0.72**	0.91**	0.99**	0.92**	0.97**
General upper sec.	−1.42**	−1.47**	−0.88**	−1.09**	−0.16	−0.13	0.19	0.21
Qualification (ref. lower secondary degree)								
No educational qualification	–	0.35**	–	0.3**	–	−0.07+	–	−0.29**
Upper secondary degree	–	−0.73**	–	−0.88**	–	0.48**	–	0.65**
A-level	–	−0.44**	–	−1.03**	–	0.16**	–	0.31**
Tertiary degree	–	−1.14**	–	−1.96**	–	0.73**	–	0.8**
Events	5 679	5 679	6 198	6 198	23 991	23 991	24 414	24 414
Total episodes	1 680 882	1 680 882	1 775 201	1 775 201	54 541	54 541	58 308	58 308
Censored episodes	1 675 203	1 675 203	1 769 003	1 769 003	30 550	30 550	33 894	33 894
Log likelihood	−44 130	−40 867	−47 431	−44 539	−43 080	−39 800	−44 841	−42 167

Notes: ** p < 0.01, * p < 0.05, + p < 0.10. In our models, we additionally control for birth cohort, age, age squared, and migrant status.

Source: Own calculations based on the IDA.

level of education improves individuals' labor market chances and supports their chances of leaving unemployment.

Direct career mobility

The results of our final longitudinal analyses, the investigation of individuals' direct career mobility chances, are reported in Table 11.3. The table also consists of two panels: The left panel describes the persons' chances of upward career mobility, whereas the right panel presents the risk of downward career mobility.

First of all, the table shows that participating in vocational upper secondary education increases both men's and women's chances of salary gains and decreases their risk of income loss. Second, participation in formal adult learning also has a similar positive correlation with income mobility, but only for men. For women, the correlation is not significant. Third, the table shows that non-formal adult learning is rather unfavorable since this type of training increases persons' risk of income loss and decreases their chances of improving their income. Fourth, concerning participating in tertiary education (which was a good predictor of improving individuals' labor market chances in our previous analyses), we find that it has both a positive and a negative impact on individuals' income mobility. Participating in adult learning at the tertiary level increases both the chances of upward mobility and the risk of downward mobility, which suggests that persons who participate in tertiary education are more mobile in general. Fifth, attending general upper secondary education negatively affects men's income chances, whereas the results for women are mixed. For women, general upper secondary adult training increases both the chances of upward mobility and the risk of downward mobility. Thus, while the effects of participating in adult learning are pretty clear-cut for persons' risk of becoming unemployed and their chances of leaving unemployment, the effects of adult learning on income mobility are rather mixed. With respect to individuals' initial level of education, we generally find that a higher level of education positively impacts on individuals' income chances since it reduces their risk of becoming downwardly mobile and improves their chances of upward mobility. The only exception in this case is that we find that persons holding an A-level display a greater risk of downward mobility than do persons with lower secondary degrees. However, this result might be explained by the fact that compared with persons with a lower secondary degree, individuals holding A-levels potentially have more to lose than do lesser-qualified individuals.

Table 11.3   Direct career mobility (logistic regression models)

	Upward mobility				Downward mobility			
	Men		Women		Men		Women	
	1	2	1	2	1	2	1	2
Constant	1.97**	2.49**	1.32**	1.79**	−2.55**	−2.92**	−2.31**	−2.74**
Adult learning								
Formal adult learning	0.06**	0.09**	0.00	0.03**	−0.08**	−0.1**	0.00	−0.01+
Non-formal adult learning	−0.06**	−0.04**	0.02*	0.04**	0.05*	−0.01	0.09**	−0.01
Tertiary education	0.02**	−0.04**	0.07**	0.06**	0.41**	0.34**	0.43**	0.28**
Vocational upper sec.	0.72**	0.82**	0.73**	0.84**	−0.44**	−0.48**	−0.36**	−0.39**
General upper sec.	−0.27**	−0.23**	0.00	0.09**	0.58**	0.56**	0.26**	0.28**
Qualification (ref. lower secondary degree)								
No educational qualification	–	−0.15**	–	−0.18**	–	0.06**	–	0.03**
Upper secondary degree	–	0.19**	–	0.25**	–	−0.07**	–	−0.03**
A-level	–	0.15**	–	0.18**	–	0.15**	–	0.28**
Tertiary degree	–	0.61**	–	0.51**	–	−0.31**	–	−0.08**
Events	4 990 209	4 990 209	4 526 855	4 526 855	1 302 525	1 302 525	1 063 878	1 063 878
Total episodes	7 533 289	7 533 289	6 912 175	6 912 175	7 533 289	7 533 289	6 912 175	6 912 175
Censored episodes	2 543 080	2 543 080	2 38 5320	2 385 320	6 230 764	6 230 764	5 848 297	5 848 297
Log likelihood	−6 729 916	−6 556 460	−6 274 307	−6 170 953	−3 825 389	−3 749 374	−3 263 762	−3 224 079

Notes: ** p < 0.01, * p < 0.05, + p < 0.10. In our models, we additionally control for birth cohort, age, age squared, and migrant status.

Source: Own calculations based on the IDA.

CONCLUSION

The aim of our empirical study was to investigate patterns of adult learning as well as its impact on labor market outcomes in Denmark. In accordance with our first hypothesis, the analyses show that adult learning activities in Denmark are strongly frequented due to the fact that about 77 per cent of our sample participated at least once in some kind of adult learning after labor market entry. Those who took part in adult learning were mainly between 26 and 40 years old, followed by the age group 25 or younger. We also found that formal activities are the most popular and that the average person taking part in adult learning was between the ages of 26 and 40. Furthermore, as we hypothesized, it is not uncommon that persons are able to significantly upgrade their initial level of qualification by reentering the mainstream educational system. Regarding the gender perspective, we found that Danish women are more likely to participate in adult learning than men, which is in line with the gendered participation hypothesis. Another interesting finding in relation to the chances of participating in adult learning is that less-qualified individuals holding a lower secondary degree almost consistently show a higher probability of participation in adult learning. Therefore (and as expected by our second hypothesis), it can be said that adult learning in Denmark not only fosters gender equality, but it also leads to a partial equalization of previously experienced educational inequalities.

With regard to labor market returns to adult learning, the results confirm our third hypothesis, which predicted that gains from both formal adult learning and mainstream educational programs should prove to be the greatest. Our findings indicate that attending formal activities pays off most of all, and this fact applies to all of the examined outcomes and almost always to both genders.

Concerning adult learning in the form of returning to the educational system, vocational upper secondary education constitutes the most valuable type of educational upgrading. Interestingly, non-formal adult learning only plays a significant role in terms of upward mobility, on which it exerts a negative effect among men and a positive one in the case of women. Finally, for all three labor market outcomes studied, more highly qualified individuals profited from the most ideal conditions. As a result of our investigation, it is obvious that investing in education from the outset is an important means of enhancing labor market returns.

REFERENCES

Andersen, Torben M. and Michael Svarer (2006), 'Flexicurity – the Danish labour market model', *Working Paper*, University of Aarhus, Denmark.

Andersen, T. M. and M. Svarer (2007), 'Flexicurity – labour market performance in Denmark', *CESifo Economic Studies*, **53** (3), 389–429.

Bredgaard, T., F. Larsen, P. K. Madsen and S. Rasmussen (2009), 'Flexicurity und atypische Beschäftigung in Dänemark' (Flexicurity and atypical employment in Denmark), *WSI-Mitteilungen*, **62** (1), 31–8.

Commission of the European Communities (ed.) (2011), *Progress towards the common European objectives in education and training. Indicators and benchmarks 2010/2011*, Luxembourg: Publications Office of the European Union.

Cort, P. (2002), 'Das Berufsbildungssystem in Dänemark' (The occupational training system in Denmark), *Cedefop panorama series*, Luxemburg: Amt für amtliche Veröffentlichungen der Europäischen Gemeinschaften.

Cox, R. H. (1998), 'From safety net to trampoline. Labor market activation in the Netherlands and Denmark', *Governance*, **11** (4), 397–414.

Danish Agency for Universities and Internationalisation (ed.) (2011), *The Danish Education System*, published with support from the European Commission.

Dieckhoff, M. (2007), 'Does it work? The effect of continuing training on labour market outcomes: a comparative study of Germany, Denmark and the UK', *European Sociological Review*, **23** (3), 295–308.

Ebralidze, Ellen (2008), 'Weaker entries – lower risk of unemployment: labor market entry trends in Denmark between 1981 and 2003' (together with Søren Leth-Sørensen), in Hans-Peter Blossfeld, Sandra Buchholz, Erzsébet Bukodi and Karin Kurz (eds), *Young Workers, Globalization and the Labor Market Comparing Early Working Life in Eleven Countries*, Cheltenham, UK and Northampton, MA, USA: Edward Elgar, pp. 259–85.

Eriksson, Tor and Niels Westergaard-Nielsen (2008), 'Wage and labor mobility in Denmark, 1980–2000', in Edward P. Lazear and Kathryn L. Shaw (eds), *The Structure of Wages: An International Comparison,* University of Chicago Press, pp. 101–23.

Georgiadis, F. and A. Zisimos (2010), 'South/North "dichotomies" of lifelong learning discourses: traditionalism versus modernism in Greek and Danish adult education policies', *Occasional Papers in Education and Lifelong Learning – an international journal*, **4** (1&2), 5–30.

Grunow, Daniela and Søren Leth-Sørensen (2004), 'Women's employment in Denmark: Are Danish women's careers marked by globalization?', *GLOBALIFE Working paper series*, No. 52, Bamberg University, Germany.

Hoheisel, Miriam (2007), 'Gleichstellungspolitik in Dänemark' (Equal opportunities policy in Denmark), GenderKompetenzZentrum, Humboldt-University, Berlin, Germany.

Jørgensen, Jan Reitz (ed.) (2007), 'Denmark's strategy for lifelong learning– Education and lifelong skills upgrading for all', *Report to the European Commission*, Danish Ministry of Education, Department of Adult Vocational Training, Division for Lifelong Learning.

Keogh, Helen (2009), *The state and development of adult learning and education in Europe, North America and Israel,* Regional synthesis report, Hamburg: UNESCO Institute for Lifelong Learning.

Kildal, Nanna (ed.) (2001), *Workfare Tendencies in Scandinavian Welfare Policies,* Geneva: International Labour Office.

Kulawik, Teresa (2005), 'Wohlfahrtsstaaten und Geschlechterregime im internationalen Vergleich' (Welfare states and gender regimes in international comparison), *gender...politik...online.* January 2005, online: »http://web.fu-berlin.de/gpo/pdf/kulawik/kulawik.pdf« (1.9.2013).

Kvist, J. and B. Greve (2011), 'Has the Nordic welfare model been transformed?', *Social Policy & Administration,* **2** (45), 146–60.

Madsen, Per Kongshøj (1999), 'Denmark: flexibility, security and labour market success', *Employment and Training Working Papers,* No. 53, ILO, Geneva, Switzerland.

Madsen, Per Kongshøj (2002), 'The Danish model of flexicurity: a paradise – with some snakes', in Hedva Sarfati and Giuliano Bonoli (eds), *Labour Market and Social Protections Reforms in International Perspective: Parallel or Converging Tracks?* Aldershot: Ashgate, pp. 243–65.

OECD (2011), *Education at a Glance 2011: OECD Indicators,* Paris: OECD Publishing.

Plougmann, Peter and Per Kongshøj Madsen (2002), 'Flexibility, employment development and active labour market policy in Denmark and Sweden in the 1990s', *CEPA Working Paper,* Center for Economic Policy Analysis, New School University, New York, USA.

Powel, M. and A. Barrientos (2004), 'Welfare regimes and welfare mix', *European Journal of Political Research,* **43** (1), 83–105.

Sprogoe, Jonas (ed.) (2003), *Comparative Analysis of Lifelong Learning Strategies and their Implementation in Denmark, Estonia, Finland, Iceland, Latvia, Lithuania, Norway, Sweden,* Copenhagen: The Danish University of Education.

UNESCO Institute for Lifelong Learning (ed.) (2009), *Global Report on Adult Learning and Education,* Hamburg: UNESCO Institute for Lifelong Learning.

12. Reinforcing Social Inequalities? Adult Learning and Returns to Adult Learning in Germany

Sandra Buchholz, Julia Unfried, and Hans-Peter Blossfeld

INTRODUCTION

Attention toward education has strongly increased in Germany, especially since the disappointing results of PISA 2000. As a consequence, public investments in education have grown over the past years. However, it must be mentioned that up to now, reforms and debates have mainly addressed early childhood education, schooling, and tertiary education (Deiss 2011). So far, little attention has been paid toward improving adult learning and educational opportunities for persons who have already entered the labor market – surprisingly enough, though, such efforts would target the largest part of the population.

From an economic point of view, neglecting education for adults is not very forward-looking for modern societies since it has become more and more important for countries to keep the qualifications of the workforce up to date over its whole life course. Ongoing accelerated economic change and tertiarization under globalization have increased the economic need for adult and lifelong learning (Buchholz, Hofäcker and Blossfeld 2006). Additionally, demographic aging structurally enforces the necessity for continued training due to the fact that labor markets will face significant labor shortages in coming years (Buchholz 2008; Blossfeld, Buchholz and Kurz 2011). Furthermore, the latest pension reforms, which expect older persons in Germany to prolong their working life, demand growing investments in the constant (re)training of adults in order to secure their employability (Buchholz 2008; Buchholz et al. 2011).

In addition to these economic needs, adult learning is also highly important from a social inequality point of view. It is well known and well documented that education has a powerful impact on individuals' life chances in modern societies, such as on their labor market trajectories (Müller and Shavit 1998). Adult learning can serve as a powerful mechanism for reducing previously experienced educational inequalities. Social inequalities can be reduced in countries that allow individuals at all points in life to upgrade the level of education and to correct previous educational decisions later in life. In contrast, in countries that have no or only highly selective adult learning systems, previously experienced educational inequalities are persistent and can increase over the course of life. It is also highly important for policy-makers to understand which programs of adult learning and training are successful and which are not.

Though some research on adult learning and further training in Germany already exists (Wilkens and Leber 2003; Bundesministerium für Bildung und Forschung 2010), it is notable that there has not yet been a systematic empirical study that simultaneously investigates both *patterns* of adult learning and *returns* to adult learning. Our chapter thereby aims to analyze adult learning patterns and returns to adult learning in Germany. Specifically, we analyze what forms of adult learning and training are predominant in Germany, who has access to the various programs of adult learning, and how participation in adult learning and training improves individuals' labor market chances. Our analyses are based on the adult cohort of the National Educational Panel Study (NEPS),[1] which offers detailed information on individuals' educational, training, and employment biographies for successive birth cohorts.

In this chapter, we proceed as follows: First, we describe the German institutional setting and its influence on shaping adult learning patterns and labor market returns to continued training. Based on this institutional description, we derive general hypotheses of our empirical analyses. After presenting our research design, data, and methods, we introduce the results of our analyses and then conclude with a summary and discussion of our findings.

INSTITUTIONAL CONTEXT

Educational System, Adult Learning, and Occupational Boundaries

The German educational system is known for being highly standardized and stratified (Allmendinger 1989). This applies to both the general schooling system as well as to the system of vocational training. In school, stratification starts at a comparatively early age, i.e., around 10. At this stage, pupils are sorted into three different tracks of secondary schooling – i.e., lower secondary schools (*Hauptschulen*), middle secondary schools (*Realschulen*), and upper secondary schools (*Gymnasien*). Young persons usually achieve access to tertiary education by completing upper secondary schooling; however, there are also new, alternative routes to entering a university through vocational training.

General schooling is usually followed by vocational training or attendance at a college or university. Compared with other modern societies, the share of those with tertiary education in Germany is still relatively low because this sector concentrates on academic education only. Thus, the vocational training sector is comparatively strong and equips participants with high-quality certificates that function as signals for employers in the labor market. Vocational training usually takes place within the so-called dual system, which combines practical learning in a firm with theoretical learning in vocational schools. Successful participants of the German vocational training system receive a standardized occupational certificate, which allows them to move easily between firms. However, this system also hinders mobility between occupations because the training is highly occupation-specific and the strong standardization and stratification of occupational certificates creates hurdles for those without certificates as well as for those without the appropriate certificate. Consequently, occupational boundaries are very strong in the German labor market. Furthermore, internationally comparative research has shown that Germany belongs to those countries in which educational inequalities are strongly reproduced in the labor market (Müller and Shavit 1998). Though all countries display strong job prestige differences between various educational levels, Germany is among the countries with the highest labor market returns to initial education.

In addition, the educational system in Germany is characterized by being strongly youth-oriented (Blossfeld and Stockmann 1999). Fully-qualifying educational and vocational training usually takes place at young ages. Against this background, it is not surprising that the share of working-age persons participating in education and training in Germany is very low and decreases with individuals' age (Eurostat 2013). Instead, learning and education after labor market entry take place primarily outside the formal educational and training system. While the level of standardization of education is high during the youth phase, this is not the case with respect to adult learning and training. As a consequence, programs tend to be very heterogeneous. On the one hand, there are welfare-supported training programs, the so-called vocational preparation courses. These training programs, offered by employment agencies, mainly target persons with labor market problems and do not equip participants with fully-qualifying professional degrees. On the other hand, there are occupation-specific add-on training programs. While such add-on trainings also fail to equip participants with fully-qualifying professional degrees, they are much more widely recognized by employers, especially if these add-on trainings are standardized and equip participants with valuable signals for the highly occupation-specific German labor market. It must be noted, however, that these occupational add-on trainings are usually closely tied to the workplace and aim at complementing participants' previously achieved occupational degrees. Hence, such trainings mainly target persons who obtained a vocational training certificate during their youth, and they allow participants to expand upon their already-existing vocational degree. As a matter of fact, access to such courses is strongly dependent on persons' initial educational level.

Welfare Regime, Support for Vulnerable Sub-Groups, and Gendered Careers

Germany belongs to the so-called conservative welfare regime. This regime is characterized by a strong transfer-orientation and to a lesser extent by a full-employment ideology (Esping-Andersen 1990, 1999). This means that the German welfare state puts little emphasis on active labor market programs that promote the (re)employment chances of persons with labor market problems and is instead oriented toward paying generous transfers to vulnerable labor market groups. Typical examples of the strong transfer-orientation of the German welfare state include comparatively generous early retirement payments and long-lasting unemployment benefit payments.[2] Public expenditures on different labor market programs thus mainly support out-of-work income maintenance rather than adult learning or activating employment schemes.

Moreover, the German welfare state hardly supports reentering the regular and formal educational and vocational training system for adults. Instead, the welfare state has built up a parallel system with very heterogeneous training programs that are mainly offered by regional and local employment agencies. These programs are hardly standardized and, as a result, these trainings do not equip participants with recognized certificates or clear labor market signals. Additionally, participation in these courses does not qualify persons to get access to jobs that demand occupational training within the German vocational training system (this applies to the majority of qualified jobs in Germany). Hence, these training programs only offer qualifications below the qualifying level for an occupation. Since occupational definitions and boundaries are very strong in Germany, participants in such courses receive certificates that exhibit minimal exchange value in the occupationally highly standardized and specified German labor market.

Besides the low emphasis on active labor market policies, the conservative welfare regime is characterized by a specific and rather traditional gender contract that is marked by the assumption that women will take over unpaid care-giving tasks for the family (Esping-Andersen 1990, 1999; Orloff 1993). Typical examples of the German welfare state's support of this traditional gender contract include relatively generous maternity leave regulations, tax legislations favoring the male breadwinner or the 1.5 earner model instead of the dual earner model for families, low early childcare coverage rates, and a mostly half-day oriented kindergarten and schooling system. As a consequence, women's careers in Germany tend to be marked by employment interruptions as well as by high rates of part-time employment after family formation. This applies especially to West Germany, whereas in East Germany – because of its socialist past – women's labor market attachment tends to be significantly higher (see, for example, Falk and Schaeper 2001; German Statistical Office 2006). In sum, a trade-off between work and family is characteristic of female labor market participation in Germany (Buchholz and Grunow 2006; Grunow 2006). Women's mid-career phase is not defined as clearly as is the case for men (Mayer 1991; Lauterbach 1994).

Type of Economy, Employment Structures, and the Unequal Distribution of Training Opportunities

Germany belongs to the coordinated market economies (Mayer 1997; Soskice 1999). Such economies tend to have rather regulated labor markets that display a low level of general labor market mobility and employment flexibility. In contrast to uncoordinated economies (which are typically found in Anglo-Saxon countries), labor market partners invest in long-term and trust-based relationships. Employers are encouraged to maintain lasting relationships with their employees, and the state plays a framework-setting role of protecting persons with continuous employment careers. Typical institutional characteristics of the German economy include influential unions and works councils, strong employment protection regulation, seniority systems, and an active role of employers in educating and training their employees.

However, as a consequence of the aforementioned structural characteristics, these economies can be characterized as so-called insider/outsider labor markets with closed employment relationships, especially if the state does not actively support (full) employment. Employers tend to invest in securing and privileging the labor market insiders with strong ties to the labor market and the work organization. These insiders are typically middle-aged men with continuous employment careers in Germany (Mills, Blossfeld and Bernardi 2006). On the other hand, employers offer less-favorable positions and working conditions to outsiders of the labor market, especially to those with discontinuous employment careers, those who lack work experience, and those with weaker ties to work organizations and firms (such as women and/or mothers and the unemployed). Hence, work experience and being an insider of the labor market are crucial factors that pay off in Germany.

Additionally, the closed employment structures in Germany have a strong impact on employers' decisions regarding the parts of their workforce to which they offer additional occupational training. This training is, in contrast to state-supported training, of comparatively high importance for adults in Germany. However, due to the dominance of long-lasting employment relationships, it is in the employers' interest to invest in their permanent employees' skills development (Dieckhoff, Jungblut and O'Connell 2007). These permanent employees tend to consist of men as the classical insiders of the German labor market. For the outsiders, however, the situation is very different. Since their ties to the labor market are weaker and they cannot easily access internal labor markets, they are likely dependent on publicly offered adult learning opportunities, which are, as outlined above, hardly recognized by employers. Furthermore, there is a high risk that initial educational degrees lose their value once a person becomes non-employed.

HYPOTHESES

Based on the German institutional setting, we have derived the following general hypotheses for our empirical analyses:

1. Because of the strong youth-orientation of the general education and vocational training system, we expect that most persons in our sample do not participate in any form of structured or formalized learning after their entry into the labor market.
2. Participation in educational programs that would allow persons to upgrade their initial level of qualification (by entering secondary schooling or tertiary education) should be rather rare. Instead, further training should mainly take place through participation in certified occupational trainings that are, however, strongly bound to persons' workplaces and to their employers. These trainings display a strong practical orientation; therefore, we expect that such trainings do not usually target persons with tertiary education but mainly persons holding a medium level of education at labor market entry. Welfare-supported training programs (so-called vocational preparation) should, on the other hand, mainly concentrate on those least qualified.

3. As a result of rather traditional gender roles in Germany, we expect women in our sample to participate less in additional education and training. Instead, it should be men, the classical insiders of the labor market, who receive the most valuable additional training after labor market entry.
4. Gains from adult learning should be high for those participating in standardized occupational training programs since only such courses equip participants with recognized certificates. In contrast, gains from welfare-supported (re)training programs (i.e., vocational preparation courses) should be very low. Such trainings are very heterogeneous and hardly standardized. Moreover, they are not embedded in the regular and recognized German vocational training system. As a consequence, such trainings do not equip participants with valuable labor market signals. Instead, participation in such programs might even be disadvantageous for persons because it could be interpreted as a negative signal by employers.
5. Taking these expectations together, Germany should thus display a strong tendency to perpetuate inequalities over the life course.

RESEARCH DESIGN, DATA, AND METHODS

The aim of our empirical study is to analyze adult learning patterns and labor market returns to various forms of adult learning in Germany. Our empirical analyses are based on the adult cohort of the National Educational Panel Study (NEPS). This dataset is a panel study with detailed retrospective monthly information for about 11 000 persons of working age. The NEPS adult cohort contains detailed longitudinal information on the individuals' educational and training trajectories, their employment careers, family histories, and inactivity spells (such as retirement, parental, and sick leave), among other items. The NEPS data covers the birth cohorts from 1944 to 1988.

To study patterns of and returns to adult learning, we defined the risk set for our analyses as follows: To catch episodes of adult learners in Germany, we only included individuals' transitions and events after labor market entry. To properly define individuals' labor market entry, we closed small gaps of up to six months between educational episodes in order to make sure that the persons were actually available in the labor market and not in a 'waiting line' for continuing education – e.g., after school graduation and before starting university or vocational training (Buchholz 2008). For East Germany, we only included persons who experienced their labor market entry after reunification. Based on these definitions, our sample of adult learners consists of persons who experienced their first significant labor market entry (either employed or unemployed) after having left formal education for a minimum of at least seven months. Our sample includes 8 392 individuals.

In our empirical study, we proceed as follows: In the first step, we study patterns of adult learning and inequalities in participating in adult learning in Germany. Specifically, we analyze whether persons in our sample entered training or education after labor market entry. Since the programs of adult learning are very heterogeneous in Germany, we differentiate between the following types of adult learning in our analyses:

1. *Formal secondary schooling* indicates that persons returned to upper secondary schools after labor market entry (for example, to complete the Abitur, which is the major university entrance qualification in Germany).
2. *Vocational preparation courses* are trainings offered by the regional and local employment agencies for persons with labor market problems that equip participants with rather basic qualifications as opposed to fully-qualifying occupational training certificates.
3. *Certified occupational trainings* equip participants with a standardized and recognized vocational certificate. On the one hand, these certified trainings can indeed be fully-qualifying vocational trainings obtained in the dual training system, in full-time vocational schools, or at universities and colleges. On the other hand, these certified trainings can also be occupation-specific add-on trainings that complement a person's already existing, fully-qualifying vocational degree. For example, a computer scientist could obtain a network administrator license; a dental nurse could complement her initial vocational degree with a license for professional tooth cleaning; or a skilled warehouseman could acquire a license for the operation of a forklift. Moreover, certified occupational trainings could refer to trainings that equip persons with a professional mastership certificate that allows them to train apprentices and to use the title *Meister* in Germany. For example, a hairdresser could obtain a mastership in hairdressing or a mechanical engineer could acquire a mastership in mechanical engineering. The *Meister* certificate holds an intermediate position between the two extremes of fully-qualifying certified trainings on the one hand and certified occupation-specific add-on trainings on the other hand. Though our definition of certified occupational trainings includes a broad range of trainings at different levels, we have integrated all these trainings into one category since all of them have in common the fact that they equip participants with standardized and nationally recognized professional certificates, a fact that is very important in the German labor market with its strong occupational boundaries.

4. *Uncertified occupational trainings* are more diffuse and less standardized than certified trainings. Examples for such uncertified trainings include courses offered by employers' organizations (such as the Chamber of Industry and Commerce) in which participants acquire general knowledge, e.g., in marketing, conflict management, or in using new software in an occupational field.

In the second step of our analyses, we investigate labor market returns to these various forms of adult learning by using methods of event-history analysis (Blossfeld and Rohwer 2002). Specifically, we analyze (a) persons' risks of becoming unemployed, (b) their chances of becoming employed after unemployment, and (c) their direct career mobility chances. To study career mobility, we refer to a person's CAMSIS scores. Upward career mobility is characterized by an increase in CAMSIS of at least 5 points; downward career mobility is classified by any decrease in CAMSIS.

We use product limit estimations as the descriptive method for our longitudinal analyses. In our multivariate event history analyses, we implement an approximation of the piecewise constant exponential model by using logistic regression models. In order to take the specific process dynamics into account, we include dummy variables for the different 'time pieces' of the observed processes in our regression models. To account for the effect of gendered career trajectories, we estimate these models separately for men and women.

We include a number of covariates in our multivariate analyses – namely process dynamics (i.e., dummies for the duration of the observed process), birth cohorts, age and age squared, characteristics of the previous employment career (e.g., labor force experience, number of previous unemployment episodes, number of previous jobs), job characteristics (e.g., permanent or fixed-term contract as well as working hours), and region (East and West Germany). While we estimate the effects for all mentioned variables, as a matter of simplicity we only display the effects for persons' educational level and participation in different forms of adult learning in our tables since these are the relevant variables to our research question.

RESULTS

Participation in Various Forms of Adult Learning

Figure 12.1 gives a descriptive overview of whether or not persons in our sample reentered education or training at least once after labor market entry. As

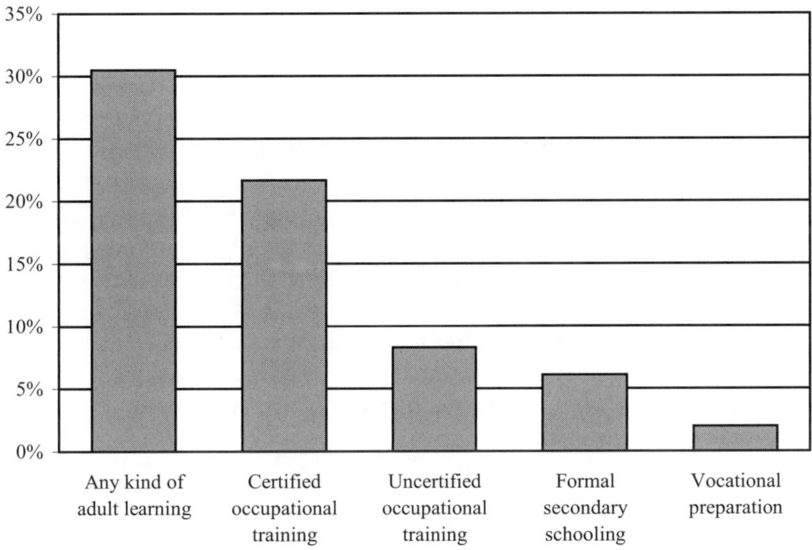

Notes: Figure 12.1 displays persons in our sample who reentered education at least once in their lives after labor market entry. Persons may have entered more than one form of adult learning after their labor market entry, and they may have participated in programs more than once.

Source: Own calculations based on the NEPS adult cohort.

Figure 12.1 Participation in different forms of education and training after labor market entry

can be seen, only about 30 per cent of our sample entered any kind of training after labor market entry. Additionally (and as expected), adult learning in Germany rarely takes place by means of formal secondary schooling. Only 6 per cent of the persons in our sample upgraded their initial educational degree by reentering secondary schooling after labor market entry (and these persons were usually very young; see below). Vocational preparation courses are also very rarely attended. Such courses are welfare-supported trainings that only provide training below the professionally qualifying level and specifically target persons with labor market problems as well as the unemployed. Only about 2 per cent of our sample participated in such courses after labor market entry. A bit more common, though also not very widespread, are uncertified occupational trainings, in which about 8 per cent of our sample participated after labor market entry. Additional analyses reveal that such trainings are mainly courses offered by employers' organizations, e.g., the Chamber of Industry and Commerce.

Certified occupational trainings are clearly the most common form of education in which persons participate after their labor market entry. About 22 per cent of the persons in our sample participated at least once in certified occupational trainings after their labor market entry. Further analyses reveal that the vast majority of certified occupational trainings in which employed persons participated were not fully-qualifying professional trainings. Additionally, if a transition to fully-qualifying occupational training occurred at all after persons' labor market entry, it was mainly very young persons who entered such fully-qualifying training. Later in life and when persons have already spent some years in the labor market, such certified trainings are mainly occupation-specific add-on trainings that do not equip participants with a fully-qualifying vocational degree, but 'only' complement participants' already-existing occupational degrees (mainly by enabling them to acquire an additional occupation-specific license or the *Meister* certificate).

All in all, our results support that learning and training after labor market entry is usually related to the workplace in Germany and allows persons to further specialize in their occupational field without having to change their occupation. Moreover, our results show that the majority of the persons in our sample, i.e., about 70 per cent, never participated in any kind of additional education or training after having entered the labor market.

Figure 12.2 presents our empirical results for the age of participants in the various educational and training programs. As can be seen, participants in education and training after labor market entry are mainly persons up to the age of 35, and participation strongly decreases with increasing age. In particular, entering training becomes rare after the age of 45. Very young persons (up to the age of 25 years) are overrepresented in formal secondary schooling. This result can be explained by the fact that reentering the highly youth-oriented German schooling system is easiest for this group. However, youths and young adults are also slightly overrepresented among vocational preparation courses. Though vocational preparation is in principle open for persons of all age groups, German social security legislation puts special efforts into training younger persons up to the age of 25. Persons aged 26 to 35 years are overrepresented among occupational trainings, particularly among uncertified occupational trainings. These descriptive results are also supported by additional multivariate analyses in which we include both age and age squared into our models.

Following this descriptive overview, Table 12.1 presents our multivariate findings for persons' chances of participation in any kind of adult learning (Model 1) as well as in different forms of adult learning (Models 2 to 5) after labor market entry. All in all, the results indicate that adult learning in Germany partially equalizes previously experienced educational inequalities. Persons

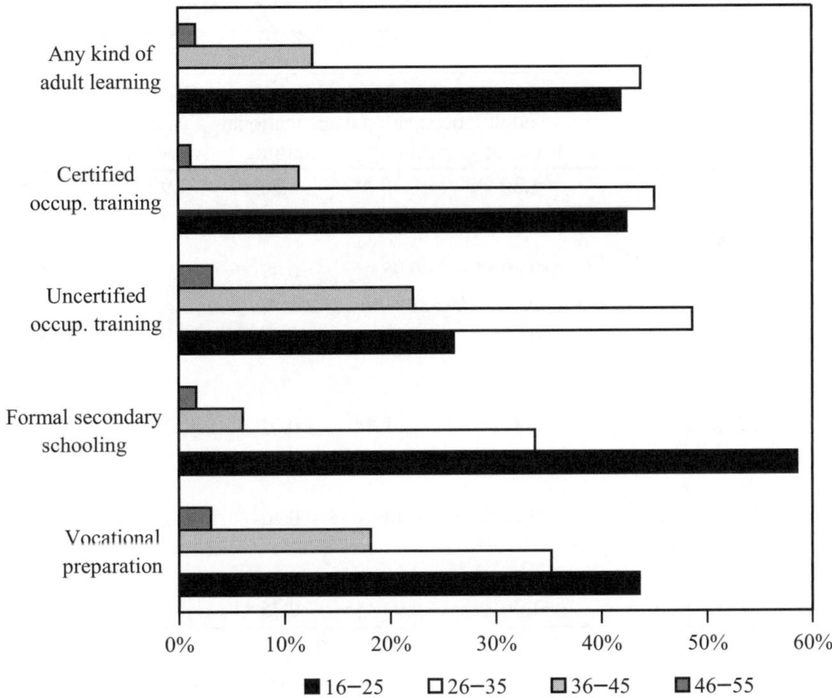

Notes: Persons aged 56 years and older did not participate in any kind of education or training. Therefore, results for persons beyond the age of 55 years are not displayed in our figure.

Source: Own calculations based on the NEPS adult cohort.

Figure 12.2 Participants' age in different forms of education and training

with tertiary education (who already display the highest level of education that individuals can achieve) participated significantly less in adult learning after their labor market entry, whereas persons who held a medium qualification degree at labor market entry were most likely to receive valuable education or training thereafter (Model 1). Compared with individuals holding a lower secondary degree with vocational training at labor market entry, persons holding middle or upper secondary school degrees were most likely to upgrade their initial educational level by participating in certified occupation-specific training or reentering formal secondary schooling (Models 2 and 4). Indeed, persons with middle or upper secondary degrees and without vocational training were most likely to try to upgrade their initial level of education by earning

Table 12.1 Chances of participating in different forms of education and training after labor market entry (logistic regression models)

	Any kind of adult learning	Certified occupational training	Uncertified occupational training	Formal sec. schooling	Vocational preparation
Constant	−1.20 **	−0.38 **	−1.76 **	−1.92 **	−4.08 **
Gender (ref. men)					
Women	−0.89 **	−0.98 **	−0.47 **	−0.97 **	0.06
Qualification (ref. lower secondary degree with vocational training)					
Lower secondary without vocational training	0.21	0.10	−0.24	0.29	1.73 **
Middle or upper secondary without vocational training	0.82 **	1.08 **	−0.02	−0.20	0.36
Middle or upper secondary with vocational training	0.17 *	0.13	0.16	0.28 *	−0.20
Tertiary degree	−1.00 **	−0.94 **	−0.45 **	−4.73 **	−0.88 *
Individuals	8 392	8 392	8 392	8 392	8 392
Log likelihood	−4 486	−3 617	−2 245	−1 692	−660

Notes: ** p < 0.01, * p < 0.05, + p < 0.10. In our models, we additionally control for birth cohorts and region (East vs. West Germany).

Source: Own calculations based on the NEPS adult cohort.

a tertiary degree shortly after their labor market entry. However, it must be noted that the share of these persons was very low. Among our entire sample, only about 6 per cent of persons entered tertiary education after having left the educational system for at least six months. For vocational preparation courses, our results support the assumption that these trainings mainly concentrate on persons with labor market problems, namely the least-qualified persons who hold only a lower secondary schooling degree without vocational training.

Regarding gender differences, our multivariate findings show that women's chances of participation in adult learning after labor market entry are significantly lower than those of men (with the exception of vocational preparation courses, for which we do not find significant gender differences). All in all, we thus find that adult learning in Germany contributes to establishing gender inequalities. Men, who are part of the core workforce within the closed German insider/

outsider labor market, succeed most often in acquiring additional education or training after labor market entry.

Labor Market Returns to Various Forms of Adult Learning

In the next step of our empirical study, we investigate the labor market returns to various forms of adult learning in Germany by applying techniques of event history analysis.

Risks of unemployment

Table 12.2 presents the results of our longitudinal analyses for individuals' risk of becoming unemployed. For men, we find a clear pattern: Participating in certified occupational training significantly reduces their risk of becoming unemployed. As noted above, such trainings for employed persons are mainly occupation-specific add-on trainings, not fully-qualifying occupational trainings. All in all, the significant influence of certified occupational trainings supports our assumption that certified adult training pays off to the greatest extent in the occupationally highly specific and standardized German labor market. For women, however, we do not find a strong and clear effect of certified occupational training. Women not only have worse chances than men to receive such training (see our results presented in Table 12.1), but they also profit less from such training since they are not able to convert participation in certified occupational training into a significant reduction of their unemployment risk. This result highlights the fact that the German labor market works very differently for men and women.

Vocational preparation courses generally increase men's and women's risk of becoming unemployed (Model 1). Participating in such courses, which are welfare-supported trainings that offer training below a fully-qualifying professional degree, is clearly worse than not participating in any kind of further education and training at all. Hence, these subsidized trainings fail at securely integrating persons with labor market problems into the labor market. Such courses even increase participants' risk of becoming unemployed (again).

Regarding persons' level of education (Model 2), our results show that a higher qualification significantly reduces the risk of becoming unemployed for men. This finding supports our assumption that Germany has a strong tendency to transfer educational inequalities to the labor market. Individuals are hardly able to significantly upgrade their initial level of education (see our results presented above), and unemployment risks are clearly stratified by the (initial) level of individuals' qualification. For women, the effect of qualification is less pronounced. We find a substantial negative effect only for those with tertiary

Table 12.2 Unemployment risks (logistic regression models)

	Men		Women	
	1	2	1	2
Adult learning (ref. no further education or training)				
Certified occupational training	−0.73 **	−0.69 **	−0.37 +	−0.32
Uncertified occupational training	−0.07	−0.07	0.23	0.26
Formal secondary schooling	−0.29	−0.31	0.31	0.33
Vocational preparation	2.77 *	2.68 *	1.76 *	1.82 *
Qualification (ref. lower secondary degree with vocational training)				
Lower secondary without vocational training	−	0.60 **	−	−0.03
Middle or upper secondary without vocational training	−	−0.27 +	−	−0.26 +
Middle or upper secondary with vocational training	−	−0.27 **	−	−0.15
Tertiary degree	−	−0.78 **	−	−0.35 *
Events	2 594	2 594	2 813	2 813
Total episodes	8 799	8 799	11 684	11 684
Censored episodes	6 205	6 205	8 871	8 871
Log likelihood	−6 325	−6 237	−6 572	−6 510

Notes: ** p < 0.01, * p < 0.05, + p < 0.10. In our models, we additionally control for the duration in the current employment episode, birth cohorts, region (East vs. West Germany), age, age squared, contract (fixed-term vs. permanent contract), and working hours.

Source: Own calculations based on the NEPS adult cohort.

education. Women are clearly unable to gain from adult learning, and they demonstrate lower returns to initial education.

Though the effects are not displayed in Table 12.2, it must be noted that duration in employment pays off differently for men and women in Germany. Whereas men experience a significant reduction of unemployment risks with increasing employment experience, this trend is less the case for women. Women also face a relatively high risk of becoming unemployed even after a longer time in employment. Apparently, it is harder for women to transform their employment experience into employment security and protection against unemployment. This finding is also supported by additional product-limit estimations. Again, this result supports our assumption that gender-specific logics exist in the German labor market.

Table 12.3 Employment chances of the unemployed (logistic regression models)

	Men		Women	
	1	2	1	2
Adult learning (ref. no further education or training)				
Certified occupational training	−0.19	−0.20	0.13	0.01
Uncertified occupational training	−0.55 +	−0.57 +	−0.37	−0.41
Formal secondary schooling	0.32	0.30	0.77 **	0.75 **
Vocational preparation	−0.84 *	−0.85 *	−0.39	−0.39
Qualification (ref. lower secondary degree with vocational training)				
Lower secondary without vocational training	−	−0.81 **	−	−0.04
Middle or upper secondary without vocational training	−	−0.32 +	−	0.15
Middle or upper secondary with vocational training	−	0.04	−	0.38 **
Tertiary degree	−	0.37 **	−	0.74 **
Events	2 853	2 853	3 122	3 122
Total episodes	3 881	3 881	4 413	4 413
Censored episodes	1 028	1 028	1 291	1 291
Log likelihood	−3 459	−3 366	−4 303	−4 241

Notes: ** p < 0.01, * p < 0.05, + p < 0.10. In our models, we additionally control for the duration of the current unemployment episode, birth cohorts, region (East vs. West Germany), age, age squared, previous labor force experience, the number of previous unemployment episodes, and the characteristics of the previous job (fixed-term vs. permanent contract and working hours).

Source: Own calculations based on the NEPS adult cohort.

Employment chances of the unemployed

In the next step, we focus on the chances of unemployed persons to become employed. The results of our longitudinal analyses are reported in Table 12.3. As our analyses show, certified occupational training, which substantially reduces men's risks of becoming unemployed (see Table 12.2), does not help unemployed men to become employed. Acquiring additional certified occupational training is obviously only valuable for men if they are labor market insiders. Participating in uncertified occupational training during unemployment even slightly worsens unemployed men's chances of becoming employed. We again find that vocational preparation worsens men's labor market chances. Men who participate in such welfare-supported training courses have a significantly higher risk of remaining unemployed than do men who do not participate in any kind of training while unemployed. For unemployed women, we find a significantly positive effect for participation in secondary schooling during unemployment. Women are obviously able to escape unemployment by reentering secondary schooling.

Again, the initial level of individuals' qualification significantly impacts their chances of leaving unemployment. This is true for both men and women. It must be noted, however, that there is less variance among men with different levels of initial qualification for ending unemployment, whereas there is much more variance for the risks of becoming unemployed (see Table 12.2). Therefore, the initial level of qualification also seems to lose some of its promotional value once men become unemployed in the German insider/outsider labor market. Though the coefficients are not displayed in Table 12.3, it must be noted that men's previous employment status also strongly impacts their chances of becoming employed. If men have been permanently employed (i.e., have been labor market insiders), they enjoy significantly better chances of leaving unemployment again. This, however, is not the case for women. If women have been permanently employed before, they are not able to improve their chances of leaving unemployment.

Direct career mobility

In the final step of our analysis, we investigate individuals' direct career mobility chances. Table 12.4 presents the results for upward and downward career mobility.

For men, participation in vocational preparation courses significantly decreases both upward and downward mobility. This result can be explained by the fact that vocational preparation for men is often followed by unemployment (see Table 12.2). Consequently, participation in vocational preparation hinders any kind of direct career mobility among men. For women, the picture is different. Women participating in vocational preparation courses show higher chances of both upward and downward career mobility. However, in contrast to men, women do not show a higher risk of unemployment after participating in vocational preparation courses (see Table 12.2 above). Additionally, we find a positive effect of certified occupational training on women's upward career mobility. For women, this kind of occupational training improves their career chances. For men, we do not find such an effect.

Taking these findings together with our analyses of unemployment risks (Table 12.2), we can thus summarize the role of certified occupational training as follows: While men's participation in this kind of training increases their level of employment security (since it significantly reduces their unemployment risks; see Table 12.2), certified occupational training improves women's career chances (see Table 12.4) but not their level of employment

Table 12.4 Direct career mobility (logistic regression models)

	Men		Women	
	1	2	1	2
	Upward mobility			
Adult learning (ref. no further education or training)				
Certified occupational training	−0.06	−0.08	0.55 *	0.49 *
Uncertified occupational training	−0.29	−0.28	−0.32	−0.35
Formal secondary schooling	0.22	0.16	−0.18	−0.19
Vocational preparation	−14.50 **	−14.40 **	2.03 **	2.37 **
Qualification (ref. lower secondary degree with vocational training)				
Lower secondary without vocational training	−	−0.62 +	−	−0.60 *
Middle or upper secondary without vocational training	−	0.16	−	0.21
Middle or upper secondary with vocational training	−	0.41 **	−	0.34 *
Tertiary degree	−	0.87 **	−	1.01 **
	Downward mobility			
Adult learning (ref. no further education or training)				
Certified occupational training	−0.23	−0.15	−0.45	−0.45
Uncertified occupational training	−0.72	−0.71	−1.31	−1.31
Formal secondary schooling	−13.86 **	−13.84 **	−0.40	−0.39
Vocational preparation	−14.29 **	−13.85 **	2.58 **	2.78 **
Qualification (ref. lower secondary degree with vocational training)				
Lower secondary without vocational training	−	0.42	−	0.22
Middle or upper secondary without vocational training	−	−0.87 **	−	−0.13
Middle or upper secondary with vocational training	−	−0.28 *	−	−0.18
Tertiary degree	−	−0.51 **	−	−0.38 +
Upward mobility events	1 758	1 758	1 320	1 320
Downward mobility events	1 781	1 781	1 334	1 334
Total episodes	17 461	17 461	17 572	17 572
Censored episodes	13 922	13 922	14 918	14 918
Log likelihood	−21 756	−21 647	−17 985	−17 898

Notes: ** p < 0.01, * p < 0.05, + p < 0.10. In our models, we additionally control for the duration in the current the job episode, birth cohorts, region (East vs. West Germany), age, age squared, contract (fixed-term vs. permanent contract), working hours, previous number of jobs, labor force experience, and CAMSIS of the current job.

Source: Own calculations based on the NEPS adult cohort.

security (see Table 12.2). While certified occupational training is important for women's career chances, men significantly profit from participation in formal secondary schooling while employed. Formal secondary schooling substantially reduces men's risk of downward mobility.

A higher level of qualification significantly improves both men's and women's chances of being upwardly mobile. Individuals who hold middle or upper secondary degrees with vocational training as well as those with tertiary education have better chances of upward mobility compared with persons holding a lower secondary degree with vocational training. In contrast, the least qualified (i.e., persons holding only a lower secondary degree without vocational training) are the least upwardly mobile. While a higher level of qualification improves men's and women's upward career chances, higher qualification has a protective function against downward mobility only for men. Women are instead either not or far less able to use their initial level of education as a safeguard against downward career mobility.

CONCLUSION

The aim of our empirical study was to investigate adult learning patterns and returns to adult learning in Germany. Our analyses show that the majority of individuals in our sample, i.e., about 70 per cent, never reenter any kind of structured and more formalized education or training after labor market entry. Additionally, those 30 per cent who receive education or training after their labor market entry mainly participate in occupation-specific training, which is usually certified. This fact is not surprising since the German labor market is well-known for holding certificates in high regard. It must be noted that such occupational training in adult life is mainly occupation-specific add-on training and hence does not allow persons to change their occupational field. Instead, such training 'only' complements persons' initial vocational training certificates. Entries into educational programs that would allow persons to significantly upgrade their initial educational level (by aspiring to a higher secondary schooling degree or by entering tertiary education) are very rare once persons have left the educational system for more than six months. If such educational programs are begun at all, it is mainly very young persons who (re)enter secondary schooling or tertiary education. Moreover, those who are least qualified at the time of their labor market entry are least likely to receive valuable additional training and education afterward. Instead, the least-qualified persons are dependent on welfare-supported training programs that, however, are not well-recognized in the labor market. Indeed, our analyses show that participation in such welfare-supported training programs is even worse than not receiving any additional training at all, especially for men.

In terms of returns to adult learning, our analyses demonstrate that participating in certified occupational training is quite valuable. However, even more significant than participating in further education or training is a person's initial level of education. Moreover, our analyses reveal that being continuously employed (as a method of learning informally on the job) is a crucial factor in Germany. Once persons become unemployed or if persons are (perceived as) potential outsiders (as is the case for women), educational degrees seem to pay off less. All in all, our results indicate that the German system prolongs and partly even reinforces already-existing social inequalities. Adult learning is not able to substantially reduce previously experienced educational inequalities since those who would need further training (i.e., persons who display very low qualification at the time of labor market entry) hardly receive valuable additional training thereafter.

NOTES

1. This paper uses data from the National Educational Panel Study (NEPS): Starting Cohort 6 – Adults (Adult Education and Lifelong Learning), doi:10.5157/NEPS:SC6:1.0.0. The NEPS data collection is part of the framework program for the promotion of empirical educational research, funded by the German Federal Ministry of Education and Research and supported by the Federal States.
2. However, there have been cutbacks in both early pension regulations and unemployment benefit payments in the more recent past. Still, even after these cutbacks, the German welfare state continues to offer relatively generous transfer payments.

REFERENCES

Allmendinger, J. (1989), 'Educational systems and labor market outcomes', *European Sociological Review*, **5** (3), 231–50.

Blossfeld, Hans-Peter and Götz Rohwer (2002), *Techniques of Event History Modeling*, London: Lawrence Erlbaum Associates.

Blossfeld, H.-P. and R. Stockmann (1999), 'The German dual system in comparative perspective', *International Journal of Sociology*, **28** (4), 3–28.

Blossfeld, Hans-Peter, Sandra Buchholz and Karin Kurz (eds) (2011), *Aging Populations, Globalization and the Labor Market: Comparing Late Working Life and Retirement in Modern Societies*, Cheltenham, UK and Northampton, MA, USA: Edward Elgar.

Blossfeld, Hans-Peter, Hans-Günther Roßbach, and Jutta von Maurice (eds) (2011), 'Education as a Lifelong Process – The German National Educational Panel Study (NEPS)', *Zeitschrift für Erziehungswissenschaft*: Special Issue 14.

Buchholz, Sandra (2008), *Die Flexibilisierung des Erwerbsverlaufs: Eine Analyse von Einstiegs- und Ausstiegsprozessen in Ost- und Westdeutschland* (The Flexibilization of Employment Careers: An Analysis of Entry and Exit Processes in East and West Germany), Wiesbaden: VS Verlag für Sozialwissenschaften.

Buchholz, Sandra and Daniela Grunow (2006), 'Women's employment in West Germany', in Hans-Peter Blossfeld and Heather Hof*Meister* (eds), *Globalization, Uncertainty and Women's Careers: An International Comparison,* Cheltenham, UK and Northampton, MA, USA: Edward Elgar, pp. 61–83.

Buchholz, Sandra, Dirk Hofäcker and Hans-Peter Blossfeld (2006), 'Globalization, accelerating economic change and late careers. A theoretical framework', in Hans-Peter Blossfeld, Sandra Buchholz and Dirk Hofäcker (eds), *Globalization, Uncertainty and Late Careers in Society,* London, UK and New York, USA: Routledge, pp. 1–23.

Buchholz, Sandra, Annika Rinklake, Julia Schilling, Karin Kurz, Paul Schmelzer and Hans-Peter Blossfeld (2011), 'Aging populations, globalization and the labor market – Comparing late working life and retirement in modern societies', in Hans-Peter Blossfeld, Sandra Buchholz and Karin Kurz (eds), *Aging Populations, Globalization and the Labor Market: Comparing Late Working Life and Retirement in Modern Societies,* Cheltenham, UK and Northampton, MA, USA: Edward Elgar, pp. 3–32.

Bundesministerium für Bildung und Forschung (2010), *Bildungsreport 2010 – Bildung in Deutschland 2010* (Educational Report 2010 – Education in Germany 2010), Bonn: Bundesministerium für Bildung und Forschung.

Deiss, Richard (2011), 'Measuring systems outcomes in the context of Education and Training 2020 and Europe 2020. The strategy of the European Commission', *Conference on effective policies for the development of competencies of youth in Europe,* Warsaw, available at: http://ec.europa.eu/education/lifelong-learning-policy/doc/report10/report_en.pdf (accessed 16.1.2012).

Dieckhoff, Martina, Jean-Marie Jungblut and Philip J. O'Connell (2007), 'Job-related training in Europe: Do institutions matter?', in Duncan Gallie (ed.), *Employment Regimes and the Quality of Work,* Oxford: Oxford University Press, pp. 77–103.

Esping-Andersen, Gøsta (1990), *The Three Worlds of Welfare Capitalism,* Princeton, NJ: Princeton University Press.

Esping-Andersen, Gøsta (1999), *Social Foundations of Postindustrial Economies,* Oxford: Oxford University Press.

Eurostat (2013), 'Statistiken über lebenslanges Lernen – Statistics explained' (Statistics on lifelong learning – statistics explained), available at: http://epp.eurostat.ec.europa. eu/statisticsexplained/index.php/Lifelong_learning_statistics/de   (accessed 12.2.2013).

Falk, Susanne and Hildegard Schaeper (2001), 'Erwerbsverläufe von ost- und westdeutschen Müttern im Vergleich: ein Land – ein Muster?' (Comparing employment careers of East and West German mothers: one county – same pattern?), in Claudia Born and Helga Krüger (eds), *Individualisierung und Verflechtung. Geschlecht und Generation im deutschen Lebenslaufregime* (Individualization and Integration. Sex and Generation in the German Life Course Regime), Weinheim/München: Juventa Verlag, pp. 172–201.

German Statistical Office (2006), *Leben und Arbeiten in Deutschland – Vereinbarkeit von*

Familie und Beruf. Ergebnisse des Mikrozensus 2005 (Life and Employment in Germany – Compatibility of Family and Work, Results of the Micro Census 2005), Wiesbaden: Statistisches Bundesamt.

Grunow, Daniela (2006), *Convergence, Persistence and Diversity in Male and Female Careers. Does Context Matter in an Era of Globalization? A Comparison of Gendered Employment Mobility Patterns in West Germany and Denmark*, Opladen: Barbara Budrich Publishers.

Lauterbach, Wolfgang (1994), *Berufsverläufe von Frauen (Employment Careers of Women)*, Frankfurt, Main and New York: Campus Verlag.

Mayer, Karl Ulrich (1991), 'Berufliche Mobilität von Frauen in der Bundesrepublik Deutschland' (Women's occupational mobility in the Federal Republic of Germany), in Jutta Allmendinger, Karl Ulrich Mayer and Johannes Huinink (eds), *Vom Regen in die Traufe: Frauen zwischen Beruf und Familie* (Jumping out of the Frying Pan into the Fire: Women Between Work and Family), Frankfurt, Main and New York: Campus Verlag, pp. 57–91.

Mayer, K. U. (1997), 'Notes on a comparative political economy of life courses', *Comparative Social Research*, **16**, 203–26.

Mills, Melinda, Hans-Peter Blossfeld and Fabrizio Bernardi (2006), 'Globalization, uncertainty and men's employment careers: a theoretical framework', in Hans-Peter Blossfeld, Melinda Mills and Fabrizio Bernardi (eds), *Globalization, Uncertainty and Men's Careers: An International Comparison*, Cheltenham, UK and Northampton, MA, USA: Edward Elgar, pp. 3–37.

Müller, W. and Y. Shavit (1998), 'Bildung und Beruf im institutionellen Kontext – Eine vergleichende Studie in 13 Ländern' (Education and occupation in institutional context – a comparative study for 13 countries), *Zeitschrift für Erziehungswissenschaften*, **4**, 1–39.

Orloff, A. S. (1993), 'Gender and the social rights of citizenship – the comparative analysis of gender relations and welfare states', *American Sociological Review*, **58** (3), 303–28.

Soskice, David (1999), 'Divergent production regimes: coordinated and uncoordinated market economies in the 1980s and 1990s', in Herbert Kitschelt, Peter Lange, Gary Marks and John D. Stephens (eds), *Continuity and Change in Contemporary Capitalism*, Cambridge: Cambridge University Press, pp. 101–34.

Wilkens, Ingrid and Ute Leber (2003), 'Partizipation an beruflicher Weiterbildung – Empirische Ergebnisse auf Basis des Sozio-Ökonomischen Panels' (Participation in continued education – empirical results on the basis of the socio-economic panel), *Mitteilungen aus der Arbeitsmarkt- und Berufsforschung*, Institute for Employment Research (IAB).

13. Adult Learning in Hungary: Participation and Labor Market Outcomes

Gábor Csanádi, Adrienne Csizmady, and Péter Róbert

INTRODUCTION

This chapter investigates the predictors of participation in adult learning as well as the labor market outcomes of adult learning in post-communist Hungary. The issues are discussed in the frame of the country's institutional settings. More information is available on the first research topic because participation in lifelong learning has been investigated nationwide by the Hungarian Central Statistical Office (KSH 2004, 2010). Moreover, Hungary was part of the Adult Education Survey (AES, Eurostat) as well as of an EU FP6 project, entitled "Towards a Lifelong Learning Society in Europe: The Contribution of the Education System".[1] The chief finding of these previous studies is that participation in lifelong learning is low in Hungary. The present chapter goes beyond the existing studies and employs the Hungarian Household Panel Study carried out by TARKI, Inc., and the analysis of the data provides more insight into the predictors of participation in adult learning in Hungary.

The second research topic, i.e., the labor market consequences of lifelong learning, has hardly been investigated in Hungary – though economists have analyzed income returns to human capital investments (Kertesi and Köllő 2002, 2005). Results from this part of the chapter deal with labor market outcomes, in particular with job mobility. This analysis puts a large emphasis on how various levels of schooling affect the chances of mobility. In fact, two options can be distinguished for lifelong learning. The first option is that participants receive relatively little initial education, in which case adult learning is a way of compensating for previous disadvantages in educational attainment caused chiefly by inequalities in learning opportunities due to social origin. This function of adult learning was characteristic of Hungary between the 1950s and 1970s, when lifelong learning contributed to educational and occupational mobility for the masses (Kolosi and Róbert 1985). The other option for lifelong learning is that participants receive a relatively high level of initial education and return to learning in order to revise previous educational decisions and to obtain additional skills and a second tertiary degree with better labor market prospects. Lifelong learning in Hungary is selective, and the second option seems to be more typical under the current market conditions.

NATIONAL INSTITUTIONAL SETTINGS

The Welfare State

Post-communist countries, including Hungary, generally tend to fall under the radar of well-known international welfare maps. The theoretical constructions and typologies (social democratic, liberal, corporatist/conservative/ Bismarckian, Latin/Mediterranean) can only be applied to the formerly socialist states to some extent. Given their wide social policies and safety nets, these societies used to belong to the social democratic type; however, they moved in different directions after the collapse of communism. Hungary has experienced significant downsizing of the welfare state. Based on an overview of the existing data on social expenditures and changes in government policies, Lelkes (2000) argues that Hungary has become more of a liberal type. At the same time, she also recognizes signs of a corporatist regime. In a comparative perspective based on employment-sustaining policy measures, Bukodi and Róbert (2007) classified the CEE countries, including Hungary, closer to the conservative-corporatist type, in contrast to the Baltic countries, which they viewed as being closer to the liberal type. Given Hungary's traditional connections to Austria and Germany, this move seems to be realistic.[2]

Very few empirical studies on welfare typologies have included former socialist countries. One exception is Fenger (2007), who performed a cluster analysis that placed Hungary in a group with Slovakia, Poland, and Bulgaria, which was close to the Czech Republic and Croatia. Based on the applied indicators, the CEE countries seem to resemble the conservative-corporatist regime, but the governmental program measures score below the values observed in the Western European countries of the type.[3] It is also difficult to speak about a coherent welfare regime in Hungary because preferences for welfare spending and for policy measures (labor market policy includes active and passive measures and unemployment benefits; family policy includes childcare and a taxing system) have varied with governmental changes and cycles in the last decades.[4]

Educational System

Generally speaking, the Hungarian school system has several features in common with the German one, including tracking, selection at an early age, vocational specificity, and standardization of the curriculum. Many of these features changed after the collapse of communism. A more detailed overview is given in Bukodi, Róbert, and Altorjai (2008), Bukodi and Róbert (2008), and Halász and Lannert (2006), but the main processes are as follows: The school system has become more stratified due the (re)established private and church-run schools at the primary, secondary, and tertiary levels. From time to time, changes in the system of administration occur, regardless of whether schools are financed by the local or the central government, and these changes have an impact on school quality. Given the large variety of the 8+4, 6+6, and 4+8 curricula for the primary and secondary schools that pupils can attend between ages 6 and 18, the school system contains more tracks (parallel paths) than before and the impact of early age selection has increased, making the practice and regulation of school choice more important (Lannert, Mártonfi and Vágó 2006). Vocational specificity has declined and the vocational track has become less popular in contrast to secondary schools, which make students eligible for tertiary education.[5]

Educational expansion, particularly at the tertiary level, was strong in the 1990s and the early 2000s, but slowed afterward. In the 1990s, democratization and marketization of the school system were at the heart of the policy: The curriculum became less standardized, lots of new school books and teaching materials were published, and teachers had more freedom to choose between programs. This process has slowed down and reversed since 2000, at which point the system of the national school curriculum was reestablished. At the same time, the content of the curriculum has been under constant criticism for not being adequately competence based and for putting too much emphasis on accumulating large amounts of lexical information – a fact that is also revealed by Hungary's low placement in the PISA study rankings.

Adult Learning in Hungary

Adult learning has a clear legislative basis in Hungary. Act CI of 2001 was established with the purpose of ensuring the transparency and accountability of the system in a regulated form and of providing a basis for the state support system for adult learning. Additional laws that also apply to adult education refer to and regulate it in relation to the various forms and levels of schooling.[6]

While lifelong learning refers to the formal and non-formal training of adults, legislation is more defined and elaborated for formal educational activities. Tasks regarding taking responsibility for formal adult education and informal adult learning are shared by various public bodies and ministries. The Ministry of Education and the Ministry of Labor were originally responsible for these tasks; currently, however, the Ministry of National Resources plays the chief role. The National Vocational Training and Adult Training Council is another national body that assists the Minister in carrying out tasks related to adult education. Its duties also include the preparation of professional decision making, proposals, and evaluations. The Adult Education Accrediting Body is responsible for the qualification and accreditation of institutions and programs of adult education. Additional relevant umbrella associations and national (service) organizations include the National Institute of Vocational and Adult Education (NIVE), which deals with regional and national research related to adult learning, content development of vocational and adult education, and the handling of tenders. Nine regional training centers contribute to these activities in the form of a national network. From the perspective of civil control, the Association of Adult Educators and the Civilian Adult Education Network deserve mentioning.

In 2010, there were 7 987 registered institutes of formal adult education and informal adult learning. Of these, 1 469 were accredited institutes and 6 365 were accredited adult formal and informal learning programs. Together, these institutes and programs offered 39 406 courses, of which 17 470 were accredited courses in 2009.

Adult learning in Hungary is financed by various sources. Central and local government funds include training for both public servants and disadvantaged groups and offer complete or partial financing to national and local development programs. Employment and training-related funding come from the Labor Market Fund, which is the chief funding provider for adult learning. This fund offers support for the training of persons registered as unemployed or at risk of becoming unemployed. A third type of financial source is the permitted vocational training contribution for vocational education for adults inside and outside the school system. In addition, EU sources, i.e., the Human Resources Development Operational Programme (2005–08), the Social Renewal Operational Programme, and Social Infrastructure Operational Programme (2007–10), tend to contribute to the costs of adult learning. Official statistics claim that public expenditure on formal education was about 4–5 per cent of the GDP in the 2000s. Zachár (2010, p. 12) reports a rate of 5–6 per cent in total without separating formal adult education. Expenditure on non-formal adult education is below 1 per cent according to the same source.

The Labor Market and Employment Systems

The Hungarian labor market has become heavily deregulated since the collapse of communism. It is a typical transitional labor market (Cazes and Nesporova 2003) with a high level of flexibility. Characteristic forms of flexible and atypical employment in Hungary include part-time work, working with fixed-term contracts, self-employment, and distance work (Hárs 2012). While an unemployment rate of about 10 per cent is not extreme at the European level, employment is the lowest in the EU, at about 55 per cent. Nevertheless, the unemployment rate is probably underestimated because the eligibility period continues to be shortened and individuals continually disappear from the system. In terms of active labor market programs (ALMP), both public work and job retention subsidies deserve mentioning, whereas wage subsidies or spending on (re)training have declined (Fazekas and Molnár 2011).[7]

The Hungarian labor market used to be an insider economy, but employment protection legislation (EPL) has deteriorated. The role of collective work agreements has become more limited, and those in employment enjoy much less job safety. Employment in the private sector has become more uncertain and flexible since the collapse of communism. Recently, forms of atypical employment and a decline in job safety have also become typical for those working in public employment. More risks were shifted to the employees in the new Hungarian Labor Code of 2012, and industrial relations now tend to be in favor of employers.

Technological change in the economy is an important feature of post-communist Hungary and has led to a growing demand for an educated labor force. Between the 1990s and the 2000s, this technological change led to good opportunities for workers as a result of a wage premium, despite the increasing number of graduated job-seekers in the labor market. At the same time, due to strong educational expansion, young job-seekers with a higher level of schooling now beat their lesser-educated counterparts even at those jobs that do not require a diploma. Consequently, education has become a weaker predictor of occupational success in the labor market, and job status has decreased for each given level of schooling (Róbert 2009; Bukodi and Goldthorpe 2010).

Linking the Elements of the Institutional Settings and Our Hypotheses

According to the quoted literature, Hungary belongs to some extent to both the corporatist and liberal welfare regimes. On these grounds, we do not find the Hungarian adult learning system to be very widespread and equal because equalizing access to adult learning, using the system of social redistribution to support adult learners, and increasing the level of participation usually do not occur in these types of regimes. This view is in line with the bounded agency model by Rubenson and Desjardins (2009), who assume that there is an interaction between the structurally and individually based barriers to participation in lifelong learning.[8] These barriers are handled to a different extent by the various welfare regime types (Green 2011; Riddell and Weedon 2012).

Since retaining the existing differences characterizes the conservative-corporatist regime type, the previous level of schooling and labor market integration should be strong predictors of adult learning. At the individual level, the hypothesis derived from the welfare regime type is in accordance with the Matthew effect assuming that individuals with better education and in better occupational positions should accumulate further advantages in adult learning. We expect a quite linear relationship between education, employment, and the probability of studying (situational barriers). Thus, even the *"partial equalization hypothesis"* (see Chapter 1) may not hold for Hungary. The *"Matthew effect hypothesis"* has already found support for formal adult education in Hungary (Róbert 2011).

Equalization in adult learning cannot be expected due to institutional barriers. The programs, particularly in formal adult education, are usually long, lasting 1–3 years and requiring more commitment from learners in terms of time. As a result, not everyone can afford the required time to participate. Educational institutions in Hungary are not very sensitive to the purchasing power of possible adult learners. Since schools suffer from low budgeting from the state, they use formal adult education as an extra source of funding.[9] At the same time, the content of the accredited learning programs (the curriculum) is not in accordance with employers' needs, which leads to a decline in the vocational specificity or the occupational labor market character of the linkage between education and the labor market.[10]

Regarding the impact of demographics, we expect to find a strong age effect: The odds of returning to any school or training program should be significantly lower as individuals age. The *"gendered participation hypothesis"* for Hungary posits that women most likely participate in both formal and non-formal adult learning more frequently than men. This assumption is based on the fact that men and women try to overcome the barriers of participation in adult learning. In terms of financial barriers, there are no gender differences. In terms of time constraints to participation in further learning activities, a clear gender variation exists in Hungary. For women, the barrier involves combining studies and family obligations; for men, the barrier involves combining studies and (additional) working activities. It seems that women are able to study despite their family obligations. On the contrary, men in

Hungary are not able to study because they tend to have a second (or third) job in order to financially support the family.

Based on the previously cited studies, it is apparent that higher levels of schooling lead to wage premiums and to a decreased risk of losing a job. However, the effect of the original education and that of further adult learning has not been evaluated in previous analyses. Nevertheless, we expect that lifelong learning has an additional positive impact on labor market and employment outcomes.

RESULTS

Participation Rates in Adult Learning

Hungary ranks low in lifelong learning participation in a comparative perspective. According to the data from the Adult Education Survey (AES) organized by Eurostat, Hungary occupies the lowest position in the league table of 25 EU nations with a participation rate of 9 per cent in formal and non-formal learning (the EU average is 36 per cent) (Boateng 2009).[11] According to the LFS data from 2005 and 2009, Hungary performs well below the EU benchmark level, and its lifelong learning participation rate has even been declining.[12] The most recent data on Hungary confirm that adult learning tends to be vocationally oriented. Nearly 33 per cent of adult learners participate in some vocational training and about 16 per cent study for a state-accredited vocational qualification. A similarly large proportion (14 per cent) of learners attend a language course. Another group of students (12 per cent) attend school in order to receive a qualification required by their job. Training for a public service-type qualification, IT trainings, and business-skill trainings are also popular. Only 10 per cent of adult learners participate in general adult education (KSH 2010).

Participation in formal and non-formal adult learning is shown in Figure 13.1 by gender and age group with a distinction between employer-sponsored and non-employer-sponsored forms.[13] Non-employer-sponsored non-formal training is the most frequent form of adult learning activity for both sexes, followed by non-employer-sponsored formal education (in the younger age groups). The decline by age, however, is steeper for non-employer-sponsored formal education. Employer-sponsored non-formal learning is thereby the second most frequent form for age groups above 35.

Regarding gender differences, women participate more in adult learning than men, the only exception being for employer-sponsored formal education.

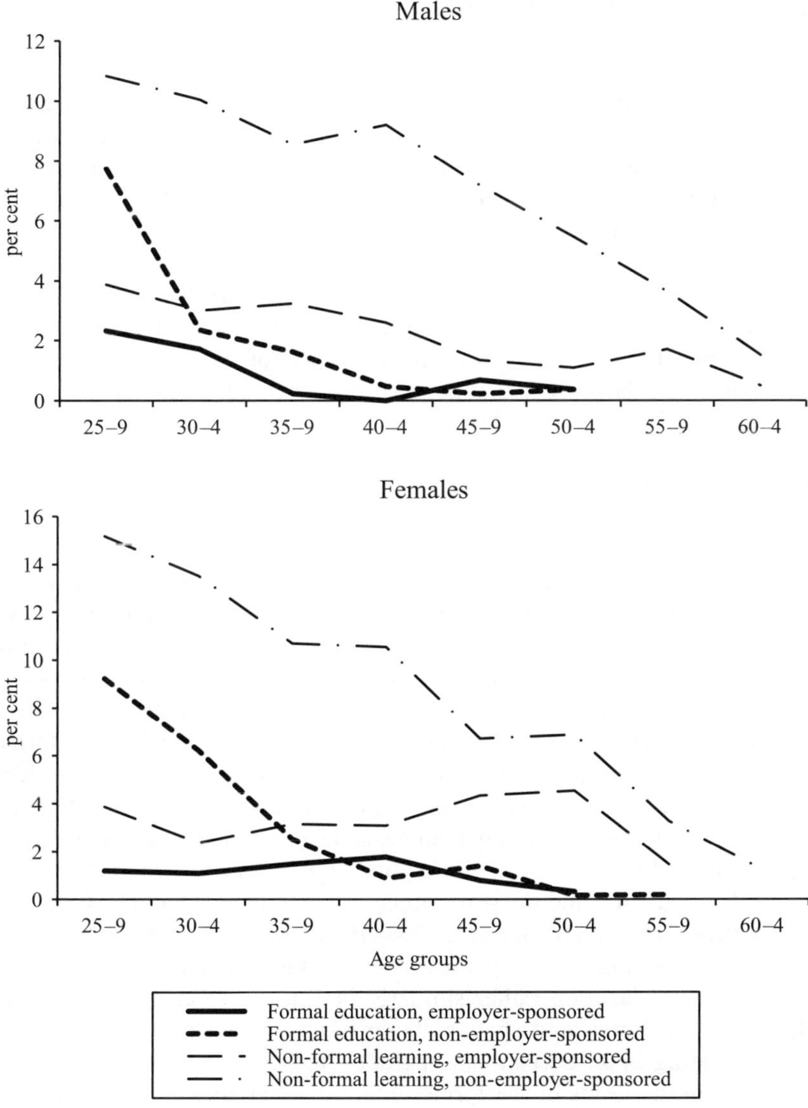

Notes: Learning is sponsored if employers provide full or partial financial support or if the activity occurs fully or partially during working hours. Education that does not require tuition is considered not sponsored.

Source: Own calculations based on the Adult Education Survey (2006).

Figure 13.1 Rates of participation in adult learning for persons aged between 25 and 64 by type of activity (per cent)

Predictors of Educational Upgrades

In this section, we analyze panel data of the Hungarian Household Panel, conducted by TARKI. In the panel, 2 600 households were surveyed on a yearly basis between 1992 and 1997. The research focuses on certain aspects of the labor market, income inequalities, the life prospects of various strata of the population, and the financial and economic strategies of households. Ten years after the completion of the HHP's research on 7 200 persons, TARKI found 2 690 original respondents in the framework of the Living Condition of Hungarian Households Project. This project examined the period between 1992 and 2007 with the help of retrospective data and merged these data with the original HHP sources.[14] From the viewpoint of our analysis, the main limitation of the database is that there are few specific questions concerning adult learning, and these questions are limited to adult education. As a result, we can only analyze formal adult education. A similar problem is that there are few questions about the labor market situation. We have no data, for example, about the change in position or salary during the period our respondents were employed at the same workplace.

In Table 13.1, we examine the factors affecting the participation in and successful educational upgrading through formal adult education. We consider as an 'adult' a person who has completed a given level of education at least three years after the normal completion age. We run binary logistic regression models for men, women, and the whole population. In these models, the dependent variable is adult educational upgrade through formal education, and the predictive variable set consists of age, highest (initial) level of education, labor market status, having children, rural or urban residential location, logarithm of the family income, and gender (in the case of the whole population model). The models have good explanatory power in the case of the whole population and the sub-samples divided by gender: The Cox-Snell R^2 is between 0.24 and 0.26, and the Nagelkerke R^2 is between 0.42 and 0.44.

The results support our hypotheses that upgrades that are gained through adult education function rather similarly in Hungary: Persons with higher educational attainment and a better labor market situation have a better chance of participating in an educational upgrade. At the same time, an important difference in the levels of the former educational attainment is visible: The effect is not linear. The disadvantage in participation of upper secondary school graduates compared with those with higher education is not significant. On the other hand, the two lower levels of educational attainment (i.e., vocational and compulsory education) result in a substantial disadvantage in participation in adult education. The impact of the labor market status is more interesting from a gender perspective. Compared with those in stable jobs,

Table 13.1 Predictors of an educational upgrade, 1992–2007 (logistic regression model, dependent variable: gained an upgrade in formal adult education)

	All	Men	Women
Age	0.08	−0.03	0.16*
Age squared	0.00*	0.00	−0.00*
Initial education (ref. university degree)			
Compulsory	−3.05**	−3.42**	−2.91*
Vocational	−0.81*	−0.99*	−0.87**
Upper secondary	0.07	−0.28	0.19
Labor force status (ref. employed in stable job)			
Employed in precarious job	−0.58*	−0.88*	−0.42
Unemployed	−0.47*	−0.82*	−0.10
Inactive (except students)	−0.68*	−0.47	−0.69*
Full-time students	−1.88*	−2.42*	−1.32*
Marital status (ref. single, living alone)			
Cohabiting	0.29	0.84*	0.03
Married	0.39*	1.12*	0.13
Other	0.62	1.00	0.64
Children in the household (ref. no children)			
Under three years	0.50*	−0.19	0.89**
Over three years	−0.22	−0.69*	−0.06
Living in rural area	0.02	0.54*	−0.41*
Log of household income	0.00	0.19	−0.11
Male	−0.43*	−	−
Constant	−0.19	−0.07	−0.85
Individuals	2 680	1 176	1 504
Cox & Snell R^2	0.24	0.24	0.26
Nagelkerke R^2	0.42	0.43	0.44

Notes: **$p < 0.01$, *$p < 0.05$.

Source: Own calculations based on the HHP.

the other options reveal a significant disadvantage in becoming involved in adult learning, and there is a difference between men and women. In the case of men, unemployment and a precarious job are disadvantageous, whereas in the case of women, these labor-force indicators do not result in a significant disadvantage compared with the chances of individuals in stable jobs for an educational upgrade. For women, other forms of inactivity have a similar effect, yet these factors do not have significant effects in the case of men.

Marital status yields a significantly higher chance of an adult educational upgrade in the case of married men compared with singles. At the same time, another family status variable, having children below three years old, has a significant positive effect compared with childless respondents. This effect is not significant in the case of families with older children. The above-mentioned result comes entirely from the female part of the sample. Thus, childbearing shows significant positive effects on participation in adult education compared with childlessness among women, yet we do not find a similar effect among men. However, the effect is reversed in the case of older children: Men with older children have a significantly smaller chance of participating in a formal educational upgrade, whereas having older children in the family does not significantly affect women's participation.

The effects are also different by gender for rural residential locations. Living in rural areas negatively affects women's chances compared with urban residential locations, whereas the effect of living in rural areas is positive for men. This observation can be explained by the gender difference in the structure of adult education. As we know from our data, men have a higher chance of attending compulsory and vocational schools than do women, who usually look for learning programs that offer high school graduation or a connection to professional training. At the same time, a higher proportion of compulsory and vocational schools are located in smaller towns, whereas higher-level schools that provide education in women's professions tend to be located in cities. The urban location of these kinds of schools may be the reason why women living in smaller towns have lower chances of participating in adult education than do women living in urban areas.

The Effects of Formal Adult Educational Upgrades in the Labor Market

Following the analysis of the inequalities of participation in adult education, we now examine the hypothesis of the positive effects of adult educational upgrades on the labor market situation. To measure the labor market effects of educational upgrades, we cannot use the standard event history analysis due to the features of our database and the software available to us. At the same time, standard logistic regression methods could help us carry out a significant part of the analysis similarly to an event history analysis (except for the analysis of the time factor).

Do formal adult educational upgrades affect exiting unemployment?

We have to consider two additional limitations regarding the relationship between getting out of unemployment and educational upgrades. On the one hand and as indicated above, our data for a certain part of the examined period does not come from regular annual surveys. In the case of the unemployed, it is not always possible to examine whether or not they were still unemployed at the time of the next data collection. The other, more important reason is that the number of cases of educational upgrades during unemployment was so low that further covariate effects were impossible to analyze.

Table 13.2 Length of unemployment of upgraded and non-upgraded adults (in years)

		Mean
Male	Non-upgraders	2.11
	Upgraders	3.77
	Total	2.33
	Post upgrading – unemployed period (year)	3.46
Female	Non-upgraders	2.25
	Upgraders	2.72
	Total	2.30
	Post upgrading – unemployed period (year)	1.45
Total	Non-upgraders	2.18
	Upgraders	3.29
	Total	2.31
	Post upgrading – unemployed period (year)	2.54

Source: Own calculations based on the HHP.

In spite of these limitations, Table 13.2 reveals that especially in the case of male respondents, the length of unemployment seems to be longer among those who gained an educational upgrade than among those who did not study during their unemployment period: 3.8 versus 2.1 years for male and 2.7 versus 2.2 years for female respondents. At the same time, we can also calculate that educational upgrades among men occur in the first part of unemployment. After gaining an educational upgrade, men spend an average of 3.46 years in unemployment, whereas this period is shorter among women (1.44 years). This phenomenon is related to the fact that men who participate in adult education are more likely to only finish the compulsory level, whereas women gain a higher level of schooling during the period of unemployment.

It is important to be careful in our conclusions based on the limitations of our database; however, it appears obvious that our analysis confirms that adult educational upgrading can help individuals get out of unemployment. However, this only occurs if an individual can find a form of adult educational upgrading that is useful in the labor market.

Does a formal adult educational upgrade affect labor market position?
Now we examine how the processes of a changing labor market situation develop among those who could stay in the labor market, i.e., those from the 'insider' group. In other words, we investigate how labor market mobility processes are related to educational upgrades. In our models, the independent variable is whether or not there was any change in a person's occupational status during job changes, and if so, in what direction. To measure this, we use the ISCO occupational codes and the ISEI values they produce.

Thus we defined the upward and downward mobile groups according to the change in ISEI values.

We use two types of binomial regression models. First, we examine the relationship between upward and downward mobility and adult educational upgrades as a whole in one model each, controlling for age, educational attainment (before the upgrade), household income, and settlement type. We examine these models separately among men and women and also in the whole sample. Second, we analyze how much the different types of adult educational upgrades differ from one another in their effects on labor market status changes.

As we can see from the two models in Table 13.3, participation in formal adult education is positively related to labor market success. Those who use this opportunity have a better chance of obtaining a favorable labor market position with higher ISEI than do those who do not make use of this opportunity. Based on Model 2, we can also see that the risk of downward mobility decreases with participation in adult education in the case of the whole population, but this effect is significant only in the case of men and not among women.

Table 13.3   Returns to adult educational upgrades as a whole

	All	Men	Women
Model 1. Upward mobility			
Adult education upgrade	0.74+	0.91+	0.70*
Model 2. Downward mobility			
Adult education upgrade	−0.49*	−0.79*	−0.36

Notes: * p<0.05, + p<0.10. Reference category: no upgrade in formal adult education. Controlling for age, educational attainment (before the upgrade), household income, and settlement type.

Source: Own calculations based on the Hungarian Household Panel Study.

Related to the different effects for men and women, we can assume that the educational attainment of those earning formal adult educational upgrades may differ by the level of the educational upgrade. The results presented in Table 13.4 confirm this assumption, demonstrating that completing compulsory education does not have the same effect as higher levels of educational upgrades, which are directly useful in the labor market.

Table 13.4   Returns on different types of adult educational upgrades

	All	Men	Women
Model 3. Upward mobility			
Adult education upgrade levels (ref. no upgrade)			
Compulsory	0.67	0.68	0.71
Vocational	0.91+	0.88*	1.03*
Upper secondary	0.60*	0.64	0.65+
Higher education	0.79+	1.33+	0.50
Model 4. Downward mobility			
Adult education upgrade levels (ref. no upgrade)			
Compulsory	0.04	0.10	0.02
Vocational	−0.25	−1.14*	0.28
Upper secondary	−0.84*	−1.44*	−0.64*
Higher education	−1.22*	−1.65	−1.22*

Notes: * p<0.05, + p<0.1. Controlling for age, educational attainment (before the upgrade), household income, and settlement type.

Source: Own calculations based on the HHP.

Based on Model 3, we can see that not all of those who gain an adult educational upgrade have a better chance of improving their labor market situation. Finishing compulsory education (which is often available to the lowest status groups) does not have a significant effect on labor market upgrades among either men or women. Observed differences between the two genders can probably be explained by the effects of labor market segmentation. Higher education (for men) and upper secondary education (for women) are the best forms of adult educational upgrades and offer the most important and significant improvements. The vocational level of educational upgrades may be particularly beneficial for women because of its relative rarity.

We can more clearly see the influence of formal adult educational upgrades on downward mobility in Model 4. The chance of decreasing in labor market status is not significantly smaller among those who finish compulsory education compared with the chances of those who do not upgrade at all. Even participation in vocational education leads to a decreased risk of losing labor market status for men (but not for women). Only among men does earning a vocational educational upgrade decrease the risk of losing a labor market position. Higher levels of educational upgrades further decrease the chances of a downward occupational move, and the pattern is stronger for women than for men. An educational upgrade at the tertiary level has no significant impact on downward mobility among men.

SUMMARY

For the first research issue, we were able to confirm that participation in adult education is determined by social forces: Individuals with a higher social status have a better chance of participating than do those from lower-status groups. One of the underlying reasons for this trend is the dichotomy of the Hungarian system, for adult education is not uniform in Hungary. There are types of adult education that help individuals adapt to changing circumstances, types that help with labor market integration, and types that help with status stabilization or even with the increase of social status. Higher-status groups often utilize these options more successfully. Moreover, there are types of adult education that only formally function in this manner (i.e., only according to their proclaimed principles), while they are actually unable (or only able in a very limited way) to help improve or stabilize the labor market position of participants. In sum, we found a strong Matthew effect associated with formal adult upgraders, and the *"partial equalization hypothesis"* could not be confirmed in Hungary.

Regarding further assumptions on gender differences in adult learning, we found interesting patterns. On the one hand, the male breadwinner hypothesis is supported for Hungary: Married or cohabitating men have higher odds of participating in an educational upgrade compared with their single counterparts. Differences in marital status turned out to be insignificant for women, for whom household composition matters more. Women with at least one child below three years old have a higher probability of studying. At the same time, having older children can be a barrier to returning to adult education for men. We can interpret these results as a modified version of the "motherhood penalty/fatherhood premium" explanation (Correll, Benard and Paik 2007). Mothers with small children do not seem to be penalized, but as children grow older, men have to do more work to support their family and have a smaller chance of participating in a formal educational upgrade than do men without children. This type of 'bonus' does not offer a real advantage to men because it means more work in the form of second jobs, overtime, etc., and not simply an upgrade of labor market status. In other words, men have already achieved their highest educational attainment by the time of having children, and their participation in adult learning cannot occur until their children move out. The higher adult learning activity of women with smaller children can be explained by the fact that they have the chance to compensate for their lower educational attainment in normal school ages as a result of their life situation. Hungary's various maternity-leave support options can also have substantial effect.

For the second research issue on the impact of educational upgrades on labor market outcomes, we can say that our data confirmed the hypothesis that formal adult education can improve one's labor market position and can prevent labor market decline. In this regard, we found positive effects on upward mobility and negative effects on downward mobility in terms of job change measured by ISEI scores. At the same time, the level of participation in formal adult education has also had an effect on labor market outcomes. Our analysis provides evidence that the different forms of adult education reflect different options in the labor market and in the structure of the institutional system. The higher-status groups can use their already-existing knowledge and education to choose the type of adult education that actually helps them improve and stabilize their position and thereby protect themselves from the risk of labor market deterioration. For them, participation in higher education or in upper secondary schooling is more advantageous. In contrast, the already-existing disadvantages of low-status groups are amplified by this system. Individuals in these groups can study at compulsory level or (at best) in vocational training programs, but these forms are less helpful in the labor market.

The pattern of gender difference is also interesting for labor market outcomes. The analysis reveals a strong positive effect on upward mobility for men if they study at the tertiary level. The same form of educational upgrade is significantly negative for women's downward mobility. This means that the best form of educational upgrade leads to a direct advantage for men, whereas it 'only' has an indirect benefit for women in the sense that it spares them from downward mobility.

NOTES

1. For more details, see http://lll2010.tlu.ee.
2. Bohle and Greskovits (2007) also confirm the liberal character of the Baltic States but find Slovenia to be the only example of the corporatist type. They claim that Hungary belongs to an "embedded liberal" category.

3. Leibrecht, Klien, and Onaran (2011) also show that social protection expenditures as a share of total public expenditures are significantly higher in both the social democratic and the conservative welfare nations as compared with the liberal, Southern, and CEE countries.
4. For further details, see also Bukodi and Róbert (2008).
5. Since grammar schools provide the greatest chance of receiving higher education, most students try to attend this type of school.
6. These are Act 76 of 1993 on vocational education, Act 79 of 1993 on public education, Act 86 of 2003 on vocational education contributions, and Act 139 of 2005 on higher education. See also Róbert, Ayupova, and Altorjai (2013).
7. When examining the national spending of the Labor Market Fund in 2011, the largest share (40 per cent) was devoted to the support of job searches for the unemployed. Adult education and vocational training received 10 per cent of the total budget distributed by the Labor Market Fund in 2011.
8. The types of barriers can be situational, institutional, or dispositional. Situational barriers are related to previous schooling, the current job, and family circumstances. Institutional barriers refer to a person's inability to find an appropriate study course that he or she would be interested in attending. Dispositional barriers include a person's belief in their low ability, negative previous experiences with learning activities, and the feeling of being too old to study (Cross 1981).
9. Subproject 5 of the LLL2010 EU FP6 project investigated the national educational institutions that provide formal adult educational programs. For Hungary, see Róbert, Ayupova, and Altorjai (2013).
10. Subproject 4 of the LLL2010 EU FP6 project investigated the SMEs from the viewpoint of their attitudes and practices regarding lifelong learning. In fact, it is rare for employers in Hungary to contribute to the costs of their employees' formal learning activities in financial terms. If a company finds some training important for the employees, it tends to organize an appropriate course offered to them for free. The company can apply to have the costs of the course covered by the Labor Market Fund (Ayupova and Róbert 2010).
11. This survey was carried out between 2005 and 2007 and is representative of the population aged 25-64, and participation refers to learning activities in the 12 months previous to the data collection. For a comparative analysis of the data, see also Róbert (2012).
12. The rate was 3.9 for 2005 and 2.7 for 2009. This indicator refers to persons aged 25 to 64 who stated that they received education or training in the four weeks preceding the survey.
13. This result differs from the one shown in Chapter 2 due to different variable definitions. Rates are higher here because learning is not restricted to being job related.
14. See http://www.tarki.hu/en/research/index.html#Hungarian_Household_Panel_Survey.

REFERENCES

Ayupova, Saida and Péter Róbert (2010), 'Formal adult education in small- and medium-sized enterprises. The case of Hungary. SP4 – national report', *LLL2010 Working Paper*, No. 25, Institute for International and Social Studies, Tallinn University.

Boateng, Sadiq Kwesi (2009), 'Significant country differences in adult learning', *Statistics in Focus* 44, Eurostat, Luxembourg.

Bohle, D. and B. Greskovits (2007), 'Neoliberalism, embedded neoliberalism and neocorporatism: towards transnational capitalism in central-eastern Europe', *West European Politics*, **30** (3), 443–66.

Bukodi, E. and J. H. Goldthorpe (2010), 'Market versus meritocracy: Hungary as a critical case', *European Sociological Review*, **26** (6), 655–74.

Bukodi, Erzsébet and Péter Róbert (2007), *Occupational Mobility in Europe. Analysis of Eurobarometer Data on Mobility*, Dublin: European Foundation for the Improvement of Living and Working Conditions.

Bukodi, Erzsébet and Péter Róbert (2008), 'Hungary', in Irena Kogan, Michael Gebel and Clemens Noelke (eds), *Europe Enlarged. A Handbook of Education, Labour and Welfare Regimes in Central and Eastern Europe*, Bristol: Policy Press

Bukodi, Erzsébet, Péter Róbert and Szilvia Altorjai (2008), 'The Hungarian educational system and the implementation of the ISCED-97', in Silke L. Schneider (ed.), *The International Standard Classification of Education (ISCED-97) An Evaluation of Content and Criterion Validity for 15 European Countries*, Mannheim: MZES, pp. 200–15.

Cazes, Sadrine and Alena Nesporova (2003), *Labour Markets in Transition: Balancing Flexibility and Security in Central and Eastern Europe*, Geneva: ILO.

Correll, S. J., S. Benard and I. Paik (2007), 'Getting a job: is there a motherhood penalty?', *American Journal of Sociology*, **112** (5), 1297–339.

Cross, K. Patricia (1981), *Adults as Learners: Increasing Participation and Facilitating Learning*, San Francisco: Jossey-Bass.

Fazekas, Károly and György Molnár (eds) (2011), *The Hungarian Labour Market. Review and Analysis 2011*, Budapest: Institute of Economics, HAS.

Fenger, H. J. M. (2007), 'Welfare regimes in Central and Eastern Europe: Incorporating post-communist countries in a welfare regime typology', *Contemporary Issues and Ideas in Social Sciences*, **3** (2), 1–30.

Green, A. (2011), 'Lifelong learning, equality and social cohesion', *European Journal of Education*, **46** (2), 228–243.

Halász, Gábor and Judit Lannert (2006), *Jelentés a magyar közoktatásról* (Report on the Hungarian Public Education), Budapest: Országos Közoktatási Intézet.

Hárs, Ágnes (2012), 'Az atipikus foglalkoztatási formák Magyarországon a kilencvenes és a kétezres években' (Atypical employment in the 1990s and 2000s in Hungary), *Budapest Working Papers BWP* 2012/7, Institute of Economics, Hungarian Academy of Sciences, Budapest.

Kertesi, Gábor and János Köllő (2002), 'Economic transformation and the revaluation of human capital – Hungary, 1986–1999', in Andries de Grip, Jasper van Loo and Ken Mayhew (eds), *The Economics of Skills Obsolescence: Theoretical Innovations and Empirical Applications*, Research in Labor Economics Vol. 21, Bingley, UK: Emerald Group Publishing Ltd, pp. 235–73.

Kertesi, Gábor and János Köllő (2005), 'The expansion of higher education high-skilled unemployment, and the returns to college/university diploma', *Budapest Working Papers on the Labour Market*, No. 3, Institute of Economics, Hungarian Academy of Sciences, Budapest.

Kolosi, Tamás and Péter Róbert (1985), 'Die Rolle des Abend- und Fernstudiums bei der gesellschaftlichen Mobilität', in Manfred Kaiser, Reinhard Nuthman and Heinz Stegmann (eds), *Berufliche Verbleibsforschung in der Diskussion*,

Nürnberg: IAB, pp. 335–65.

KSH (2004), *Az élethosszig tartó tanulás* (Lifelong Learning), Budapest: Hungarian Central Statistical Office.

KSH (2010), Részvétel a felnőttképzésben (Participation in Adult Education), *Statisztikai tükör* (Statistical Mirror), Vol. 4, No. 87, Budapest: Hungarian Central Statistical Office.

Lannert, J., G. Mártonfi and I. Vágó (2006), 'The impact of structural upheavals on educational organisation, attainment and choice: the experience of post-communist Hungary', *European Journal of Education*, **41** (1), 71–84.

Leibrecht, M., M. Klien and O. Onaran (2011), 'Globalization, welfare regimes and social protection expenditures in Western and Eastern European countries', *Public Choice*, **148** (3), 569–94.

Lelkes, O. (2000), 'A great leap towards liberalism? The Hungarian welfare state', *International Journal of Social Welfare*, **9** (2), 92–102.

Riddell, Sheila and Elisabet Weedon (2012), 'Lifelong learning and the wider European socioeconomic context', in Sheila Riddel, Jörg Markowitsch and Elisabet Weedon (eds), *Lifelong Learning in Europe. Equity and Efficiency in the Balance,* Bristol: The Policy Press, pp. 17–38.

Róbert, Péter (2009), 'The consequences of educational expansion for returns to education in Hungary', in Andreas Hadjar and Rolf Becker (eds), *Expected and Unexpected Consequences of the Educational Expansion in Europe and the US,* Bern, Stuttgart, Wien: Haupt Verlag, pp. 201–11.

Róbert, Péter (2011), 'Predicting the probabilities of participation in formal adult education in Hungary. SP2 – national report', *LLL2010 Working Paper*, No 69, Institute for International and Social Studies, Tallinn University.

Róbert, Péter (2012), 'The sociodemographic obstacles to participating in lifelong learning across Europe', in Sheila Riddel, Jörg Markowitsch, and Elisabet Weedon (eds), *Lifelong learning in Europe. Equity and Efficiency in the Balance*, Bristol: The Policy Press, pp. 87–101.

Róbert, Péter, Saida Ayupova and Szilvia Altorjai (2013), 'Why are the participation rates in lifelong learning so low in Hungary?', in Ellu Saar, Odd Bjorn Ure and John Holford (eds), *Lifelong Learning In Europe. National Patterns and Challenges,* Cheltenham, UK and Northampton, MA, USA: Edward Elgar, pp. 280–303.

Rubenson, K. and R. Desjardins (2009), 'The impact of welfare state regimes on barriers to participation in adult education', *Adult Education Quarterly*, **59** (3), 187–207.

Zachár, László (2010), *A felnőttképzés az OKKR kidolgozása tükrében* (Adult education in the frame of developing OKKR), Budapest: Oktatáskutató és Fejlesztő Intézet.

14. Adult Learning in the Czech Republic: A Youth- and Female-Oriented System?

Dana Hamplová and Natalie Simonová

INTRODUCTION

This chapter focuses on adult learning in the Czech Republic in the last two decades. In it, we search for answers to two research questions: (1) What are the main characteristics of the participants in adult learning in the Czech Republic? and (2) What are the outcomes of adult learning? At present, there are only a few available analyses on adult learning and its consequences in the Czech Republic. The lack of interest in the subject might be partly explained by the dearth of appropriate data or – to some degree – by a low public interest in the issues of lifelong learning in general. Despite the fact that adult education was very common in the past and that adult students represented a significant share of all students during the socialist era, adult learning has not been a priority of any of the Czech Republic's post-communist governments.

Our chapter begins with a short overview of the institutional context in which adult learning takes place. We first briefly describe the main features of the Czech Republic's labor market and the main changes it underwent in the last two decades. Afterward, we describe the educational system in the country with a special emphasis on the options available to adults who decide to participate in learning activities. The empirical part of the chapter is divided into two parts. The first part focuses on our first research question and explores the characteristics of individuals who participate in adult learning, while the second part examines the labor market consequences for individuals who decide to participate in further education. We specifically address the question of how adult learning affects the chances for prestige mobility.

INSTITUTIONAL SETTING

The Czech Republic can be classified among countries with a coordinated labor market economy (Soskice 1999). In general, the Czech labor market is characterized by low levels of income inequality, moderate levels of unemployment, and medium employment protection. These low levels of income inequality seem to be a rather long-term and stable feature of the Czech labor market. Former Czechoslovakia was known for very high wage equality, even in comparison with other socialist countries (Večerník 1999), and despite the substantive increase of income inequality in the early transition period, the overall levels of wage differentiation have remained relatively stable since the mid-1990s. Consequently, the Czech (and Slovak) Republic still has one of the lowest GINI coefficients among EU-countries (Mysíková 2011).

Unemployment was an unknown phenomenon during the socialist era due to the policy of full and compulsory employment. In the first half of the 1990s, during the first years of transformation, unemployment levels were kept low (at less than 5 per cent) due to relatively generous early retirement schemes and a transformation strategy based on a low-wage/low-unemployment trade-off (Oreinstein and Hall 2001). However, unemployment began to increase in the second half of the 1990s and had spread to 8.7 per cent of the labor force by 2012 (Czech Statistical Office; for more on the economic transformation, see, e.g., Hamplová and Kreidl 2006). Levels of employment protection are intermediate in the Czech Republic and comparative levels can be found, e.g., in the Netherlands, Finland, Estonia, and Austria (see OECD 2008). The usage of fixed-term contracts is legally limited to a maximum cumulative duration of 24 months. Afterward, the fixed-term contract is automatically transformed into a permanent contract.[1] A redundancy claim (business restructuring) is probably the most commonly used method of laying off workers. In this case, the employer must pay a severance equal to at least three times the worker's average earnings.

Despite the relatively low increase in the level of income inequality, returns to education rose significantly during the post-socialist transformation process. During the socialist era, the financial pay-offs of schooling were low and higher education attracted mainly individuals from educated families who valued other aspects of education over a financial reward. However, the labor market value of education has dramatically changed in the last two decades. The financial returns to education have doubled and education has begun to play an important role in upward mobility, income stability, and as a protection against unemployment (Boguszak, Matějů and Peschar 1990). Currently, one year of additional schooling is linked with an approximate increase in wages of 8.4 per cent among men and 10.2 per cent among women compared with 4 per cent and 5 per cent, respectively, during the socialist era (Večerník 2012).

Given the increasing importance of education in the labor market, lifelong learning might seem a solution to marginalization, social exclusion, and long-term unemployment (Matějů 1993). Despite the fact that official Czech documents and declarations seem to accept this position, public support for lifelong learning is quite low and the system of adult education is rather fragmented and underdeveloped (see MŠMT – Ministry of Education 2001). The Czech educational system is clearly youth-oriented. Czechs tend to leave the system of formal education sooner than their peers in other OECD countries (OECD 2012) and those who would like to return to a standard educational institution face considerable difficulties and costs.

THE CZECH EDUCATIONAL SYSTEM

The Czech educational system is based on highly standardized certificates and diplomas. The system is organized into three principal levels: elementary schools, secondary schools, and tertiary-level institutions.[2] The program in elementary schools is further divided into two stages. The first stage lasts for five years and corresponds to the primary level in the ISCED classification (ISCED 1); the second stage lasts for four years and corresponds to lower secondary education in the ISCED classification (ISCED 2). The standard program in elementary school takes nine years altogether, but a student can transfer into an academic track at a multi-year gymnasium (secondary school) upon finishing the first stage of the elementary school.

The majority of students who graduate from the second stage of elementary school continue into upper secondary education. Only 8 per cent of the population aged 25–64 has not completed upper secondary school, compared with the average of 25 per cent among all OECD countries (OECD 2012). The upper-secondary-school system is highly stratified and the principal dividing line lies between the three-year (or in some cases two-year) programs leading to nationally recognized occupation-specific certificates (ISCED 3C) and the four-year programs leading to high-school diplomas (ISCED 3A, 3B, 4A). The four-year programs are further divided into schools with an academic program (gymnasia) and different types of vocational schools or professional secondary schools with various emphases on practical learning. Thus, occupation-specific training can be obtained in a three-year program in a vocational school (without a high-school diploma) or in a four-year program in a technical/professional school (with a high-school diploma, the so-called *maturita*). In general, the Czech Republic can be classified as a country that combines theoretical and practical learning in a dual system. Currently, approximately 33 per cent of students attend vocational schools without a high-school diploma, 47 per cent are enrolled in the vocational schools with high-school diplomas or in secondary professional schools, and 21 per cent attend gymnasia (11 per cent are enrolled in the four-year track and 10 per cent in multi-year gymnasia) (Source: personal communication at the Ministry of Education).

Tertiary-level education is offered by universities (ISCED 5A, 6) and tertiary professional schools (ISCED 5B). University-level education is divided into three cycles: undergraduate (bachelor studies: 3–4 years), masters (1–3 years), and doctoral studies (3–8 years). Tertiary professional schools provide three-year programs with advanced technical training and the graduate becomes a "specialist with a diploma" (DiS.). It is important to note that the proportion of the population with a tertiary degree is relatively low in the Czech Republic; however, the educational opportunities at the tertiary level have been expanding in recent years. The number of universities has grown by nearly 40 per cent in the last 10 years (from 52 institutions in the academic year 2002/03 to 72 institutions in 2011/12). At the same time, previously existing universities have significantly increased their number of students. Although some of the expansion can be attributed to the accelerated development of private universities, most of the growth has occurred within the public system (Simonová 2011).

Adult Learning in the Czech Republic

The Czech Republic's educational system is clearly youth-oriented and the system of adult learning is rather fragmented. Both formal and non-formal adult learning are offered by standard educational institutions (elementary and secondary schools and universities), employers, commercial institutions, NGOs, foundations, trade unions, churches, professional associations, and other institutions (Czesaná, Matoušková and Havlíčková 2006; Matoušková and Žáčková 2008; EACEA 2010). Different ministries are responsible for different programs and many courses offered by commercial institutions are not regulated. In general, the Czech Republic can be categorized among countries with occupation- and employer-related models of lifelong learning similar to models in more conservative and Southern European countries.

Formal adult education at the secondary level is organized along two main pathways: "follow-up technical studies" in secondary professional schools (ISCED 4A) and educational upgrading through a set of exams defined by the national system of qualifications. Follow-up study in secondary professional schools represents the most traditional method of educational upgrading. Typically, the program is attended by graduates from vocational schools who wish to earn a high-school diploma. At the same time, it can serve as a means to obtaining a new vocational certificate in a different field. The program usually lasts for two years on a full-time basis or for three years on a part-time basis.

Some limited options are also available for those with only primary education, but the follow-up study is usually significantly longer in their case (4–5 years).

The so-called National System of Qualifications has been under development since 2006. It is a publicly accessible register that defines skills required to obtain an occupational certificate. The occupational standards are used for both early and adult education and are set up by employers and representatives of educational institutions. One of the goals of the system is to test and certify skills gained outside of the standard educational system through a set of exams. Each exam leads to a certificate of partial qualification and the participant has to complete a final exam at a vocational or secondary school. So far, the National System of Qualifications has not been widely used as a means to acquire a vocational certificate or secondary-school diploma because the public awareness of this opportunity is very low. Moreover, students obtaining certificates of partial qualification might incur considerable costs,[3] even though the final exam is free of charge. Nevertheless, the fact that employers participate in setting occupational standards makes it likely that the certificates of partial qualifications will be more widely used in the future.

Formal adult education at the post-secondary level includes post-secondary non-university programs (ISCED 5B) and distance learning at the university level (ISCED 5A, 6).

Non-formal adult learning includes a variety of different options. Retraining courses, which are the main governmental instrument of the active labor market policies, play a specific role in this field. Retraining programs were introduced in 1991 at the beginning of the economic transformation and are usually offered through job centers. Participants are eligible for reimbursement of tuition fees and in some cases receive financial aid to cover the cost of travelling, accommodation, and meals. The courses can be attended by both employed and unemployed individuals. Since 2009, retraining courses have been linked with the National System of Qualifications and obtain accreditation only if they are completed with a certificate of partial qualification. However, participation in retraining is rather low and heavily skewed toward the long-term unemployed. Moreover, the reintegration of participants into the labor market has not been very successful (MŠMT – Ministry of Education 2007).

Given the fact that the system of continuing education is highly fragmented and run through a variety of institutions, it is difficult to precisely estimate total public expenditures; however, the available evidence suggests that the public support for adult learning has been generally low until recently. For example, from 2004–09, direct expenditures on retraining courses represented only 0.003 per cent of the GDP compared with the average of 0.234 per cent in the EU-27.[4] The total expenditure on active labor market policies reached around 0.010 per cent of the GDP in 2010. However, public expenditures on adult learning have been growing in the last few years. The Ministry of Education has launched several new programs,[5] and a network of centers for lifelong learning has been established to expand the opportunities for adult learning in various regions (MŠMT – Ministry of Education 2011, p. 34–5). Moreover, since 2012, indirect public support for adult learning includes financial aid to companies to enroll workers in educational activities instead of laying them off. This financial compensation covers workers' full salary for six (or in some cases 12) months.

Unlike the relatively low public investments, employers' contributions to adult learning are comparable to the OECD and EU standards. Further education is provided by nearly three-quarters of employers (71 per cent of employers in 2005, see CŠÚ – Czech Statistical Office 2008). In 2008, employers invested a sum equaling 0.39 per cent of the GDP in workers' education, which is slightly higher than the OECD or EU-21 average (0.36 per cent and 0.35 per cent, respectively). It is also critical to note that unlike the other EU or OECD countries, employers' expenditures on female adult learning surpass expenditures on male adult learning in the Czech Republic (OECD 2012, p. 419).

Participation in Adult Learning

The time series based on the LFS survey suggests that the overall levels of participation in adult learning in the Czech Republic are relatively low compared with the EU average (Figure 14.1). In 2010, only 7.5 per cent of Czech respondents aged 25–64 participated in some adult education or training in the four weeks prior to the survey compared with 10.4 per cent in the EU-15. However, these results should be interpreted with caution.

On the one hand, it is true that participation in formal adult education is low and declining in the Czech Republic. Participation rates peaked at the beginning of the 1960s, when 22 per cent of high-school students and 37 per cent of university students were adult students enrolled in part-time or distance-learning programs. However, participation in formal education has been gradually declining ever since. In the 1980s, adult students in part-time programs represented only 13–15 per cent of secondary-school students and 20–4 per cent of university students (EACEA 2010, p. 197). In 2008, only 4 per cent of the population aged 25–64 was involved in formal education compared with an average of 8 per cent among the EU countries (OECD 2012).[6] Official government documents explain the current low participation of Czechs in adult formal education by the fact that the Czech population is already relatively highly educated and upper secondary education is nearly universal (MŠMT 2007). At the same time, there are significant barriers to reentering formal

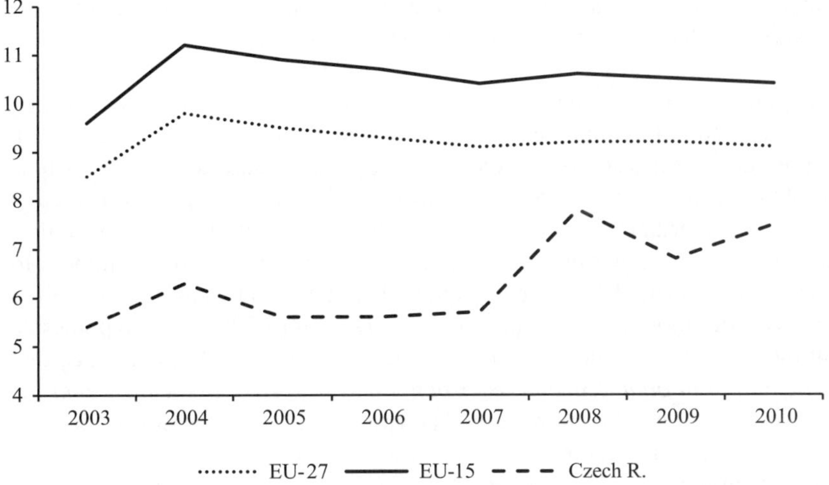

Source: Eurostat based on the LFS surveys, see OECD Employment Outlook 2012.

Figure 14.1 Participation in adult learning in the last four weeks (%)

education in adulthood, especially on a full-time basis. For example, students above 26 years of age are not eligible for any student benefits and have to pay their health and social insurance out of pocket if they are not simultaneously working (Czesaná 2010; Žáčková 2010).

On the other hand, it is necessary to note that the overall levels of participation in adult learning reported in Figure 14.1 are underestimated as the LFS data from this period do not fully capture participation in non-formal learning. In the last quarter of 2011, LFS data corrected a possible bias and used more-specific measures of adult learning. Consequently, participation levels nearly doubled (see more in the data section). The new measures from the LFS 2011 seem to be more plausible since relatively high levels of non-formal learning were also observed in other surveys. For example, according to estimates based on the AES survey, the Czech Republic is close to the OECD average (34 per cent and 33 per cent of the population aged 25–64, respectively, OECD 2012).[7]

HYPOTHESES

The empirical part of this text seeks an answer to two main questions: (1) What are the main characteristics of the participants in adult learning in the Czech Republic? and (2) What are the outcomes of adult learning? In this section, we outline some hypotheses regarding the characteristics of adult learners and the potential impact of adult learning on labor market outcomes. The outcomes are measured as chances of upward and downward mobility.

To study the characteristics of the adult learners, we focus on two key socio-demographic variables that are likely to be linked to the participation and outcome of adult learning: gender and the level of education already achieved. Past research clearly shows that the level of previous educational attainment is one of the strongest predictors of participation in adult learning. Several factors seem to be important in explaining the so-called "Matthew effect". For instance, individuals with higher education have already demonstrated a readiness to learn but are also more likely to work in higher-status and knowledge-intensive jobs that offer more training opportunities (Dieckhoff 2007). We hypothesize that the "Matthew effect" is relatively strong in the Czech Republic, i.e., that *participation in adult learning is strongly and positively associated with the level of education already achieved* (Hypothesis 1). The reason is that the educational system channels children into the academic and occupational tracks at early ages and the barriers between both types of educational careers are quite strong, which is likely to strengthen the "Matthew effect". Moreover, past research indicates that the relative difference between educational groups has been increasing (Czesaná 2010).

The link between gender and participation in adult learning is more complicated. Some studies have found that women are more likely to get involved in adult learning while others emphasize the relative advantage of men in the access to training. The relative gender differences appear to be linked with the type of learning measured but also with the type of welfare regime. We expect that *participation in adult learning will be skewed toward women in the Czech case* (Hypothesis 2) for two reasons. First, women from recent cohorts are more likely to achieve higher education than men, and educational attainment is by far the strongest predictor of participation in further education (Boudard and Rubenson 2003). Second, the Czech Republic has the lowest level of maternal employment among the OECD countries, and the majority of mothers drop out of the labor market for several years after the birth of their children. We assume that this long employment interruption depreciates women's human capital, and further training is often a necessity to be able to catch up.

Regarding the hypothesis predicting the association between adult learning and labor market outcomes, we expect that *participation in learning activities will increase the chances of upward mobility* (Hypothesis 3). Moreover, we predict that *adult learning will have a buffering effect against downward mobility since it might enhance the levels of human capital and function as a positive signal to employers* (Hypothesis 4). Furthermore, we hypothesize that *the association between learning activities and labor market outcomes will be stronger among women* (Hypothesis 5). It is likely that, given the tendency to drop out of the labor market for family reasons, an educational upgrade might be necessary to be able to make an upward career move.

ANALYTICAL SECTION

Data

As no survey of the Czech Republic provides a comprehensive picture of adult learning, this chapter relies on three different data sources. First, we use the Adult Education Survey from 2008 (AES 2008), which collected detailed information on educational activities during the preceding 12 months. Unfortunately, the Czech study left out all the questions about the labor market situation at the beginning of the reference period. Consequently, it is possible to study the characteristics of the participants in adult learning only for those who were continuously employed with the same employer. For others, it is not possible to distinguish individuals who changed a job from those who reentered the labor market after an unemployment spell or parental leave. In total, 5 802 respondents (61 per cent of the sample) were continuously employed in the same job for at least one year.

The Labor Force Survey (LFS) gathers more-detailed information on the employment situation even though, in this case, the information on educational activities is limited. However, a pilot that tested new measures of adult learning was run in the last quarter of 2011. The previous Czech LFS surveys directly asked whether the respondent participated in non-formal learning, but it is likely that most respondents did not know what "non-formal" learning stood for. The 2011 pilot used three questions and asked specifically about participation in training courses, seminar workshops, and private lessons during the preceding four weeks, and the measure of non-formal learning is derived from these three questions. These data will enable us to include the unemployed and other non-working individuals in our study.

Finally, to study the outcomes of adult learning, we rely on the Social Cohesion Survey from 2005/06 (SCS 2006). This questionnaire included a calendar with information about the respondents' labor market statuses for the whole post-communist period (from 1989 to 2005/06). Respondents were asked to indicate their economic status, type of occupation (if employed), year of the beginning of the status, year when the status ended, whether they were self-employed, the number of subordinates, and reason for the change. Unfortunately, the survey provides only yearly data, which might lead to an underestimation of job mobility since short-term and temporary jobs were not reported. Moreover, interviewers were instructed to record only the most significant changes, and unemployment was recorded only if the jobless spell lasted more than half a year. As a consequence, unemployment spells are rather rare in the dataset. Information on adult learning is limited to the question of whether the respondent finished some other school- or educational training and to the year of the last educational upgrading. Respondents were specifically asked two questions: (1) "Have you completed any other schooling or technical course, either at home or abroad, which extended your primary level of education?" and (2) "In what year did you last broaden (expand or extend) your education?" No additional information on the type of education (formal/non-formal) is available. The relatively rough measures of job statuses and further education in the SCS 2006 survey do not allow us to study the consequences of adult learning in detail. However, the analysis might disclose some general trends concerning the outcomes of adult learning. In total, 1 654 men and 1 806 women participated in the survey, 765 (22 per cent) of whom participated in further education, 414 doing so after 1989.

Participation in Adult Education and Learning – Descriptive Statistics

Table 14.1 displays the proportions of respondents aged 26–64 who participated in formal and non-formal learning in the last quarter of 2011 based on the LFS survey. For comparative reasons, information from the AES 2008 is also included. Formal education includes both full-time and part-time programs. Non-formal education comprises private lessons and courses, courses conducted through open and distance education, seminars, workshops, and guided on-the-job trainings. Table 14.1 shows that participation in formal education is low in both cases. Only 3.9 per cent of respondents were enrolled in the preceding 12 months in the AES and only 2 per cent in the preceding four weeks in the LFS surveys. Furthermore, the table shows that formal adult learning is more common among women, whereas men are more likely to participate in non-formal learning. However, it is important to note that these crude proportions do not take into account labor force participation. As we will later show, the relatively high proportion of men in non-formal learning can be explained by their higher labor force participation.

Enrollment in formal education rapidly declines with age, and formal educational activity in the preceding 12 months was reported by less than 1 per cent of respondents in the age group 45+. Older individuals are also less likely to participate in non-formal training. We must also note that the effect of education is strong and consistent across all sub-groups. The higher the educational level an individual has, the more likely he or she is to participate in adult learning. In other words, further education attracts mainly individuals who already enjoy the benefits of relatively high education and is only rarely

Table 14.1 *Proportion of respondents that participated in adult learning in the last 12 months (weighted %)*

| | AES | | | | | | LFS – last 4 weeks | | | | | | LFS – last 12 months | | | | | |
| | Formal | | | Non-formal | | | Formal | | | Non-formal | | | Non-formal | | |
	M	W	All	M	W	All	M	W	All	M	W	All	M	W	All
Age groups															
26–34	9.3	10.3	9.8	44.2	31.4	38.0	4.8	6.1	5.4	17.8	18.0	17.9	41.6	34.7	38.3
35–44	3.0	4.3	3.6	47.3	39.8	43.5	1.2	2.7	1.9	15.7	17.5	16.6	42.1	36.6	39.4
45–54	1.0	2.1	1.5	41.1	38.6	39.8	0.6	0.9	0.7	12.6	16.6	14.5	36.1	34.8	35.5
55+	0.1	0.5	0.3	26.1	16.9	21.4	0.1	0.1	0.1	7.9	7.9	7.9	23.5	17.0	20.1
Education															
Primary	0.0	0.6	0.4	16.7	31.2	11.3	0.3	0.4	0.4	4.0	3.3	3.5	17.2	8.7	11.5
Vocational	0.9	1.1	0.9	34.0	16.6	26.8	0.4	0.8	0.5	6.5	6.8	6.6	27.5	17.2	23.3
High school diploma	5.3	5.7	5.5	42.9	40.8	41.7	3.0	3.1	3.0	16.3	19.0	17.9	41.2	38.9	39.9
Tertiary	8.4	11.2	9.7	57.2	56.7	57.0	3.4	5.0	4.2	30.3	27.3	28.8	55.2	49.4	52.4
Total	3.4	4.3	3.9	39.5	31.2	35.4	1.7	2.4	2.0	13.6	14.9	14.2	36.1	30.6	33.4
Individuals	4 600	4 900	9 500	4 592	4 900	9 492	14 917	15 988	30 905	14 904	15 980	30 884	14 888	15 975	30 863

Source: Own calculations based on Adult Education Survey 2008, Labor Force Survey 2011.

293

used by disadvantaged groups to catch up and compensate for the lack of human capital.

Characteristics of the Participants in Non-Formal Adult Learning

Table 14.2 reports estimated odds from a logistic regression predicting the likelihood of participation in non-formal learning in the preceding four weeks in the LFS data from the last quarter of 2011. Given the fact that only 2 per cent of the sample participated in formal adult education, the estimates for this type of education are not reported in the table.

Three models were used to assess the characteristics of the participants in non-formal adult learning. Model 1 controls for socio-demographic characteristics of the respondents, i.e., gender, age, living with a spouse/ partner, presence of children at home, educational attainment, and economic activity (employed, unemployed, and other). Models 2 and 3 include only individuals who are employed. Model 2 controls for the socio-demographic characteristics mentioned above (except for economic activity) and Model 3 enters some characteristics of respondents' jobs, i.e., job-specific experience measured by the number of years spent in the job, permanency of the contract, and sector. The last variable distinguishes employees in industry, commercial services, public and cultural services, and other.

Table 14.2 demonstrates that participation in non-formal training declines with age and is strongly dependent upon education, which corroborates Hypothesis 1. For example, men and women with tertiary education have 12 and 8 times higher odds, respectively, of being involved in adult learning activities than their peers with just primary education. Moreover, the table shows that if we control for employment status and educational attainment, women are more likely to get further training than men, which confirms Hypothesis 2. However, the relative advantage of women loses significance if the sector of employment is controlled for. In other words, women's higher participation in adult learning can be explained by the fact that they are more likely to work in sectors where training is more common.

Furthermore, employed individuals are the most likely to get trained, and the model does not indicate that non-formal learning is a typical pathway out of unemployment. We should note that participation in adult learning is especially low among unemployed men. Even though the employment status matters per se, the length of the employment and permanency of the contract do not influence participation in adult learning. However, it is important to note that both of these variables were significant in the AES data (results not reported here). One of the potential explanations of this lies in the reference period. The LFS data collects information on the four weeks prior to the

Table 14.2 Coefficients from logistic regression with dependent variable "participation in non-formal education"

	Men			Women		
	M1	M2	M3	M1	M2	M3
Constant	0.12 **	0.09 **	0.07 **	0.12 **	0.08 **	0.08 **
Age	0.98 **	0.98 **	0.98 **	0.98 **	0.99 **	0.98 **
Living with a partner	0.96	0.97	0.96	0.95	0.95	0.99
Children at home (ref. none)						
Children 0–5	0.97	0.95	0.95	0.89 +	0.95	0.92
Children 6–18	0.99	0.98	0.96	0.91 +	0.89 *	0.84 **
Education (ref. primary)						
Vocational	1.35	1.81 *	2.24 *	1.72 **	1.93 **	1.67 *
High school diploma	3.50 **	4.72 **	5.77 **	5.53 **	6.88 **	5.76 **
Tertiary	7.64 **	10.40 **	11.60 **	8.48 **	10.70 **	7.69 **
Activity (ref. employed)						
Unemployed	0.47 **	–	–	0.80 +	–	–
Other	0.26 **	–	–	0.26 **	–	–
Years in the job	–	–	1.02	–	–	0.99
Permanent contract	–	–	0.88	–	–	1.22
Sector (ref. industry)						
Services	–	–	1.37 **	–	–	1.28 **
Public and cultural	–	–	1.48 **	–	–	1.58 **
Other	–	–	0.78	–	–	2.25 **
Male – coefficient from models with both genders	0.78 **	0.79 **	0.94	–	–	–

Notes: **$p < 0.01$, *$p < 0.05$, +$p < 0.10$. N (men) = 14 904, N (women) = 15 980.

Source: Own calculations based on Labor Force Survey, last quarter 2011.

survey, and the respondents are likely to remember and report even shorter and less-significant training sessions that might not be observed in the AES data. Given the fact that these short-term courses or seminars are likely to have a lesser impact on labor market outcomes, their inclusion might pulverize the overall effect of non-formal learning. As mentioned above, the sector of employment is an important predictor of participation in non-formal learning, and those working in the industrial sector are the least likely to participate. Notably, participation is relatively high in the "other" sector and in public and cultural services. This finding corroborates previous research suggesting that the incidence of training is usually the highest in non-market services such as health and education (Boudard and Rubenson 2003).

Outcomes of Adult Learning: Upward And Downward Mobility in Prestige

To estimate the outcomes of adult learning in terms of prestige mobility, a discrete-time survival analysis is estimated using the SCS 2006 data (see above). Table 14.3 shows that approximately 14 per cent of respondents reported some further education in the dataset after 1989 and confirms that participation in further education was typical for higher educational groups. No difference between men and women with respect to further education was observed in the SCS data. Unfortunately, there is no information on the nature of this further education (see data section). It is also necessary to note that only the last educational upgrading is recorded in the data.

Table 14.3 Participation in further education by education before the upgrade from 1989 to 2006 based on the SCS data, descriptive statistics (%)

	Primary	Vocational	High school diploma	Tertiary	All	N
Men	5.0	8.1	20.9	28.8	14.1	1 445
Women	2.5	6.0	22.1	26.8	13.2	1 605

Notes: Further education is measured as a positive answer to question "Have you finished any other school or a professional course in the country or abroad to expand your primary educational career?"

Source: Own calculations based on the Social Cohesion Survey 2006.

Upward mobility is defined as a five-point increase on the adjusted CAMSIS scale[8] (Lambert 2003); downward mobility as a five-point decrease on the same index. If the respondent was still in the given job at the time of the survey, the observation is censored (censoring was set to 2004). Only job-to-job moves are included in the analysis; other moves are censored and spells that began in 2005 are excluded. In total, 2 442 job-to-job moves are recorded in the roster, of which 15 per cent are upward and 9 per cent downward. Around three-quarters of moves are to a job with a similar prestige.

As repeated events with multiple records per respondent are analyzed, random effect logit models are estimated using the discrete-time event-history data structure (Cleves, Gould and Gurierrez 2004; Rabe-Hesketh and Skrondal 2008). These models will assist us to treat jobs as being nested within individuals and will account for the relative similarity of each respondent's job spells. The rationale for choosing the random-effects models rather than fixed effects is that a substantial proportion of the sample is not mobile. These individuals would be dropped out of the sample in a fixed-effects model. Moreover, the time-constant covariates cannot be included in the fixed-effects models. This feature would be problematic with our dataset, which provides only little retrospective information besides the job roster.

Participation in further education is the main explanatory variable in our analysis. It is treated as a time-varying covariate and we test two alternative measures. The first option assumes that educational upgrading sets an individual on an upward trajectory and increases the likelihood of upward mobility in all future jobs ("long-term outcome"). This means that the variable indicating educational upgrading is set to 1 for all years under observation following the participation in adult learning. The second option assumes that educational upgrading helps an individual to move from a job with a lower prestige to a job with a higher prestige, but the effect of additional education is exhausted in the first transition. To experience further upward mobility, an individual would need further educational upgrading ("short-term outcome"). In this case, the dummy for adult learning will be set to 1 at the time of the educational upgrading but reset to 0 at the beginning of the next job.

The models further control for job tenure, i.e., duration of the job in years (time-varying: since the beginning of the job or since 1989), age in years (time-varying), highest level of education (distinguishing between primary, vocational, complete secondary, and university education) (time-constant), employment status (differentiating between employed and self-employed) (time-constant for the given job), and time period (1989–95, 1996–99, 2000–04).

Results – upward mobility
The estimated coefficients from logistic regression with upward mobility as the dependent variable are reported in Table 14.4 ("short-term mobility" – see above). Model 1 controls for duration of the job, gender, age, education, and employment status. Given the low odds of upward mobility in the first year, a dummy indicating the first year in the job is included along with the linear measure of job duration. Model 1 indicates that the likelihood of upward mobility is higher among younger individuals, men, and those who are employees compared with the self-employed. In contrast, education and job tenure do not seem to be important predictors of upward mobility. Moreover, the effect of the socio-demographic variables is similar among men and women.

Model 2 directly tests whether participation in adult learning changes the odds of upward mobility. It shows that the effect is significant and positive

Table 14.4 Coefficients from logistic regression with dependent variable "upward mobility" (xtlogit)

	Men				Women			
	M1	M2	M3	M4	M1	M2	M3	M4
Constant	−6.98 **	−6.98 **	−6.79 **	−6.78 **	−5.47 **	−5.55 **	−5.31 **	−5.31 **
Duration	0.01	0.00	0.05 *	0.05 *	−0.01	−0.02	0.02	0.03
First year in job	−1.16 **	−1.16 **	−1.04 **	−1.05 **	−1.18 **	−1.17 **	−1.08 *	−1.07 *
Age	−0.01	−0.01	−0.01	−0.01	−0.01	−0.01	−0.01	−0.01
Education (ref. primary)								
Vocational	0.75	0.74	0.71	0.71	−0.02	−0.04	0.00	−0.02
High school diploma	1.04 +	1.02 +	1.02 +	1.02 +	−0.02	−0.12	−0.07	−0.08
Tertiary	1.01	1.01	0.98	0.98	−0.10	−0.17	−0.10	−0.08
Employee	2.90 **	2.90 **	2.76 **	2.77 **	2.15 *	2.16 *	1.96 *	1.98 *
Further education	−	0.48 +	0.53 *	0.41		0.93 **	1.01 **	1.47 **
Time period (ref. 1989–95)								
P2: 1996–99	−	−	−0.31 +	−0.30	−	−	−0.51 *	−0.49 *
P3: 2000–04	−	−	−0.81 **	−0.84 **	−	−	−0.71 *	−0.60 *
*Period*Further education*								
Period2*Education	−	−	−	0.04	−	−	−	−0.44
Period3*Education	−	−	−	0.31	−	−	−	−0.98
Male – coefficient from models with both genders	0.26 *	0.27 *	0.26 *	0.26 *	−	−	−	−

Notes: **p < 0.01, *p < 0.05, +p < 0.10. N (men) = 842, N (women) = 700.

Source: Own calculations based on the Social Cohesion Survey 2006.

for both genders even though it is stronger among women. Thus, women who participate in further education increase their chances of upward mobility 2.5 times (by 250 per cent), whereas men's chances only increase by 60 per cent. Moreover, it is necessary to note that the effect of educational upgrading is only marginally significant among men (at the 0.10 significance level). Model 3 includes a set of dummies controlling for the time period. It takes into account the fact that the labor market was rather turbulent and characterized by high job mobility during the first years of post-communist transformation (Večerník 1996, p.13). When the time period is controlled for, the effect of adult learning slightly increases for both men and women. However, the conclusion that the effect is much stronger among women holds (estimated odds of 1.5 for men and 2.7 for women). Our analysis therefore corroborates Hypothesis 3, which predicted that participation in adult learning would increase the likelihood of upward job mobility. Moreover, the analysis supports Hypothesis 5, which indicated that the effect would be gendered and more pronounced among women.

The fact that the effect of adult learning increased when the time period was entered into the model suggests that educational upgrading might have had a different impact in different time periods. The final model therefore includes an interaction effect between the period and adult learning. However, the likelihood ratio test comparing models both with and without interactions does not confirm the expectations.

The same models were used to estimate the long-term effects of educational upgrading. In other words, the models test whether the effect of educational upgrading extends even to future jobs; however, the analysis did not confirm this assumption (results not shown, available upon request from the authors).

Results – downward mobility

The same strategy that was used to model upward mobility was applied to estimate downward mobility (see Table 14.5). Model 1 again controls only for the socio-demographic variables. It suggests that men and women do not differ in their odds of downward mobility and that older individuals are less likely to move to a job with a worse prestige than the job they currently hold. Unlike the models for upward mobility, the first year in the job is not significantly different from other years, but the odds of downward mobility gradually decrease with job duration. The striking result is that the self-employed have significantly higher odds of being downwardly mobile if they move to a different status; however, this result is partly driven by the fact that the self-employed are assigned a higher prestige score in the CAMSIS scale than are employees, even if they work in the same occupation. The transition

Table 14.5 Coefficients from logistic regression with dependent variable "downward mobility" (xtlogit)

	Men				Women			
	M1	M2	M3	M4	M1	M2	M3	M4
Constant	−2.18	−2.24	−2.62 +	−2.61 +	−4.66 +	−3.98	−6.36 *	−6.42 *
Duration	0.35 **	0.36**	0.30 **	0.30 **	0.22 **	0.22 **	0.21 **	0.20 **
First year in job	−0.16	−0.17	0.08	0.07	−0.09	−0.09	0.02	0.01
Age	−0.47 **	−0.47**	−0.13 **	−0.13 **	−0.34 **	−0.34 **	−0.14 **	−0.14 **
Education (ref. primary)								
Vocational	−2.08	−2.02	−2.28 +	−2.27 +	−1.13	−0.90	0.27	0.41
High school diploma	0.29	0.23	−0.80	−0.83	6.22 *	6.06 *	5.06 **	5.08 **
Tertiary	3.17	3.26	−0.21	−0.25	−4.62 +	−4.03	−2.12	−2.11
Employee	−2.50 **	−2.53**	−2.08 **	−2.10 **	−6.27 **	−6.17 **	−6.30 **	−6.29 **
Further education	–	−0.34	−0.34	−0.72	–	0.06	0.01	−0.25
Time period (ref. 1989–95)								
P2: 1996–99	–	–	−1.93 **	−1.98 **	–	–	−0.92 **	−0.94 **
P3: 2000–04	–	–	−3.49 **	−3.46 **	–	–	−2.75 **	−2.77 **
*Period*Further education*								
Period2*Education	–	–	–	1.15	–	–	–	0.43
Period3*Education	–	–	–	−32.54	–	–	–	0.45
Male – coefficient from models with both genders	0.19	−0.24	0.20	0.25				

Notes: **p < 0.01, *p < 0.05, +p < 0.10. N (men) = 842, N (women) = 70

Source: Own calculations based on the Social Cohesion Survey 2006.

from self-employment to employment is therefore associated with downward mobility by default.

Model 2 adds the effect of further education. Table 14.5 shows that educational upgrading does not have any impact on the odds of downward mobility. In other words, we cannot confirm the Hypothesis 4, which suggested that further education might protect workers from the risk of downward mobility. Model 3 enters the time period into the equation and shows that the odds of downward mobility were highest in the early 1990s and have been decreasing since. The final model adds the interaction effects between the period and further education but does not confirm that the effect of educational upgrading changes over time.

CONCLUSION

The Czech Republic's educational system is youth-oriented and the system of adult learning is both fragmented and underdeveloped. Going back to school is difficult and uncommon and only approximately 4 per cent of the Czech population continues to be enrolled in formal education after age 26. These low participation rates might be partly attributable to the institutional obstacles facing formal adult education. In contrast to low enrollment rates in formal education, participation in non-formal or informal education seems to be on a similar level as that in other OECD or EU countries.

Our analysis indicates that participation in non-formal education is closely linked with the level of education already achieved, employment status, gender, age, and sector of employment among those who are already employed. The LFS data suggest that the opportunity to upgrade education or skills is primarily used by individuals with higher education. Adult learning only rarely serves as a means to improve training or skills among groups with lower levels of education. Similarly, participation is more common among those who are already employed, whereas the unemployed are less likely to upgrade their skills through participation in adult learning. Among employed individuals, the sector of employment is an important predictor of enrollment in further education, and those working in non-market services are the most likely to get trained. If employment status is controlled for, women are more likely to participate in adult learning. This finding holds, even if educational attainment and the sector of employment are controlled for. The analysis thus corroborates our first hypothesis that participation in adult learning is skewed toward women in the Czech Republic. As for other predictors, participation in further education declines with age but does not seem to be influenced by the duration of the job or the type of contract.

Analyzing the outcomes of further education, we found that the likelihood of upward mobility is higher among younger individuals, men, and those who are employed compared with the self-employed. At the same time, education and job tenure do not seem to be important predictors of upward mobility. In contrast, men and women do not differ in their odds of downward mobility, and downward mobility is less common among older workers. In both cases, the effect of the socio-demographic variables is similar among men and women. Furthermore, we found that participation in educational activities increases the chances for upward prestige mobility but does not protect against downward mobility. The results also suggest that the positive effect of further education on upward mobility is stronger among women than among men. If the time period is controlled for, the effect of adult learning slightly increases for both men and women, but the effect is still much stronger among women.

It is also important to note here that employers tend to invest in female employees' education more than in men's education (OECD 2012, p. 419). There are two possible explanations for this unusual finding: (1) Women work in professions where further education is more common and (2) The relatively high returns of further education for women might be linked to their tendency to drop out of the labor market when they become mothers. The employment of Czech (and Slovak) mothers with small children is low, even when compared with conservative or Southern European countries. For example, less than 20 per cent of mothers with children under three years of age are in paid employment in the Czech Republic compared with around 50 per cent of German, Italian, and Spanish mothers and around 70 per cent of Swedish mothers (OECD 2008). It is possible that such a long stay out of the labor market depreciates their human capital and that these women thereby have a low chance for upward mobility unless they upgrade their skills.

NOTES

1. The limitation of 24 months does not apply if the individual on the fixed-term contract temporarily replaces an absent employee, or when there are serious operational reasons or reasons relating to the special nature of the work (ILO – Employment protection legislation database).
2. More information on the Czech educational system is available in Eurydice materials, e.g., those accessible at http://eacea.ec.europa.eu/education/eurypedia.
3. There is a considerable variability in the price of the certificates but it may be up to 20,000 CZK, which corresponds to the median monthly income of a qualified manual worker.
4. These expenditures include only direct costs of retraining courses but not investment incentives for employers to retrain their employees. Since 2008, the expenditure includes also the EU-funded retraining programs. For more information, see www.dvmonitor.cz, published by the Ministry of Education, Youth and Sport.

5. These programs include "Educate yourself for growth", "Educate yourself for stability", and "Educate yourself".
6. Web page: statlinks.oecdcode.org/962012031P1T191.xls.
7. These numbers refer only to the proportion of individuals who participate in non-formal learning.
8. Unlike the original CAMSIS scale (available at http://www.camsis.stir.ac.uk), directors and managers of small companies were included among professionals (CAMSIS value of 98.57).

REFERENCES

Boguszak, Marek, Petr Matějů and Jules L. Peschar (1990), 'Family effect on educational attainment in Czechoslovakia, the Netherlands and Hungary', in Jules L. Peschar (ed.), *Social Reproduction in Eastern and Western Europe: Comparative Analyses on Czechoslovakia, Hungary, the Netherlands and Poland*, Nijmegen: OOMO, pp. 211–62.

Boudard, E. and K. Rubenson (2003), 'Revisiting major determinants of participation in adult education with a direct measure of literacy skills', *International Journal of Educational Research*, **39** (3), 265–81.

Cleves, Mario A., William W. Gould and Roberto G. Gurierrez (2004), *An Introduction to Survival Analysis Using Stata*, College Station: Stata Press.

Czesaná, Věra (2010), 'Nerovnosti účasti v dalším vzdělávání' (Inequality in the Participation in Further Education), in Petr Matějů, Jana Straková and Arnošt Veselý (eds), *Nerovnosti ve vzdělávání. Od měření k řešení* (Inequality in Education. From measuring to solving), Prague: Slon, pp. 353–75.

Czesaná, Věra, Zdeňka Matoušková and Věra Havlíčková (2006), 'Další vzdělávání v ČR' (Further education in the Czech Republic), *NVF-NOZV 6/2006 Working Paper*, Prague: National Training Fund.

ČSÚ (2008), *Continuing Vocational Training Survey 3*, Prague: ČSÚ (Czech Statistical Office).

Dieckhoff, M. (2007), 'Does it work? The effect of continuing training on labour market outcomes: a comparative study of Germany, Denmark, and the United Kingdom', *European Sociological Review*, **23** (3), 295–308.

EACEA (2010), *Organizace vzdělávací soustavy České republiky 2009/2010* (Organization of the Czech Republic's Educational system 2009/2010), available at: http://eacea.ec.europa.eu/ education/eurydice/documents/eurybase/ eurybase_full_reports/CZ_CS.pdf.

Hamplová, Dana and Martin Kreidl (2006), 'The winners in a globalizing world. Mid-career men in the Czech Republic', in Hans-Peter Blossfeld, Melinda Mills and Fabrizio Bernardi (eds), *Globalization, Uncertainty, and Men's Careers: An International Comparison*, Cheltenham, UK and Northampton, US: Edward Elgar, pp. 269–95.

Lambert, Paul S. (2003), *CAMSIS for the Czech Republic,* (electronic file, version 1.0, date of release: 21.3.2003), retrieved 8.10.2012 from http://www.camsis.stir.ac.uk/Data/ CzechRepublic.html.

Matějů, Petr (1993), 'Who won and who lost in a socialist redistribution in Czechoslovakia?', in Yossi Shavit and Hans-Peter Blossfeld (eds), *Persistent Inequality. Changing Educational Attainment in Thirteen Countries*, Oxford: Westview Press, pp. 251–71.

Matoušková, Zdeňka and Hana Žáčková (2008), *Angažovanost podniků ve vzdělávání zaměstnanců* (Participation of Businesses in Employees' Training), Prague: National Training Fund.

Mysíková, Martina (2011), *Personal Earnings Inequality in the Czech Republic,* Prague: UK FSV.

MŠMT (2001), *Národní program rozvoje vzdělávání v České republice. Bílá kniha* (National Program of Educational Development of the Czech Republic. The White Book), Prague: MŠMT (Ministry of Education, Youth, and Sports).

MŠMT (2007), *Strategie celoživotního učení ČR* (Strategy of Life-long Training in the Czech Republic), Prague: MŠMT (Ministry of Education, Youth, and Sports).

MŠMT (2011), *Dlouhodobý záměr vzdělávání a rozvoje vzdělávací soustavy ČR (2011–2015)* (Long-term Plan for Education and the Development of Educational System of the Czech Republic (2011-2015)), Prague: MŠMT (Ministry of Education, Youth, and Sports).

OECD (2008), *Indicators on Employment Protection,* Paris: OECD Publishing.

OECD (2012), *Education at a Glance*, Paris: OECD Publishing.

Oreinstein, Mitchell A. and Lisa E. Hall (2001), 'Corporatist renaissance in post-communist central Europe?', in Christopher Candland and Rudra Sil (eds), *The Politics of Labor in a Global Age: Continuity and Change in Late-Industrializing and Post-Socialist Economies*, Oxford: Oxford University Press, pp. 258–308.

Rabe-Hesketh, Sophia and Anders Skrondal (2008), *Multilevel and Longitudinal Modeling Using Stata,* College Station: Stata Press.

Simonová, Natálie (2011), *Vzdělanostní nerovnosti v české společnosti. Vývoj od počátku 20. století do současnosti* (Educational Inequality in the Czech Society. From the Beginning of the 20th Century to the Present Day), Prague: Slon.

Soskice, David (1999), 'Divergent production regimes: coordinated and uncoordinated market economies in the 1980s and 1990s', in Herbert Kitschelt, Peter Lange, Gary Marks and John D. Stephens (eds), *Continuity and Change in Contemporary Capitalism*, Cambridge, UK and New York, US: Cambridge University Press, pp. 101–34.

Večerník, Jiří (1996), *Změny na trhu práce a v materiálních podmínkách života v České republice v období 1989–1995* (Changes in the Labor Market and Life Conditions in the Czech Republic in the Period 1989–1995), Prague: Národohospodářský ústav.

Večerník, Jiří (1998), *Občan a tržní ekonomika: Příjmy, nerovnost a politické postoje v české společnosti* (Citizen and Market Economy: Income, Inequality, and Political Attitudes in the Czech Society), Prague: Lidové noviny.

Večerník, Jiří (1999), 'Inequalities in earnings, incomes and household wealth', in Jiří Večerník, Petr Matějů (eds), *Ten Years of Rebuilding Capitalism: Czech Society after 1989*, Prague: Academia, pp. 115–36.

Večerník, Jiří (2012), 'Earnings disparities and income inequality in CEE countries: An analysis of development and relationships', *Eastern European Economics,* **50** (3), 27–48.

Žáčková, Hana (2010), 'Bariéry účasti na dalším vzdělávání' (Barriers for further education), in Petr Matějů, Jana Straková and Arnošt Veselý (eds), *Nerovnosti ve vzdělávání. Od měření k řešení* (Inequality in Education. From measuring to solving), Prague: Slon, pp. 376–402.

15. Participation in Adult Learning in Spain and Its Impacts on Individuals' Labor Market Trajectories

Daniela Vono de Vilhena and Pau Miret Gamundi

INTRODUCTION

With its strongly segmented labor market, Spain is among the EU countries with the lowest rates of upward employment mobility. Within this system, work experience is the main element that contributes to the progress of careers, and formal education processes finish at young ages, with very few individuals returning to education as adults. The country is also characterized by cyclical unemployment periods and faced major changes in its macro-economic scenario during the first decade of the 2000s. In these years, we can find both the lowest and highest unemployment rates since 1976, beginning at around 8 per cent during the initial years and rising to 26 per cent in 2013. The combination of a segmented labor market with cyclical unemployment periods has been interpreted as Spain's strongest barrier toward the decrease of inequalities. Using data for the period between 2002 and 2009 from the Catalonian Inequality Panel, which encompasses both prosperity and crisis scenarios, we explore participation patterns in different types of adult learning as well as the role of adult learning regarding inequality patterns and its consequences on labor market trajectories. We aim specifically at answering the following research questions: (1) What are the predictors of participation in adult learning? (2) Does participation in adult learning increase the likelihood of the unemployed to return to employment? (3) Does participation in adult learning influence occupational-class mobility? (4) Does participation in adult learning influence the probability of getting out of precarious jobs?

NATIONAL INSTITUTIONAL SETTINGS

The Welfare State

The Spanish welfare state is part of the Southern European welfare system (Ferrera 1995; Rhodes 1997; Ferrera 2005). Among its most salient characteristics are a delayed modernization process, the insider-outsider divide, the generational bias, universal social benefits combined with an overlap of public and private provisions, inefficient states, and clientelism. These aspects have a direct impact on the configuration of societies, which exhibit high proportions of the population at risk of poverty, high levels of inequality, and a rigid and segmented labor market (Guillén and León 2011).

Focusing on the last four decades, Spain has moved away from the "underdeveloped version of the Bismarckian model" (Guillén and León 2011), which characterized Franco's dictatorship period, and toward a gradual process of universalization of social benefits (mainly education and health), which culminated in the 1980s. Nonetheless, social expenditures in the following years have also been gradually reduced, affecting the protective intensity but not the coverage of social protection. This relatively low intensity of social protection has led to both an increase in the participation of private welfare providers and a reinforcement of the role of families for the protection of individuals – the so-called welfare mix (Montagut 2011). Second, a decentralization process can be observed toward autonomous communities' competences regarding planning and policy implementation, particularly in the cases of educational and labor policies, despite the fact that the financial system is mostly centralized. This decentralization also implies an increase in territorial disparities with respect to the availability of services (Rodríguez Cabero 2004). A third characteristic relevant to this analysis is the Europeanization of social policies that took place after Spain joined the European Union, a process that has been characterized as "deep and intense" (Moreno and Serrano 2011). This process is particularly relevant in the case of the initiatives on employment policy (unemployed individuals are expected to become active, which includes participation in non-formal training) and more recently for policies on gender equality.

An important remark should be made on the changing role of women inside the Spanish welfare state. As in other European countries, the activation of female employment and the educational level achieved by women have increased enormously in the last decades despite the fact that female labor force participation rates in Spain are among the lowest in the EU. In the same way, women still lag behind men in terms of employment rates and job status attained, and married women and mothers are more often found in precarious employment compared with their single and childless counterparts. Although there have been significant improvements regarding the reconciliation of family and work in recent years, family protection policies are still very weak, which reinforces the traditional division of labor. In this context, the educational improvements achieved by women do not necessarily impact on the structures of inequality in the labor market (Salido 2011).

The Educational System, Standardization, and Stratification

The Spanish educational system is moderately standardized: There is a common and shared curriculum throughout the country that is determined by the Ministry of Education; nonetheless, there is a certain degree of sovereignty among autonomous communities in implementing extra courses, although these courses need to be previously authorized by national institutions. The educational system is also only somewhat stratified considering the fact that no selection procedures take place at early stages of educational careers (Martínez-Pastor, Bernardi and Garrido 2008). In countries with comprehensive school systems like Spain, secondary-school graduates have been found to require relatively little non-formal training to adapt to technological change (Bassanini et al. 2005).

In general terms and following a largely universal trend, the maximum education level achieved among Spain's population has increased considerably in the last decades. For instance, the percentage of individuals between 25–64 years old with a university-level education (completed or not) increased from 9.8 per cent in 1987 to 18.3 per cent in 2010 for men and from 7.4 per cent to 21.9 per cent for women. Educational expansion seems to be associated with a decrease in the class inequality of educational opportunities (Ballarino et al. 2009) and with upward social mobility across generations, which is particularly strong in Catalonia (Martínez and Marín 2011). Nonetheless, the process is strongly concentrated among younger cohorts and no relevant changes can be observed in the educational levels of older cohorts. In other words, educational expansion has not been accompanied by a substantive increase in formal adult learning, although a few initiatives in this direction have been implemented. Regarding formal adult learning, the main barrier to reentering as an adult is not driven by the characteristics of the educational system itself, but by this system's openness in relation to the participation of mature individuals. In closed systems, where enrollment as an adult is rare, participation is expected to be more 'scarring' for adults than is the case in an open system, where participation is much more frequently observed (Kilpi-Jakonen et al. 2012).

Adult Education and Lifelong Learning

In this chapter, adult learning refers to all types of educational activities that individuals participate in as adults, whereas adult education refers to formal activities only. The first act regarding the promotion of adult education in Spain was promulgated in 1838 but had very little impact. It was only in 1857, with the *Moyano Act*, that real importance was given to the promotion of an adult literacy policy in order to deal with the illiteracy rate of 81 per cent of the total population. Until 1970, the vast majority of initiatives were concentrated in literacy programs. The first act that also considered formal education for adults with different levels of education was promulgated during the last years of Franco's dictatorship regime, in 1970 (LGE Act), and implemented through the Permanent Program for Adult Education three years later.

Continuing training for adult workers was formally institutionalized in 1978 with the creation of the National Institute for Employment. Nonetheless, various programs already existed in non-governmental institutions. Among them, the programs developed by unions during the 1960s (*Programas de Promoción Profesional Obrera*) are of particular importance (Sarramona 1985). Community Universities (*Universidades Populares*), which originated during the beginning of the 20th century, were another important initiative regarding adult learning. Both organizations were formally incorporated into the structure of the state during the 1970s and mostly offer non-formal educational activities.

The LOGSE Act, promulgated in 1990, was the first legislative effort to reorganize formal adult learning after Franco's regime and to reframe it under the concept of continued learning. The law also aimed at promoting the participation of adults in different educational levels, albeit in very general terms. It was only with the LOE Act in 2006 that specific regulations were elaborated to promote adult participation in formal education. Key among these were the promotion of preparatory training to access vocational training and university courses, increased availability of distance learning at all educational levels, more flexibilization in terms of participation modalities, and regulations to increase participation in vocational training (Rodríguez 2008).

Regarding non-formal education, the important change in participation levels occurred in 1985, when funding for job-related training increased substantially. Regulations and policies offered by the state for the training of employed and unemployed individuals were developed together under the same framework of job-related training until 1993, when they were separated. Although general regulations in this field are much less specific in comparison to formal education, a much stronger effort toward the increase in participation rates in non-formal activities can be observed when compared with formal activities.

Currently, adult learning is officially defined as "continuing education and training for adults". In this case, adults are either individuals older than 18 or both older than 16 and employed (Ministerio de Educación 2011). The concept is operationalized and developed through three different systems within public institutions: education for adults (education administration) as well as training for unemployed individuals and continuing training for employed workers (labor administration). This national system is relatively decentralized and autonomous communities are responsible for implementing adult learning-related acts as well as organizing and offering activities. In other words, all policies regarding adult learning are currently implemented by autonomous communities. The adult learning regime is characterized by a relatively large number of learning centers available in the country (particularly in the case of non-formal activities), selectivity as a means of accessing formal adult education, and low participation rates (INEM 2007). Non-governmental institutions also play an important role in offering adult learning activities, as is particularly the case with unions, which act as intermediaries between the state, firms, and workers.

Data on adult learning activities offered by the educational administration shows that 454 000 individuals were enrolled in different courses in 2009/10, 53 per cent of whom were in formal education (Ministerio de Educación 2011). Regarding job-related training, 4 803 529 employed and unemployed individuals participated in some educational activity in 2010, amounting to 21 per cent of the active population in the country. Although the number of firms that offer job-related training increased tremendously during the last decade – from 33 000 in 2004 to 432 00 in 2011 – these activities were concentrated in big firms with more than 250 workers (50.6 per cent) (SEPE 2011; Fundación Tripartita 2012). Regarding the content of training programs, more than 30 per cent is related to health and safety issues and 15 per cent to the management of human resources. These are followed by informatics (14 per cent), foreign languages (11 per cent), and food handling (8 per cent) (Fundación Tripartita 2011). It is important to highlight that the different data sources reveal that the levels of participation in adult learning activities in Catalonia are very similar to the national average levels.

The Spanish Labor Market: Low Mobility in a Strongly Segmented Institutional Setting

As previously mentioned, the Spanish labor market has a strongly dual structure. On the one hand, there are the insiders: individuals who are typically mid-career employees in standard employment (i.e., with permanent working contracts) and strongly protected by the state (Blossfeld, Buchholz and Hofäcker 2006). On the other hand, those who have not succeeded at finding a stable job or who are altogether unemployed – the so-called outsiders – are the ones who struggle for stability. In other words, the insider-outsider model of job relations prevails and both instability and vulnerability are concentrated among outsiders and particularly among young workers. The spread of precarious jobs (mostly those with fixed-term contracts) was a strategy originally used to increase employment rates during the economic crisis of the 1980s but it currently creates a structural problem in Spain. According to this logic, seniority is the main driving force of upward mobility among the insiders, whereas evidence suggests that it is difficult for those who start working in precarious jobs to eventually find good jobs. Instead, a 'churning' dynamic has been observed: Workers occupy similar, precarious positions over time and job mobility occurs much more frequently than for insiders (MacInnes 2009).

The structure of the labor market is also characterized by a persistently high unemployment rate in comparison with the EU average. Spain's unemployment rate has always been among the highest in Europe, although its level has varied substantially in the last decades, ranging from 5 per cent in 1978 to 17 per cent in 1985 and later dropping to 13 per cent in 1990 only to rise again to more than 19 per cent in 1994. From 1994 to 2007, unemployment decreased to a level of 8 per cent following the prosperity years of the Spanish economy (Bentolila, Dolado and Jimeno 2012, based on OECD harmonized data). Nonetheless, with the world economic crisis, the unemployment rate is currently very high at around 25 per cent. Relevant to this study is the fact that after a period of strong economic crisis, Spain entered into its 'golden years' in terms of economic growth from 1994 to 2007, a period that encompasses most of the years available for the survey we explore in this chapter (2002–09).

This combination of a segmented labor market with a strongly cyclical unemployment rate is the most important barrier to the expansion of social protection and the decrease of inequalities between insiders and outsiders, gender, and cohorts (León and Guillén 2011).

HYPOTHESES

In Spain, education takes place early in life and to return to formal educational activities at atypical ages is a rather marginal phenomenon. In general terms and due to Spanish institutional settings, we expect to find low participation rates (with participation being concentrated among young adults) and a clear accumulated advantage pattern, also known as a Matthew Effect (Merton

1968). In other words, the more advantaged individuals, particularly regarding educational attainment, are those who are expected to participate more in education as adults. In these terms, instead of contributing to a decrease in inequality, adult learning may reinforce it.

Spain is characterized by widespread use of early retirement (Radl and Bernardi 2011), which makes it possible for workers with outdated qualifications to leave the workforce rather than having to retrain themselves. Therefore, there is less pressure on older individuals to participate in further education and lifelong learning in comparison with younger citizens. Additionally, the majority of the middle-aged are insiders with stable jobs. Thus, we expect lower levels of participation among older individuals in all types of adult learning. We also expect that single individuals participate more than individuals with other marital statuses in all types of education except employer-sponsored training, which is expected to be less influenced by events in individuals' life courses. As previously mentioned, mothers are still penalized in the labor market in comparison with childless women and men. Therefore, we expect children, in particular those under three years old, to have a negative effect on participation. This expectation is grounded on Spain's weak family protection policies.

Regarding gender, we follow the general *"gendered participation hypothesis"* elaborated in the conceptual framework. It is well-known that younger cohorts of women participate more in education in comparison with men, which is also true for the Spanish case. Specific to adult learning, it has also been shown that job interruptions due to maternity leave contribute to higher participation rates among women as a catch-up strategy to return to the labor market (Dieckhoff and Steiber 2011). In this way, we expect a higher risk of participation for women than men with the exception of employer-sponsored training, in which men should prevail. In terms of an educational profile, we expect to find a prevalence of the Matthew effect, whereby more educated individuals are more likely to have completed adult learning. All models control for place of residence because those living in rural areas are expected to be less likely to participate in adult learning.

For formal upgrading, we also control for labor force status and household income. As previously mentioned, the educational expansion was not accompanied by a substantial increase in formal adult learning. Formal upgrading is expected to be a very marginal phenomenon among the Spanish population and concentrated among young and wealthy individuals. We therefore hypothesize that those with higher household incomes and full-time students are more likely to upgrade as adults. In the case of employer-sponsored training, we include firm characteristics as controls. For firm size, we expect that the higher the number of workers is, the higher the probability of participating in training, as previous studies have demonstrated. Moreover, insiders are expected to have a higher likelihood of being trained compared with those in precarious jobs. Nonetheless, because we control for the insider/outsider divide, we expect to find a more equal pattern in the likelihood of participation among different occupational classes. We also expect non-formal non-employer-sponsored learning to be the type of adult learning in which vulnerable groups (particularly unemployed individuals and those in precarious jobs) are more likely to participate due to the relatively high offering of free courses, the short length of course duration, and the specificity of their contents, which seek to adapt the workforce to employers' needs.

Using human capital theory to hypothesize about the returns to adult learning, we can assume that changes in individuals' productivity (namely skills and experience) lead to job mobility (assuming no additional constraints). Based on this theory, adult learning would therefore be expected to impact positively on career progress. Nonetheless, considering the Spanish institutional settings, we have modified this hypothesis by using the dual labor market theory. In general terms, this theory predicts little intersegmental mobility, particularly regarding upward occupational mobility from the secondary (outsiders) to the primary (insiders) segment. Career progress in the primary segment is mostly a consequence of seniority, whereas the length of employment or an educational upgrade in the secondary segment does not necessarily lead to upward mobility. The theory also highlights that the availability of jobs is crucial for explaining probabilities of advancement in employment careers (Piore 1975). Additionally, women are considered as disadvantaged in the labor market, regardless of other factors such as human capital or previous labor experience (Vono and Vidal 2012). Therefore, women are expected to face greater obstacles toward upward mobility. In other words, we expect that an improvement in educational attainment or the completion of non-formal training have a positive impact on employment careers. Nonetheless, we also expect that this effect may be constrained by the institutional setting in Spain.

Concretely, in the case of formal upgrading, seeing as we expect low participation in general and a Matthew effect, those who upgrade are expected to be a small and privileged sector of the population who indeed benefit from the upgrade. We also expect a positive impact in the case of non-formal activities, particularly employer-sponsored training and non-formal activities for unemployed individuals. Considering the institutional efforts toward active labor market policies and based on previous findings (Arrazola and Hevia 2006), our assumption is that these kinds of training provide unemployed individuals with a positive short-term effect. However, due to Spanish institutional settings, we expect no effects of non-formal non-employer-sponsored training on employed individuals. Finally, the effect of adult learning is assumed to be non-significant for women although they may participate more, in comparison to men.

DATA AND METHODS

We used the Panel Survey on Inequalities in Catalonia (PaD), from which data are available from 2002 to 2009. This is the best available longitudinal dataset for the study of adult learning and its impacts on labor market outcomes in Spain and it is very similar to the structure of the British Household Panel Study (BHPS). The survey is representative of Catalonia and focuses on social structures and inequalities (Pineda and Puerto 2006). The total sample includes 3 266 households, 9 544 individuals, and 37 956 observations. Regarding our sample selection, a sub-set was created that includes only those individuals at risk of being an adult learner. This means that all individuals who were above the retirement age or who were studying for an age-appropriate qualification in an age-appropriate educational institution were excluded. Different samples were used depending on the population under analysis and final sample sizes thereby vary in each model.

Adult learning was studied based on the following typology: (1) adult upgraders in formal education, where as adults we include all individuals above age 25 as well as those who are at least three years older than the national median for completion of the specific level of education; (2) participants in non-formal adult learning whose training is not funded by employers (with separate analyses only for those employed); and (3) participants in non-formal adult learning who are employed and whose training is funded by their employer. We only considered individuals who completed their learning activities. In the case of formal education, this was measured by an increase in educational attainment between waves. For non-formal adult learning, the variable used reports on whether an individual had finished any activity within the preceding 12 months.

In the models related to the consequences of upgrading on labor market outcomes, we avoided causality problems by defining a formal upgrade as an event when it occurred in a wave before the change in our dependent variables. In the same way, the conclusion of a non-formal activity in the preceding 12 months was taken from the preceding wave backward. All waves were used for formal upgrades, whereas data were only available for non-formal learning beginning in 2005. The data limitation was also the reason we applied separate models for the different types of adult learning.

The individual characteristics included in the logistic multilevel regressions on predictors of the conclusion of education or training refer to the wave preceding the upgrade or the obtained training. These characteristics are age, age squared, gender, educational level, labor force status, marital status, children in the household, logarithm of household income, place of residence, and wave. For models restricted to employed individuals (Table 15.1, Models 2 and 3), we also included firm size, occupational class (ESeC), branch of industry, and a dummy to identify being in a precarious job. Branch of industry is based on a modified version of Singelmann's classification, in which transformative and distributive industries are collapsed into one category, personal service and producer service industries into another, and communicative industries into a third (Schmelzer 2012).

To analyze the role of adult learning on different types of labor mobility (leaving unemployment, occupational-class mobility, and leaving a precarious job), we applied discrete-time event-history models for repeated events. The dependent variable for leaving unemployment was defined as being unemployed in the current wave and employed in the next one. In the case of an occupational-class upgrade, the movement referred to any upward or downward movement between waves. Finally, for the models regarding leaving precarious jobs and based on the typology elaborated by Vosko, Zukewich and Cranford (2003), the following categories were considered precarious jobs: working without a contract; involuntary and voluntary part-time jobs; fixed-term contracts; self-employed without employees; self-employed or full-time worker with a second job; and full-time, working poor.

Among the control variables included in the models on returns to adult learning were age, gender, highest previous educational qualification for formal upgrade, current educational attainment for non-formal education, labor force status, marital status combined with household structure, children in the household, place of residence, wave, and duration of the spell. In order to deal with left-censored cases and to control for the length of job or unemployment spell, a self-reported start date of the current job/ unemployment (in calendar months and year) was used. For models regarding upward mobility of employed individuals, we included firm size, occupational class (ESeC), and branch of industry. We ran models considering two different definitions for formal education: (1) an upgrade at any (preceding) point of time during the survey or (2) a set of lagged dummies (upgrade during the preceding year, two years before, and three or more years ago) – the latter strategy was prioritized as far as the data allowed. For non-formal activities, the lagged definition was applied in each model. Finally, we controlled for missing information in the lags.

RESULTS

Who Participates in Adult Learning Activities?

In Spain, as we expected, formal adult upgraders are mostly young adults. Figure 15.1 shows the proportion of individuals eligible for a certain upgrade in formal education who indeed upgraded in the age range specified. It can be seen that obtaining educational qualifications at a mature age, specifically after the age of 40, is a rare phenomenon and those who do so are at the university level. In the case of non-formal learning, the age distribution of those who concluded an activity is less concentrated than in the previous case; nonetheless, the majority are younger than 50 (Figure 15.2).

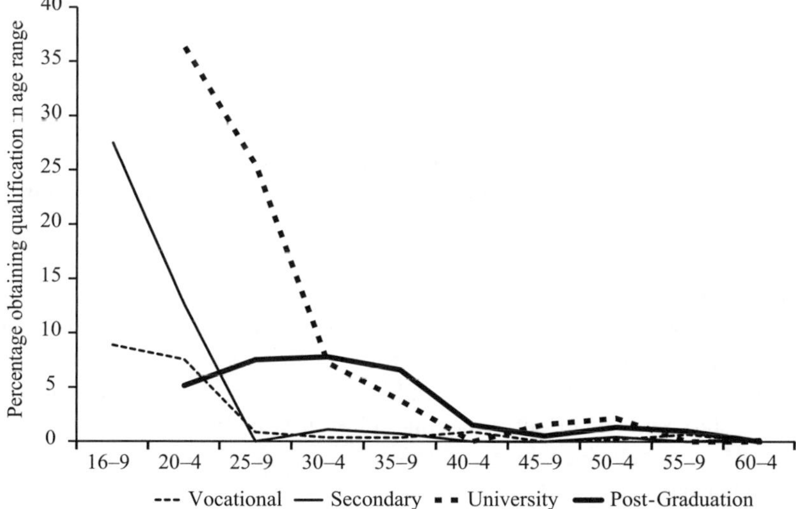

Source: PaD 2002–09.

Figure 15.1 Proportion of educational upgraders within age range by level of qualification obtained

The analysis of the characteristics associated with formal education upgraders shows no significant differences between men and women in the probability of upgrading. Individuals with a university degree have higher estimates in comparison with lower educational levels; however, the difference is only significant for individuals with vocational training. In comparison with those employed, full-time students are more likely to obtain a new

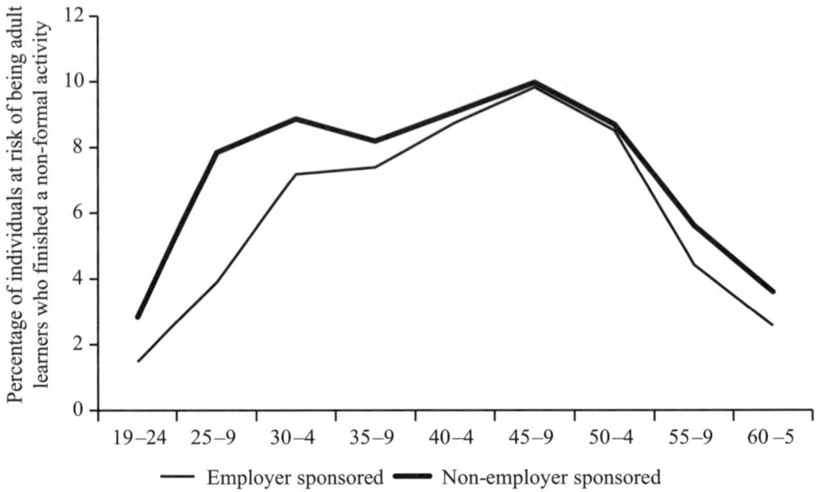

Source: PaD 2002–09.

Figure 15.2 Percentage of individuals who finished a non-formal learning activity in the 12 months preceding the interview among those at risk of being adult learners, by age

formal qualification. Differences by gender were found in the role of age, marital status, and household income – whereas these characteristics are not significant for men, they do play a role for women. Women who are single and living alone are more likely to upgrade in comparison with women of other marital statuses. The effect of having children is not significant. A positive effect of household income on educational upgrade for women can also be observed (Table 15.1, Model 1).

Model 4 (Table 15.1) examines the characteristics of individuals who participated in employer-sponsored training. Our findings confirm what has been already found in previous research for other European countries (Dieckhoff, Jungblut and O'Connell 2007; Dieckhoff and Steiber 2011): namely that men, highly educated individuals, and workers in big firms holding stable jobs are more prone to complete this type of learning. For men and women, the probability is estimated to increase until age 48 and 47, respectively, at which point it begins to decrease.

As expected, non-employer-sponsored training is the type of adult learning in which those less advantaged in the labor market are more likely to participate. The probabilities are higher for those who are unemployed or in a precarious job in comparison with those employed in good jobs or inactive. Nevertheless, educational inequalities are very strong.

Table 15.1 Predictors of educational upgrade and participation in non-formal training later in life (results as log odds ratios)

	All individuals		Employed individuals	
	Formal adult learning	Non-employer-sponsored	Non-employer-sponsored	Employer-sponsored
	Model 1	Model 2	Model 3	Model 4
Age	−0.27*	0.22**	0.15*	0.22**
Age squared	0.00*	−0.00**	−0.00**	−0.00**
Female	0.24	0.44**	0.27*	−0.26*
Highest (previous) educational qualification (ref. university degree)				
Postgraduation	Excluded	0.61**	0.55**	−0.08
Upper secondary	−0.07	−0.55**	−0.20	−0.51*
Vocational	−1.49**	−0.54**	−0.21	−0.31+
Compulsory	−0.44	−1.19**	−0.69**	−0.72**
Labor force status (ref. employed in a stable job)				
Precarious employment	−0.32	0.35**	0.26*	−0.37**
Unemployed	0.13	0.61**	–	–
Inactive (except students)	−0.39	0.09	–	–
Full-time students	3.89**	−0.16	–	–
Constant	−1.62	−7.15**	−6.33**	−7.06**
Observations	8 869	9 792	5 249	5 330
Number of individuals	2 685	3 662	2 070	2 101
Number of events	239	895	565	698

Notes: **p < 0.01, *p < 0.05, +p < 0.10. Additional controls in all models: children in the household, logarithm of household income, place of residence and wave. Models restricted to employed individuals also control for firm size, occupational class (ESeC), and industry.

Source: Own calculations based on the PaD (2002–09 for formal activities and 2005–09 for non-formal).

Regarding gender differences, women are more likely to participate in comparison with men. The probabilities of concluding non-employer sponsored training increases until around age 40 for both genders and then begins to taper. Marital status only has a significant effect in the case of married men, who are less likely to participate in comparison with unmarried men living alone, and having children less than three years old has a negative effect, but only for women (Table 15.1, Model 2). When analyzing non-employer-sponsored training only among employed individuals, all covariates behave in similar ways to those in previous models (Table 15.1, Model 3).

The Impact of Adult Learning on Labor Market Outcomes

With regard to leaving unemployment, we did not find any type of adult learning to have a significant effect, thus contradicting our initial hypothesis (Table 15.2, Models 5 and 6).

Table 15.2   Returns to different types of adult learning in the form of leaving unemployment (discrete-time model for repeated events, results as log odds ratios)

	Model 5		Model 6
	Women	Men	All individuals
Non-formal activities			
Non-formal adult learning	0.47	0.69	–
Non-formal adult learning, lagged 1	0.68	1.45	–
Non-formal adult learning, lagged 2	−0.58	0.08	–
Formal education			
Upgrade preceding year	–	–	−0.01
Upgrade two years before	–	–	0.94
Upgrade three years ago or more	–	–	−0.41
Observations	470	405	894
Number of individuals	318	285	615
Number of events	137	142	284

Notes: **p < 0.01, *p < 0.05, +p < 0.10. Models control for duration of the spell, missing information in lags for adult learning, current educational attainment in model 5 and educational attainment before formal adult education in model 6, gender, age, place of residence (rural or urban areas), marital status combined with household structure, and wave.

Source: Own calculations based on the PaD (2002–09).

In terms of occupational-class mobility, when it came to upward mobility, we found a significant and positive effect of formal adult upgrade that occurred three years or more before the mobility, and only for men. This shows that the effect of upgrading is not immediate but rather slow, although positive. (Table 15.3, Models 7 and 9). No significant effect was found for non-formal activities.

Regarding downward mobility, the models show a negative effect for non-formal education only for men (Table 15.3, Model 8). In other words, non-formal activities help men to stay in their job positions, preventing downward mobility. The effect was found for both employer-sponsored and non-employer-sponsored training, the latter having an effect with a lag of three years. The preventive effect of a formal upgrade was also found only for men and only when the variable used was an upgrade at any point in time during the survey (Table 15.3, Model 10). We additionally explored the effect of a formal upgrade within different occupational-class categories. The only case in which a preventive effect was found was among directors and high-earning professionals, which shows, once more, the prevalence of a strong Matthew effect in the role of formal adult education in Spain (Table 15.3, Model 11).

For precarious jobs, our results tend to corroborate previous findings regarding the difficulties in moving from outsider to insider: No effect was found for either formal or non-formal adult learning on the probability of leaving precarious employment when analyzing the whole population, which confirms our initial hypothesis (Table 15.4, Models 12 and 13). However, when analyzing only individuals younger than 36 years old, we found a positive and significant effect of a formal adult upgrade (Table 15.4, Model 14). Individual models for men and women showed no differentiated effects. Moreover, the effect found was only significant when *upgrading at any preceding time point during the survey* was used as the independent variable. No effect was found for the lagged set of covariates.

SUMMARY AND CONCLUSION

The aim of this chapter was to analyze the role of adult learning as an equality-enhancing instrument in Spanish society. Additionally, we aimed at exploring the impact of concluding a learning activity on individuals' labor market trajectories, particularly regarding leaving unemployment, moving across occupational categories, and leaving precarious jobs. We studied adult learning, taking into account different types of activities, namely a formal educational upgrade, a conclusion of non-employer-sponsored non-formal activity, and a conclusion of employer-sponsored non-formal training.

We first explored the characteristics of individuals concluding different types of learning activities by gender. For formal education, we found a strong effect of being a full-time student in comparison with other labor force statuses, which was interpreted as an indication of prolonged educational trajectories among young cohorts. The fact that single individuals living alone are at a higher risk of upgrading, particularly among women, confirms the significance of being wealthy. We found some hints indicating the presence of a Matthew effect: Individuals upgrading from university degrees have slightly higher estimates in comparison with other educational levels; however those

Table 15.3 Returns to different types of adult learning upgrade in the form of occupation class (ESeC) mobility (discrete-time model for repeated events, results as log odds ratios)

Non-formal adult learning	Upward mobility Model 7	Downward mobility Model 8	
	All	Women	Men
Employer-sponsored	−0.10	−0.43	−0.75+
Employer-sponsored, lagged 1	0.43	−0.25	0.12
Employer-sponsored, lagged 2	−0.61	−0.10	−0.14
Non-employer-sponsored	0.12	−0.49	0.46
Non-employer-sponsored, lagged 1	0.22	−0.30	0.03
Non-employer-sponsored, lagged 2	0.52	−0.40	−0.99+
Observations	8 682	5 166	5 040
Number of individuals	2 362	1 340	1 323
Number of events	248	421	350

Table 15.3 Continued

Formal adult upgrade	Upward mobility Model 9		Downward mobility Model 10		Downward Model 11
	Women	Men	Women	Men	only highest ESeC
Upgrade at any point of time during the survey	–	–	0.06	−0.81+	−1.37*
Upgrade preceding year	0.66	−0.07	–	–	–
Upgrade two years before	−24.06	0.76	–	–	–
Upgrade three years ago or more	0.59	1.77*	–	–	–
Observations	3468	3 349	4 993	4 867	1 315
Number of individuals	1106	1 044	1 297	1 278	331
Number of events	74	72	331	250	66

Notes: **p < 0.01, *p < 0.05, +p < 0.10. Models control for duration of the spell, missing information in lags for adult learning, current educational attainment in models 7 and 8 and educational attainment before formal adult education in models 9, 10 and 11, gender, age, place of residence (rural or urban areas), marital status combined with household structure, wave, children under three years old in the household, firm size, and industry.

Source: Own calculations based on the PaD (2002–09).

Table 15.4   Returns to different types of adult learning in the form of leaving precarious jobs (discrete-time model for repeated events, results as log odds ratios)

Model 12: Non-formal adult learning	All
Employer-sponsored	−0.29
Employer-sponsored, lagged 1	−0.21
Employer-sponsored, lagged 2	−0.28
Non-employer-sponsored	0.22
Non-employer-sponsored, lagged 1	0.28
Non-employer-sponsored, lagged 2	−0.41
Observations	3 552
Number of individuals	1 457
Number of events	649
Model 13: Formal upgrade	
Upgrade at any point of time during the survey	0.29
Observations	3 420
Number of individuals	1 406
Number of events	628
Model 14: Only individuals younger than 36 years old	
Upgrade at any point of time during the survey	0.48+
Observations	1 293
Number of individuals	635
Number of events	270

Notes: **p < 0.01, *p < 0.05, +p < 0.10. Models control for duration of the spell, missing information in lags for adult learning, current educational attainment in model 12 and educational attainment before formal adult education in models 13 and 14, gender, age, place of residence (rural or urban areas), marital status combined with household structure, wave, children under three years old in the household, firm size, occupational class (ESeC), and industry.

Source: Own calculations based on the PaD (2002–09).

effects were mostly not significant. The exceptions were individuals holding vocational degrees, who are significantly less likely to upgrade than the university educated.

Our results reveal a typical accumulated advantage pattern among participants in non-formal employer-sponsored adult learning since more-highly educated individuals are more likely to conclude an activity. Our results for employer-sponsored activities corroborate existing findings for other countries: Men, individuals in stable jobs, and workers in big firms have the highest chances of being trained. The type of adult learning in which vulnerable groups have a higher likelihood of participation relative to other groups is non-formal non-employer-sponsored training. Although those with higher educational levels are more prone to finish an activity, our results indicate that unemployed individuals and those in precarious jobs are more likely to conclude activities in comparison with those in stable jobs, and that women have higher probabilities of concluding activities than do men. We at least partially attribute this fact to the relatively strong active labor market policies that were implemented during the past several years and were heavily influenced by a Europeanization process. In this sense (and coming back to our initial hypothesis), we indeed find Matthew-effect patterns in terms of participation in non-formal adult learning: The most advantaged individuals, particularly in terms of educational attainment, are those more prone to participating in education as adults.

Secondly, we analyzed the impacts of adult learning on individuals' labor market trajectories. Despite the fact that Spain is among the European countries with the lowest levels of upward job mobility (Andersen et al. 2008) and although participation in adult learning is low and concentrated among the most privileged sectors of the society, we showed that participation in adult learning has a positive impact on labor outcomes, which is particularly relevant among young adults. Nonetheless, the positive impact is only visible for men, revealing that the improvements achieved by women in terms of educational careers do not impact on the structures of inequality in the labor market. We found an effect of formal adult upgrades on occupational-class mobility, both in terms of enhancing probabilities of upward mobility and preventing downward movements. The effect was also positive for getting out of a precarious job, albeit only for those under 36 years old, but no impact was found in the case of leaving unemployment, which partially confirms our initial hypothesis. Our hypothesis on gender differences was also supported: We expected no returns for women in comparison with men and found positive returns only for men.

The period analyzed in this chapter was mostly one of economic prosperity in which few macro-economic constraints were in place and insiders were strongly protected. Taking into account the strong economic crisis during the last four years and the reforms that have made it easier to fire insiders, we expect some major changes regarding our findings to occur in the future. First, we expect an increase in participation rates, particularly in formal education. Our results show that participation tended to increase from 2007 to 2008 for this type of adult learning, and we assume this tendency will continue. Second, the theory of the dual labor market highlights the fact that the availability of jobs is a key element when explaining the probabilities of advancement in employment careers. With the creation of new jobs, we expect updating skills to have an impact on the return to employment. For occupational class and leaving precarious jobs, we expect that, with insiders less protected, the need for updating skills and the impact of these skills on employment careers will increase in the coming years.

REFERENCES

Andersen, Tine, Jens Haahr, Martin E. Hansen and Mikkel Holm-Pedersen (2008), *Job Mobility in the European Union: Optimising its Social and Economic Benefits*, Denmark: Danish Technological Institute, Centre for Policy and Business Analysis.

Arrazola, M. and J. Hevia (2006), 'Gender differentials in returns to education in Spain', *Education Economics*, **14** (4), 469–86.

Ballarino, G., F. Bernardi, M. Requena and H. Schadee (2009), 'Persistent inequalities? Expansion of education and class inequality in Italy and Spain', *European Sociological Review*, **25** (1), 123–38.

Bassanini, Andrea, Alison Booth, Giorgio Brunello, Maria De Paola and Edwin Leuven (2005), 'Workplace training in Europe', *IZA Discussion Paper*, No. 1640, Institute for the Study of Labor, Bonn, Germany.

Bentolila, Samuel, Juan J. Dolado and Juan F. Jimeno (2012), 'Reforming an insider-outsider labor market: the Spanish Experience', *Serie Capital Humano y Empleo – Cátedra Fedea-Santander*, 2012–01, Fedea, Madrid.

Blossfeld, Hans-Peter, Sandra Buchholz and Dirk Hofäcker (eds) (2006), *Globalization, Uncertainty and Late Careers in Society*, London, UK and New York; USA: Routledge.

Dieckhoff, M. and N. Steiber (2011), 'A re-assessment of common theoretical approaches to explain gender differences in continuing training participation', *British Journal of Industrial Relations*, **49** (s1), 135–57.

Dieckhoff, Martina, Jean-Marie Jungblut and Philip O'Connell (2007), 'Job-Related Training in Europe: Do Institutions Matter?', in Duncan Gallie (ed.), *Employment Regimes and the Quality of Work*, Oxford: Oxford University Press, pp. 77–103.

Ferrera, Maurizio (1995), 'Los Estados del Bienestar del Sur de la Europa Social'

(The Southern Welfare States of the Social Europe), in Sebastià Sarasa and Luis Moreno (eds), *El Estado de Bienestar en la Europa del Sur* (The Welfare State in Southern Europe), Madrid: CSIC, pp. 85–112.

Ferrera, Maurizio (2005), *Welfare State Reform in Southern Europe: Fighting Poverty and Social Exclusion in Italy, Spain and Greece*, London, UK and New York, USA: Routledge.

Fundación Tripartita (2011), *Formación para el empleo: balance de resultados 2010* (Training for Employment: Results in 2010), Madrid: Fundación Tripartita.

Fundación Tripartita (2012), *Formación para el empleo: balance de resultados 2011* (Training for Employment: Results in 2011), Madrid: Fundación Tripartita.

Guillén, Ana Marta and Margarita León (2011), 'Introduction', in Ana Marta Guillén and Margarita León (eds), *The Spanish Welfare State in European Context*, Farnham: Ashgate, pp. 1–16.

INEM (2007), *Continuing education and training for adults in Spain*, Madrid: Servicio Público Empleo Estatal.

Kilpi-Jakonen, E., D. Vono de Vilhena, Y. Kosyakova, A. Stenberg and H.-P. Blossfeld (2012), 'The impact of formal adult education on the likelihood of being employed: a comparative overview', *Studies of Transition States and Societies*, **4** (1), 48–68.

León, Margarita and Ana Marta Guillén (2011), 'Conclusions', in Ana Marta Guillén and Margarita León (eds), *The Spanish Welfare State in European Context*, Farnham: Ashgate, pp. 305–12.

MacInnes, John (2009), 'Spain: continuity and change in precarious employment', in Leah Vosko, Martha MacDonald and Iain Campbell (eds), *Gender and the Contours of Precarious Employment*, Oxon, UK and New York, USA: Routledge, pp. 159–76.

Martínez, Xavier and Antonio Marín (2011), *Educació i mobilitat social a Catalunya* (Education and Social Mobility in Catalonia), Barcelona: Fundació Jaume Bofill.

Martínez-Pastor, Juan Ignacio, Fabrizio Bernardi and Luis Garrido (2008), 'Increasing employment instability among young people? Labor market entries and early careers in Spain since the mid-1970s', in Hans-Peter Blossfeld, Sandra Buchholz, Erzsébet Bukodi and Karin Kurz (eds), *Young Workers, Globalization and the Labour Market: Comparing Early Working Life in Eleven Countries*, Cheltenham, UK and Northampton, MA, USA: Edward Elgar, pp. 129–53.

Merton, R. (1968), 'The Matthew effect in science', *Science*, **159** (3810), 56–63.

Ministerio de Educación (2011), *Informe sobre el Estado y Situación del Sistema Educativo: curso 2009/2010* (Report on Current Trends and Characteristics of the Spanish Educational System, 2009/2010), Madrid: Ministerio de Educación.

Montagut, Teresa (2011), 'Assessing the welfare mix: public and private in the realm of social welfare', in Ana Marta Guillén and Margarita León (eds), *The Spanish Welfare State in European Context*, Farnham: Ashgate, pp.119–38.

Moreno, Luis and Amparo Serrano (2011), 'Europeanization of Spanish welfare: the case of employment policy', in Ana Marta Guillén and Margarita León (eds), *The Spanish Welfare State in European Context*, Farnham: Ashgate, pp. 39–58.

Pineda, Laia and Laura Puerto (2006), 'The PaD, the first longitudinal survey of Catalonia', *Paper at the Conference of the European Panel Users Network*, 8–9 May, Barcelona, Spain.

Piore, Michael J. (1975), 'Notes for a theory of labor market stratification', in Richard Edwards, Michael Reich and David Gordon (eds), *Labor Market Segmentation*, Lexington, Massachusetts: Heath, pp. 125–50.

Radl, Jonas and Fabrizio Bernardi (2011), 'Pathways from work to retirement and old age inequality in Spain', in Hans-Peter Blossfeld, Sandra Buchholz and Karin Kurz (eds), *Aging Populations, Globalization and the Labor Market: Comparing Late Working Life and Retirement in Modern Societies*, Cheltenham, UK and Northampton, MA, USA: Edward Elgar, pp. 121–47.

Rhodes, Martin (1997), 'Southern European welfare states: identity, problems and prospects for reform', in Martin Rhodes (ed.), *Southern European Welfare States. Between Crisis and Reform,* London: Frank Cass and Co., pp. 1–22.

Rodríguez, M. (2008), 'Evolución de la oferta educativa para adultos: de la educación a distancia a los centros de segunda oportunidad' (Trends in adult learning: from distance learning to centers of second oportunities), *CEE Participación Educativa*, **9**, 30–52.

Rodríguez Cabero, Gregorio (2004), *El Estado del bienestar en España: debates, desarrollo y retos* (The Welfare State in Spain: Debates, Development and Challenges), Madrid: Editorial Fundamentos.

Salido, Olga (2011), 'Female employment and policies for balancing work and family life in Spain', in Ana Marta Guillén and Margarita León (eds), *The Spanish Welfare State in European Context*, Farnham: Ashgate, pp. 187–208.

Sarramona, J. (1985), 'Situación de la educación de adultos en España' (Current trends of adult education in Spain), *Revista Interamericana de Educación de Adultos*, **1** (2), 61–73.

Schmelzer, P. (2012), 'Consequences of job mobility for the subsequent earnings at the beginning of the employment career in Germany', *European Sociological Review*, **28** (1), 82–95.

SEPE – Servicio Público de Empleo Estatal (2011), *Informe Anual 2010* (Annual Report 2010), Madrid: SEPE.

Vono, D. and E. Vidal (2012), 'The impact of informal networks on labour mobility: immigrants' first job in Spain', *Migration Letters*, **9** (3), 237–47.

Vosko, L., N. Zukewich and C. Cranford (2003), 'Precarious jobs: a new typology of employment', *Perspectives on Labour and Income*, **4** (10), 16–26.

16. Italy: A Segmented Labor Market with Stratified Adult Learning

**Paolo Barbieri, Giorgio Cutuli,
Michele Lugo, and Stefani Scherer**

INTRODUCTION

This chapter provides an overview of the main characteristics of adult learning in Italy and focuses specifically on predictors of adult learning and its effects on labor market outcomes, such as individual careers and occupational advantages in terms of quality and employment security.

Several elements are chiefly responsible for determining the potential relevance of adult learning as well as its criticalities. Italy is characterized by traditionally low employment rates (57 per cent), especially among women (47 per cent), and inactivity is rapidly increasing to the extent that being "neither in employment nor in education and training" (NEET) has become a mass phenomenon among young persons – the discouraged 'outsiders' (2.2 million according to ISTAT). Moreover, a series of factors hindering Italy's ability to recover economically in a reasonable time have led to a rather gloomy scenario. Among these factors are high levels of the youth unemployment rate (over 36 per cent), the high incidence of long-term unemployment, low levels of education (OECD 2011b), a poorly qualified occupational structure with a limited trend toward upgrading, the insider-outsider segmentation of the labor market (Barbieri 2009, 2011), and low growth in labor productivity (Lucidi and Kleinknecht 2010).

We begin this chapter with a brief overview of the structure of the Italian lifelong learning system, its development, its main organizational features, and their connected consequences. We take a closer look at the Italian formal educational system and at the role played by other agencies and actors responsible for the provision and promotion of learning activities: welfare and the labor market. Some descriptives concerning the factual (ir)relevance of adult learning are then presented in order to identify the relevant types and policies.

We use panel and event history analysis models to analyze the predictors of participation in adult learning and the effects of adult learning – mainly on on-the-job training (OJT) – on several labor market outcomes: individual prestige and occupational mobility, protection from unemployment or career instability, and the employability of the unemployed.

OVERVIEW OF THE INSTITUTIONS

The Educational System

The Italian educational system can be characterized as standardized, having a medium level of internal differentiation (Schizzerotto and Barone 2006), and having de facto (but not formally) relatively high levels of stratification. The educational system is almost entirely public, with only a small share of private (often religious) schools, which are generally of a lower quality than the public ones (Bertola, Checchi and Oppedisano 2007). Enrollment in public education is free, with merely a minor contribution being required for upper-secondary schools and quite modest fees for education at the tertiary level. During the past four decades, the Italian educational system has been structured in five levels: primary school (five years), lower secondary school (three years), upper secondary school (either three or five years; all five-year programs provide access to tertiary education since 1969), university, as well as doctoral programs (since 1981). In order to increase participation and completion of university tracks and thereby reduce dropout and long-term student rates, a three-level structure for university education was implemented based on the Bologna Process: a first-level (BA) degree (*Laurea triennale*, three years), a second-level (MA) degree (*Laurea magistrale*, two years), followed by doctoral studies (*Dottorato di ricerca*, three years).

Figures on the amount of public expenditure on education reveal that the distribution of the public investment in education in Italy is quite unbalanced despite the fact that spending is not too dissimilar from other major EU countries (but still below the EU average). Expenses are disproportionally devoted to financing the lower levels of education and consequently leave the tertiary level with relatively much less resources (OECD 2011b). The low spending is partly the result of low participation. In fact, overall levels of educational attainment are rather low in international comparison, with tertiary education falling far behind other EU countries (OECD 2011b). Educational expansion has so far concerned mainly upper secondary education and only currently reaches the tertiary level (Scherer 2013). In line with what has occurred in other countries, Italian women have surpassed men in terms of their educational attainment.[1]

Adult Learning in Italy

Lifelong learning and especially adult learning might represent relevant mechanisms to promote full employment (O'Connell and Byrne 2012) and social mobility and to foster productivity growth and economic progress. They might become even more relevant when the economy has to face the negative consequences of exogenous economic downturns (Scarpetta, Sonnet and Manfredi 2010). Nevertheless, adult learning still represents a very limited phenomenon in modern Italy, particularly when considering older individuals' reentry into the regular educational system for the purpose of acquiring some formal educational degree. The limited propensity to participate in adult learning can be partly attributed to the absence of any incentives that would favor the recovery of individuals' human capital. No paid leaves or monetary facilities are provided for workers who interrupt their labor market participation to acquire further education. Moreover, the scarce diffusion of part-time work as well as the limited expected returns from further education for the employment career represent additional disincentives (Ballarino and Scherer 2013). Formal adult education is therefore a marginal phenomenon, generally limited to evening classes (most common in vocational or technical schools) and mainly devoted to individuals who have previously dropped out of school. At the university level, participation in later stages of life is quite rare, except for (sometimes part-time) students who take longer than normal to pass the mandatory exams and complete university courses. Indeed, the share of individuals that participate in a 'de-standardized educational career'[2] is statistically irrelevant, amounting to around 1.5 per cent of individuals in all possible educational upgrading programs during their entire career (between the ages of 15 and 64).

Extending the perspective toward other forms of adult learning and considering all kinds of employment-related learning opportunities for the unemployed and employed, there are two major providers of adult learning: the state and private employers. Other possible training agencies as well as self-imposed, self-financed, and self-directed adult learning activities are virtually non-existent (ISTAT 2008, own calculations).

Regarding training provided by the state/public, (re)activation courses co-financed by the European Social Fund (ESF) have been introduced in the last two decades to reduce regional imbalances in the labor market, thereby facilitating the occupational integration of women, young persons, and disadvantaged workers as well as promoting the retraining of (displaced) labor force members (European Commission 2010; ECORYS 2011). Since these courses have been traditionally organized at the local (regional or even municipality) level, they are characterized by low standardization, and abide by quite heterogeneous goals, eligibility rules, and quality standards.

Only very limited expenses are dedicated to active labor market policies (ALMP), particularly to training programs aimed at improving individual employability. In fact, in terms of GDP, public spending for ALMP is among the lowest in Europe (0.5 per cent of the GDP in 2010, OECD 2012). Moreover, labor policies are strongly unbalanced towards passive LMP and are mainly targeted at labor market insiders. The very limited active LMP programs are targeted at the unemployed or closely-related groups (OECD statistics).

It is therefore not surprising that Italy ranks at the bottom of lifelong learning coverage, adult learning diffusion (regardless of the particular age group selected for the international comparison), and adult educational intensity (Eurostat 2011). National survey data show that, in more than 85 per cent of cases, lifelong learning and adult learning activities concern employed persons (ISFOL 2008), whereas the unemployed and inactive individuals have far lower participation rates.

Adult learning mainly takes the form of on-the-job training (OJT) if not provided by the state or by any other public agency. Consequently, in most cases (80 per cent), training activities are strictly firm- or even workplace-specific and are mainly scheduled during working hours (ISTAT 2008). However, even this OJT (employer-sponsored activity) is very limited. According to the OECD, the total annual labor cost of employer-sponsored non-formal education amounts to 0.18 per cent of the GDP as compared with an OECD average of 0.36 per cent (OECD 2011a).

In addition to being limited in its diffusion, access to adult learning and training is also very unequally distributed. These inequalities follow well-known inequality patterns, such as regional disparities, socio-educational cleavages, and relevant labor market dimensions (ISTAT 2008). Access to on-the-job training, for instance, is highly stratified, and higher-educated workers as well as those in high-skilled positions enjoy greater training opportunities (Cutuli and Guetto 2012). This "Matthew effect" (Merton 1995) of OJT adds to already-existing labor market inequalities. We find this effect in countries with poor public support for programs fostering employment chances and skills of the low-skilled workforce, e.g. in Italy and Spain.

In addition, the framework of the work agreement in which persons are hired turns out to be relevant. The labor market deregulation "at the margins", which was implemented in the 1990s, mainly aimed at favoring strategies of labor cost reduction between medium and small-sized firms and has increased labor market segmentation. Workers of the secondary labor market (FTC holders, pseudo-self-employed, temporary agency workers, etc.) are often employed as a sort of cheap "labor buffer" (Barbieri and Cutuli 2010) to cope with business cycle variations. These workers have much lower chances of receiving training than the core workers (Cutuli and Guetto 2012).

Firm size is another factor that shapes (re)training opportunities. Large firms have the economic advantage of being able to invest in the training activities of their internal workforce. This is not in itself a peculiarity of the Italian labor market. Nonetheless when dealing with firm-based training in this country one should keep in mind the structure of the productive system (Amatori, Bugamelli and Colli 2011). Large companies (>100 employees) amount to less than 2.5 per cent of all firms, and out of 4.5 million active firms in 2009, 95 per cent had fewer than 10 employees yet supplied about 47 per cent of all jobs (ISTAT 2012). This small and micro-asset of the vast majority of the productive system strongly affects a series of structural phenomena and labor market related issues, such as wages, mobility opportunities, female employment, work turnover rates, overall innovation capacity, and firms' strategies in international competition. It also affects firms' incentives to invest in training their workforce instead of opting for more opportunistic strategies of labor poaching, labor raiding, or eventually outsourcing the most innovative and skill-based activities. This results, among other things, also in a reduction of the need for firm-internal training.

The Sub-Protective, Double-Distorted Welfare State and a Highly Segmented Labor Market

The Italian occupational welfare state is characterized by its "double distortion", which is both functional and distributive (Ferrera, Fargion and Jessoula 2012). The functional distortion underlines the displacement of the welfare toward pensions, which almost exclusively benefit the older generations.[3] Such functional displacement is reinforced by decades of early retirement practices, which de facto forced social policies (pensions) to play the role of policies of labor supply reduction as a way of dealing with the restructuring of the manufacturer productive system from the 1970s to the 1990s. Such choices, indeed not uncommon among the continental EU countries, heavily contributed to fostering an increase in public expenses, thus deteriorating the public debt/GDP ratio. Italy currently demonstrates the highest expense rates in pensions in Europe (15.5 per cent of the GDP in 2012, OECD SOCX database), whereas other forms of social and family policies are residualistic.

The distributive distortion of the Italian welfare state has to do with the strong targeting of welfare interventions (mainly transfers) toward insiders. This was further reinforced by reforms in the 1990s that shifted the pension system from a defined-benefit scheme to a much less generous defined-contribution scheme – a reform that is applied only to the post-1995 cohorts of labor market entrants; older cohorts of insider workers remain fully sheltered. The distributive distortion perpetuates a situation of undue privilege and leads to institutionally originated social inequality. The result of such a situation is that the present welfare is still largely distorted toward the protection of the "industrial and manufacturer" constellation of social risks (and the related social groups), while the new, "post-industrial" social risks (and the related social groups) are left largely unsheltered. The mid-1990s bore witness to coincidental pension (1992, 1995, 1997) and labor market reforms (1997, 2001, 2003) that were both "partial and targeted", i.e., institutionally tailored to deepen the age-based, insider-outsider cleavage. This led to a strong labor market segmentation between the primary, well-protected, and socially secure sector and the marginal sector (Barbieri 2011). As a result, no policies concerning universalistic unemployment benefits, the activation of labor or the retraining possibilities for unemployed outsiders, minimum income schemes, families and housing, or child benefits are de facto disposable. The 2008 financial crisis exacerbated the institutionally originated situation of welfare-bias and posed extremely tight budget constraints. As a result, the veto power of the insider seems de facto insurmountable.

In contrast to other major EU countries, Italy continues to suffer greatly from the consequences of the 2008/09 financial crisis, yet its economy has been stagnant since at least the beginning of the new century (in terms of GDP per capita). In the meantime, the labor share (dependent workers) dropped from 70 per cent in the mid-1970s to about 40 per cent at the end of the 2000s, while the public debt/GDP ratio rocketed to 126 per cent in 2012 (it was about 60 per cent in 1980). Overall, employment protection legislation (EPL) lies within the EU average (and is slightly lower than in Germany), but the divide between the amount of protection that shelters permanent workers and the lack of guarantees that affect the (young and female) precarious secondary labor market workers is among the highest in the EU (Barbieri and Cutuli 2012). Much as is the case with generational cleavage, the labor market is segmented along traditional lines, such as gender and region; female employment is 47.2 per cent compared with an EU average of 58.6 per cent (ISTAT 2012), and the center-north/south divide represents a long-term, unresolved issue. The current economic crisis contributes to accentuating the existing cleavages. In addition, the upgrading of the occupational structure and therefore of social and occupational mobility chances, is rather moderate (Ballarino and Barbieri 2012). In the last years, white-collar positions have grown mainly for women. This fact has consequences for returns to education, which are now experiencing a notable decline, mainly for those with upper secondary education (Ballarino and Scherer 2013; Scherer 2013). This decline further diminishes individuals' incentives for human capital investment.

The long-lasting negative economic situation and the increased flexibility in labor relations realized over the past 20 years, while curbing wage growth and enhancing some employment gains, have led to a crisis in the trend of labor productivity growth. The shift toward a low-productive and labor-intensive growth path – which is quite problematic against the background of an aging population (Lucidi and Kleinknecht 2010) – is matched with scarce mobility chances and a work incomes restraint. Such a situation will inevitably lead to a rise in occupational and labor market inequality. Compared with occupationally segmented regimes (such as Germany), Italy (as well as Spain) is far less characterized by an "occupational labor market" because its educational system remains quite general in nature. As a result, entering the labor market takes very long, and young entrants often enter the "secondary, flexibilized labor market" even if they are well qualified (Barbieri and Scherer 2008, 2009).

DATA AND METHODS

We use data from the five waves of the Italian Household Longitudinal Survey (ILFI, *Indagine Longitudinale sulle Famiglie Italiane*) carried out from 1997 to 2005 on a representative sample of families. The panel information was completed by retrospective information on the life course. For the purposes of this chapter, we observe individual work histories since the first job search after having left the formal educational system. We concentrate on individuals born after 1940, aged between 15 and 64.[4] Training refers to attending a course or learning program in concomitance to employment.[5]

We investigate training exposure[6] by a longitudinal random-effects probit model and we employ panel fixed-effects models (linear and logit models) to study the effects of on-the-job-training. Fixed-effects models are most adequate for discovering possible causal effects. Consequences of job training are assessed on the basis of different occupational outcomes including the occupational prestige score, occupational mobility, employment stability (operationalized as the event of leaving an uninterrupted employment spell), and unemployment exit. Occupational prestige is measured by the CAMSIS prestige score (Lambert and Prandy 2012).[7] Occupational mobility is measured as changes in prestige scores, more precisely as a five-point upward increase or any downward decrease in the CAMSIS score. Fixed-effects panel models allow controlling for individual, time-constant, unobserved heterogeneity, which is relevant given that access to job training is most likely issue to selection processes based on unobserved individual ability.[8] Repeated training events and lagged training variables (t–1 and t–2) have been taken into account. The independent variables are educational attainment, labor force experience, firm size, private/public sector, working time, contract type, industrial branch, marital status, and presence of child/children. Where the number of cases allows, we stratify by gender.

To analyze employment stability, event history piecewise constant exponential models are employed. Because of the relatively low number of job training spells, the time dependency of training effects cannot be analyzed. As before, however, repeated events of training are considered. The effects of training on employment stability and unemployment risks are treated by means of a set of lagged (t–1, t–2, t–3) job training variables, which allow for examining the extent to which any training event effect persists over the following 36 months.[9] We use the same method to assess the effects of job training on the chances of leaving unemployment. The limited occurrence of retraining episodes (training events occurring within unemployment spells) does not allow us to separate models by gender in this case.

RESULTS

Descriptive Results

The picture depicted thus far, with very modest coverage rates of adult learning and training provision and even lower learning chances for labor market outsiders, is confirmed by our own analysis. Table 16.1 offers a snapshot of the exposure to lifelong learning for different labor market groups. Those who experienced at least one training event during their entire career do not exceed one-third of the interviewees, whereas training episodes during or in response to unemployment spells (retraining) cover around 5 per cent of the unemployment episodes.

Adult learning in terms of returning to formal education is marginal. We use two criteria to identify individuals receiving formal adult education: Criterion A considers all persons who are at least three years older than the national median upon completion of the given level of formal education (6.4 and 4.6 per cent for men and women, respectively). Our results reveal that 75 per cent of these individuals never leave the educational system. Criterion B encompasses persons who return to education after having left for at least two years, during which time they were active in the labor market (1.8 and 1.6 per cent for men and women, respectively). Only the stricter criterion B can be used to properly identify adult education since we would otherwise

Table 16.1   Adult learning coverage in the Italian labor market (%)

	Individuals		Employment spells		Unemployment spells	
	Men	Women	Men	Women	Men	Women
Training						
Total	33.1	34.1	–	–	–	–
Job Training	31.0	29.6	25.1	21.9	–	–
Retraining	1.2	2.0	–	–	4.0	6.0
Formal education						
Criterion A	6.4	4.6	4.4	2.3	0.8	1.2
Criterion B	1.8	1.6	1.2	0.9	0.0	0.0
N	3 358	3 051	4 223	4 279	1 006	1 036

Source: Own calculations based on the ILFI.

include working students still formally enrolled in the educational system. Unfortunately, due to the very small number of cases (which mirrors the substantial irrelevance of formal adult education in the population), we cannot estimate any reliable statistical model for the predictors and the effects of formal adult education. As a result, we focus on job-related training. As mentioned previously, training chances are concentrated in selected groups, and education strongly stratifies these chances. The probability of experiencing (additional) job training is highest among the highly educated (53 per cent), followed by those with intermediate levels of education (42 per cent), and finally by those with the lowest educational levels (21 per cent).

Predictors of Job Training

Table 16.2 depicts the predictors of job training for the entire sample of Italian (dependent) workers (M1) and distinguishes the results by gender (M2 & M3). Results are in line with the descriptive evidence, confirming a highly-selective allocation of individuals in job training programs. Gender does not seem to play any specific role in shaping individuals' chances of accessing training courses, but the influence of some of the other factors depend on gender. Being married comes with less training participation, and the presence of children reduces training for women.

Education (especially at the tertiary level) is by far the strongest predictor of job training. This finding can be read as the result of at least two mechanisms: (1) a positive relationship between job qualification and the need for updated skills and (2) the level of education as a signal of individuals' learning capacity.

Table 16.2 Predictors of job training (random-effects panel probit model)

	M1	M2	M3
	All	Males	Females
Female	0.00	–	–
Education level (ref. primary)			
Secondary	0.49**	0.48**	0.46**
Tertiary	0.78**	0.72**	0.74**
Resident in South (ref. not)	−0.29**	−0.31**	−0.29**
Married (ref. not married)	−0.20**	−0.18**	−0.20**
Children in household (ref. not)	−0.03	0.08	−0.14*
Prestige score	0.00**	0.00	0.01**
Labor market experience (years)	−0.00+	−0.01**	0.00
Non-permanent contract (ref. permanent)	−0.04	−0.08*	0.01
Working hours (ref. full time)			
Part-time, voluntary	−0.07	−0.15	−0.06
Part-time, involuntary	0.01	0.00	0.01
Employment sector (ref. private)			
Public	0.43**	0.36**	0.46**
Industry (ref. primary)			
Secondary	0.24	0.22	0.27
Tertiary	0.38*	0.38+	0.39
Firm size (ref. 1–5)			
6–15	−0.04	0.01	−0.15*
16–49	−0.01	0.00	−0.01
50–99	−0.12	−0.13	−0.06
100–250	0.12	0.15	0.06
>250	0.16*	0.28**	−0.26*
Observations	75 070	42 870	32 200
Individuals	4 989	2 606	2 383

Notes: ** $p < 0.01$, * $p < 0.05$, + $p < 0.10$.

Source: Own calculations based on the ILFI.

Firm size and service sector employment appear to increase job training chances. Large companies and firms operating in the service sector – possibly operating in open-market business and activities – invest more in training their workforce, though this is true only for men. Women are actually penalized by firm size. Their training opportunities particularly profit from working in the public sector. No statistical confirmation can be found for the negative effects of part-time work (voluntary or involuntary) in the literature, though the sign of the effects is in line with the findings of other studies.

The lower training incidence among secondary labor market male workers is also in line with the literature. Labor market experience, which is highly correlated with age, exerts only a small negative effect that is slightly stronger and significant for males and thus suggests that less-experienced young male workers might have greater opportunities of entering job training programs at the beginning of their career. On this point, it might be argued that in a context of high permanent contract stability, low overall training coverage, and very low quotas of workers repeatedly exposed to training, the few job training episodes are most likely concentrated in the very initial phases of the working career.

Moreover, the strong and negative effect of living (and working) in Southern Italy confirms how (net of individual characteristics) macro-level factors as well as differences in institutions and the productive and economic system account for a large share of training differentials.

Job Training Effects on Occupational Prestige and Mobility

Now that we have considered the (unequal) distribution of job training opportunities, we turn to the medium-term impact of job training on occupational prestige and mobility. Table 16.3 reports the results. Fixed-effects models are based on individual within-variation. Thus, only individuals who effectively experience some changes in the occupational prestige score over time contribute to the analysis. For the same reason, no individual time-constant characteristics (such as gender) can be inserted into the models.

Results from Tables 16.3 and 16.4 are substantively in line with our expectations. Participation in training increases a person's occupational prestige, indicating an important advantage for those acquiring training. More specifically, considering the effects of job training and its timing in the current occupational position (Table 16.3) suggests two things: First, the unfolding of a possible effect takes some time – the strongest effects appear to be those referring to job training up to 24 months before the interview – and second, women profit more from training. Looking at occupational upward mobility (Table 16.4), we find clear confirmation of an occupational prestige premium, yet there seems to be no effect on (reducing) downward mobility. In sum, on the one hand, our findings support the positive impact of adult learning in Italy. On the other hand, especially when considering the stratification of the access to training distribution, the results indicate even higher occupational disadvantages for those who are already in less-favorable situations and who, due to their personal characteristics or their labor market situation (primary versus secondary labor market workers), are less likely to benefit from any training opportunity.

Training obviously is not the only predictor of occupational mobility. As expected, also labor market experience, moving to the service or private sector, moving to a large firm as well as augments in educational credits come with an increase in occupational prestige. The presence of children instead lowers downward mobility for men somewhat.

Table 16.3   Occupational prestige score (CAMSIS, fixed-effects panel models)

	M1	M2	M3
	All	Males	Females
Training up to 24 months ago	0.33**	0.21+	0.47**
Training up to 12 months ago	0.09	0.14	0.08
Education level (ref. primary)			
Secondary	6.37**	7.63**	3.00**
Tertiary	7.97**	10.05**	4.18**
Resident in South (ref. not)	0.23	−0.44*	1.38**
Married (ref. not married)	0.26**	0.32**	0.08
Children in household (ref. not)	−0.11+	0.16*	−0.40**
Labor market experience (years)	0.06**	0.04**	0.05**
Working hours (ref. full time)			
Part-time, voluntary	−0.99**	2.56**	−1.47**
Part-time, involuntary	0.06	0.31	−0.01
Employment sector (ref. private)			
Public	2.40**	2.85**	1.99**
Industry (ref. primary)			
Secondary	5.02**	5.09**	5.50**
Tertiary	9.51**	10.06**	9.04**
Firm size (ref. 1–5)			
6–15	−0.22*	−0.18	−0.13
16–49	−0.50**	−0.47**	−0.60**
50–99	−0.22+	0.65**	−2.22**
100–250	−0.34**	0.14	−1.67**
>250	0.47**	0.85**	−0.93**
Observations	75 417	42 661	32 756
Individuals	5 015	2 596	2 419

Notes: ** $p < 0.01$, * $p < 0.05$, + $p < 0.10$.

Source: Own calculations based on the ILFI.

*Table 16.4 Occupational mobility, upward (M1–M2), downward (M3–M4)
        (fixed-effects logit panel models)*

	Upward mobility		Downward mobility	
	M1	M2	M3	M4
	Males	Females	Males	Females
Training up to 24 months ago	0.68**	0.31+	0.21	−0.03
Training up to 12 months ago	−0.26	0.58**	0.00	0.15
Education level (ref. primary)				
Secondary	0.73*	0.20	−0.20	1.04
Tertiary	0.37	2.17*	1.88+	1.74*
Resident in South (ref. not)	−0.32	−0.76	0.18	−0.86
Married (ref. not married)	−0.08	−0.49**	0.25+	−0.38*
Children in household (ref. not)	0.00	−0.25	−0.35*	−0.27
Labor market experience (years)	−0.12**	−0.09**	−0.12**	−0.11**
Working hours (ref. full time)				
Part-time, voluntary	−0.96	−0.11	−1.21*	0.78*
Part-time, involuntary	0.22	−0.57+	−1.14*	−0.47
Employment sector (ref. private)				
Public	0.88**	1.61**	0.83**	1.07**
Industry (ref. primary)				
Secondary	1.10*	1.88+	−1.77**	−1.47*
Tertiary	1.79**	1.94+	−2.35**	−1.47*
Firm size (ref. 1–5)				
6–15	0.30+	0.23	0.01	0.31
16–49	0.35+	0.43	0.20	0.21
50–99	1.31**	0.46	0.27	0.68+
100–250	0.73**	0.34	0.44+	1.58**
>250	1.06**	0.48	0.14	1.30**
Observations	16 465	8 002	12 611	6 847
Individuals	769	443	572	393

Notes: ** p < 0.01, * p < 0.05, + p < 0.10.

Source: Own calculations based on the ILFI.

Employment Stability

Another important labor market outcome likely influenced by job training
events is employment stability. Indeed, if an educational upgrade can have
positive consequences on occupational mobility, one should not necessarily
expect that it will produce the same effect on employment stability.
Theoretically, job training could increase both the chances of having an

Table 16.5 Employment stability and unemployment risks (EHA piecewise constant exponential models)

	Employment stability		Unemployment risk	
	M1	M2	M3	M4
	Males	Females	Males	Females
Time period (years)				
1–5	−7.63**	−5.73**	−7.6**	−7.13**
6–10	−8.44**	−6.18**	−8.45**	−7.93**
11–20	−8.82**	−6.73**	−8.84**	−8.52**
21–30	−8.59**	−6.90**	−8.68**	−8.32**
31+	−7.94**	−6.51**	−8.01**	−8.07**
Training up to 12 months ago	−0.33	−0.19	−0.50+	−0.22
Training up to 24 months ago	−0.30	−0.41*	−0.19	−0.36
Training up to 36 months ago	−0.51+	−0.60**	−0.57+	−0.85*
Female (from model with all)	–	0.92**	–	0.28**
Education level (ref. primary)				
Secondary	0.20*	−0.15**	0.14+	−0.09
Tertiary	−0.24	−0.73**	−0.35+	−0.51**
Age	0.00	−0.03**	0.00	−0.02+
Cohort (ref. 41–50)				
51–60 cohort	0.41**	−0.05	0.40**	0.21*
61–70 cohort	0.62**	0.27**	0.57**	0.71**
71–80 cohort	0.72**	0.24**	0.69**	0.70**
Resident in South (ref. not)	0.34**	0.11+	0.41**	0.03
Married (ref. not married)	−0.34**	0.38**	−0.29*	−0.04
Children in household (ref. not)	0.16	−0.12+	0.19	−0.04
Labor market experience (years)	−0.02	−0.03	−0.02	−0.06
Working hours (ref. full time)				
Part-time, voluntary	0.04	−0.23*	−0.46+	−0.61**
Part-time, involuntary	0.46**	0.10	0.43*	0.15
Non-permanent contract (ref. permanent)	1.19**	1.00**	1.16**	1.29**
Employment sector (ref. private)				
Public	−0.33*	−0.47**	−0.42**	−0.03
Firm size (ref. 1–5)				
6–15	0.30**	0.09	0.32**	0.13
16–49	0.30**	0.09	0.27*	0.01
50–99	0.24+	−0.13	0.25+	0.09
100–250	0.21	0.08	0.30*	0.09
>250	−0.10	−0.27*	−0.15	−0.15

Table 16.5   Continued

	Employment stability		Unemployment risk	
	M1	M2	M3	M4
	Males	Females	Males	Females
Industry (ref. primary)				
Secondary	0.65**	0.92**	0.65**	1.08**
Tertiary	0.52**	0.79**	0.50*	0.92**
Observations	656 722	481 702	656 722	481 702
Episodes	3 795	3 857	3 795	3 857

Notes: ** p < 0.01, * p < 0.05, + p < 0.10.

Source: Own calculations based on the ILFI.

internal career (and thus have a stabilizing impact) as well as an individual's opportunities in the job market.

Labor market returns from job training in terms of higher employment stability and lower unemployment risks are displayed in Table 16.5. Models 1 and 2 display the analysis of the risk of leaving an "uninterrupted" employment spell (defined as employment stability).[10] Models 3 and 4 report the analysis of the risk of leaving a job to become unemployed.[11] Piecewise constant exponential models are applied to study both the length of uninterrupted employment episodes and the length of unemployment spells. For both outcomes, we run models for the full sample divided by gender.

Upon first glance, job training appears to have a positive effect on employment stability since it reduces the likelihood of leaving an employment spell. Once again, the effect of job training requires some time to be fully effective. Job training reaches its maximum level for both genders after around three years. Additionally, job training also protects from unemployment risks and, again, the effect increases with time. Regarding the effects of the main socio-demographic covariates, some (well-known) groups appear to be more vulnerable to the risks of having an unstable career. Younger cohorts, persons living in Southern Italy, poorly educated persons, and individuals working in small firms and with fixed-term contracts show shorter employment spells and higher unemployment risk. As already shown, many of these characteristics also penalize persons in the access to job training programs. This means that the risks of having an unstable and insecure employment career come together with the risks of not being entitled to job training, thereby leading to a concentration of adverse occupational conditions for the same social groups.

This is the case, for instance, for women, who (see M1–2 in Table 16.5) have lower employment stability and shorter uninterrupted employment spells than men. In particular, gender-specific models allow us to recognize gender differences regarding the relevance of education on employment stability. Whereas for men the level of education is not an important predictor of employment stability, higher levels of education clearly protect women against employment exit, underlining the importance of education for women's career stability. This effect might be originated by gendered differences in labor market participation patterns. In fact, men's work career is almost always continuous, regardless of individual characteristics. This frame seems to also include the effect of adult learning. In fact, we see that the positive effect of job training on employment stability is weaker for men than for women. Also when analyzing unemployment risks, the impact of training differs by gender. In addition to some differences in timing, the consequences of training are stronger for women.

Overall, job training positively affects employment stability for both men and women, but the impact appears to be stronger for women. We should stress, however, that the same characteristics that influence participation in job training also result in more stable employment careers in the primary labor market sector. Consequently, adult learning could turn out to be a specific mechanism through which the segmentation of the Italian labor market is maintained.

Unemployment Exit

We conclude our analysis by examining the impact of job training on the chances of leaving unemployment. As stressed in the introduction, job training and adult learning targeted at unemployed persons are a rather rare phenomenon in Italy. For this reason, we do not present distinct models for men and women. Table 16.6 shows the piecewise constant exponential model for unemployment duration. Notwithstanding the relatively limited numbers, our analysis reveals how receiving job training during unemployment has a clear positive and overall significant effect on individuals' chances of leaving unemployment to enter a new employment spell, both in the short- and medium-term. Moreover, the effect of training is strong and matches with the effect of formal education, which reveals that the amount of human capital possessed by individuals does represent a highly valuable resource to escape from social and labor market exclusion.

As already stressed, individual-level characteristics that decrease the opportunity of leaving unemployment reproduce the usual pattern of predictors of labor market exclusion in Italy. Being a woman, being young, living in Southern Italy, being poorly educated, and not being admitted to any training activity definitely increase the risks of remaining trapped in unemployment.

Table 16.6   Unemployment exit (piecewise constant exponential model)

	All
Time period (years)	
One	−1.41**
Two	−2.13**
Three	−2.45**
Four or more	−2.96**
Training up to 12 months ago	0.42*
Training up to 24 months ago	0.54+
Training up to 36 months ago	0.27
Female	−0.40**
Age	−0.05**
Cohort (ref. 41–50)	
51–60 cohort	−0.04
61–70 cohort	−0.14
71–80 cohort	−0.35**
Resident in South (ref. not)	−0.64**
Education level (ref. primary)	
Secondary	0.30**
Tertiary	0.81**
Labor market experience (years)	0.00
Married (ref. not married)	−0.12
Children in household (ref. not)	−0.01
Observations	48 137
Episodes	1 423

Notes: ** $p < 0.01$, * $p < 0.05$, + $p < 0.10$.

Source: Own calculations based on the ILFI.

CONCLUSIONS

The aim of this chapter was to provide an overview of the main characteristics and consequences of adult learning in Italy by looking at adult learning's distribution and predictors, and its effects on individuals' labor market outcomes. Given the very limited social investments in (active) labor market policies, the overall weak welfare support, and the low share of employer-sponsored non-formal education, Italy maintains an overall residual coverage rate of adult learning and job training within a strong insider-outsider segmented labor market.

This situation applies to both the low incentives for returning to formal education and acquiring an additional educational degree at adult age as well as to on-the-job training. Limited returns to education and modest overall career mobility (net of seniority) plausibly work as disincentives for returning to school at older age. Formal adult education therefore remains a relatively marginal phenomenon. On the other hand, adult learning outlined as on-the-job training and related activities has proven to be highly concentrated in the insider, permanently employed, and already-qualified workforce due to the combination of the meager public investment in labor policies and of a sub-protective welfare state support for ALMP implementation.

Notwithstanding the scarcity of public and institutional attention paid to lifelong training strategies, adult learning and work-related training play an effective role – at least from a medium-term individual perspective – in reducing unemployment risks, promoting employability, and fostering job quality and upward occupational mobility.

The dark side of this situation has to do with the fact that training enrollment follows a rather selective mechanism that de facto excludes not only job-seekers but also a large share of the employed workforce (likely those persons who would most need and might largely benefit from training and retraining) due to both the strong labor market segmentation and the peculiar characteristics of the national productive structure. Empirical evidence confirms the existence of a "Matthew effect" for the Italian case. Low-qualified individuals, marginal workers, employees of (very) small firms, and persons living and working in poorly competitive contexts are de facto excluded from training opportunities.

In order to both pursue a better reallocation of workers to job opportunities and to re-distribute employment chances among socially differentiated groups, it would therefore be important to guarantee a larger investment and a wider diffusion of training activities among the more disadvantaged individuals and the social groups that face higher labor market risks and poorer career prospects.

NOTES

1. Educational expansion also came with some changes for social mobility and the inequality of educational opportunities, though the debate is still open. Some authors (Ballarino et al. 2009; Barone, Luijkx and Schizzerotto 2010) argue for a generalized trend of reduced inequality in educational attainment. Others are more skeptical (Barbieri and Scherer 2011). Moreover, when considering both vertical and horizontal educational inequality trends (Van de Werfhorst and Luijkx 2010; Munk and Thomsen 2012), the Italian situation appears nuanced. Lower social classes clearly have increased chances on the secondary level but not on the tertiary one. Moreover, the reduction in inequality on the secondary level has come with increased inequality in a horizontal

dimension of school-track differentiation, with the lower classes being relocated to technical and professional tracks.

2. Considered to be formal adult education takers who return to the educational system after leaving it for at least two years, during which time they were active in the labor market.

3. About 61 per cent of the national welfare budget is directed to paying for occupational and survivor pensions, compared with an average 45 per cent for the EU15 (Eurostat 2013). We should also note that the share of the GDP spent on social expenses in Italy – 28.1 per cent in 2012 (OECD 2013) – has apparently grown during the past years due to the reduction in the denominator.

4. The self-employed have been excluded from the analysis since learning measures represent on-the-job, not self-financed training.

5. The question on training in the questionnaire reads as follow: "After entering the labor market did you attend at least one professional training, re-training or updating course? Could you please indicate the period in which you attended it/them?" (Up to five training episodes could be recorded in the retrospective window.) Even if ILFI data do not allow for distinguishing training programs during/after working hours, cross-references with other comparative Italian datasets render us confident that our training measures detect to a great extent training episodes that occur on the job.

6. Independent variables included in the analyses are gender, marital status, presence of children in the household, place of residence, educational level, labor force experience measured as time since labor market entry, firm size, private/public sector, working time, contract, industrial branch, and prestige score of the current occupation. All panel models control for period effects. Age has been excluded given its high collinearity with labor market experience.

7. We performed a robustness check using the standard Italian occupational scale.

8. When running models on the predictors of job training and the effects of training on occupational prestige and on occupational mobility, the ILFI dataset was organized according to a yearly-person-spell data structure.

9. Independent variables included are gender, age, cohort, place of residence, educational level, labor force experience measured as time since labor market entry, firm size, private/public sector, working time, contract, industrial branch, marital status, and presence of children.

10. With "uninterrupted employment spell", we indicate one or more continuous job spell(s) with no breaks in between, due to any reason (unemployment or inactivity). We consider "employment spells" and not single "job episodes" in our analyses.

11. We also recode episodes of "cassa integrazione" and "liste di mobilità" as unemployment.

REFERENCES

Amatori, Franco, Matteo Bugamelli and Andrea Colli (2011), 'Italian firms in history: size, technology and entrepreneurship', *Economic History working paper,* No. 13, Banca d'Italia.

Ballarino, Gabriele and Paolo Barbieri (2012), 'Disuguaglianze nelle carriere lavorative' (Inequalities in working careers), in Daniele Checchi (ed.), *Disuguaglianze diverse (Different inequalities)*, Bologna: Il Mulino, pp. 79–98.

Ballarino, G. and S. Scherer (2013), 'More investment – less returns? Changing returns to education in Italy across three decades', *Stato e Mercato*, **96**, 359–86.

Ballarino, G., F. Bernardi, M. Requena and H. Schadee (2009), 'Persistent inequalities? Expansion of education and class inequality in Italy and Spain', *European Sociological Review*, **25** (1), 123–38.

Barbieri, P. (2009), 'Flexible employment and inequality in Europe', *European*

Sociological Review, **25** (6), 621–28.

Barbieri, Paolo (2011), 'Italy: no country for young men (and women)', in Hans-Peter Blossfeld, Sandra Buchholz, Dirk Hofaecker and Kathrin Kolb (eds), *Globalized Labour Markets and Social Inequality in Europe*, Houndmills, UK and New York, US: Palgrave Macmillan, pp. 108–46.

Barbieri, P. and G. Cutuli (2010), 'A uguale lavoro, paghe diverse; Differenziali salariali e lavoro a termine nel mercato del lavoro italiano' (Equal job, unequal pay. Fixed-term contracts and wage differences in the Italian labor market), *Stato e Mercato*, **90**, 471–504.

Barbieri, Paolo and Giorgio Cutuli (2012), 'Employment protection legislation, labor market dualism and inequality in Europe', Paper presented at the ECSR/EQUALSOC Conference "Economic change, Quality of Life and Social cohesion", Stockholm, September.

Barbieri, Paolo and Stefani Scherer (2008), 'Flexibilizing the Italian labor market. Unanticipated consequences of partial and targeted labor market deregulation', in Hans-Peter Blossfeld, Sandra Buchholz, Erzsébet Bukodi and Karin Kurz (eds), *Young Workers, Globalization and the Labor Market: Comparing Early Working Life in Eleven Countries*, Cheltenham, UK and Northampton, MA, USA: Edward Elgar, pp. 155–80.

Barbieri, P. and S. Scherer (2009), 'Labour market flexibilisation and its consequences in Italy', *European Sociological Review*, **25** (6), 677–92.

Barbieri, Paolo and Stefani Scherer (2011), 'Non-Persistent Inequalities (NPI) or Effectively Maintained Inequality (EMI) or Inequalities Maintained through Horizontal educational choices (IMH)? The Italian case study', Paper presented at the NEPS Seminar, July.

Barone, C., R. Luijkx and A. Schizzerotto (2010), 'Elogio dei grandi numeri: il lento declino delle disuguaglianze nelle opportunità di istruzione in Italia' (In praise of large numbers: inequalities in educational opportunities slowly decreasing in Italy), *Polis*, **24** (1), 5–34.

Bertola, Giuseppe, Daniele Checchi and Veruska Oppedisano (2007), 'Private school quality in Italy', *IZA Discussion Paper*, No. 3222, Bonn University, Germany.

Cutuli, Giorgio and Rafaelle Guetto (2012), 'Fixed-term contracts, economic conjuncture, and training opportunities: a comparative analysis across European labour markets', *European Sociological Review*, **29** (3), 616–29.

ECORYS (2011), *Evaluation of the ESF support to Lifelong Learning*, Rotterdam, available at http://sbnlo2.cilea.it/bw5ne2/opac.aspx?WEB=ISFL&IDS=18879 (accessed 7.10.2013).

European Commission (2010), *Employment in Europe*, Directorate-General for Employment, Social Affairs and Equal Opportunities, Luxembourg: Publication Office of the European Union.

Eurostat (2011), *Adult Education Survey*, http://epp.eurostat.ec.europa.eu/portal/page/portal/microdata/adult_education_survey (accessed 7.10.2013)

Eurostat (2013), *European System of Integrated Social Protection Statistics (ESSPROS) database*, http://epp.eurostat.ec.europa.eu/portal/page/portal/social_protection/data (accessed 7.10.2013).

Ferrera, Maurizio, Valeria Fargion and Matteo Jessoula (2012), *Alle radici del welfare all'italiana: origini e futuro di un modello sociale squilibrato* (The Roots of the Italian Welfare State: the Origins and Future of an Unbalanced Social Model), Venezia: Marsilio.

Isfol (2008), *PLUS – Participation, Labour, Unemployment, Survey*, http://www.isfol.it/temi/Lavoro_professioni/mercato-del-lavoro/plus (accessed 7.10.2013).

ISTAT (2008), *Labour Force Survey*, http://en.istat.it/lavoro/lavret/forzedilavoro (accessed 7.10.2013).

ISTAT (2012), *Struttura e dimensione delle imprese (Structure and size of firms)*, available at http://www.istat.it/it/archivio/64179 (accessed 7.10.2013).

Lambert, Paul S. and Ken Prandy (2012), CAMSIS project webpages: Cambridge Social Interaction and Stratification Scales, http://www.camsis.stir.ac.uk/ (accessed 7.10.2013).

Lucidi, F. and A. Kleinknecht (2010), 'Little innovation, many jobs: an econometric analysis of the Italian labour productivity crisis', *Cambridge Journal of Economics*, **34** (3), 525–46.

Merton, R. K. (1995), 'The Thomas theorem and the Matthew effect', *Social Forces*, **74** (2), 379–424.

Munk, Martin D. and Jens P. Thomsen (2012), 'Horizontal stratification in access to Danish university programs by institution and field of study', *VBN Working Paper*, Aalborg University, Denmark.

O'Connell, P. J. and D. Byrne (2012), 'The determinants and effects of training at work: bringing the workplace back in', *European Sociological Review*, **28** (3), 283–300.

OECD (2011a), *Education at a Glance 2011: OECD Indicators*, OECD Publishing, available at http://dx.doi.org/10.1787/eag-2011-en (accessed 7.10.2013).

OECD (2011b), *OECD Employment Outlook 2011*, OECD Publishing, available at http://www.oecd-ilibrary.org/employment/oecd-employment-outlook-2011_empl_outlook-2011-en (accessed 7.10.2013).

OECD (2012), 'Public expenditure on active labour market policies', *Employment and Labour Markets: Key Tables from OECD*, No. 9.

OECD (2013), 'Social expenditure', SOCX database, available at http://stats.oecd.org/Index.aspx?QueryId=4549 (accessed 7.10.2013).

Scarpetta, Stefano, Anne Sonnet and Thomas Manfredi (2010), 'Rising youth unemployment during the crisis: How to prevent negative long-term consequences on a generation?', *OECD Social, Employment and Migration Working Papers*, No. 106, OECD Publishing.

Scherer, Stefani (2013), 'Bildungserträge im Arbeitsmarkt – das Beispiel Italiens' (Returns to education – the Italian example), in Rolf Becker, Patrick Buehler and Thomas Buehler (eds), *Bildungsungleichheit und Gerechtigkeit: Wissenschaftliche und Gesellschaftliche Herausforderungen* (Educational Inequality and Justice: Scientific and Societal Challanges), Bern: Haupt, pp. 141–62.

Schizzerotto, Antonio and Carlo Barone (2006), *Sociologia dell'istruzione* (Sociology of Education), Bologna: Il Mulino.

Van de Werfhorst, H. G. and R. Luijkx (2010), 'Educational field of study and social mobility: disaggregating social origin and education', *Sociology* **44** (4), 695–715.

PART IV

Conclusion

17. The Promise and Reality of Adult Learning in Modern Societies

Daniela Vono de Vilhena, Elina Kilpi-Jakonen, Susanne Schührer, and Hans-Peter Blossfeld

INTRODUCTION

Despite the fact that the topic of adult learning is not a new one (see, e.g., Jarvis 1995), its relevance has only relatively recently been recognized inside academic and political spheres as one of the main issues in contemporary global and aging societies. Due to the acceleration of technological change caused by processes of globalization, generational change is becoming insufficient as a mechanism for adapting the workforce to new demands (Janossy 1966; Blossfeld and Stockmann 1999). Instead, individuals are required to continuously update their skills to be prepared for rapidly changing requirements of the labor market. In particular, adult learning has been identified as a potential strategy to enable older workers to stay employed longer, thereby also reducing the pension burden of welfare states (OECD 2004a; Schuller and Watson 2009; D'Addio, Keese and Whitehouse 2010; European Commission 2011).

Furthermore, the debate on inequality of educational opportunities has resurfaced, partly as a result of the PISA studies (see, e.g., OECD 2004b; see also OECD 2013 for new evidence on skill inequalities among adults). These studies have highlighted the extent of educational inequalities within and among nations, which has triggered a large amount of political attention and changes that have the aim of improving the quality and equality of education. However, these initiatives have hardly touched upon adult learning, despite the fact that this type of learning is an important way of giving individuals a second chance in education as well as in the labor market.

Notwithstanding the potential importance of adult learning for reducing social inequalities over the life course, the available evidence so far seems to often point in the opposite direction: Adult learning opportunities accumulate disproportionately to advantaged individuals (the so-called Matthew effect). This effect has often been explained from an economic point of view, whereby employers have greater incentives to train their more-highly skilled employees due to lower training costs and higher pay-offs (Dieckhoff 2007; see also Oosterbeek 1998; Korpi and Tåhlin 2009). It is also possible that the jobs held by these employees require more-constant minor adaptations to technological change, whereas low-skilled jobs may remain more stable in their required tasks but have a greater risk of becoming obsolete in the long run due to technological innovations (OECD 2013). On the other hand, the accumulation of learning has also been explained from the perspective of individuals, with greater barriers seen for the participation of the lower educated. This trend may be due to both the way that learning is organized and the prior skill or qualification requirements that are placed on participants (Gorard et al. 1998; Field 2000).

Although the importance of adult learning has been widely acknowledged, empirical evidence on the topic is still scarce, particularly from cross-national comparative research. In this sense, the aim of this book has been to contribute to this field of research by exploring patterns of participation in different adult learning activities and the consequences of participation on individuals' labor market trajectories using a life-course approach. The key to this perspective is the use of longitudinal data in all the included countries and the use of appropriate modeling for analyzing causal mechanisms over the life course (Mayer 2009). We have investigated how adult learning is organized in different countries, how successful countries are in terms of encouraging participation, and whether adult learning activities have a positive impact on individuals' labor market outcomes.

Our introductory chapter set out a number of hypotheses related to the general nature in which adult learning was expected to operate over the life course. However, we also expected that there were likely to be important country differences in our results due to national differences in institutional arrangements. In order to address these issues, this book includes an extensive number of country studies based on national longitudinal data as well as internationally comparative studies based on cross-national datasets. In this concluding chapter, we summarize the main findings of the book. We first give an overview of the chapters in terms of datasets and the issues they analyze. Following this, we discuss results regarding participation levels. We then discuss our initial hypotheses presented in the conceptual framework based on the results obtained from the analyses, with a focus both on the characteristics of participants and on returns to adult learning. We concentrate on results related to educational levels, employment patterns and gender because these formed the focus of our expectations and were analyzed in all chapters. However, it should be noted that individual chapters also include many results that relate to other life-cycle factors such as parenthood. We conclude with a discussion of the main results in terms of policies.

OVERVIEW OF ANALYZED DATASETS AND OUTCOMES

This book began with two cross-national chapters, followed by in-depth case studies. Although the majority of countries analyzed are part of Europe, we also included the United States and Australia as non-European examples of liberal societies. As can be seen in Table 17.1, all country studies are based on longitudinal data. However, cross-sectional data are also explored in the two comparative chapters (the Adult Education Survey in Chapter 2 and the International Adult Literacy Survey in Chapter 3) and are additionally included in the chapters on Australia, the Czech Republic, Estonia, and Hungary.

To understand the mechanisms of adult learning, it is crucial to recognize that the definitions of activities are strongly related to national institutional settings. Due to the variety of school systems and labor market structures, no one adult learning system is identical to another. Therefore, the construction of the measurement of adult learning in the datasets is country-specific due to both the specific structures of educational systems as well as dataset definitions and the extent to which they can be extended or changed. This is also why it has been important for us to limit the scope of activities analyzed in this volume in a way that enables cross-nationally comparative research to be undertaken (cf. Jarvis 1994).

In general, "formal education" refers to education that takes place either in educational institutions that are also attended by young persons or in institutions that mirror the content taught to young persons and that lead to qualifications that are comparable with the standard qualifications obtained along the normal educational pathway. In some countries, adult learners attending formal education can only be identified when they upgrade their educational level, whereas in other countries, qualifications at the same (or even at a lower) level – often indicating a change in the field of study – can also be identified. In turn, "non-formal learning" denotes any other form of organized learning outside of the educational system (such as on-the-job-training); this type of learning can also be certified. The variety of measurements among countries mirrors the variety of educational possibilities available in different countries. In some cases, the data additionally offered the possibility of dividing learning between employer-sponsored and non-employer-sponsored types.

Notwithstanding national differences in how the different types of learning were classified, our interest in all countries was on learning related to the labor market. Therefore, other types of learning were excluded from our analyses as far as possible. Although individuals participate in adult learning for a variety of motives, many of which do not relate to the labor market, it is important to study the ways in which adult learning is related to the labor market given the centrality of (paid) employment in modern societies.

The main concern of the book has been on understanding the mechanisms affecting participation in adult learning and adult learning's impact on individuals' life courses by prioritizing both the longitudinal approach and the respect for country specificities. Moreover, the aim of the book has been to analyze participation patterns of adult learning and its possible effects on labor market outcomes in different country contexts. In particular, while the study of adult learning is already established in Nordic and liberal countries, literature on the majority of Southern and Eastern European societies is rare. In some cases, this book even provides the first available analyses. Overall, we believe that cross-national comparisons that are based on studies from a life-course perspective and that take country specificities into account are the best way to understand the mechanisms of long-term changes from a comparative point of view.

HETEROGENEITY IN PARTICIPATION RATES

Among the patterns explored in this book, participation rates in adult learning certainly display the greatest heterogeneity among countries. In Chapter 2, four groups of countries were identified according to patterns of participation in different types of adult learning, namely formal and non-formal employer-sponsored activities on the one hand and formal and non-formal non-employer-sponsored activities on the other hand.

The first group of countries includes Denmark, Finland, Norway, Slovenia, and Sweden and is characterized by high participation rates in all types of activities. The second group represents those cases in which participation rates are at moderate levels in the EU context and includes Austria, Estonia, Germany, Lithuania, and the Netherlands. The third group is formed by countries in which the participation rates are relatively low in all activities, including Bulgaria, Croatia, the Czech Republic, Cyprus, France, Greece, Hungary, Italy, Latvia, Poland, Portugal, Romania, the Slovak Republic, and Spain. The fourth and final group is formed by Belgium and the UK and is characterized by high participation rates in formal education but low rates in non-formal adult learning. We expect that Australia and the USA – countries included in our book but not in the AES – would most likely fall into the second group and that Russia would possibly belong to the third group.

As expected in the introductory chapter, countries with higher levels of education also tend to have higher participation rates in adult learning. The high participation rates of the Nordic countries may also reflect the relatively

Table 17.1   Overview of country studies: data, observation window, and processes under study

Country group	Country	Data	Observation window	Processes under study
Comparative studies	Participation in adult learning in Europe	Adult Education Survey (AES)	Between 2005 and 2008	– Participation in formal and non-formal adult learning
	Returns to adult learning in a comparative perspective	International Adult Literacy Survey (IALS)	Between 1994 and 1998	– Income
Liberal countries	USA	National Longitudinal Study of Youth (NLSY79)	1979–2010	– Participation in formal and non-formal adult learning – Income – Career progress – Unemployment risks
	Australia	Household Income and Labour Dynamics in Australia (HILDA)	2001–10	– Participation in formal and non-formal adult learning – Career progress
	Great Britain	British Household Panel Study (BHPS)	1991/98–2008	– Participation in formal and non-formal adult learning – Career progress

Table 17.1 Continued

Country group	Country	Data	Observation window	Processes under study
Liberal countries	Russia	Russia Longitudinal Monitoring Survey (RLMS-HSE)	2000–10	– Participation in formal and non-formal adult learning – Career progress – Exit from precarious labor market positions
	Estonia	Adult Education Survey 2007 (AES), Family and Fertility Survey 2004/2005 (FFS)	2005 retrospective	– Participation in formal and non-formal adult learning – Career progress
Nordic countries	Sweden	Register data from Statistics Sweden (LISA)	1990/94–2010	– Participation in formal adult learning only – Employment chances – Income
	Finland	Register data from Statistics Finland	1987–2007	– Participation in formal adult learning only – Income – Unemployment risks
	Denmark	Integrated Database for Labor Market Research (IDA)	1981–2009	– Participation in formal and non-formal adult learning – Career progress – Unemployment risks – Reemployment chances

Table 17.1   Continued

Country group	Country	Data	Observation window	Processes under study
Central European countries	Germany	National Educational Panel Study (NEPS)	2011 retrospective	– Participation in formal and non-formal adult learning – Career progress – Unemployment risks – Reemployment chances
	Hungary	Adult Education Survey (AES) 2007, Hungarian Household Panel Study (HHP, TARKI)	1992–2007	– Participation in formal adult learning only – Career progress
	Czech Republic	Adult Education Survey (AES) 2008, Labour Force Survey 2011 (LFS), Social Cohesion Survey 2005/2006 (SCS)	1989–2005	– Participation in non-formal adult learning only – Career progress
Southern European countries	Spain	Panel Survey on Inequalities in Catalonia (PaD)	2002–2009	– Participation in formal and non-formal adult learning – Career progress – Exit from precarious labor market positions
	Italy	Indagine Longitudinale sulle Famiglie Italiane (ILFI)	1997–2005	– Participation in non-formal adult learning only – Career progress – Employment stability – Unemployment risks – Reemployment chances

Source: Own illustration.

unstratified nature of initial education in these countries, which leads to both greater training needs and more-trainable populations, as is discussed in the introductory chapter.

In all countries studied in Chapter 2, non-formal employer-sponsored training is the most common type of job-related adult learning (the total participation rate is 16.3 per cent), followed by non-formal non-employer-sponsored training (4.0 per cent), formal non-employer-sponsored education (3.9 per cent), and formal employer-sponsored education (2.4 per cent). Interestingly, non-formal employer-sponsored activities are the only type of adult learning for which differences in participation rates among countries are substantively high and country groups are clearly separable. Participation is rather low in other types of activities, with the exception of a few cases (often Nordic or Central European countries). There is still much to do in order to increase participation levels in Europe. We are particularly concerned with low levels of participation in formal education due to its importance as an instrument for decreasing inequality within societies. In particular, the results in this book often highlight the effective role of this type of adult learning in promoting improvements in individuals' careers, especially when compared with non-formal activities. We return to these results later in this chapter.

Governmental investments were found to have a considerable impact on participation rates, despite the fact that most adult learning is sponsored by employers. For instance, public expenditures on education, research and development, and social protection tend to have a positive effect on participation levels in all types of adult learning activities, with the exception of formal employer-sponsored education (Chapter 2). The way in which adult learning is organized within a country also affects participation levels in all types of activities.

CHARACTERISTICS OF PARTICIPANTS

Our introductory chapter set out two general hypotheses about the individual-level factors that influence participation: one related to non-formal and the other related to formal adult learning. In this section, we present our results based on these general hypotheses. It should be noted that the results that we refer to in this and the following sections are from multivariate models; in other words, they take the impact of other individual characteristics into account.

Non-Formal Adult Learning – A Matthew Effect

First, we expected that more-highly educated individuals and those in better occupational positions would be more likely to participate in non-formal adult learning ("*Matthew effect hypothesis*"). With regard to education, the hypothesis has been systematically corroborated by analyses in most of the countries (Australia, the Czech Republic, Estonia, Great Britain, Italy, Russia, and the USA), with the exception of Germany and Denmark. In these two countries, results have shown that those with tertiary degrees are least likely to participate in uncertified learning. Additionally, among employed men in Estonia, those with vocational secondary and post-secondary education are more likely to participate than higher-educated men.

With regard to occupational positions, a positive effect of occupational status (or prestige) on the likelihood of participation was found in Australia, Estonia, Great Britain, Russia, and Spain, as well as only for women in Italy. In a number of countries, individuals with permanent contracts were also found to have a higher likelihood of participation than those without such contracts (Australia, Spain, and men in Britain and Italy). However, no significant difference based on contract type was found in the Czech Republic (or for women in Britain and Italy).

There is some evidence that these inequalities are reversed or at least attenuated when focusing on non-formal learning that is not employer sponsored. This may be to some extent due to the prevalence of training that is related to active labor market programs within this category. More specifically, some evidence has been found that those in poor job positions (e.g. individuals with fixed-term contracts) and the unemployed are equally or more likely to participate in this type of learning than those in good labor market positions (Great Britain, Russia, and Spain). Additionally, in Germany, individuals with a lower-secondary qualification but without vocational training demonstrate the greatest likelihood of participating in vocational preparation courses (active labor market related activities). However, these courses tend to give participants only relatively basic qualifications.

Therefore, the general trend is that the highly educated and those in good employment positions are more likely to participate in non-formal learning. In other words, participation displays a Matthew effect of cumulative advantage. The partial exception to this pattern is non-formal learning that is not sponsored by employers. However, this type of learning is less common than the employer-sponsored type, and the exception mainly relates to employment position rather than to education.

Formal Adult Learning – Partial Equalization?

Regarding formal activities, we expected that medium-educated individuals and those in lower or less-stable employment positions would be most likely to participate in formal adult education ("*Partial equalization hypothesis*"). The evidence here is more mixed. The country studies that support the hypothesis with regard to educational level are Denmark, Finland, and Germany. Moreover, in Russia and the USA (with descriptive evidence), the lower one's educational attainment is, the higher the likelihood of participating in formal adult education. Partial support for the educational-level part of the hypothesis also comes from countries where differences between educational levels are very small or not significant. This is the case among women in Estonia, between most educational levels in Spain, and between upper-secondary school graduates and those with higher education in Hungary.

Moving on to labor force status and job-related characteristics, support for the partial equalization hypothesis was found in Australia, Finland, and Sweden, where lower personal incomes lead to a higher propensity of entering formal adult education (though only for women in Australia), and the same is the case for household incomes in Australia and Great Britain (though only for women in Britain). In Finland, unemployment experiences in the preceding year increase entry probabilities. In Australia and Britain, individuals outside the labor force have an equal probability (or even higher in Britain) to enter formal adult education compared with the employed. In Spain and for men in Russia, labor force status hardly has an effect on formal adult education (though it should be noted that formal adult education is measured differently in these two countries than in the other countries discussed here).

However, we also found a number of results that contradict the partial equalization hypothesis. Results from the comparative study presented in Chapter 2 show that in all countries those with higher educational levels have higher probabilities of participating in adult learning when compared with lower-educated individuals (independent of the country analyzed). Nevertheless, differences in the likelihood of participating in non-employer-sponsored formal adult education between these two educational levels are small in Liberal, Nordic, and Central European countries. In Southern European countries, the differences are more pronounced, independent of whether learning is employer-sponsored.

In country studies, higher educational levels were associated with higher probabilities of obtaining formal adult education in Australia, the Czech Republic, Estonia (for men), Great Britain, Hungary (with the exception of no difference between the two highest levels of education mentioned above), and Sweden. With regard to labor market characteristics, individuals with higher occupational statuses (among the employed) were found to have higher propensities to participate in adult education in Australia, Estonia, and Russia. Finally, employed individuals in Estonia and those with stable jobs in Hungary have the highest likelihoods to participate in formal adult education.

Therefore, our preliminary conclusion is that in a number of countries, participation in formal adult education is highest among the medium or lower educated and/or those in worse labor market positions. Nevertheless, in some countries, neither of these results appears. Overall, support for our hypothesis that formal adult education leads to (partial) equalization differs by country. We return to a discussion of these differences in the following section.

Gender Differences

In addition to socio-economic characteristics, we are interested in gender differences both within and among countries. At the outset, we expected that *women would be more likely than men to participate in formal adult education.* Results from the comparative study presented in Chapter 2 confirm this hypothesis. The only exception is participation in employer-sponsored formal adult education in Central European countries, for which men have a higher probability of participating in comparison with women. In the country studies, the results also tend to confirm the initial hypothesis. In particular, this is the case in Australia, Denmark, Estonia, Finland, Great Britain, Hungary, and Sweden. In Spain and Russia, there are no gender differences, and in Germany, an advantage for men prevails (with the exception of vocational preparation, where no differences were found). The male advantage in Germany may be related to the fact that formal education is usually initiated by employers, whereas individuals in other countries may be more likely to initiate education themselves.

For non-formal adult learning, we expected *men to be more likely to participate in employer-sponsored learning but women to be more likely to participate in non-employer-sponsored learning.* Results from the comparative study (Chapter 2) confirm the hypothesis that women are more likely to participate in non-formal non-employer-sponsored activities. The same pattern of higher female participation was found with regard to employer-sponsored training, thereby contradicting our hypothesis, yet the Central European countries provide an exception.

Results from the country chapters are diverse; however, due to data restrictions, very few studies were able to analyze non-formal activities while also taking their sponsor into account. For instance, no gender difference was found for employer-sponsored activities in Britain, Italy, or Russia, and an advantage for men was found in Spain. For non-employer-sponsored learning, our initial hypothesis is supported: Women are more likely than men to participate in the countries for which this type of learning has been analyzed (Britain, Russia, and Spain). In countries for which non-formal activities have been examined without the previously mentioned distinction, men have higher probabilities of participating in Germany, whereas the opposite is the case in the Czech Republic, Denmark, and Estonia. In the Czech Republic, the difference in participation rates between men and women disappears after taking the sector of employment into account, which means that women tend to be employed in sectors in which training is more prevalent, most notably the public sector. Furthermore, in Australia and Italy, the probability of participating in non-formal learning is also relatively equal for both genders.

Overall, either women tend to be more likely to participate in adult learning than men or there are no gender differences (with only some exceptions – most notably Germany). Women's participation relative to men's is particularly high when learning decisions are more likely to be initiated by individuals themselves rather than employers. Our findings suggest that women have higher probabilities of participation (particularly in formal education) due to their need to update their skills after periods of human capital depreciation, irrespective of the typical length of employment interruptions for family formation (see also the literature cited in Chapter 2). Despite women's already higher participation level, we expect that there is likely to be unmet demand among women and that participation could be further promoted with more public support for parents' reconciliation of work, studying, and family responsibilities.

Age Profiles

The general pattern with regard to age profiles is for participation in all types of activities to be concentrated among young adults and the probability of enrollment to decrease with age. The exact functional form differs among countries and learning activities. In some cases, the decrease over age is monotonic, whereas in others, the rate at which participation decreases changes over the life course. More specifically, participation in non-formal learning is relatively equally distributed among different age groups in a number of countries (though sometimes only for women), whereas participation in formal education reduces dramatically as individuals age.

For example, in Estonia, participation in non-formal learning peaks for women around age 35–45, and in Spain, non-formal learning is highest around age 40–50. In Italy, labor market experience (which can be taken as a proxy for age) does not reduce women's participation. In Great Britain, the age effect tends to be relatively flat for non-formal learning. In Germany, the proportion of older participants is highest in uncertified occupational training. Finally, in Australia, there is a surprising finding that the likelihood of participation in non-formal learning increases with age. On the other hand, trends for formal education in Sweden show that period effects (in this case a deep recession and a strong government program supporting formal adult education) can be so strong that even the normal pattern of reduced participation as individuals age can be disrupted.

A NEW COUNTRY TYPOLOGY FOR PARTICIPATION IN ADULT LEARNING

Contrary to the initial expectation that the characteristics of participants would vary depending on national institutional settings, we found that these characteristics tend to be rather similar among the countries analyzed, which suggests that in many cases, similar life-course factors influence participation decisions. Nevertheless, some differentiated results were found. The results discussed here concern the social inequality patterns of participation in formal education.

For formal adult learning, three types of patterns can be discerned: (1) partial equalization, in which the highest educated are not the most likely to participate and labor market disadvantages increase the likelihood of participation (Finland and Russia; in Denmark, Germany, and the USA, the educational inequalities fit the pattern, but labor market disadvantages were not measured); (2) increasing educational inequality, although labor market disadvantages increase participation (Australia, Britain, Spain, and Sweden); and (3) persistent (dis)advantages with regard to both education and the labor market (Hungary; also Estonia with the partial exception of women and educational inequalities). In the Czech Republic, participation in formal adult education is associated with increasing educational inequality, but labor market factors influences were not measured.

The countries analyzed do not fall into these categories based on the institutional groupings that we set out in the introductory chapter. Liberal countries, which were expected to display rather inequitable access to adult learning, can be found in all three groupings. Nordic countries with strong welfare states that should promote equality in access can also be found in two different groups. Moreover, one of the expectations in the introductory chapter was that the youth orientation of the educational system would influence social inequalities in participation. However, this effect cannot be the driver of these results due to the way that even systems with many opportunities for adult learners and high participation rates still reproduce earlier educational disadvantages (namely Australia, Britain, and Sweden).

A more-plausible explanation is likely to come from the perceived need of lower-educated adults to acquire additional education. For example, the equalization effect in Russia is explained as a catching-up mechanism used by low-educated individuals to improve their opportunities in a labor market dominated by highly educated workers, whereas in Germany, workers without occupational certificates have a strong need to gain them. The exceptionalism of employed Estonian women can possibly also be explained by the new certification needs imposed upon them in some female-dominated occupations.

More generally, the grouping of the countries also tends to map the educational level of the adult population, with more-highly educated countries tending to have lower levels of social inequality in terms of formal adult education (see Figure 1.2 in Chapter 1). As suggested above, high educational levels can lead to the perceived need for individuals who have been left behind either educationally or occupationally (or both in the most highly educated countries) to catch up by obtaining new credentials. It is also possible that high educational levels do not cause more equality in educational opportunities, but rather that equality of opportunity in formal adult education leads to higher educational levels. This is likely to be part of the big picture, but in most cases, adult learners are unlikely to account for such a large proportion of the highly educated as to be able to fully account for this association.

THE ROLE OF ADULT LEARNING IN CAREER PROGRESS

Improved Outcomes from Formal Adult Education

The studies presented in this book have shown that formal adult education almost always has a positive influence on employment outcomes when compared with non-participation ("*Improved employment outcomes hypothesis*"). Apart from helping upward mobility, adult learning may also have an important role in preventing downward mobility. However, this is not the case in all countries since some display no effects regarding specific outcomes.

In the Czech Republic and Great Britain, further education and new qualifications have a positive effect on upward mobility but no effect on downward mobility. The same is the case in Hungary, with the exception that men additionally benefit through a reduced likelihood of downward mobility. In Estonia, only an effect on women's upward mobility was found. In Russia, new tertiary-level qualifications were found to increase upward mobility chances, reduce downward mobility risks, and increase the likelihood of exiting a precarious labor market position. In Spain, formal upgrades were found to increase men's likelihood of experiencing upward mobility and decrease their likelihood of downward mobility, with no effect for women. In addition, a positive effect was found for exiting precarious employment for those under 36, whereas no effect was found for moving from unemployment to employment. In Germany, certified occupational training reduces unemployment risks for men and increases upward mobility chances for women. In Denmark, adult learning was found to impact both upward and downward mobility as well as the additionally analyzed outcomes of unemployment risks and reemployment chances for the unemployed, though the results were not always in the expected direction. Overall, the clearest and most beneficial outcomes were found for vocational upper-secondary studies.

New qualifications also increase occupational status in Australia. In Finland, adult education tends to lead to slightly reduced unemployment experiences as well as to higher income levels, though the latter only appear for those graduating at the tertiary level. In Sweden, upgrading tends to increase both employment probabilities and earnings for the employed. In the USA, additional education obtained by adults increases prestige when measured at age 45 but does not affect wages or the incidence of long unemployment spells. Moreover, the effect on prestige depends on the age at which the additional education was obtained, with a more positive effect resulting from education obtained at younger ages.

The comparative study (Chapter 3) examined short-term income returns to formal adult education and found these returns to be higher in Eastern European countries in comparison with Nordic and Central European countries. However, although we cannot compare returns in our single-country studies, evidence has shown that positive outcomes are relatively high and persistent over time almost everywhere. Moreover, a number of studies show the evolution of returns over time, taking as their point of departure either entry into formal adult education (Sweden) or graduation (Australia, Finland, Great Britain, Russia, and Spain). In a number of cases, it can be seen that returns to formal adult education take at least a few years to fully materialize, particularly for income. However, when measuring mobility chances, the positive effect of further education in the Czech Republic only involves making the first upward move but does not have a long-term consequence, and in Russia, the positive effects from new tertiary-level qualifications are mostly evident only up to three years after graduation.

In terms of differentiation within formal adult education, we found that returns to tertiary education tend to be higher when compared with other educational levels (Finland, Great Britain, and Russia, and for men in Hungary and Sweden). In other words, returns are higher for the more advantaged. The exceptions are for Denmark and women in Hungary. In Denmark, individuals participating in general upper-secondary education benefit the most in terms of preventing unemployment. In the case of upward and downward income mobility, those who participate in vocational upper-secondary education display the highest returns. In Hungary, women upgrading from vocational education show the highest returns in terms of upward mobility.

Improved Outcomes Following Non-Formal Adult Learning

Non-formal adult learning and employment outcomes were also found to be positively related in some cases. However, some caution needs to be taken with regard to assessing their causal impact due to unmeasured individual characteristics (*"Indeterminate employment outcomes hypothesis"*). Nevertheless, even when using fixed-effects panel models, which control for individual-level heterogeneity, positive effects were found in both Britain and Italy, though the size of the effects was quite small in both cases. More generally, non-formal learning in Italy was found to have a positive impact on occupational status, upward mobility chances, employment stability, and the reduction of unemployment risks. However, no effect was found on downward mobility risks. In Britain, some beneficial effects from non-formal learning on mobility chances were also found, and additional analyses also indicate that training is associated with mobility such that either mobility occurs shortly after training participation or mobile employees are trained in their new positions.

In Russia, employer-sponsored training was found to have a positive effect on all three outcomes measured, though this was limited in most cases to the first year after training. In the USA, job-training spells are associated with increased wages and prestige (measured at age 45) and reduce the incidence of long unemployment spells for men. In Spain, non-formal learning was found to only reduce men's risks of downward mobility, with no effect for women or for the other outcomes under consideration. In Denmark, non-formal learning has a relatively negligible relationship with the four outcomes studied. In Germany, uncertified occupational training is not associated with the outcomes studied, and the outcomes following vocational preparatory courses tend to even be negative. More specifically, these German courses were found to lead to increased unemployment risks, reduced reemployment chances for men, fewer career moves for men (less upward and downward mobility), and more career instability for women (more upward and downward mobility).

Gendered Outcomes

Returns to adult learning were also found to vary by gender (*"Gendered outcomes hypothesis"*). Overall, women benefit more than men from participation in adult learning. This result was confirmed by both the comparative analysis presented in Chapter 3 as well as by the chapters on the Czech Republic, Great Britain, Italy, and Sweden. In Germany and Russia, the results depend on the type of adult learning as well as on the outcome in question, but the general picture in Germany is that women profit more from adult learning in terms of career progress, while it contributes more in terms of job security for men. In Denmark, most of the effects were relatively similar for both genders, with women's upward mobility being slightly more-positively influenced by adult learning than men's. In the USA, effects also tend to be relatively similar for both genders. In Spain, on the contrary, women have higher probabilities of participation in adult learning activities, but they do not benefit from them, and the tendency in Finland is for women to lag behind their male counterparts in income levels. This heterogeneity is also confirmed by previous research (see discussion in Chapter 3).

GROUPING COUNTRIES BASED ON ADULT LEARNING OUTCOMES

The most widespread beneficial effects of formal adult education were found in Australia, the Czech Republic, Finland, Great Britain, Hungary, and Sweden, whereas less-widespread beneficial effects (but nevertheless beneficial for certain groups, certain types of formal education, and/or certain outcomes) were found in Denmark, Estonia, Germany, Russia, Spain, and the USA. In general, widespread beneficial effects tend to go hand in hand with more-prevalent formal adult education, as was expected in the introductory chapter, but this is not always the case. Nevertheless, it seems that when adult education is highly prevalent, it is less likely to be associated with stigmatizing effects and therefore likely to be more beneficial to the individual. On the other hand, there are also some hints that when formal adult education is rather rare (as in Hungary and the Czech Republic), the few individuals who do participate benefit from it, possibly because they are positively selected.

On the other hand, a negative relationship between participation rates at the country level and short-term returns to adult learning measured by income levels was reported in the comparative study (Chapter 3). However, the contradictory evidence with the country chapters may be due to the time frame analyzed. Chapter 3 also found that short-term returns to formal adult education are correlated with returns to initial education, with Nordic countries displaying relatively low returns and post-Socialist countries showing high returns.

It is also interesting to note that the results for social inequalities regarding participation in formal adult education and those for the effects of this type of learning in the labor market do not go hand in hand. Countries from all three groupings of the former can be found in each of the two groupings of the latter. This means that an equitable distribution may be achieved together with a high outcome, which is also shown in studies on learning outcomes of 15-year-olds (OECD 2004b) and, more recently, with regard to the literacy skills of the adult population (OECD 2013). However, widespread beneficial effects in the labor market can also accompany a cumulative disadvantage in participation.

Relatively widespread positive effects from non-formal learning were found in Italy and the USA; slightly more-patchy results were found in Britain, Russia, and Spain; and quite weak results were found in Denmark and Germany. Part of the reason for the weak results in the last two cases may be the importance of certificates in these countries, as well as the possibility that the data do not capture uncertified learning very well (with register data having been used in Denmark and retrospective data in Germany). The comparative chapter found more widespread short-term returns to non-formal learning than to formal education and fewer between-country differences.

Overall, these results do not strongly support the expectations put forward in the introductory chapter, namely that non-formal learning would not be beneficial in countries in which certificates have a strong signaling function or that training would mainly pay off for insiders but not for outsiders in countries with strong insider-outsider labor markets. The latter may be the case, but our models did not directly test for this. On the other hand, the comparative chapter also reported that internal and external training tend to have similar returns in all countries, which throws some doubt on our initial hypothesis since it could be expected that insiders receive more internal training and outsiders receive more external training. Nevertheless, it seems that between-country differences in the benefits from attending non-formal learning tend to be less pronounced compared with those of attending formal adult education, with possibly more heterogeneity within countries depending on personal and employment characteristics.

FINAL REMARKS: THE PREVALENCE OF A MATTHEW EFFECT AND ITS CONSEQUENCES IN AGING SOCIETIES

In this final section, we highlight our most important findings, particularly those that should be taken into account for policy-making purposes. First, we have found the prevalence of a Matthew effect to a greater or lesser extent in terms of who participates in adult learning and its impact on employment careers. So far, those able to update their skills later in life are not the most disadvantaged within societies; rather, they tend to be already-successful, highly-skilled individuals. Accordingly, those with higher educational attainment are also more likely to participate in learning activities as adults. In general terms, the mechanisms of the adult-learning system reproduce and reinforce the mechanisms of the original educational system to a great degree. Consequently, adult learning is currently associated with the perpetuation of social inequalities and educational disparities that prevail in earlier phases of the life course. Despite the potential promise of adult learning to reduce social inequalities over the life course, the reality is that adult learning tends to increase these inequalities.

In addition, our results indicate that participants in adult learning are mostly young adults, particularly in the case of formal education. The young profile added to the prevalence of a Matthew effect signalizes that adult learning is often an individual choice made to boost initial career trajectories. In other words, adjustments in individuals' educational levels as a mechanism for adapting the workforce over the lifespan to possibly new demands in the workplace have not been the main driving force of the process so far. Moreover, the role of adult learning as a potential strategy to enable older workers to stay employed for longer was not observed in our studies. In this sense, efforts should be made not only to increase the number of participants in adult learning activities, as has often been claimed, but also to democratize the process in terms of participants' characteristics (cf. Coffield 1999; Cruikshank 2002).

Regarding non-formal learning activities, we found evidence that individuals with low educational attainment, those in poor labor market positions, and the unemployed are more likely to participate in *non-formal non-employer-sponsored training* (which is mostly related to active labor market policies), thereby showing the positive role of active labor market policies in some countries that are concerned with both increasing participation rates and including those less advantaged among the workforce. However, the effect of active labor market policies was also found to be not significant and even negative for specific employment-related outcomes (in Germany and Denmark) and is, therefore, not necessarily a solution for reintegrating 'outsiders' back into the labor market, at least not in the policies' current form. This may be related to the fact that some participants in these types of learning have been obliged to take part, which means that they are less likely to be motivated to learn (Field 2000; Illeris 2003), or to the way in which unemployment experiences themselves may be scarring (Gangl 2006; Dieckhoff 2011).

Current policy recommendations related to adult learning are mostly focused on increasing participation rates. For instance, Badescu, D'Hombres and Villalba (2011) have suggested that strengthening schooling is a potent way of encouraging adult learning. Our analyses indeed found that in countries in which the adult population is highly educated, participation rates in adult education also tend to be high. However, our results show that high participation rates are not necessarily associated with more-equal participation in (formal) adult learning (as, for example, in Britain and Sweden). Moreover, critical commentators have also warned against credential inflation and new social divisions within educational levels as educational participation increases (Coffield 1999; Fuller 2001; see also Brooks and Everett 2008). On the other hand, a higher level of education in the population also tends to be related to lower social inequalities in participation.

In other words, public provision of adult learning does not guarantee higher participation of disadvantaged groups or a decrease in social inequalities per se. In this sense, public policies should explicitly target older, less-educated, and less-skilled workers, as well as immigrants and unemployed individuals because in a market-based system these groups tend to be overlooked (see also OECD 2013). Age-based learning policies are one step in this direction (Schuller and Watson 2009), but a broader conception of different life-cycle-based needs is also necessary (Billet 2010).

Therefore, states are expected to be the protagonists of the process of adult learning by creating and managing a set of learning opportunities for disadvantaged subgroups of adults and by offering incentives for increasing participation rates, either by compensating for lost income during the time of study or by allowing the reconciliation between family duties and learning. Additionally, cooperation between public and private actors should be strengthened in order to increase on-the-job training opportunities among workers. The OECD (2002) recommends that both formal and non-formal activities should be as flexible as possible in order to attract adults with busy lifestyles. Courses should be available in the evenings and on the weekends, and it should be possible to complete part-time studies (see also Schuller and Watson 2009).

On the other hand, the agency of individuals should not be undermined. If adults do not choose learning for themselves, they are unlikely to be motivated to learn (Illeris 2003; Billett 2010; see also Gorard et al. 1998; Gorard 2000). In general, we cannot exclude the possibility that unmeasured characteristics of individuals, such as motivational factors or the personal drive to learn, influence both participation in adult learning and labor market outcomes. Motivation can also be increased by knowledge about the returns to further education, which is higher among the higher educated. Therefore, policy-makers should consider providing information to disadvantaged groups about the long-term advantages of adult learning (cf. OECD 2013).

Cross-national research has found that in countries where there is greater pressure to participate in learning, participants tend to be less satisfied with their courses (Boeren et al. 2012). Nevertheless, since much of the policy discourse related to adult learning places the emphasis on individuals to keep their skills up-to-date and constantly develop themselves, our message is that states need to take more responsibility in distributing opportunities for learning equitably and promoting the learning of individuals who are not intrinsically motivated, which may involve diversifying the types of learning that are on offer (Gorard et al. 1998; Coffield 1999; Field 2000). The recent recession also seems to have improved equality in access to training provided by employers in a number of countries, though this has come through a combination of reduced training incidence among the highly educated and increased training incidence among the lower educated (Dieckhoff 2013).

Overall, our analyses on returns to adult learning reveal a positive scenario: Acquiring new qualifications contributes to career progress in almost all societies, independent of the value of certificates in national contexts. This suggests that in addition to providing credentials, adult learning is likely to represent evidence of high motivation, which supports individuals in the labor market. For non-formal activities, we generally found sparser returns. In terms of policies, we interpret this evidence as an indicator of a greater need for reforms in course content in this type of training in comparison with formal education, though it is probable that some of the benefits of increased productivity coming from employer-sponsored training are captured by employers. Lastly, in countries in which it was possible to measure differences in returns according to educational level, we found that returns tend to be higher for those already advantaged.

Our country studies offer a detailed analysis of the characteristics of participants and the outcomes related to participation in adult learning. These studies constitute an excellent starting point for all policymakers who aim at improving national adult learning systems from an equality-enhancing perspective. We also wish to note that although our focus has been solely on individuals and their labor market careers, adult learning is likely to be associated with more-widespread beneficial effects, e.g., in terms of increasing civic participation or health (e.g., Feinstein and Hammond 2004; Sabates 2008). Our other exclusion of informal learning should also be mentioned here; much work-related learning takes place in ways that is not institutionalized as formal or non-formal learning (Coffield 1999; Billett 2010). Large-scale longitudinal studies of informal learning are needed in order to assess the role that it plays in the labor market and more broadly (Allmendinger et al. 2011).

Our analyses suggest that no institutional constellation is inherently more suitable for promoting adult learning, ensuring an equal distribution of learning opportunities, or stimulating widespread beneficial effects from learning. We also do not wish to suggest that any particular countries necessarily have institutions or policies that other countries should copy – or that the same policies should even be implemented in all countries (Boeren et al. 2012). What our analyses do show is that adult learning can be promoted in many different types of policy regimes and that when education and adult learning are promoted to a large extent and in an equitable manner, the benefits of participation are also reflected in the labor market.

REFERENCES

D'Addio, A. C., M. Keese and E. Whitehouse (2010), 'Population ageing and labour markets', *Oxford Review of Economic Policy*, **26** (4), 613–35.

Allmendinger, Jutta, Corinna Kleinert, Manfred Antoni, Bernhard Christoph, Katrin Drasch, Florian Janik, Kathrin Leuze, Britta Matthes, Reinhard Pollak and Michael Ruland (2011), 'Adult education and lifelong learning', in Hans-Peter Blossfeld, Hans-Günther Roßbach and Jutta von Maurice (eds), *Education as a Lifelong Process: The German National Educational Panel Study. Special Issue 14/2011 of Zeitschrift für Erziehungswissenschaft*, Wiesbaden: VS Verlag, pp. 283–300.

Badescu, Mircea, Béatrice D'Hombres and Ernesto Villalba (2011), 'Returns to education in European Countries. Evidence from the European Community Statistics on Income and Living Conditions (EU-SILC)', *JRC Scientific and Technical Reports*, Publications Office of the European Union, Luxembourg.

Billet, S. (2010), 'The perils of confusing lifelong learning with lifelong education', *International Journal of Lifelong Education*, **29** (4), 401–13.

Blossfeld, H.-P. and R. Stockmann (1999), 'The German dual system in comparative perspective', *International Journal of Sociology*, **28** (4), 3–28.

Boeren, E., J. Holford, I. Nicaise and H. Baert (2012), 'Why do adults learn? Developing a motivational typology across 12 European countries', *Globalisation, Societies and Education*, **10** (2), 247–69.

Brooks, R. and G. Everett (2008), 'The impact of higher education on lifelong learning', *International Journal of Lifelong Education*, **27** (3), 239–54.

Coffield, F. (1999), 'Breaking the consensus: lifelong learning as social control', *British Educational Research Journal*, **25** (4), 479–99.

Cruikshank, J. (2002), 'Lifelong learning or re-training for life: Scapegoating the worker', *Studies in the Education of Adults*, **34** (2), 140–55.

Dieckhoff, M. (2007), 'Does it work? The effect of continuing training on labour market outcomes: a comparative study of Germany, Denmark, and the United Kingdom', *European Sociological Review*, **23** (3), 295–308.

Dieckhoff, M. (2011), 'Scar effect of unemployment on subsequent job quality in Europe: a comparative study of four countries', *Acta Sociologica*, **54** (3), 233–49.

Dieckhoff, Martina (2013), 'Continuing training in times of economic crisis', in Duncan Gallie (ed.), *Economic Crisis, Quality of Work, and Social Integration: The European Experience*, Oxford: Oxford University Press, pp. 88–114.

European Commission (2011), *Progress towards the common European Objectives in education and training. Indicators and benchmarks 2010/2011*, Brussels: European Commission, available at: http://ec.europa.eu/education/lifelong-learning-policy/doc/report10/report_en.pdf (accessed 16.1.2012).

Feinstein, L. and C. Hammond (2004), 'The contribution of adult learning to health and social capital', *Oxford Review of Education*, **30** (2), 199–221.

Field, John (2000), *Lifelong Learning and the New Educational Order*. Stoke on Trent and Sterling: Trentham Books.

Fuller, A. (2001), 'Credentialism, adults and part-time higher education in the United Kingdom: An account of rising take up and some implications for policy', *Journal of Education Policy*, **16** (3), 233–48.

Gangl, M. (2006), 'Scar effects of unemployment: an assessment of institutional complementarities', *American Sociological Review*, **71** (6), 986–1013.

Gorard, S. (2000), 'Adult participation in learning and the economic imperative: a critique of policy in Wales', *Studies in the Education of Adults*, **32** (2), 181–94.

Gorard, S., G. Rees, R. Fevre and J. Furlong (1998), 'Learning trajectories: travelling towards a learning society?', *International Journal of Lifelong Education*, **17** (6), 400–10.

Illeris, K. (2003), 'Towards a contemporary and comprehensive theory of learning', *International Journal of Lifelong Education*, **22** (4), 396–406.

Janossy, Ferenc (1966), *Das Ende der Wirtschaftswunder* (The End of the Economic Miracle), Frankfurt am Main: Campus.

Jarvis, Peter (1994), 'Problems in developing the study of international comparative adult education', in Peter Jarvis and Franz Pöggeler (eds), *Developments in the Education of Adults in Europe*, Frankfurt am Main: Peter Lang, pp. 145–55.

Jarvis, Peter (1995), *Adult & Continuing Education: Theory and Practice*, 2nd edition, London, UK and New York, USA: Routledge.

Korpi, Tomas and Michael Tåhlin (2009), 'A tale of two distinctions: the significance of job requirements and informal workplace training for the training gap', *Paper prepared for the EQUALSOC conference*, available at: http://www2.sofi.su.se/~mta/docs/Lifelong_learning,_job_requirements_and_informal_training.pdf (accessed 31.10.2013).

Mayer, K. U. (2009), 'New directions in life course research', *Annual Review of Sociology*, **35**, 413–33.

OECD (2002), *Beyond Rhetoric: Adult Learning Policies and Practices*, Paris: OECD

Publishing.

OECD (2004a), *Completing the Foundation for Lifelong Learning: an OECD survey for upper secondary schools*, Paris: OECD Publishing.

OECD (2004b), *Learning for Tomorrow's World: First Results from PISA 2003*, Paris: OECD Publishing.

OECD (2013), *OECD Skills Outlook 2013: First Results from the Survey of Adult Skills*, Paris: OECD Publishing.

Oosterbeek, H. (1998), 'Unravelling supply and demand factors in work-related training', *Oxford Economic Papers*, **50** (2), 266–83.

Sabates, Ricardo (2008), 'The impact of lifelong learning on poverty reduction', *IFLL Public Value Paper*, No. 1, National Institute of Adult Continuing Education, Leicester.

Schuller, Tom and David Watson (2009), *Learning through Life: Inquiry into the Future for Lifelong Learning (IFLL)*, Leicester: National Institute of Adult Continuing Education.

Index